Emirate, Egyptian, Ethiopian

Modern Intellectual and Political History in the Middle East
Fred H. Lawson, *Series Editor*

Select titles in Modern Intellectual and Political History of the Middle East

Becoming Turkish: Nationalist Reforms and Cultural Negotiations in Early Republican Turkey, 1923–1945
Hale Yılmaz

Ethnicity, Identity, and the Development of Nationalism in Iran
David N. Yaghoubian

Jurji Zaidan and the Foundations of Arab Nationalism
Thomas Philipp

Mirror for the Muslim Prince: Islam and the Theory of Statecraft
Mehrzad Boroujerdi, ed.

Pax Syriana: Elite Politics in Postwar Lebanon
Rola el-Husseini

Raging Against the Machine: Political Opposition under Authoritarianism in Egypt
Holger Albrecht

Syria from Reform to Revolt, Volume 2: Culture, Society, and Religion
Christa Salamandra and Leif Stenberg, eds.

The Urban Social History of the Middle East, 1750–1950
Peter Sluglett, ed.

Emirate, Egyptian, Ethiopian

Colonial Experiences in Late Nineteenth-Century Harar

Avishai Ben-Dror

Syracuse University Press

First Edition 2018

18 19 20 21 22 23 6 5 4 3 2 1

∞ The paper used in this publication meets the minimum requirements of the American National Standard for Information Sciences—Permanence of Paper for Printed Library Materials, ANSI Z39.48-1992.

For a listing of books published and distributed by Syracuse University Press, visit www.SyracuseUniversityPress.syr.edu.

ISBN: 978-0-8156-3566-6 (hardcover)
978-0-8156-3584-0 (paperback)
978-0-8156-5431-5 (e-book)

Library of Congress Cataloging-in-Publication Data

Names: Ben-Dror, Avishai, author.
Title: Emirate, Egyptian, Ethiopian : colonial experiences in late nineteenth-century Harar / Avishai Ben-Dror.
Description: Syracuse, New York : Syracuse University Press, 2018. |
Series: Modern intellectual and political history of the Middle East
Identifiers: LCCN 2018024812 (print) | LCCN 2018026677 (ebook) | ISBN 9780815654315 (e-book) | ISBN 9780815635666 (hardcover : alk. paper) | ISBN 9780815635840 (pbk. : alk. paper)
Subjects: LCSH: Hārer (Ethiopia)—History—19th century. | Hārer (Ethiopia)—Colonization—19th century. | Egypt—Colonies—Africa.
Classification: LCC DT390.H3 (ebook) | LCC DT390.H3 B46 2018 (print) | DDC 963.204—dc23
LC record available at https://lccn.loc.gov/2018024812

Manufactured in the United States of America

To the memory of my father, Eli Ben-Dror

Contents

Illustrations and Tables

Illustrations

Tables

Acknowledgments

I would like to express my warmest gratitude to numerous individuals and institutions that assisted me in completing this book.

I am thankful to my friends and colleagues in the Open University of Israel, The Harry S. Truman Research Institute for the Advancement of Peace at the Hebrew University of Jerusalem, and the program of Africa Studies at the Ben-Gurion University of the Negev, who provided me with the support necessary for research and writing.

I owe immeasurable gratitude to Professor Steven Kaplan from the Hebrew University, Professor Ami Ayalon from Tel-Aviv University, and Professor Jonathan Miran from Western Washington University, whose critical comments, advice, and support during the years of research for this book and writing it are unequalled.

I am also grateful to Professor Heather J. Sharkey from the University of Pennsylvania and Professor James De Lorenzi from John Jay College, City University of New York, for their critical comments on the earlier versions of the book. Their comments and suggestions were crucial in making this a better book.

I wish to thank Professor Mustafa Kabha from the Open University of Israel for his kind assistance, advice, and encouragement. For his friendship and encouragement I thank Dr. Tal Shuval from the Open University of Israel.

Thanks are due to Professor Haggai Erlich from Tel-Aviv University for planting the seed of curiosity about the history of Ethiopia.

I would like to acknowledge the research authority of the Open University of Israel for its ongoing generous support of my research. I also wish to thank The Harry S. Truman Research Institute for the Advancement of

Peace at the Hebrew University of Jerusalem, which provided generous support that enabled me to complete this study.

Research for this book was conducted in Ethiopia (the Institute of Ethiopian Studies at Addis Ababa University and in Harar), London (Public Record Office/National Archives, Royal Geographical Society Archive and British Library), Paris (Archives des Capucins, Bibliothèque Nationale de France) and Rome (Società Geografica Italiana, Istituto Italiano per L'Africa e L'Oriente). I am indebted to the staff members of all these institutions for their kind assistance and gracious hospitality.

I am also very grateful to Alison M. Shay, the acquisitions editor at Syracuse University Press, and to Kelly L. Balenske, the assistant editor, for their invaluable advice and encouragement.

Finally, I wish to express my deepest gratitude to my beloved family.

Timeline

1200s	Sheikh Abadir ʻUmar ar-Riḍa establishes Harar
1525–1543	Ahmad b. Ibrahim al-Gazi "Gragn" religious wars against Ethiopia
1551–1567	Rule of Imam Nur b. Mujahid in Harar
1647	ʻAlī b. Da'ud initiates an emir's dynasty in Harar
1805–1849	Rule of Mehmet (Muhammad) ʻAlī Pasha in the Ottoman province of Egypt
1863–1879	Rule of Khedive Ismaʻīl in Egypt
1865	Turco-Egyptian gain control of the coastal cities of Sawakin and Massawa
1869	Khedive Ismaʻīl inaugurates the Suez Canal
Oct.–Nov. 1875	Turco-Egyptian occupation of Harar; the murder of Harar's emir; Ra'uf Pasha appointed governor of the Egyptian *hikimdariya* of Harar
Nov. 1875	Battle of Gundet
Mar. 1876	Battle of Gura
1877	Khedive appoints Charles Gordon as the governor of Sudan
1878	Gordon dismisses Ra'uf Pasha, Raduan Pasha becomes governor of Harar
1879	Khedive Ismaʻīl is dismissed; Khedive Tawfiq is appointed in Egypt
1880	Nadi Pasha becomes governor of Harar
1880	European traders and missionaries first settle in Harar

1881	Ahmad ʻUrabi's rebellion in Cairo and Alexandria
1882	British occupation of Egypt
1882	ʻAlī Riḍa Pasha becomes governor of Harar
1884	Raduan Pasha becomes governor of Harar; waves of Egyptian withdrawals from Harar; Egyptian retreat from the Somali coastal towns
May 1885	ʻAbdullahi's Emirate in Harar
January 1887	Battle of Callanqo; Menilek, king of the Ethiopian kingdom of Shewa, conquers Harar; Ras Makonnen Walda-Mikael is appointed as the first Ethiopian governor of the town
1889	Menilek becomes emperor of Ethiopia

Emirate, Egyptian, Ethiopian

Introduction

Harar is an ancient East African city situated in what is now Ethiopia. For centuries it was a major commercial center, and today is one of Ethiopia's most important political and economic hubs. Before 1875, the city had been an independent emirate; after 1887 it was conquered by and incorporated into Shewa, one of the kingdoms of Ethiopia. In the twelve years between 1875 and 1887, it was occupied by the Turco-Egyptians.

During the last two decades of the twentieth century, municipal authorities in Harar began a restoration and renewal program for the ancient city. But this program paid little attention to the twelve-year period from 1875 to 1887, when Harar was ruled by military delegates of the Mehmet ʿAlī Pasha dynasty of Egypt, itself an autonomous satellite of the Ottoman Empire. Publications that surveyed the history of Harar acknowledged Egyptian construction during this period in a very general way, mostly through mention of the mosque and a bank that the Turco-Egyptian rulers erected in the city. But in general, the accomplishments of the Turco-Egyptians from 1875 to 1885 were largely overlooked by planners and researchers. The decade of their presence was presented merely as a short interval that served as preparation for the Ethiopian occupation of the city.

The Turco-Egyptian era was, in fact, a significant period in the history of Harar. This book demonstrates the importance of this neglected period and its significance and relevance to contemporary times and the entire twentieth century. Historical events during this period set the stage for many major processes in the formation of the societies of Harar and its neighbors. The book introduces the Turco-Egyptian decade as a dramatic period of transitions that had far-reaching social consequences.

The occupiers from Egypt put in place many innovations and developments. They changed the coinage, encouraged and sometimes forced conversions to Islam, extended urban systems, built roads, reconfigured political offices, and more. In so doing, they established a quasi-colonial inter-Muslim and inter-African regime at the same time as, or just before, the "Scramble for Africa"—the period when European powers were occupying, dividing, and colonizing the Horn of Africa and the Gulf of Aden basin. The events in Harar during the Turco-Egyptian occupation thus resembled, and in some aspects anticipated, the colonial regimes that European powers were beginning to establish throughout Africa.

The Turco-Egyptian occupation of Harar came to an end when financial troubles in Egypt contributed to the regime's collapse. It was the Ethiopian kingdom of Shewa, rather than a European power, that conquered and absorbed Harar, underscoring the important role of non-European imperialists in shaping the history of the Horn of Africa and the Red Sea basin.[1]

This book is a systematic exploration of an inter-Muslim and inter-African colonial case study. While the study of such issues in other areas around the globe has been an arena of lively scholarly endeavor for several decades, in the Egyptian/African/Ethiopian contexts the first substantive study of this kind is yet to appear. With this in mind, the book uses a broad approach, considering issues of political and cultural tradition, social norms, concepts of education and religious faith—issues that were shaped during transitions in the identities of both occupiers and occupied. This book thus serves as an introductory account for similar studies on other Ottoman, Middle Eastern, and African (Muslim and Christian) societies.

The book analyzes a dramatic twelve years, from the start of the Turco-Egyptian conquest in October 1875 until the Ethiopian conquests in January 1887. The core of this discussion presents the various dimensions of the Muslim Turco-Egyptian conquest and continues until slightly after this period. One of the main and immediate results was the short-term return of Emir ʿAbdullahi, a scion of the local emir's dynasty of Harar immediately following the Turco-Egyptian conquest of the city.

The term Turco-Egyptian requires explanation. The occupation of Harar should also be seen in the Ottoman-Egyptian context. It sheds light on the emerging identity of the local Egyptian elite, which was trying to negotiate a regional role for an autonomous, though still Ottoman, Egypt. The Turco-Egyptian identity was formed "together with the loyalty to the house of Mehmet Ali, a commitment to live and serve in Egypt, and a sense of belonging the Ottoman culture and Ottoman Empire."[2] However, the term Turco-Egyptian is the correct one when discussing Egyptian rule in the Sudan, the Red Sea basin, and Harar during the last four decades of the nineteenth century. The majority of Harar's Muslim inhabitants, as well as the Oromo and the Somali populations, did not differentiate between Ottoman and Turkish. Most of them referred to Harar's conquerors from Egypt as Turks, or Arabs. Furthermore, the origin of the high-ranking Egyptian officers and administrators in Harar, Zeila, and Berbera was Turco-Circassian, Berberian, and Sudanese. Most of them spoke Arabic as well, but the locals related to them as Turks, not Ottomans.[3]

This book is a culmination of years of research on the history of Harar and the Somali coast during the second half of the nineteenth century. It is the product of archival and library research in Ethiopia (the Institute of Ethiopian Studies at Addis Ababa University), London (Public Record Office/National Archives, Royal Geographical Society Archive, British Library), Paris (Archives des Capucins, Bibliothèque Nationale de France) and Rome (Società Geografica Italiana, Istituto Italiano per L'Africa e L'Oriente). The book is based on a variety of published and unpublished sources in French, English, Italian and Arabic. Primary sources include Harari and Ethiopian chronicles and reports on oral research conducted in Harar, and official Egyptian correspondence containing reports, maps, and discussions of the town and also its hinterland. Other primary archival sources include British, French, and Italian correspondence, as well as diaries and letters of agents, traders, and missionaries who visited the town. Secondary sources include the vast literature on the history of Harar as well as that of Egypt, the Somalis, the Oromo, and Ethiopia. The more general studies contained useful sources regarding the traditional and new scholarly perspectives on colonial and regional studies, as well as transregional, national, and global perspectives.

A Colonial Case Study

In recent years there has been growing scholarly and public interest in colonialism as a transreligious and transnational phenomenon. The interactions between colonialism and Islam, especially during the latter years of the Ottoman Empire, are also part of cutting-edge research in African and Middle Eastern studies.

Various theoretical approaches have testified to the complexity of the colonial phenomenon and clarify that it can be analyzed and investigated in more than one way. Contrary to the well-known image of the colonialist, and as opposed to the conclusions of accepted theories, the conquerors of Harar were not white Christians, natives of some European superpower. They did not arrive in Harar after crossing oceans, were not necessarily emissaries of a mother country with a well-defined identity, and did not settle in Harar only for economic considerations.[4]

Turco-Egyptian colonialism at the end of the nineteenth century can be understood in this context. It suggests a certain break with the traditional monolithic view of colonialism in Africa as a white Christian European colonialist project that conquered areas and exploited societies in "black" Africa.

The book presents an instance in which colonial interactions took place between two African Muslim societies. According to the analyses of Jürgen Osterhammel, or those of Edward Said in his book *Culture and Imperialism*, Turco-Egyptian colonialism in the Nile Valley and the Horn of Africa was characterized by a controlling relationship between a local majority and a minority of foreign invaders.[5] However, similar to white Christian European colonial projects, this is a case of fundamental decisions that were made and carried out by colonial rulers in order to realize interests set in a far-away metropolis—in this case, Cairo—which influenced the lives of the peoples who were ruled. In the case of Egypt at the end of the nineteenth century, the colonial rulers rejected cultural compromise with the population under their rule out of a sense of cultural superiority and a belief in their right to rule. These interpretations include reference to political control and economic exploitation of another land, but they also take into account the assumptions of the colonialists (who in this case are the Egyptians) regarding the cultural superiority of the colonial rulers over their subjects.

What makes colonialism in modern times unique among situations in which one group of people rules over another is that we are not only talking about a master-servant relationship, or one nation achieving political hegemony over another. Colonialism diverts an entire society from its path of historical development and manipulates it from outside, transforming it according to the needs and desires of its colonial rulers. An additional characteristic of this phenomenon in modern times is the unwillingness of rulers to make any cultural concessions to the societies over which they rule. Similar to the expansion of Europe in the nineteenth century, the Egyptian expansion was also based upon an attitude of superiority to African cultures.

Nevertheless, like in other arenas, the Turco-Egyptian conquerors did not live in a "bubble." Cultural interactions took place between the conquerors and the conquered—there was intermarriage, and there were mutual cultural influences. Historiographical changes that have occurred in the study of colonialism shift the spotlight of research away from the writings of colonial officers and officials, which tend to emphasize the many benefits that colonial rule brought to the conquerors and the conquered, toward alternative narratives. During the last decades, the new historiography focused more on the cultural aspects of colonialism than on its political and economic aspects. The emphasis on the common man attempted to break the dichotomy between ruler and subject. It showed how vague these borders are and emphasized the limits of power—power that was mainly cultural—of colonial regimes.[6]

In recent years, criticism has also been directed at scholars' emphasis on the social and cultural aspects of colonialism. Ann Stoler and Frederic Cooper claim, for example, that in the modern approach, it is problematic to ignore political and social subjects, and it is important to find a way to integrate the new approach with the old. They also call for more dynamic connections between academic research into the history of certain colonies and research into colonialism as part of the history of the colonial powers. According to this approach, one should see the mother country and the colonies as one analytic study. A segment of African researchers also oppose the focus on the social and cultural aspects of colonialism. They claim that stressing the limits of power of colonial regimes distorts the historical picture of political repression and violence where, in their view, those colonial powers played the principal part.[7]

An additional characteristic of modern colonialism is connected to the ideological interpretation given to the relationship between the rulers and those over whom they ruled. The Egyptians saw themselves as fulfilling a universal mission, both religious and secular, of civilizing "barbarians" or "savages" in Africa. During the nineteenth century, other non-European nations that had undergone processes of modernization to one degree or another also regarded adopting the colonial discourse as an admission ticket to the club of cultured nations. A good example is Japan after the Meiji restorations of 1868 to 1912.[8]

Khedival Egypt: From Semi-Independent Ottoman Province to the British Occupation

From the sixteenth to the eighteenth centuries, Egypt was a semiautonomous Ottoman province that occasionally experienced transformations in governance in tandem with the Ottoman imperial center. It was the first Ottoman Arab-speaking country to be colonized by a European power—the French Napoleon Bonaparte's occupation of 1798. Mehmet (Muhammad) ʿAlī Pasha, a Turkish-speaking Ottoman officer (r. 1805–48), was a servant of the Ottoman sultan, although he aspired to his own imperial hegemony in the region.[9] He was the founder of a dynasty that lasted until the revolution of July 1952 in Egypt.[10]

In 1866, Ismaʿīl Pasha (r. 1863–79), Mehmet ʿAlī Pasha's grandson, was declared by the sultan in Istanbul as khedive (vice sultan), a title especially introduced to mark Egypt's unique status as de facto almost independent of the Ottoman empire, although it formally belonged to it until 1914. Ismaʿīl's declared vision was to integrate Egypt into the network of European empires. For this purpose he developed Egypt's economy—mainly through the export of cotton—borrowing huge sums of money from private European banks. Ismaʿīl inaugurated the Suez Canal in 1869, and this ambitious project forced him to take out further loans. His modernization efforts had tremendous social and cultural impacts. They included rapid urbanization of Cairo (in imitation of Paris), the establishment of modern education (e.g., a French-staffed school of law established in 1868) and modern newspapers (e.g., *Al-Ahram*, established in 1875), and the formation of a Council of Ministers and Council of Representatives, which shaped a new and educated Egyptian public sphere in which Turkish speakers and Arabic speakers in the civil and military sectors could actively participate in Egyptian politics.[11] Isma'īl envisioned Egypt's admission to Europe through the Nile Valley and African empire he aspired to build, "but his dreams overweighed his finance"; the Egyptian treasury could not support his ambitions for the Suez Canal and for his "African empire." The Turco-Egyptian military defeats of Gundet (November 1875) and Gura (March 1876) accelerated the collapse of Isma'īl's enterprise.[12]

By 1875 the Ottoman Empire faced bankruptcy. Egypt's credit, as an official province of the Empire, was connected to that of Istanbul, and by spring 1876 Isma'īl declared the Egyptian treasury bankrupt. By 1876, Isma'īl had to sell 44 percent of Egypt's Suez Canal shares to Britain, commencing direct European control of Egyptian finance. He was now forced to put Egypt's economy under independent Anglo-French commissions—*Caisse de la Dette Public*—which assumed the task of consolidating and administering the Egyptian debt repayments. In 1878 Britain and France forced Isma'īl to appoint a new government. The khedive struggled with the European economic and political interventions, using the unpopularity of the European commissioners to garner support for the pro-Isma'īl national party. Britain and France, encouraged by Germany and Austria, forced the Ottoman sultan to depose Isma'īl in June 1879. His son, Tawfiq, was proclaimed khedive.[13]

The military failures of the khedival army in Gundet and Gura dramatically affected many Egyptian officers, mostly Arabic-speaking. Although the political and military authorities remained in the hands of the Turkish-speaking officers and administrators of the ruling classes, many of the Arabic speakers now blamed the Turkish-speaking Circassians for the khedival government's financial difficulties and the defeats against the Ethiopians. Groups of Arabic-speaking officers who were frustrated and angry gathered under Colonel Ahmad 'Urabi and asked Isma'īl for long-delayed back pay, pensions, increases in the number of enlisted soldiers, and an end to the monopoly on senior positions long held by Turco-Circassian officers. They were turned down and started to rebel against their Turco-Circassian commanders.

In September 1881, ʻUrabi's loyal officers demonstrated in front of ʻAbdeen Palace, Khedive Tawfiq's residence in Cairo. The khedive discovered that ʻUrabi's popularity was even greater than he had estimated, and he was forced to listen to the rebels' demands. ʻUrabi was appointed as a war minister, but he and other ministers were preoccupied by their struggle with Khedive Tawfiq. ʻUrabi's rebellion gained power in Cairo and Alexandria, while at the same time a movement led by the Sudani Muhammad Ahmad—the Mahdī (the "rightly guided one")—was spreading across Turco-Egyptian Sudan.[14] The combination of ʻUrabi's rebellion and the Mahdī movement in Sudan led to the British occupation of Egypt during 1882.[15]

Because khedival Egypt was officially an integral part of the Ottoman Empire, this book is indeed part of the discourse regarding Ottoman colonialism and Orientalism, which deals with varied aspects of the Ottoman frontiers of Arabia, Syria, and the Nile Valley and the Red Sea basin.[16] This discourse focuses on the final years of the rule of the Ottoman Empire in the periphery, and points out the duality that characterized Ottoman colonialism under the rule of Sultan Abdülhamid II. Mustafa Minawi, Selim Deringil, Ussama Makdisi, and Yasemin Avçi, for instance, deal with varied aspects of the transformation of the tribal population in the Ottoman periphery becoming the target of a "civilizing mission." They refer to Islamic practices and some aspects of European culture that were imported as a survival tactic in response to powerful outside forces and a periphery that was growing stronger at the expense of the center and related to the Orientalist attitudes and practices of Ottoman officials and officers at the end of the nineteenth century in the *vilāyets* (Ottoman provinces).[17]

It is also important to point out the uniqueness of Egypt as a colonialist force that fell victim to the stronger colonialism of Great Britain in 1882, in a kind of "colonialist food chain." In this aspect the book adopts Eve M. Troutt Powell's examination of Egypt through the lens of its position as "colonized-colonizer," since the khedival semiautonomous state was an imperial power in the Nile Valley, which itself became vulnerable first to French and later to British colonialism.[18] From the time of Napoleon's conquest of Egypt at the end of the eighteenth century, the strength of the house of Mehmet 'Alī Pasha existed under the influence of empires—French, Ottoman, and British. These special circumstances continually sharpened and awakened the field of religious, local, and national identity. They also led to the creation of Egyptian knowledge, which was formulated as a consequence of the connection between Western and Orientalist bodies of knowledge in the context of Egyptian history during the colonial and postcolonial period. These bodies of Egyptian knowledge, whose source was in Harar and the Horn of Africa, included recording scientific findings in an agreed-upon "scientific" fashion through articles, research associations, academic educational institutions, and the development of departments of geography, sociology and anthropology in Cairo University in the 1920s.[19]

The colonial convergence of the Turco-Egyptians and the urban and tribal populations in Harar and its environs was a meeting of unequal partners. Any attempt to understand this relationship from the point of view of only one of the participants will miss important aspects in understanding its essence and its implications on each of the participants. These implications will remain the basis for understanding the history of the entire area for many years to come.

The Egyptians dealt a hard blow to the lifestyles and spirit of Harar's residents, and to the Afran Qallo Oromo and the Somalis. Even so, they were not the only ones to shape the historical development of the conquered populations.[20] Theoretical study in recent decades has sharpened interpretation of the many types of relationships between the colonial conqueror and the conquered population. Not only is the latter subject to physical conquest, which affects its lifestyle, but it also becomes a subaltern that is a captive in consciousness. Studies of subalterns have emphasized how conquered populations are exposed to a level of "violence against their consciousness" that erases their "otherness," silences their inner voices, and shapes their otherness according to the conqueror's needs.[21]

This book reconstructs concrete history; although it uses terms such as "conqueror" and "conquered," it has no intention of analyzing the consciousness of those conquerors and conquered. Nevertheless, it posits that a binary state did not exist between the conquerors and the conquered in Harar and its environs; that is, relationships between the two were not dichotomous but were characterized by mutual influences, and not the total oppression of a passive majority by an active minority. The book will demonstrate that the boundaries between the conqueror and conquered were reciprocal and permeable.

The question that guided this book was whether the experience of this multiparticipant encounter constituted a significant change of direction in their lives, or alternatively was just a passing episode that barely touched the surface of the existing traditional urban and tribal systems. It seems that the answer to this question is complex and leans toward the first option, both for the conquered and the conquerors. Indeed, even for the Turco-Egyptians, this was not just gentle contact with others but an experience that contributed to the molding of Egypt's national identity and historical memory.

The book presents trends of continuity alongside those of change that occurred among the conquerors and conquered in Harar during the colonial experience. The Egyptian conquest of Harar proves that the relationships between the conquerors and conquered are not an external stage that was "planted" on an existing and continuous system of beliefs, traditions, and symbols, but a part of the development of this system. The conquerors and conquered in Harar absorbed influences and underwent changes, while preserving, changing, and reinventing tradition and adapting it to new circumstances.[22] Thus, for example, the preservation of the *Afōča*—social networks comprised of men who are experienced in economic and social mutual responsibility—proves that the residents of Harar preserved their inner social organization even years after the Egyptian conquest, and indeed even after the Ethiopian conquest.[23]

The colonial encounter that occurred within Harar influenced multifaceted change and continuity on developmental processes of both the conquerors and conquered. The book presents the various encounters that occurred between the Turco-Egyptians and the local populations, as well as their implications. The conquest, which lasted ten years, had historical significance for all those involved in this process.

This book is divided into four parts. Part one summarizes the status of the participants on the eve of the encounter between them and describes the events leading up to the Egyptian control of the city. Part two describes the colonial experience in its various aspects, both in Harar and its environs. The third part outlines the forces at work in the decline of Egyptian power and the events of the Egyptian withdrawal, the Ethiopian expansion to Harar's surroundings during the 1880s, and the European imperial interests and involvement in the Somali coasts of the Gulf of Aden basin. The fourth and final part looks at the aftermath of the Egyptian period, examining the "forgotten emirate" of ʿAbdullahi, including its collapse.

The afterword, titled "Narratives in a Transitional Period," presents a historical analysis of the significant political, cultural, and religious consequences of the "Harari episode" for Egypt, Harari Muslim society, the surrounding Oromo and the Somali people and Christian Ethiopia, situating the period in the long-term history of each of the five human societies that took part in it.

PART ONE

From Emirate to Egyptian Colony

1

Harar and Its Environs Up to 1875

A Brief History of Harar

Harar is one of the oldest Muslim cities of East Africa.[1] The city is located about 325 miles east of Addis Ababa. It is often called *Madinat al-Awliya*, the "City of the Holies," and that is how it is perceived by its residents, many of whom regard themselves as the descendants of the city's holy founders.[2] There are 356 holy sites within Harar's walls, mainly tombs of emirs, religious preachers, and descendants of clerics who founded the city in the thirteenth century. Pilgrimage to these tombs was not necessarily connected to the Sufi *ziyāra* tradition and was more a central custom in the daily lives of most city residents, regardless of gender, status, and ethnic background.[3] According to their faith, the blessing of the holy ones will be preserved over the city only when all city residents call out to Allah and maintain the ceremonies, prayers, and pilgrimages to the tombs of the holy, while burning incense and chewing leaves of khat.[4]

Since the establishment of Harar by Arabs from the Arabian Peninsula during the thirteenth century, the city has been perceived as a special urban Islamic center for the entire Horn of Africa.[5] Residents of Harar and its environs regard the city as an Islamic center of learning that "uniquely merges traditional Sunni Islam within the city, Sharīʿa courts and a diverse Islamic educational system based on *Qurani* schools and commentaries on the *Quran*."[6] The Islamic practices that combine the orthodox Sunni branch of Islam, belonging to the Shafiʿi school of thought, with the adoration and sanctification of saints in the city is known in the Adari language—the vernacular of Harar—as *ãwach*.[7] The word *ãw* means "father," but this refers to a respected sheikh, elder of the tribe or holy man as well as a biological father.[8] The worship of the "founding fathers" of Harar, and other saints from Arab countries and from the Oromo and Somalis outside Harar, created a broad common denominator between city residents and their neighbors, who regard the saints as their forefathers.[9] The main religious celebrations in the city—the *'ashura*, *'arafa*, and celebrations of the birth of Muhammad—are held at the saints' burial sites and not in city mosques.[10] The saints' burial sites are dispersed around Harar, sometimes at a distance of six miles from the city wall. City residents believe that the saints protect the city. According to one common Harari belief, the founder of the city, Sheikh Abadir 'Umar ar-Riḍa, and forty-three saints settled in Harar, while 361 remaining saints settled around the city.[11] The Oromo and Somalis respected these graves even before they converted to Islam, a likely result of Harar's survival as an Islamic center of culture, where Semitic languages were spoken, and people adhered to the ethos of the saints.[12] Another factor enabling the dissemination of Islam was the activities of Oromo and Somali popular healers and religious preachers within Harar. At times of peace, the graves of the saints outside the city were used as centers for religious learning and memorization of the Quran. At times of crisis and war they were used as military centers. The graves of the saints, it seems, served as "relay stations" for the communication network centered in Harar.[13]

From its inception until the mid-sixteenth century, Harar was prominent as a religious and political center in the Horn of Africa and was the epicenter of religious dispersion.[14] It seems that already in Abadir's time, the *'ulamā'* of Harar, which was responsible for the traditional religious education systems in the city, was connected to the *'ulamā'* of the Arabian Peninsula and Yemen, and these spread Islamic education in the city and among the Oromo in the region.[15]

One of the most important chapters in Harar's history, and the history of the Muslims and Christians in Ethiopia and the entire Horn of Africa, is the case of Ahmad "Gragn." The Imam Ahmad b. Ibrahim al-Gazi (1506–43), probably a descendant of a Somali family, was born and educated in the Harar region. He was nicknamed Gragn, meaning "a left-handed person" in Amharic.[16] During the first half of the sixteenth century Gragn instigated an Islamic religious and political revolution in the Horn of Africa. Soaring on a wave of Islamic awakening, the reincarnation of the jihad spirit, and encouragement of Islamic factors in the Arabian Peninsula, Gragn succeeded in overthrowing the Walashma rulers in Harar and, for the first time, unifying all Muslims in the Horn of Africa, mainly the Somali, ʿAfar, and Gurage populations.[17] Imbued with the jihad spirit, he destroyed Christian Ethiopia through his ties with the Ottomans, who had spread around the Red Sea. The destruction of Ethiopia was followed by the coerced conversion to Islam of various populations in the Horn of Africa, and an attempt to force them to speak Arabic.[18] In 1543, Gragn was defeated, and with his downfall Harar also lost its birthright. The city's residents were now besieged within its walls and exhausted from the loss of the political, cultural, economic, and social resources that were invested there through Gragn's enterprise.

Eight years after the downfall of the political and Islamic arrangement that Gragn set up, his nephew, Imam Nur b. Mujahid (r. 1551–67) succeeded in gaining control over Harar.[19] For a while, Nur halted the crumbling of the city and upheld it as a religious and political center with regional influence. But this success was only temporary. Harar could not recover from its quick upsurge and collapse as Gragn's capital. The town became a target for plundering and looting by its Oromo neighbors, while Nur and his army were still planning their strategies.[20]

Despite the downfall, Nur was still remembered as a military, political and religious hero in Harar. His grave became the second holiest site after that of Sheikh Abadir. Nur had dedicated himself to his fellow townsmen, whose situation had worsened following the collapse of Gragn's enterprise. Harar manuscripts attributed to him miraculous talents in healing the sick, but his main efforts were invested in building the wall that stands to this day. The *jugal*, as the Harar wall was called in the Adari language, became an identifying term for those who resided within the city in contrast to the "others" who lived outside.[21]

The construction of the wall brought about internal changes as well. Nur was the first ruler of Harar who coined local currency, the main one being the *mahlak*.[22] He invested effort in applying local reforms, setting up governmental facilities, and building mosques and residential buildings within the new wall.[23] By developing the urban infrastructure, Nur laid down the foundations for the rule of the ʻAlī b. Da'ud dynasty for 212 years, during which eighteen of his descendants served as emir.[24]

Until the early nineteenth century the Harar and Oromo relationship went through many ups and downs. Despite periods of dispute between the sides, the elite of Harar maintained trade relations with the Oromo elite, which were strengthened through religious activities and marriage. But on the eve of the Egyptian conquest, Harar's political and economic hegemony among the Oromo was already cracked at the foundations.

From the beginning of the nineteenth century, with developments in the trade of coffee, saffron, cattle, salt, and khat, Harar's dependence on its neighbors increased. In order to ensure the continuation of trade with the coast and security on its roads, city emirs had to improve the conditions of the Oromo, reduce the excessive privileges of city residents, and broaden marriage possibilities.[25] Throughout this process, the involvement of the Oromo elite increased in matters within the wall, and, until the Egyptian conquest, they weakened the emirs and essentially took control of the city. In some cases, they even determined the outcome of issues pertaining to the emir's inheritance.[26] The reign of Emir Ahmad b. Abi Bakr (1852–56) was characterized by a battle between those who supported cooperation and marriage between the emirs of Harar and those who opposed the Oromo in the city.[27] The penetration of the Oromo did not paralyze the political and economic systems in Harar, which continued to function even after the political decline of the city among its neighbors. They operated through widespread and symbiotic ties of clerical echelons and connections between the Oromo elite and families of Harar's emirs and other dignitaries in the city. During these years, Islam was adopted by a growing number of Oromo as a symbolic act demonstrating their affinity to the city no less than their devotion to religion.[28]

The last emir of Harar was Muhammad b. ʻAlī b. ʻAbdashakur, who ruled from 1865 to 1875. The influence of the Oromo on the appointment of the emir and the official patronage bestowed on him during his term in office marked an unprecedented peak in Harar's history and the history of the Oromo. This was the first time that a contender for the emir's crown from Harar had willingly dedicated himself to the Oromo and their political institutions, while taking upon himself their laws, in order to win the emir's throne. The contender to the throne abandoned the unique and sovereign characteristics of the city's government and was awarded the Oromo title *mooti adari*, meaning the Adari king. With his transformation to an "Oromo by definition," the emir accumulated vast political and economic power and encouraged the Oromo people to attack his rivals. According to later Turco-Egyptian reports, the Oromo attacked Harar in 1855, demolished the coffee trees growing outside the city, and disturbed the farmers from working land outside the city.[29] By gaining power within the walls in such a way, the emir had, in fact, become a protégé of the Oromo people.[30]

The Oromo around Harar

The Oromo living in the Harar environs are generally associated with the eastern Oromo, known as Baarentuu, after the ancestor from whom their nation developed. The Oromo believe that they are descended from two main branches, with the western branch residing in the east, and the west of Ethiopia today named for its ancestor, Boorana.[31]

The Baarentuu came to the Hararge open plains in 1530–40 and settled in the regions of Chercher, Wobora, Habro, Gara Mulata, Dire Dawa, Gursum, Jijjiga, and Harar. The Baarentuu migrated from the southern-central areas of the Ethiopian plains to the Hararge district, ousting the local inhabitants toward the shores of the Red Sea. By the end of the sixteenth century they had completed occupation of the region to the southeastern section of the Awash River. The Baarentuu rejected Islam and did not accept the supremacy of the Islamic sultanates in southeastern Ethiopia.[32]

They developed independent political institutions, including the method of age groups—the *gada*—and the monarchy of the *mooti*, which were wiped out by the Turco-Egyptians.[33]

The Baarentuu that concentrated around Harar were split into various clans, or ethnic groups known in the Oromo language as *gosa*(s). The *bokku* (tribal judge or leader) headed each *gosa*.[34] The various *gosas* around Harar were Ittu, Annya, Ala, Babillee, Oborra, Jarso, and Noole. These tribes believed that they were direct descendants of Baruntu, through their affiliation with the descendants of his sons, Annya and Qallo. According to tribal traditions, Qallo had four sons: Ala, Babillee, Doga, and Oborra. Doga had three sons: Nola, Jarso, and Hume, who were the ancestors of the Oromo tribes around Harar. They united in a tribal coalition known as the Afran Qallo, which means the "Four Sons of Qallo."[35]

The Afran Qallo is the Oromo group discussed in this book. They played a central position in the history of Harar's emirate until 1875 and were influenced by the political, religious, and economic reforms heralded by Turco-Egyptian colonialism.[36]

The Afran Qallo tribes engaged in agriculture, and only leading up to the 1840s did the Babillee tribes and other Oromo and Somali groups get involved in the economy and agriculture that originated in Harar. This formed the basis for joint economic and agricultural activities that led to the strengthening of ties between the emirs of Harar and the Oromo elites and the development of marital ties between them.[37]

The Oromo people entered into this period while most of their fifty branches still enjoyed their own sovereignty in the south of the Ethiopian plateau. The populations surrounding Harar had a complex relationship with the city for generations, and on the eve of the Turco-Egyptian conquest, the Oromo in the Harar region were the dominant element in this relationship.

As will be discussed in the book, the Turco-Egyptians eradicated the elected political institutions and the Afran Qallo army, forced them to congregate in settlement blocs, imposed on them economic and political enslavement to the *Hikimdariyat Harar wa mulhaqatiha* (Governor's Office of Harar and Its Dependencies), and obligated religious conversion as part of their attempt to create a "new" Oromo people. The book examines trends of change and continuity in the relationship between Harar and these neighbors during the Turco-Egyptian conquest.

The Somali Populations

The Somalis, who belong to the family of Hamite ethnolinguistic groups, were dispersed through the eastern plains of Ethiopia and Eritrea and had a weak but constant affiliation with the Arabian Peninsula. The Somali language was greatly influenced by Arabic, which is considered a second language for the various Somali tribes.[38] The Somalis are divided into many tribes, and this book deals only with those that are relevant to the period and issues under discussion: the Dir (the Somali tribe that unites the northern tribes), the ʿIssa, and the Gadabuursi.

The ʿIssa and Gadabuursi populations live in the area of Djibouti in northern Somalia and in the eastern district of Hararge.[39] Their affinity to the Harar emirate, and from 1875 to the Turco-Egyptian *hikimdariya*, was always close and sincere. These two tribes are also divided because during some periods they fought with one another, while at other times they joined in political and economic coalitions that also relied on marriage ties.[40]

The ʿIssa and the Gadabuursi were the most significant component in the trade routes that connected Harar to the coastal towns of Berbera and Zeila. The second geopolitical area that is relevant to Harar is the Ogaden Desert, where the Somali tribes resided.[41] The trade and agricultural ties of the Somali tribes with the Afran Qallo contributed, from the fifteenth century, to political and ethnic merging, expressed in the creation of the Oromo-Somali ethnic groups: the Girri-Jarso and the Girri-Babillee, which combined Oromo methods of agriculture while adopting Somali political institutions.[42]

The development of these Somali institutions was connected to the nature of trade of the ʿIssa tribe in the Zeila region. The ʿIssa protected the lives and commodities of any person on the trade routes between Zeila and the inner regions of the country, and charged taxes for their protection. This is how the practices of the *Abban* (i.e., the tribal chief and main guarantor for his people) were institutionalized and developed.[43] The Oromo took control of the trade routes from Harar to Berbera and Zeila, close to the city, while the ʿIssa and Gadabuursi controlled the routes closer to the coast. The importance of the ʿIssa and Gadabuursi was critical along these coastal routes, as the Oromo *gosa* was for managing normal and regular trade between Harar, on the one hand, and Zeila and Berbera, on the other. The distance between the cities—fifteen to twenty-five days of riding along a route of varying conditions between the coastal plains and the hilly areas around Harar—required "transportation" and trade cooperation between the Somalis and the Oromo. The 'Issa had a monopoly on raising camels in the area and were responsible for renting them out and leading the convoys through the Oromo regions. But the camels belonging to the 'Issa were not useful in the hilly areas leading up to Harar, where it was necessary to use donkeys provided by the Oromo.[44] At the beginning of their rule, the Turco-Egyptians took forceful control over this setup and created a temporary sense of security on the roads.

The second aspect in which the Somalis integrated into the history of Harar was the ethnic and religious realm. The Somalis were connected to the first half of the sixteenth century enterprise of Gragn, whose mother, it seemed, was Somali. They were part of the Islamic revival on the coast and contributed to its political momentum. The Somali tribes merged Islam, headed by the *wadād* (the religious priest and spiritual leader) into their lives. Local beliefs survived among the Somali tribes alongside the Sharīʿa and the Quran. Even after fully adopting Islam, especially during the times of Gragn, the Somalis continued to adhere to a variety of popular beliefs, witchcraft, and sorcery.[45]

The increase of European interest in the Somali coast and the Gulf of Aden during the first half of the nineteenth century, and the development of trade in coffee and ivory, contributed to a rise in the power of local Somali leaders and their involvement in the coastal cities of Zeila and Berbera. One such leader was Haji Shirmarke 'Alī Salih, member of the Habar Yunes Somali tribe, who succeeded in taking control of the Zeila region in 1840 by taking advantage of the weakness of the Ottoman pasha in the Arabian Peninsula. British traveler Richard Burton, who visited the Somali coast in 1854, reported on the sovereignty of the Somali tribal coalition over the coast and its ports. This situation continued until the arrival of the Egyptians and, in a different form, afterward as well. Abu Bakr Pasha Shahim, the ruler of Zeila and a member of the 'Afar tribe, integrated well into the Turco-Egyptian colonial enterprise and enjoyed great hegemony among the Somali tribes in 'Issa and Gadabuursi. After being awarded the title of pasha by Egypt, he promised to ensure quiet on the coastal plain. He upheld this promise as long as the Egyptians honored his sovereignty in Zeila and its surroundings and did not interfere with his personal appointments and his continued involvement in the slave trade, in contradiction to the khedival government's declared policy. But when tensions increased between Abu Bakr and the Egyptian governor of Harar, or when there were disputes between him and other Egyptian officials, Abu Bakr initiated unrest among the Somali tribes. Members of the tribes became his "soldiers" and were a bargaining chip against any force threatening his sovereignty. In this book, Abu Bakr is portrayed as the greatest survivor of the Egyptian conquest of Harar and the Somali coast. His natural death in 1885, the year of the Egyptian evacuation, undermined order among the Somali tribes on the coast and facilitated the invasion of the superpowers into the area.

The Egyptians did not interfere in the Somali sphere, but only acted in accordance with their settlement with Abu Bakr and by bribing tribal leaders (known as *ogaz*). They made the Somali tribal leaders of ʻIssa and Gadabuursi, in the Ogaden Desert southeast of Harar, their authorized representatives and called them *wukala* (singular *wakil*).[46] In contrast to the direct and harsh dispute with the Oromo, the Egyptians chose not to clash with the Somali tribes during the first year following the establishment of the Harar *hikimdariya*.

The discussion of the tribal areas surrounding Harar in this book focuses more on the Oromo than the Somali tribes. The Turco-Egyptians were quite efficient in dealing with the Oromo, and their enterprise affected the Oromo much more. It was actually the lack of political and military organization and the many splits among the Somali tribes that allowed the Somalis to survive the Turco-Egyptian colonialism without harm. Furthermore, the Oromo elites were already connected to the emirs of Harar and had created joint administrative and political echelons with the city's leadership. The Somalis, in fact, ruled the trade routes, but they were not involved in the goings-on within the walls of the emirate. The close relationships between the Oromo and the emirs, the economic benefits that were derived from them, and their consolidated military power were detrimental to them when encountering the Turco-Egyptians, who were determined to subordinate them to the *hikimdariya*. The Somalis in Ogaden and on the coast were loyal to Egypt, or to Abu Bakr, the governor of Zeila, but did not suffer under their military and administrative rule.

The Somali tribes relevant to the geopolitical scene and the period discussed in this book were, therefore, the members of the ʻIssa, who resided in the plains between Harar and Zeila, and the coalition of tribes belonging to the Habar Awal, who resided between Harar and Berbera.[47] These two tribes were, in fact, under the rule of the Turco-Egyptian *hikimdariya* of Harar.

2

The Egyptian Colonial Path to Harar

Expansion to Coastal Cities

Many studies have analyzed the sovereignty of the dynasty of Mehmet 'Alī Pasha in Sudan, which began in the 1820s. Some have dealt with the Egyptian and Sudanese historiography that analyzed Egyptian Sudan and the state of Mahadiya (1881–98). Some have dealt with the regional connections among Egypt, Sudan, and Ethiopia in the Nile valley and along the coasts of the Red Sea.[1]

In his vision, Mehmet 'Alī Pasha's grandson, Khedive Isma'īl, saw Sudan as the political impetus and anchor for Egypt's control over Africa.[2] The crux of this vision was the aspiration to control the Nile route. Isma'īl wanted to ensure the regular flow of the river's water, and this was one of the main reasons for the reinstatement of Egyptian control in Sudan.[3] According to the modern national Egyptian perception, the idea of the United Nile Valley, which defined Sudan as an integral part of Egypt, was to become the main element in the unique self-definition that derived from attempts to expand through the river valley, the coast of the Red Sea, and other parts of Africa.[4]

The renewal of Egyptian expansion to east Sudan and the coast of the Red Sea began with gaining control over the coastal cities of Massawa and Sawakin in 1865. Isma'īl's ambition to rule over the Sudanese coastal cities was not in itself an innovation. The Pharaohs, Fatimids, Mamluks, and Egyptian rulers in the early days of the Ottomans had already invaded these expanses, and from 1811 onward, so did Mehmet 'Alī Pasha.

In 1865, the Egyptians returned to Sawakin and Massawa and abolished the position of *nā'īb* of Hergigo (deputy of Hergigo), the traditional

Ottoman position in the regions of Sawakin and Massawa.[5] In its place, they reinstated a new municipal and political order according to a European administrative scheme. They also joined the battle, together with the Europeans, against slave trade around the Red Sea.[6]

Gaining control over Massawa and Sawakin had implications on the khedive's continued expansion enterprise. It fortified his independent status against Istanbul and increased his aspiration for hegemony on the coast of the Red Sea. Isma'īl's Egypt had now become a real threat, both to the Ottoman *valī* (the governor-general) of Jedda in the east and to Christian Ethiopia in the south. The khedive and his men regarded this enterprise as the flagship of culture and modernity throughout the Nile Valley and the Red Sea.[7] According to their testimonies, flying flags of Egypt and the khedive in these coastal cities intensified the sense of Egypt's strengthened sovereignty and the awareness among the conquerors of its position as leader of a "cultural revolution" in Africa. They showered gifts upon the local dignitaries and promised to include them in the new government. Nevertheless, the varied local African populations did not regard the Egyptians as bearers of good news, but rather as people with modern arms—scheming, evil, and brutal.[8]

Sawakin and Massawa, which remained under Egyptian control until 1885, became a model of the progress that the Egyptians aspired to apply to their imperialist region throughout Africa. The establishment of an administration, based on organized registration of tax collection, development of telegraph lines and a postal system, study of the city and cartographic registration, and attempts to involve the locals in the governmental systems and to establish a modern legal system in the city and its tribal environs—all these became the foundations of the Egyptian administration in Sawakin and Massawa, and a model for continued expansion plans.[9]

The combination of "dispersing culture" and "civilizing mission" in Africa, eradicating slavery and gaining control over economic resources, strengthened the khedive's territorial aspirations.[10] After establishing Egyptian control over Sawakin and Massawa, the khedive aspired to expand his control over Sudan and become wealthy from its natural quarries.[11] Nevertheless, the route from the coastal towns to the heart of Sudan passed through northern Ethiopia, and the clash between Egypt and the Christian empire of Ethiopia was inevitable.

Defeats in Ethiopia

After the conquest of Sawakin and Massawa in 1865 and the opening of the Suez Canal in 1869, the khedive and his advisors aspired to create territorial continuity between the areas under Egyptian control. The conquest of the city of Keren, in the Bogus-Sanhit region of modern Eritrea on 25 June 1872, initiated the onset of the dispute between Egypt and Christian Ethiopia.[12]

Werner Munzinger, a Swiss mercenary of the khedive and one of his military officers, was the driving spirit behind the Egyptian conquest of the area.[13] He claimed that Keren was "a good base for all attacks on northern Ethiopia."[14] His confidence in his military strength was one of the main reasons for the decline into war with Ethiopia in 1876. He rejected accepted means of diplomacy and claimed that "peace between Yohannes IV Emperor of Ethiopia and Egypt would be established over my dead body."[15]

Munzinger's involvement in Ethiopian matters had already begun in the second half of the 1860s. His simultaneous serving as the khedive's mercenary and consul of France in the Kassala region enabled him to initiate moves in Ethiopian politics in the Hamasen region of Tigray, the chief district of northern Ethiopia.[16] His hostility toward Ethiopia increased after he received complaints from the Lazarist monks about the Ethiopians' abuse of their monasteries in the Bogos and Hamasen regions.[17]

Following Munzinger's appointment as governor of Massawa in 1871, he began to take control over the areas of Bogos and Hamasen, which he regarded as "the key to Ethiopia." (These regions were known to the Ethiopians as Marab Mellash; i.e., the areas over the Marab River.[18]) The winds of war that were fanned by Munzinger from Keren were received sympathetically in Cairo, and the khedive was trapped by his own enthusiasm. Cairo was now acting to represent Yohannes to the Europeans as a slave trader who must be stopped, and the khedive as someone fighting for modernity and culture.[19]

Practically, the conquest of Ethiopia, or at least parts of it, was perceived by Egypt as vital for realizing the dream of uniting Sudan with the Red Sea, while strengthening the telegraph and railway infrastructure throughout the Hamasen region. Gaining control over politically and economically important cities, such as Adwa, Qallabat, and Harar, was a main goal in the khedive's policy of expansion.[20] At a later stage, Munzinger emphasized the importance of conquering the coasts of Somalia, as this would ensure Egyptian control over Ethiopia's salt mines and be a source of economic profit.[21]

The growing Egyptian interest in conquering Ethiopia can also be understood in light of the global interests and the "scramble for the Horn of Africa," especially between the European forces eager to gain positions of power at the Red Sea. The khedive wished to buy himself a position equal to that of Britain, France, and Italy. Britain controlled Aden, France controlled Djibouti, and in 1869 Italy fortified its economic control in the port town of Assab, quickly accompanied by military conquest.[22]

In 1873, one year after the occupation of Keren, Munzinger annexed the region to Egypt, in the name of the khedive. The failure of diplomatic efforts to bring peace between Egypt and Ethiopia led to two battles in which the Egyptian army was defeated: the Battle of Gundet in November 1875 and the Battle of Gura during January–March 1876.[23]

The Battle of Gura abolished any practical opportunity for Egypt to gain control over Ethiopia. The heavy Egyptian losses (almost 14,000 men died in three months), the economic damage to the Egyptian economy and, above all, the Egyptian depiction of the Ethiopian warriors as having a demonic character, prevented any future Egyptian invasion of Ethiopia.[24] Even so, despite their defeat, the Egyptians continued to maintain control over Keren and its surroundings until 1885.[25]

Failures on the Somali Coast

The Egyptian strategy was intended to encircle Ethiopia from all sides. In 1875, four officers, three of whom were European mercenaries serving the khedive and one who was a native Egyptian, were given the responsibility of capturing the Somali coast and Harar. They were Henry McKillop Pasha, Munzinger, Søren Arendrup Bey, and Muhammad Ra'uf Pasha.[26]

McKillop Pasha, an admiral in the khedive's service, gave supreme importance to control over the Somali coast up to the city of Kismayu.[27] The city controlling the Juba River was, as far as he was concerned, the southern "gate" to Egyptian Sudan and an important trading zone spanning the trade routes of ivory, rubber, and various types of wood. With the slave trade continuing in the area, the khedive, "who fought against slavery together with the European forces," could justify to Britain his intention to rule in the area.[28]

The Egyptian retreat from the Somali coast began in the late 1860s. The Egyptian steam boats had flown the khedival flag from 1867 in the coastal cities of Kismaayo, Bulhar, and Berbera. In 1870, Muhammad Bey Jamal sailed to Bulhar and Berbera twice, flying the Egyptian flag. In 1872, the khedive considered capturing these cities militarily to strengthen the Egyptian presence in the Gulf of Aden.[29]

The transformation of Egypt into an active and domineering player on the Somali coast in 1870 alarmed Sultan Sa'id Barghash, the ruler of Zanzibar. The sultanate, a center of intercontinental slave trade until 1873, rushed to improve its relationship with Britain, in light of the Egyptian expansion. In order to appease London, Sa'id forbade all slave trade in 1873.[30] The British, for their part, regarded the Egyptian expansion to the Somali coast as less alarming than the French or Italian gain of control in the region.[31] At this stage, the British did not regard Egyptian movement in the region as a threat to their presence in Aden.[32]

This was the context of McKillop Pasha's journey to conquer Mogadishu and Kismayo in early October 1875, and turn them into a "bridgehead" in advance of future Egyptian conquests over the Juba River. The Egyptian army captured these cities without much resistance, but faulty planning for the long supply lines and a lack of food and fuel forced McKillop Pasha to request help from the enemy, Sultan Zanzibar. The British rushed to intervene and sent a naval force to compel the Egyptians to retreat from their loose hold on the region. The journey to capture Somalia that began with a blast of trumpets ended with very weak opposition at the end of December 1875, when the British ordered McKillop Pasha to "pack his bags and return to Egypt."[33] The failure of McKillop Pasha's journey hailed a change in the British attitude to the Egyptian plans. They expressed contempt for the Egyptian attempt, which they considered an unnecessary and unrealistic adventure.[34]

From the khedival government's point of view, the journey to conquer the salt mines in the Awasa region was even more forsaken and bitter. Munzinger, the main propagandist of the Egyptian expansion policy, ascribed to this conquest great economic and political benefit and thought that it would put an end to France's plans for expansion in the region.[35]

Another Egyptian consideration was connected to Menilek, *negus* (Ethiopian title equal to king) of Shewa, in 1875. The khedive wanted to form a temporary alliance with Menilek, Emperor Yohannes IV's internal rival.[36] In order to intensify the rift between them, the Egyptians considered sending Menilek a bishop of his own. Until that time Egypt had sent Ethiopia only one bishop who had served since the fourth century AD as head of the Ethiopian church in the diocese of the Egyptian Coptic church. Therefore, the proposal to Menilek of an alliance, which Munzinger offered, encompassed an opportunity to separate the Shewa kingdom from Yohannes's regime in terms of Christian legitimacy as well.[37]

Imbued with self-confidence, Munzinger led an Egyptian force in early 1875 from the port of Tadjoura westward toward Awassa with the intention of joining forces with Menilek. But the topographical conditions and harsh climate exhausted his men.[38] On the night of 14 November, warriors of the Somali 'Issa tribe attacked the force.[39] Munzinger, his wife, and most of the Egyptian military command were massacred, and the few survivors escaped to Tadjoura.[40] The defeat put an end to the dream of expansion at the expense of the Christian empire.[41]

The Somali Coastal Cities

Despite these two failures, the Egyptians succeeded in gaining control over the Somali coastal cities of Zeila and Berbera. Their sovereignty there was recognized by the British in an agreement signed between the British government and the khedival government on 7 September 1877. This recognition included the territory from Zeila through Berbera, Tadjoura, Bulhar, and as far as Cape Guardafui. In return, Khedive Isma'īl pledged that the ports of Bulhar and Berbera would remain open to all types of trade with all countries, excluding slave trade, and that these ports would not have any European military presence. It was also agreed that the customs rate to be charged by the khedival government at all ports would not exceed 5 percent of the value of the merchandise exported through those ports, and that the British would be entitled to open consular representation in those places.[42]

This agreement was honored by the British until April–May 1884, when the Egyptian government resolved, under British pressure, to evacuate the Somali coast and Harar. The question regarding the future of these places occupied the British, as well as the French, the Italians, and Menilek, king of Shewa.

3

The Conquest of Harar

Local Traditions, Historical Context

Many of Harar's inhabitants regarded the Egyptian occupation in September 1875, at least at its outset, as a gift from heaven that would remove the yoke of the Afran Qallo Oromo tyranny. The traditions of the people of Harar attribute the campaign of Muhammad Ra'uf Pasha,[1] commander of the Egyptian forces, to conquer the city to the request of ʿAlī Abu Bakr, uncle of Emir Muhammad b. ʿAlī b. ʿAbdashakur. ʿAlī Abu Bakr was imprisoned when ʿAbdashakur seized power in 1856, as he was a severe critic of the emir's policy of submission to the Afran Qallo Oromo. Before the haj of 1875, while still in prison, he succeeded in organizing a mission of seven pilgrims to Mecca, where they met pilgrims from Egypt. Through them, Abu Bakr sent a letter to the khedive asking him to save the city from the corrupt rulers.[2] However, while the reliability of this story may be questionable, its importance lies in the credence given to it by the residents of the city.[3]

An investigation of the totality of Egyptian interests shows a more complex picture. The Egyptians' main interests in occupying Harar seem to have been Harar's geographic location and its strategic and commercial importance; strengthening ties with Menilek, king of the Ethiopian kingdom of Shewa; establishing an Egyptian presence on the Ethiopian plateau; and ruling over the Muslims of the Horn of Africa through the city.[4] From a global perspective, the khedive, as previously mentioned, attempted to gain a strategic foothold on the Somali coast—an area that Britain, France and Italy coveted as well.

From Zeila to Harar

The failure of McKillop Pasha to build a bridgehead on the Somali coast at the end of 1875 did not damage the Egyptians' hold on Zeila and Berbera. In the summer of 1875 the Egyptians appointed Abu Bakr Ibrahim Shahim, a slave trader from Zeila, as governor. Abu Bakr, apparently a descendent of the 'Afar people, had a great deal of local influence.[5] The French in the area also valued his influence; therefore, it is almost certain that they presented him with French citizenship in the early 1860s and appointed him as their representative in exchange for the privileges that he gave to their merchants in the Zeila and Obock region. Adorned with the French citizenship, Abu Bakr strengthen his status as the strongest leader of Zeila region in the eyes of the 'Afar and the European powers.[6]

Abu Bakr, for his part, understood that the Egyptians were on their way to becoming the most powerful force in the Red Sea region from the end of the 1860s. Therefore, he accepted their offer and cooperated with them.[7] He aspired to preserve his power—and even to increase it under Egyptian patronage—without ceding his independence. This was manifested principally by the continuation of the slave trade, and by his ties to Menilek and direct correspondence with the khedive in Cairo and with European authorities.[8] The khedive reckoned that Abu Bakr was the key to their rule over the Gulf of Aden and the Bulhar region, and the British recognized his importance as well.[9] It appears that the Egyptians knew of Abu Bakr's involvement in the slave trade, even though they presented his participation in their rule as part of their war against this trade.[10]

However, it was not the first time the Egyptian administration had embraced an economically and politically powerful slave trader. In 1873, in the area of Bahr al-Ghazal in Sudan, the administration had accepted the slave trader al-Zubair Rahma Mansour and granted him the title of pasha. The Egyptians, together with al-Zubair, annexed the area, making it territory under their control, and in 1874, an army of slaves headed by al-Zubair invaded the Darfur region.[11] There are certain similarities between al-Zubair Rahma Mansour and Abu Bakr and their families. Both were prominent slave traders whom the Egyptian administration embraced at the same time in order to further the implementation of its expansionist policies. The Egyptians portrayed the inclusion of the two in their administration as part of the struggle against the slave trade, even though the sale of slaves continued in front of their eyes, with no reaction on their part. The two slave traders visited Cairo in the 1870s, a year or two after Cairo granted them the title of pasha. The Egyptians and the Europeans saw Abu Bakr, first and foremost, as a political individual of great influence in the region, and only secondarily as a slave trader.[12]

In the summer of 1875, Zeila was the principal base of the Egyptians for the future conquest of Harar. In mid-August 1875, Muhammad Ra'uf Pasha arrived there, carrying a *firman* (decree) in which the khedive ordered Abu Bakr, governor of Zeila, to assist in the organization of "the geographic scientific voyage to explore" Harar. The "scientific" camouflage derived, it seems, from the concern that the British would learn about the preparations and would see the conquest of Harar as a violation of the strategic balance in the region.[13]

In contrast with the failed missions of Munzinger and Arendrup, the mission to Harar was an Egyptian production from the first detail to the last, from planning the voyage through its completion. This was demonstrated by the handing over of command for the campaign to Muhammad Ra'uf Pasha, as well as the directives issued to Zeila to increase the Egyptian forces there and prepare them.[14] In an order that arrived from Cairo, Muhammad Ra'uf Pasha is mentioned as the governor of Zeila. It appears that upon his arrival to the city, he became the senior officer in the area, and as such, replaced Abu Bakr as governor.[15] Due to his relative independence and his exceptional successes on the Somali coast and in Harar, the character of Muhammad Ra'uf Pasha was totally suited to the modern Egyptian national narrative put forward by the twentieth-century Egyptian historian Atalla Shawqi al-Jamal. Al-Jamal described Muhammad Ra'uf Pasha and his military career as an "Egyptian" officer who was the most quickly promoted in the Equatoria administration and was well-liked by his soldiers before his return from Sudan to the Egyptian "homeland" during 1874. Ra'uf Pasha was also portrayed as an "Egyptian national hero."[16]

In actuality, Ra'uf Pasha (1832–82) was not of Egyptian origin at all. He was said to be a Berberine on his father's side, and his mother was

Ethiopian.[17] Nevertheless, he was proficient in Arabic and, in contrast to other officers, he was not imported by the khedive. He grew up in Egypt, and his military career developed within the framework of the Egyptian army. Unlike the mercenaries of the khedive, he did not arrive from the United States or Europe at the end of his career, or agree to aid the khedive in exchange for generous payment. Ra'uf Pasha represented a generation of "indigenous" officers. The ranks of these officers were still a legacy of the Ottoman ranking system, but their language was Arabic, and they communicated in that language with their soldiers and among themselves. Ra'uf Pasha, his friends, and his colleagues mirrored the changes that Egypt underwent on its way to formulating a modern national identity. During the colonial interactions with the indigenous populations in Africa in general, and in Harar in particular, the Egyptian consciousness of these officers would become stronger—and with it their self-image as representatives of progress, disseminators of culture, and establishers of new orders for their homeland.

The Surrender of the Somali 'Issa People and the Emir of Harar

The military force that Ra'uf Pasha commanded was made up of five infantry units. It had fourteen officers, 236 irregular soldiers (*başhi bozuķ*),[18] two Howitzer mountain cannons, and two rocket launchers.[19] A detailed report regarding the makeup of the Egyptian forces marching on Harar, and the acquisition of 250 camels for transport by Ra'uf Pasha in Zeila, was passed on to the British at the beginning of November 1875.[20] Later, the British reported the conquest of Harar by Ra'uf Pasha and the Egyptian takeover of the trade routes between Harar and the coastal cities. It seems that they were mainly concerned about the effect of the conquest on the trade routes in East Africa and in the region of Somalia.[21]

The Egyptian force had to traverse a great distance, filled with dangers and difficulties, between Zeila and Harar. The topography in the area of the arid Somali plain is characterized by dry and rocky valleys and the average temperature in the summer hovers around 40 degrees Celsius (104° F). There is hardly any greenery in the area and scant sources of water.[22] The area where the Egyptian forces moved was populated by the ʻIssa people. Their traditional light arms, which included lances and daggers, had an advantage over the invading army. They were familiar with the difficult field conditions and climate and, as noted, wiped out Munzinger's forces in the middle of 1875 in Awsa.

The Egyptian force set out on Saturday, 18 September 1875, from Zeila eastward. About five days later, Sheikh Rolia, head of the federation of the Somali ʻIssa tribes, presented himself. He announced his surrender and, in exchange, received the protection of the khedive's government and its flag.[23] After the surrender of the Somali ʻIssa, the military threat to the Egyptian forces was removed, and they began to move across the Somali plain on their way to Harar.

The city's surrender, even as the Egyptians were on their way toward it, was expressed in three different letters, all written in Arabic. The first letter arrived from Harar's emir, ʻAbdashakur.[24] The letter was addressed to Abu Bakr and Ra'uf Pasha, and was sent after the emir received word from Abu Bakr about the Egyptians' intention to capture the city. Ra'uf Pasha also mentioned in his report that on that same day, an important letter was sent to the emir of Harar, but he did not specify its contents.[25]

On 4 October 1875, the Egyptian forces passed through one of the strategic points on the route that connects Harar and Zeila—Gildessa, a border station that separated the territories of the Somali ʻIssa and those of the Nole Oromo people. Two days later, a delegation of Harar dignitaries appeared before Ra'uf Pasha. Their meeting took place at a location known as Sharbi, about forty-five miles west of Harar.[26]

The delegation from Harar included the following: Haj Yusef, son of Emir ʻAbdashakur; ʻAbdallah Ibn ʻAbd al-Rahman, the second *qāḍī* (judge) of the city; Haj Yusef, one of the city's dignitaries; a man named Ahmed, another dignitary of the city; and Muhammad ʻAbd al-Qadir, the emir's translator. The Egyptians received them in a manner that Ra'uf Pasha described as "fitting," and "the exalted honors of the khedivate were heaped upon them."[27] In the course of the meeting, the members of the delegation presented Ra'uf Pasha with a letter of surrender in Arabic, signed with the seal of the emir of Harar.[28] In his first letter, Emir ʻAbdashakur declared his complete surrender, of his own free will, to Ra'uf Pasha and the khedival government. In his remarks, the emir stated that this surrender included himself, the people under his control, and his country. The emir emphasized his desire to be under the rule and the protection of the khedive. As a reward, the khedive would issue a generous *firman* for him, so that the emirate would belong to him and his offspring after him.[29]

The second letter written in Arabic was addressed to the khedive and to Ra'uf Pasha. It emphasized the emir's surrender and asked for the protection of the khedive's government.[30] The third letter, written in Arabic in Harar on the evening of Wednesday, 6 October 1875, was a direct reaction to the letter sent by Ra'uf Pasha four days earlier.[31] Two messengers from the Egyptian forces, Haj Aman and Haj Omar, set out from the Egyptian force on the night of 2 October to Harar, carrying the response of Ra'uf Pasha to the emir.[32] From this letter, it appears that Ra'uf Pasha saw the Somali 'Issa people as obedient to the emir. Ra'uf Pasha only met the Afran Qallo Oromo people on 8 October.[33]

From the third letter, it is possible to follow the negotiations between the residents of Harar regarding the arrival of the Egyptians. In the beginning, the emir was going to send his son Yusef, by himself, to negotiate with the invaders. Later, he decided to put together a delegation of local dignitaries to accompany his son. It seems that the emir and his people intended to negotiate over the conditions with the Egyptians.[34]

After the exchange of letters and the first meeting between Ra'uf Pasha and the city dignitaries, the Egyptians continued on their way to Harar, crossed the border station at Gildessa, and moved to the Ogaden plateau.

First Military Clashes with the Oromo Afran Qallo people

On Friday, 8 October 1875, the Egyptians first came into contact with the Afran Qallo Oromo people.[35] The meeting, which took place some twelve miles east of Harar, began with dialogue but disintegrated into heavy fighting with the Nole and the Alla Oromo.[36] According to the Egyptians, the first conflict with the Oromo occurred between 8 and 10 October 1875.[37] However, there is another version of the story of the struggle with the Oromo and its connection to the surrender of Harar. According to the second version, based mainly on Western travelers' writings, the first military skirmish between the Egyptians and the Afran Qallo took place on 25 September 1875.[38] The Afran Qallo warriors positioned themselves upon the hills by the main road to Harar and ambushed the Egyptian force. Under the command of one of the better Afran Qallo officers, Orfo Jilo Biko, they outflanked the Egyptian force. However, the battle was hopeless in this version of the story as well, due to the Egyptian artillery. The disagreement as to when the battle took place is significant. The second version connects the military skirmish, which took place on 25 September 1875, and the meeting between the Harar dignitaries with Ra'uf Pasha on September 30. However, according to this version, this is not the delegation that was mentioned in the first version of the story. At the head of the delegation at the end of September 1875 was Abu Bakr, uncle of the emir. Abu Bakr betrayed his uncle and surrendered to the Egyptians.[39] The second version is not mentioned at all in Egyptian sources, which report the first skirmish with the Oromo as beginning only on 8 October 1875.[40] Research based on Oromo sources claimed that 'Alī Abu Bakr was imprisoned in Harar, and despite this, organized a delegation from his city that passed on the letter to the Egyptians during the Haj in Mecca, inviting them to conquer the city. He remained in prison until the conquerors freed him when they entered the city.[41] A manuscript from Harar describes the liberation of 'Alī Abu Bakr from prison by the Egyptians, after they appointed him to a position in their administration.[42]

However, the battle became a formative experience for the conquerors. The Egyptian report demonstrated cooperation between the Nole Oromo people and the emir of Harar. In the events that took place in Igu, it is possible to find the foundation of Ra'uf Pasha's rigid attitude toward them after the conquest. The Orientalist heroic—yet demonic—image of the Afran Qallo was described accurately by the Egyptians: "The Gala are dangerous warriors, who can move quickly. Perhaps they are savages, but they know how to take advantage of field conditions in battle."[43] The Turco-Egyptian officer Muhammad Muhtar described an army that was well disciplined and brave.[44] However, even if he exaggerated, the Egyptians succeeded in forcing the Afran Qallo warriors to surrender only after a series of battles that continued even after the subjugation of Harar.

Finally, on Sunday, 10 October 1875, the leaders of the Nole Oromo tribes surrendered to the Egyptian forces. Othman Yaro and 'Alī Karo, the sheikhs of the Nole, asked for pardon and begged for their lives and those of their people. Ra'uf Pasha accepted their surrender and presented them with the flags of the khedival government for them to fly over their territories.[45]

There is no record of the extent of casualties among the Egyptians and the Oromo at this series of battles. Ra'uf Pasha did not recount details of casualties on his side, and the Oromo sources did not deal with this matter. One thing is agreed: it seems that the Egyptian use of heavy artillery and missile launchers, never before seen in the area of Harar, made a huge impression on the people of Harar and their neighbors.[46]

The Egyptians Enter Harar

On 11 October 1875, the day after the surrender of the Nole's notables, Ra'uf Pasha received news that the Emir of Harar himself wanted to meet with him. Ra'uf sent two of his men to Harar. They carried two flags of the Egyptian khedivate. Immediately after their arrival in the city, the flags were raised—one on the roof of the emir's house and the second at the entrance gate to the center of town. The raising of the flag took place at 1:00 p.m. Immediately afterward, the two Egyptian officers, accompanied by the emir and his men, appeared at the Egyptian encampment outside the city.[47]

The meeting between Ra'uf Pasha and the emir and his men outside the city was brief and conducted in good spirits.[48] In the central square of Harar, Faras Magala, the representatives of the Afran Qallo people, waited for the conquerors and gave a letter of surrender to Ra'uf Pasha. The sixty-two Afran Qallo tribes that lived around the city requested protection from the khedivate for themselves and, as stated in the letter of surrender, "all Muslims in the Ifat region, with no differentiation between the veterans and those who migrated there later."[49] The Oromo tribes that surrendered to Egypt on 11 October 1875 were "all four tribes of the Nole, all twelve tribes of the Alla, all three tribes of Gala Bartar, two tribes of the Gala Babla (Babillee), the seven Gala Abiba tribes, three tribes of Hiri, three tribes of Gala Abura, six tribes of Gala Jarelo, twelve tribes of Gala Zaho and eight complete tribes of Gala Itto."[50]

It is difficult to estimate the exact number of people who surrendered to Egypt. Muhtar's estimate of two million tribal people was probably exaggerated.[51] British records from 1884 state that the tribal and urban populations in the area of Harar totaled some 454,700 people.[52] The letter of surrender detailed the names and geographic location of the tribes in relation to the city, and it was the basis for the Egyptian administrative division of the Oromo territories that was carried out in 1876.[53]

There are few details about the first meeting among the Egyptians, the city people, and the tribal representatives on the evening of 11 October 1875. One of the informants quoted in historian Mohammed Hassen's 1973 research on the relation between Harar and the Oromo told of Ra'uf Pasha's call for "equality between all human beings" during the meeting. Ra'uf Pasha's promise was engraved on the memories of those present. The local informant quoted in Hassen's work highlighted that the Hararis understood that his purpose was to emphasize to the audience that the era of inequality was over and that a new and different era was beginning.[54]

In Egypt, the conquest of Harar was officially reported only on 14 November 1875. The message about the operation also included the appointment of Emir Muhammad b. 'Alī b. 'Abdashakur as governor by the Egyptians.[55] However, this information was no longer accurate, as the emir had been executed by the Egyptians two and a half weeks earlier.

The Murder of the Emir and the Monetary Change

By the end of 1875, the Egyptians had taken a number of steps to consolidate their rule over the city. After a campaign of delegitimization of Harar's emir, Muhammad b. 'Alī b. 'Abdashakur, the Egyptians murdered him. At the same time, they tried to conceal the signs of local sovereignty, and to pacify the Afran Qallo leadership. This attempt failed and led to additional military conflict between the Egyptians and the Afran Qallo.

First and foremost, the Egyptians were dealing with the institution of emirate that had declined even before their arrival, but which still had prestige inside and outside the city. It seems that the policy of Ra'uf Pasha toward the emir was neither planned nor uniform. It is possible that the murder was caused by the lack of order within the Egyptian force, and its source was a misunderstanding between the *başhi bozuķ* and the regular army. The actual murder, it seems, was not planned as part of ongoing policy but was apparently the outcome of three factors: an ambivalent attitude on the part of the Egyptians toward 'Abdashakur, the close ties between the emir and the Afran Qallo's leadership, and the Egyptians' suspicion of the Oromo during the first days of their stay in the city.[56]

Ra'uf Pasha expressed ambivalence regarding the emir in his report. On the one hand, he portrays the emir as an unreliable "sultan" who refused to sign his own letters.[57] There is no basis to this assertion. The three original letters of the emir are signed by name and stamped with the seal of the emirate.[58] Ra'uf Pasha was aware, apparently, of the shaky relations between the emir and the people of the city. While recommending caution in dealing with the emir, he advised making use of him as well in order to deepen the divisions within the city and strengthen the rule of the Egyptians.[59]

The issue of the murder of the emir, and the abolition of the office of emir immediately afterwards, is not sufficiently documented. It is difficult to date this event, since the only version of the matter is local and is based on oral tradition rather than documents. In contemporary Egyptian correspondence, we find no relevant testimonies, and the emir simply "disappeared" from them sometime in November 1875. Later Egyptian commentary relates the "death of the emir" as part of the process of the emirate's surrender.

According to local tradition, the emir was murdered on the night of 27 Ramadan 1292, corresponding to the night between 28 and 29 October 1875.[60] Some other local informants claimed that the emir was murdered on the 27 Ramadan 1292, corresponding to 26 October 1875, between 10:00 and 11:00 a.m., while reading the Quran.[61] Another version is provided by the French trader Alfred Bardey who claimed that "the emir who tried to take over the authority, once more, was executed by beheading, or by hanging from a tall tree of the central square, or was strangled in his prison."[62]

According to the version provided by the Harari informant ʿAbd el-Rahman Abugan, it was ʿAlī Abu Bakr who incited the Egyptians to murder the emir. The Egyptians freed Abu Bakr, the emir's uncle and political rival, immediately after entering the city. He reported to Ra'uf Pasha that the deposed emir was planning a surprise attack on the Egyptian forces on the eve of the 27 Ramadan 1292. Abu Bakr said that when drumbeats were heard at the central gate of Harar, armed Afran Qallo warriors would strike while the Egyptians slept, with the help of those loyal to the emir within the city.[63] Local traditions, which were also expressed in writings of Europeans of the time—Philipp Paulitschke and Charles Gordon—pointed out that Abu Bakr did indeed deliberately deceive the Egyptians. The drumming was part of a local ceremony that marked the great night of the 27 Ramadan, *Laylat al-Qadr*. When the Egyptians heard the drumming, they broke into the emir's palace and murdered him.[64]

This description of a hasty murder does not fit in with the picture gleaned from the correspondence with Cairo. On 11 November 1875, the khedive answered Ra'uf Pasha's letter of 18 October 1875, received on 7 November.[65] It appears from Ra'uf's report that the conquerors had promised Abu Bakr a position in the Egyptian administration of Harar, but at the same time had designated a position of *wakil* [authorized representative] for the emir as well.[66]

However, the removal of the symbols of the emirate and the Egyptians' attempt to create a "new" and modern Harar began prior to the killing of the emir. It seems that the emir's murder was not a main goal but a result of the Egyptian strategy to progressively wipe out the emirate's historical symbols and institutions. The first phase of this strategy was the process of delegitimizing the emir, while simultaneously taking the city's coinage—a central symbol of the emirate—out of circulation.

In his report of 18 October 1875, Ra'uf Pasha said that he had ordered the cancellation of the *mahlak*—the local coin of Harar. The Pasha accused emir ʿAbdashakur of forgery of the authentic *mahlak*, minted during the sixteenth century.[67] It seems that the Egyptians enacted monetary changes on the day that they entered the city and forced immediate use of the Egyptian *rial*. They also set the rate of exchange: one *rial* was worth 300 *mahlak*. Immediately following the establishment of the exchange rate, the Egyptians gave 800 *rial* to the emir, 200 to his son, and 100 *rial* to the members of his family and his wife.[68]

The first monetary action of the Egyptians was not successful. Ra'uf Pasha noted that the inhabitants of the city complained about the introduction of Egyptian currency, and, as of the writing of the report, had not exchanged their money. Nevertheless, to put the monetary cycle into motion, Ra'uf Pasha requested that the khedive's government send a shipment of silver coins to be disseminated in the city, and these would gradually enter circulation.[69] Ra'uf Pasha also accused the emir of carrying out a policy of monopoly and oppression in agriculture. He noted that the dignitaries of Harar expressed happiness regarding the changes promised by the Egyptians, including the participation of city residents in planning the sowing of different types of produce and dividing the profits.[70]

From its side, the khedival government appointed Emir 'Abdashakur as "governor of Harar."[71] The khedival government ordered Ra'uf to assemble the emir and the city dignitaries and to explicitly inform them of the government's intentions regarding Harar.[72] Ra'uf was also ordered to present the emir with a personal gift—a compass on which the name "Muhammad 'Abdashakur" was engraved in Arabic.[73] In this pronouncement, the government related to the appointment of the emir and requested that the inhabitants of the city be informed of it.[74] However, the letter of appointment was sent when the emir was no longer alive.

The gap between the initial report of Ra'uf Pasha to the khedive and his response to the khedive, and what actually happened within the city walls, raises questions. The only versions of the murder story are local ones, which were recycled in later writings of European visitors. Questions on the subject remain without clear answers, and we do not know of any reaction from Cairo to the murder. What is clear is that the government of the khedive definitely did not plan the murder of the emir, and that in his letter of 11 November, the khedive designated an official position for the emir.

There is virtually no reference to the murder of Harar's emir in modern Egyptian research. In the two existing references, the "death of the emir" (*wafat al-emir* in the original) is mentioned. The first Egyptian argument mentioned that the emir was dissatisfied with the Egyptian offer of a position that was just for show and which did not guarantee that his heirs would continue his rule.[75] The second argument highlighted the emir's role in stirring up the Afran Qallo due to his frustration with the appointment that the Egyptians designated for him. According to this Egyptian argument, the emir enticed them with promises, and the Afran Qallo's warriors blocked the road between Harar and Zeila. Therefore, the Egyptians did away with the emir as part of the process of subjugating the Afran Qallo people of the Oromo.[76]

After the murder of the emir, his elder son, ʿAbdullahi Muhammad b. ʿAlī ʿAbdashakur, requested the protection of Abu Bakr Shahim Pasha, the governor of Zeila. ʿAbdullahi hoped that Abu Bakr would mediate between himself and the khedive, so that he could receive protection for his life and property. To this end, he wished to travel to Cairo.[77] Abu Bakr Pasha granted his protection to ʿAbdullahi. Abu Bakr reported to Cairo that he had given ʿAbdullahi 450 *rial* as a personal salary, as well as payments to the servants of the emir's heir. ʿAbdullahi spent time in Aden, returned to Zeila and hoped to go from there to Cairo without returning to his city.[78] In the end, it seems that ʿAbdullahi visited Cairo, but there are no additional details. All that is known is that after his visit to Cairo he returned to Zeila and settled there. From his home in Zeila, ʿAbdullahi requested that Ra'uf Pasha consider his position and watch over his property in Harar.[79] In August 1876, the khedival government asked Ra'uf Pasha to aid ʿAbdullahi. ʿAbdullahi's place of residence was limited to Zeila alone, and Ra'uf Pasha was asked "not to deprive ʿAbdullahi of his basic rights and to be lenient with him regarding the receipt of payment for all his property in Harar."[80]

The Establishment of a Colonial Hub

The annexation of Harar to the Egyptian colonial enterprise took place in several stages, beginning in 1875. The first stage was a result of Ra'uf Pasha's wish to receive official sanction for the promotion of his officers, even before firmly establishing his rule over the city. The term *hikimdariya* (governor's office) had already appeared in the first missive Ra'uf sent to Cairo on 28 October 1875. In the second stage, the khedival government appointed various officials in the city, which officially became a *hikimdariya*. As mentioned, the khedive expected that Emir Muhammad b. ʿAlī b. ʿAbdashakur would be appointed governor of the city (*muḥāfeẓ*), like Abu Bakr Pasha, governor of Zeila. But, as previously noted, Raʾuf's men murdered the emir. That left the management of the city almost entirely in Egyptian hands, with a little aid from minor local officials—much less than in other Egyptian colonial districts.

The process that Harar went through in joining the Egyptian colonial enterprise can be explored on two levels, military and civilian.

On 18 October 1875, following the city's surrender without a fight, Raʾuf Pasha asked the khedive to reward his officers by promoting them. He noted that the officers had been promised a promotion in Zeila prior to embarking on the journey. Raʾuf argued that the promise should be fulfilled, now that their worthiness had been proven. He listed their fifteen names and current ranks and the advanced ranks that he sought to bestow.[81]

Raʾuf did not ask for his own promotion, but he was rewarded for his success. On 11 November 1875, the khedive appointed him to "*hikimdar* [governor] of Harar and its dependencies."[82] Raʾuf was promoted to the rank of *fariq* (lieutenant general), and his duties were defined as "general governor of the Gala, Somalis and Harar."[83] Many of the officers whom Raʾuf Pasha had asked Cairo to promote were not given a real commitment. Most of them received general blessings of gratitude, which were not accompanied by a change in rank.[84] Nevertheless, a few officers were awarded different ranks of the *mecīdiye* (badge of courage)—a ranking system named for the Ottoman Sultan Abdül Majid (r. 1839–61), demonstrating that Ottoman culture was widespread in Egypt. Three officers merited the fourth rank of the *mecīdiye*, and two others were awarded the fifth rank of the same Ottoman decoration (including one who was not mentioned in Raʾuf Pasha's list).[85]

As part of the colonial preparations on the Somali coast, the khedive ratified the appointment of Abu Bakr Ibrahim Shahim as governor of Zeila. In the newly defined order, which began in November 1875, it was determined that, as governor of Zeila, Abu Bakr would be subordinate to the *hikimdariya* of Harar.[86]

Along with Zeila, the central port city of Berbera was also annexed to the *hikimdariya*. The khedival government planned to build a lighthouse, a police station, a hospital, and a mosque in the port of Berbera, and to develop a system for irrigation and water circulation. Following the conquest of Harar, the khedive took advantage of the opportunity to make personnel changes among the governors. Until November 1875, the ruler of Berbera was Jamali Pasha, a naval officer. But the government was not pleased with him because he failed to properly promote the aforementioned civilian enterprises. In effect, Ra'uf Pasha was appointed "governor general" of Berbera, and the khedive asked him to recommend a candidate for the post of "special governor, who would spend more time in Berbera than the previous governor had."[87]

Harar was also connected immediately with the Egyptian mail system in the Red Sea area. The correspondence between Harar and the government shows that a regional postal line connected Berbera, Zeila, and Aden. A postal circuit began every fifteen days, using ships that passed between these three cities. The khedival government wrote Ra'uf Pasha to say that the mail from Harar would be collected by ships belonging to the "Eastern society." These ships would leave Aden for Zeila and then sail to Suez. The government, in coordination with Ra'uf, decided that the mail from Harar would be collected and sent from Zeila under the supervision of Hassan 'Alī Bey, who was described as "manager of Ottoman works in Aden."[88]

The boundaries between the military and civilian sectors during the annexation of the city by an occupying army were blurry. This duality, which was expressed in both the civil and military dimensions, characterized Harar's Egyptian government until Ra'uf's dismissal by Gordon in May 1878. Throughout this time, Ra'uf was the most powerful man in the entire Somali coast region. But the khedival government also tried to place a citizen—a professional appointed on its behalf—in charge of civilians affairs in the city.

It was 'Abd al-Wahab Wahabi Bey, the khedival government's representative in the town of Beni Suef in Egypt, who was finally chosen by Cairo to serve as the link between the government and the *hikimdariya*. His role was defined as "commissioner of the Harar province" and "president of the council of the *hikimdariya*." In an order sent from Cairo, Wahabi Bey was described as being "a promising administrator with extensive experience in organization, who will greatly contribute to the Egyptian control of Harar." Furthermore, the order appointed Wahabi Bey to replace Ra'uf Pasha during the latter's absence from the city. The khedive stressed that this administrative step would be given official sanction "with the establishment of the required Council [*majlis*] under the presidency of Wahabi Bey. This council will be composed of the *qāḍīs*, the *'ulamā'*, merchants and dignified and distinguished members of the city. Suitable representatives of these groups should be made responsible for political and religious issues."[89] Councils of this sort, already existing in Sawakin and in Massawa, were the prototypes for modern urban management according to the Turco-Egyptian colonial ideology.[90]

Harar also became tied financially to the Egyptian colonial enterprise. As with military issues, the khedival government's financial policy was more moderate than Ra'uf Pasha's execution of it. The khedival government declared that it intended to gradually incorporate the Egyptian *rial* into the city's economy in an attempt to avoid unnecessary upheaval. The government also found that the exchange rate set by Ra'uf Pasha on the day he entered the city was not accurate, corrected it, and set the rate at 321 *mahlak* per *rial*. The khedival government sent 100,000 *qirsh* in silver coins and 300,000 *qirsh* in copper coins. The government also ordered Ra'uf not to use force, and to allow use of the *mahlak* until the peaceful transition to full use of the *rial*. Ra'uf Pasha had been warned that any sudden change might create difficulties for the populace and, by extension, for the khedival government itself.[91]

The insularity and distance of the Harar *hikimdariya* amplified the uncertainty of the khedival government, but it also fostered a sense of pride at this unique success. The successful hold on the city was viewed as the jewel in the crown of the entire colonial operation, sparking both elation and fear of the unknown. Harar was a manifestation of Egyptian modernity in the region and the source of much pride. Harar's transformation into the center of the Egyptian colonial project in the Somali region was made public in a statement made by the khedive to Cookson, one of the British representatives, in Cairo. At their meeting, in early July 1876, the khedive laid out his plan for the development of Zeila and Berbera as part of the modernization of the area. The khedive praised Ra'uf Pasha for being the first in the history of the area to restore order and security on the roads between Harar and the port cities. The khedive's enthusiasm caused Cookson fear and worry. The Englishman doubted the khedive's ability to completely control the area, and he advised his superiors to closely monitor the Egyptian aspirations in Harar and the Somali coastal cities because they might endanger British interests in the Red Sea and the island of Zanzibar.[92]

Several British observers in Aden reported to London about the Egyptian occupation of Harar. Some of the observers noted Ra'uf Pasha's tough nature and forceful policy toward the 'Issa and the Afran Qallo people. They were especially impressed by his success at forcing them to surrender, since he was the first ever to defeat them.[93] The same observers watched as Harar became an Egyptian colonial center, linked to the important ports of Berbera and Zeila. They reported on the balance of forces established between the Egyptians and Menilek, king of the Ethiopian Shewa kingdom, and discussed the other participants in regional activity. According to the British assessment, the Egyptians were now the strongest party in the region, and therefore their activity in the Berbera-Zeila-Harar triangle should be watched.[94]

PART TWO

The Egyptian Colonial Experience

4

Creating "Egyptian" Harar

Local and Regional Economic Interests

The khedival government was obliged to take a number of steps in Harar. The first was the dissemination of education in the city and its surroundings, "since without spreading knowledge and education, we will not arrive at the required level among the cultured nations."[1] This proclamation was, in actuality, a way of connecting Harar to Isma'īl's vision of modern education, namely, providing knowledge and professional training in a European fashion.

The second step was to "increase the agricultural yield and widen the scope of trade." The Egyptians identified the economic potential of the area and wished to "cooperate" with the residents of the city to actualize it. "Your lands are very fertile in their produce, and your country is a source of plenty and profit." The locals were required to be obedient, and the government was ordered to "pursue benevolent policies and to bestow benefits."[2]

The khedival government in Cairo related to agriculture and trade in Harar itself, but also showed interest in additional sources in the areas surrounding the city. Ra'uf Pasha was ordered to ascertain whether there were coal deposits in the area between the *hikimdariya* and the region of the Ethiopian Shewa kingdom, approximately one hundred miles from Harar. The political significance of such a discovery, and its possible influence on relations with Menilek, was clear to the government in Cairo. The Egyptian forces in Harar were ordered to check the distance of the mines from Shewa and to report their findings immediately. Ra'uf and his men were asked to avoid tension with Menilek, in accordance with the understanding that had been reached with the government of the khedive in the course of undermining the rule of the Ethiopian Emperor Yohannes IV. Similarly, the government ordered Ra'uf to protect the trade passages between Harar and Shewa.[3] Modern Egyptian historiography, however, has pointed out that there was no evidence that the Egyptians did find coal deposits in the Harar area. It seems that Ra'uf Pasha and his men did not get involved in seeking coal deposits or ascertaining their existence, due to the great distance between the mines and Harar and their proximity to Shewa.[4]

The khedival government attributed great importance to exploring Harar and its surroundings. Apparently, the khedive was very impressed by Ra'uf Pasha's early reports regarding water sources and the abundance of bananas, coffee, and khat growing in the area. Ra'uf reported to Cairo on the understandings he had reached with the city leaders regarding widening the scope of agricultural produce, especially coffee. Devoted to their typical colonial effort of disparaging Harar's precolonial past, the Egyptians claimed that the emir had enjoyed a monopoly in the field of agriculture (especially khat and coffee) and trade. Ra'uf promised the residents that this period had ended and a new era of cooperation and development was beginning.[5]

Ra'uf Pasha's enthusiasm for the economic potential of local agriculture, and the promise of Harar residents to cooperate in its development, influenced the khedive's government. This directly contributed to highlighting Harar's role in the Egyptian colonial project and to Ra'uf's appointment as *hikimdar* (governor) of Harar. At the same time, the khedival government reconfirmed the appointment of Abu Bakr as the governor of Zeila under the rule of the Harar *hikimdariya*.[6]

The government urged Ra'uf and his people to immediately organize a precise report of financial and economic activities, as well as the scope of agriculture in the city. The purpose of this request was to supervise the income from this field, and to begin to move agricultural merchandise, mainly coffee, from the port of Zeila to Cairo.[7] It seems that, due to the great importance attributed to the coffee trade, the khedival government wished to adopt the units of measure used in Cairo for use in Harar as well. To this end, the *kantar* (an Ottoman unit of measure weighing 125 pounds) was adopted in Harar.[8] The government asked Ra'uf to gather all the agricultural produce and livestock according to units of one *kantar*; later on, he was required to send coffee beans to Egypt, packed in these units.[9]

There were two reasons for setting uniform weights and currency. One was symbolic—to create an official connection between Harar, its people, and its way of life, to the Egyptian colonial system, along with an attempt to replace the emir's policies. The second reason was economic, related to the need for exact records and supervision of the scope of trade, produce, and livestock.

Establishment of Colonial Bodies of Knowledge

Modern scientific research of Harar was an integral part of what Omnia El Shakry has portrayed as "the ethnographic moment" during Khedive Ismaʿīl's regime.[10] Five months before the occupation of Harar, the Société Khédiviale de Géographie d'Egypte (the Khedival/Royal Geographical Society of Egypt) was founded in May 1875 under the khedive's auspices. His imperial ambitions in Africa and Sudan provided much of the impetus for the African focus of the Royal Geographical Society's early years.[11] The enthusiasm of the khedive's government for scientific explorations and the economic exploitation of Harar and its environs was strongly expressed in Cairo's instructions to Ra'uf Pasha.[12]

The momentum of Egyptian development in the Harar *hikimdariya* during the period 1876–77 was accompanied by broad ethnographic and cartographic research. As Foucault emphasized, there are tight and mutual connections between knowledge and power. In the Egyptian colonial context in Harar, Egyptian bodies of knowledge might contribute to the understanding of power and knowledge in general.[13] As in other Ottoman and European colonial frontiers around the world at that time, the Turco-Egyptians first of all aspired to know where they were by gaining knowledge of Harar and its surroundings, collecting various geographical and human data. They divided the region into different categories to achieve maximum colonial-economic advantage, and to lay a scientific foundation for developing the region.[14] There were only two sources of Western knowledge of Harar before its Egyptian period. The first work that presented scientific findings from Harar and its surroundings was *Highlands of Ethiopia*, written by William Harris in 1844.[15] The second one is more famous, written by the well-known Sir Richard Francis Burton, who spent ten days there in 1855. In his book *First Footsteps in East Africa, or an Exploration of Harar*, which appeared in 1866, he published data that he had gathered in the field and even sketched a map of the road from Zeila to Harar.[16] Burton's work was considered "scientific" due to his use of "scientific tools."[17]

The exploration and mapping of Harar and its surroundings by Egyptian administrators and scientists was a pioneering project. Egypt's expansion into the Sudanese and Somali coast was a precursor of modern research on the region. Drawing maps and dividing the local population into different categories helped the conquerors better understand their surroundings and take advantage of natural and human resources for their own ends and needs. The concept of *mission civilatrice* ("civilizing mission") was meant to portray the conquerors as the harbingers of military, cultural, and scientific progress in Africa. At the same time, the project of colonization and modernization was meant to present Egypt to the Europeans as a modern nation, acting according to political and scientific Western criteria and contributing to the development of Western culture and Western science.[18]

The scientific investigators in Sudan and on the Somali coast from the 1860s to 1880s were Egyptian army officers; some were of Turco-Circassian origin, and others were Arabic speakers. These explorer-officers presented their scientific findings in military and other official publications in Egypt. They were written in Arabic and French and included reports, articles, and maps. It is possible to see their contribution as the basis of modern Egyptian research and an important step for studying the area under discussion. The Egyptians were the first to be involved in modern research in Sudan and Somalia, and the use of their work by the British and Ethiopians after 1885 attests to its quality.[19] As a result of this, the Egyptian cartographic and anthropological research was integrated into Western studies of Ethiopia and the Somali coast.[20]

The Egyptian officers' investigations can be divided into three main areas: cartographic research (mainly drawing maps of the city and its environs), topographic research, and anthropological study. Egyptian cartography, topography, and ethnography projects in Harar were closely intertwined. Indeed, the focus of colonialist knowledge is almost identical to instances of other colonialist interactions in the world. Issues such as the need for geographic mapping, censuses, and estimations; the need to avoid recognizing the past history of societies in Africa, or to portray this past as "corrupt and rotten"; and the necessity for medical knowledge to recognize local diseases all were manifested in the case of Turco-Egyptian colonialism in Harar.

Cartographic Research

The main motive of Egyptian cartography in Africa was military, related to the Egyptians' need to learn and to control the relevant territories. During the 1870s there was renewed Egyptian interest in Sudan, Ethiopia, and the Somali coast. As relations worsened with Ethiopia to the point of military conflict in 1875, the Egyptians tried to increase their familiarity with the territory and widen their control in the southern Sudan region and the coast of the Red Sea. One of the ways they carried out this effort was by drawing maps of the area.[21]

The officers Muhammad Ezat Pasha, Qasim Pasha, and Majdi Pasha drew maps of the various frontiers between Sudan and Ethiopia in the second half of the 1870s.[22] The writing on these maps is in Arabic, which was already the language of the army and intelligence services of the khedive's military.[23] In the regions of the Somali coast, the cartographic work of officers Muhammad Muhtar and Fauzi Pasha is noteworthy, especially the map of Zeila and surroundings that appeared in the official journal of the Egyptian army, *Bulletin de l'Etat-Major Général de l'Armée Egyptienne*, in 1876.[24] The first map of Berbera and its surroundings was drafted by 'Abd al-Razeq Pasha and his staff.[25] Another groundbreaking cartographic achievement in the area of the Somali coast was the work of Hassan Wassef Pasha, 'Abd al-Razeq Pasha, and Sadiq Pasha, who took part in McKillop Pasha's journey to the area, during which they drafted a map of the coast and the Jubba River.[26] Five years later, in 1881, Muhtar published a map of Cape Guardafui and surroundings, on a scale of 1:40,000.[27]

At the end of January 1876, Fauzi and Muhtar sent two updated maps of the Harar region to Cairo. The maps, which bore captions in Arabic and French, were attached to a detailed scientific report that had been prepared by the two about the city, its people, and the surrounding Afran Qallo of the Oromo areas.[28] A copy of the first map was reproduced, in Arabic alone, in the publication of the Egyptian army general headquarters in Cairo in 1877.[29] It described the journey of the Egyptian forces from Zeila to Harar through drawings of the areas of the "Isa, Gala and residents of Harar." This was the first cartographic description of the area between the Somali coast and Harar. It included mention of places and settlements of military and economic significance, and the settlement areas of the Oromo and Somalis, as well as the characteristics of those areas.[30] This map served as a basis for the map of Somalia that was presented in a geographic conference in Venice in 1881 and received great praise, but eventually disappeared.[31]

The second map sent to Cairo depicted the city of Harar at a scale of 1:4,000. It included a sketch of the city walls and their five gates, as well as a sketch of the area inside the city walls, with notations of principal structures. First published in French in Cairo in 1877,[32] the map is still considered to be the first basic map of the city. Later, the map was used by Philipp Paulitschke, the Austrian traveler, who drew an updated map for the British in 1885 that included the route between Harar and Berbera.[33] The original copy of Paulitschke's map can be found in the British Library in London.[34]

Map drawing by the Egyptians in Harar was renewed at the end of 1881 as part of an attempt by the third governor of the city, Muhammad Nadi Pasha (r. June 1880–December 1882) to breathe life into the *hikimdariya*.[35] Ahmed Bey, Whadi Bey, and ʿAbd al-Qarim Ezat Effendī were put in charge of cartography. They drew two new maps of the city and its environs. In these maps, the settled areas of the Oromo and Somalis around the city were noted in detail, along with the boundaries of Egyptian rule. These maps were featured in later publications by Federico Bonola Bey and Philipp Paulitschke.[36]

The Egyptian cartography of Harar between 1876 and 1881 clearly served as the basis for administrative and military activity, as well as construction in the area. The gathering of the Oromo into settlement blocs

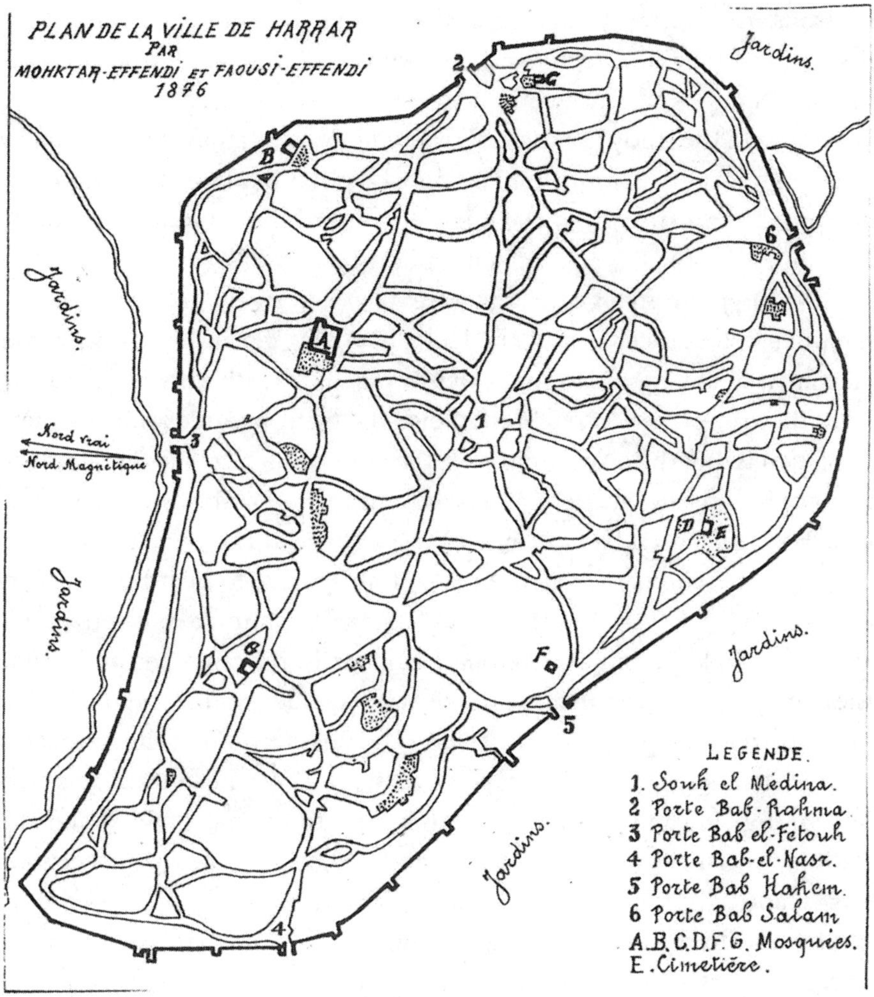

1. Map drawn by Fauzi and Muhtar, showing the city of Harar, 1876. Source: Georges Douin, *Histoire du Règne du Khédive Ismail* (Cairo: Impr. Del'Innst. Français d'Archéologie Orientale du Caire, pour La Société Royale de Géographie d'Égypte, 1938), 3:617.

and the protection of the roads between Zeila and Harar (topics that will be examined in greater detail) were based on these maps.

Mustafa Amer, an Egyptian scholar who was totally devoted to the Egyptian national narrative in 1937, emphasized the Egyptian part in establishing the cartographic bodies of knowledge of Harar and its environs. According to his claim, the European explorers Philipp Paulitschke and Luigi Robecci-Bricchetti, who were agents of European colonialism, "forgot and caused others to forget" the central role played by the Egyptians in the study of Harar. They used the foundation that was laid by the Egyptians but "forgot" to mention who put it in place. This was obviously part of an attempt by the Europeans—and the Ethiopians as well—to marginalize the Egyptian chapter in the history of Harar.[37]

The Egyptian maps of Harar were, however, a product of the Turco-Egyptian colonial context in the Horn in Africa generally and in Harar particularly. The Egyptian maps were a model *for* rather than a model of *what* they purported to represent. Since the maps became an instrument for concretizing the project on land, the maps drawn by the Egyptians in Arabic formed a new pattern and landscape in Harar. They were perceived as a scientific abstraction of reality. Nevertheless, the cartographic and ethnographic enterprises were intended, primarily, to help the conquerors to know where they were and understand the human and geographic resources in Harar and its environs. Secondarily, they were meant to serve the conquerors' mechanisms of political subjugation and economic exploitation through classification, mapping, and observations of the conquered in order to take maximum advantage of them. Thus, the foundations were laid for policing and overseeing in Arabic, for the purpose of taxation and military recruitment. Through the maps, the Egyptians could achieve power, administer it, and gain judicial legitimacy.[38]

Similar to the events in other colonial arenas in Africa and Asia, the scientific mechanisms in Harar in the 1870s and 1880s were also a central element in imagining, in Arabic, not only Harar but also the "homeland in Egypt." The attempt to form a "Cairo-like" Egyptian urban space transformed Harar into a "new Cairo," as it was described by the Egyptians.[39]

The Egyptian maps in particular, and the research in general, transformed Harar from a "mystical" entity to a city in the eyes of the European visitors who preceded the Egyptians. When Burton and Harris "discovered" Harar, their descriptions of it expressed clearly Eurocentric and Orientalist views. According to them, Harar was a mystical entity built with undefined Muslim urban and religious contours. They hardly differentiated between the city residents and the Oromo and Somalis, and for the most part, viewed the different groups of people there as a homogeneous community of Muslims. The Egyptians were the ones who made these distinctions for the first time, even documenting them in their maps.

Topographic Research

The studies by Turco-Egyptian officers included topographic sketches, mapping of water sources, and an attempt to investigate plant life and the climate. They integrated new findings together with previously known information, and they built an updated knowledge body regarding the city and the groups of people in and around it. Even during their journey from Zeila to Harar, they reported on the stops along the way and identified sites such as Gildessa, which they described as the boundary of "the land of the Nole Gala."[40] They identified the mountain overlooking Harar from the south—Jabl Hakim—and requested that the khedive's government send reinforcements to set up a military outpost on its peak.[41]

These examples are testimony to the early research of the terrain for the purposes of navigation and consolidation. In addition, Muhtar and Fauzi wrote a report that included the main geographical and anthropological findings, along with—as per the government's request—clarifications regarding the Oromo and their customs, as well as the local climate.[42]

Muhtar and Fauzi divided their report into three main parts. The first related to the "Land of the 'Issa." It seems as though data about the type of soil in the region, the water, and the flora were gathered by the Egyptians while they were on their journey from the coast to Harar. Praise for the head of the force and his functioning under the difficult conditions of the terrain were included in the topographical description.[43]

The mention of water sources and the distance between them is evidence of precise notation and is connected directly to the Egyptian agricultural development plans. The Egyptians attributed the backwardness of agriculture in the area to the failure to locate water sources and the character of the corrupt emir's rule. Thus, alongside the topographic and agricultural data are remarks from which one can learn about the ideology that guided the Egyptians, and the methods of putting it into practice. The Egyptian report directly connected the backwardness of the region with the policies of the emir, which were based on monopolies and the Harar residents' fear of the Oromo. This was the first evidence that the conquerors knew what had occurred prior to their arrival.[44]

The second section of the geographical report of Muhtar and Fauzi dealt with what they called the "Nole Land." The khedival government requested clarifications about the Oromo in particular.[45] However, the report from Harar hardly related to the Oromo, either from the geographical or the anthropological standpoint. Possible explanations for this are the difficulty in reaching these areas, and the sense of danger felt by the conquerors in the city at the end of January 1876 (the Oromo were subjugated by the Egyptians only in March 1876). However, Muhtar and Fauzi essentially described the "Nole Land," its climate, and its agricultural potential.[46]

The third part of the report relates to Harar itself. This was the most detailed part of the research, covering its geographical location and much additional data characterizing the city and its inhabitants.

The Egyptians were the first to locate the city in modern geographical terms:

> Harar is the only city that the traveler comes upon after leaving Zeila, Berbera or Tajura. It is located several English miles from Zeila, at forty-eight, thirty-three and nine northern latitude, and at fifteen, twenty and forty-two eastern longitude, in relation to the initial meridian passing through Greenwich. The area of the city is 481,812 square meters. It is surrounded by a wall on all sides. The wall is between three and four meters tall and there are twenty-four towers. The wall is built of rocks, which originated in the mountains surrounding Harar. The wall was built in a uniform manner, but the rocks are of different types all mixed together, one stone upon another as if one unit, attached to one another with mortar and red mud, which is fired for 24 hours and then hardens. And if it does not harden and connects two stones, then the material is not good. The geometric shape of the city is not ordered.[47]

The very detailed description of Harar's *jugal* was not coincidental. It had a crucial part in the processes of creating a modern "Egyptian city" while simultaneously strengthening Ra'uf Pasha's image as the first modernizer, the president of "new Harar."

Immediately after presenting this data, Ra'uf Pasha's makes reference to the city walls and gates: "The opinion of His Honor, the *ra'is* [president] is to temporarily allow the wall to remain, until sandstone can be found in the area and checked. When the sandstone is found, that which is required will be done, around the order and organization of the city in the future. There are five gates in the wall that bear foreign names. His Honor, the president changed their names to the following: Bab-al-Hakim, Bab al-Futouh, Bab-al-Nasser, Bab-al-Rahmah, Bab-al-Salam."[48]

All five Arabic names of Harar's gates were the names of old Cairo's gates, with which Ra'uf Pasha was familiar. The "foreign names" described by the Egyptians were the names of the city gates in the local Harari traditional Adari language. The meaning of the term *bari* in Adari is quarter or gate. The name of the main entrance of the city is Asmaddin Bari. The Egyptians changed the name to Bab-al-Nasser, and the locals often termed it Bab al-Turk. Badri Bari became Bab-al-Hakim, since the gate faces Mount Hakim, south of Harar. Saqutat Bari became Bab-al-Salam in the Egyptian period. Argob Bari became Bab-al-Rahmah, and Assum Bari became Bab al-Futuch or Bab al-Zayla, north of the city.[49]

The changes in definition should be considered in relation to the changing role of Ra'uf—from *hikimdar* (governor) to *ra'is* (president). Ra'uf received the title *hikimdar* from the government of the khedive, and he was promoted to the rank of *fariq* following his success in the conquest of the city, but he is not called "president" in any other official document. Ra'uf Pasha's attitude toward the Harar city wall as "temporary," and his desire to change the names of its gates, did not necessarily emanate from considerations that were architectural. It is obvious that, as "president," he wished to completely uproot the formal symbols of the precolonial independent emirate. He acted according to the same logic when he immediately abolished the *mahlak* coin. The *mahlak*, along with the city walls and their gates, had been a distinct symbol of the 'Alī b. Da'ud dynasty in Harar since the seventeenth century.

The report of the Egyptians presented detailed information about construction within the city:

> The houses in the city are all built from unprocessed stone, as mentioned, and whitewashed inside in gray. The roofs of the houses are made of boards and straw, similar to those of Egyptian houses. But the houses of Harar have one story, and they have no windows. We chided them about this. But we found that there is a real reason for it. One of the house owners explained to us that this is due to the severe cold at night. There are few temporary structures in the city. There are 9,560 houses and 346 temporary buildings. The city is divided into streets and neighborhoods. The quarters are disorganized. Some parts of the city are 25 meters higher than others, as shown by the map drawing. There is room in the city for additional three or four thousand souls in addition to those who live there, who number 35,000.[50]

An important aspect of the report touched upon the study and mapping of water sources flowing into the city: "The distance of the four streams [from the city] is 6,000 meters. The distance of the five other streams is less. They are about 2,000 meters from the city. The depth of one of these streams is forty centimeters. Its width differs in relation to the nature of its flow, ranging between four and eight meters. When we fought in Gala Nole, they sent their women to draw water from another spring."[51] Accordingly, the Egyptians detailed their modern hydrological project:

> The *ra'is* ordered a channel to be dug that would divert the water of the other spring so that its waters would flow into the city. The length of this diversion channel will be about 50 meters. Its waters will reach, among other places, Ra'uf's orchard in the city. The name of the channel will be the "Isma'īli Stream." The new stream will contribute to the welfare of the inhabitants, and it will guard the self-respect of many of them, thanks to its proximity to them. The water is sweet and good to drink, and similar to the water of the Nile. It is gathered from the rain water that comes down from the mountains near Harar.[52]

The water diversion project in the name of the khedive was intended to free the city of dependence on springs that were distant from the city, and to provide a regular flow of drinking water in times of peace and war.

Nevertheless, it was an integral part of the Egyptian modern vision of creating a "new" and modern Harar, according to their vision. The modern colonial vision of the hydrological aspect was immediately connected to the exploitation of the local Harari agriculture. The Egyptian officers were also interested in the possibility of developing agriculture within the city walls, and they organized a study of its gardens:

> There are many fruits in Harar, including bananas, sour lemons, oranges, quince, peaches, and pomegranates. There are fourteen vineyards in the city. Among the vegetables are types of sweet potato, but only a few. Among the spices there are red and white roses, jasmine, basil and mint. When His Honor the *ra'is* was present, he began to act on sowing all sorts of vegetables and watermelons, different types of cucumbers, melons and other sorts of fruit like oranges, sweet lemons, apricots and others.[53]

As part of their interest in the local plants, the Egyptians first found khat, one of the most prominent symbols of consumerism and the leisure culture of Harar.[54] They were both curious about yet terrified of the plant: "This is different from anything else that is planted in the land of the Nile. Khat is a narcotic plant. It is difficult to go into detail, since we have not received the opinion of the scholars of botany and chemistry. Samples of the plant will be sent to chemists for study and analysis to determine its chemical makeup. Khat, it would appear, is useful. The inhabitants of this city say that it strengthens the body and helps digestion, and they use it to treat every illness." However, Ra'uf Pasha forbade the chewing of khat. The Egyptians questioned its medical efficacy, and the Ra'uf Pasha explained the logic behind the decree to the residents of the city: chewing khat "addles the brain."[55]

The pasha's decision is interesting for several reasons. The narcotic influence of khat did not fit in with the Egyptians' vision of civilizing the region. They had never come across khat before and did not succeed in working out what it was using their scientific instruments. Although khat was an integral part of Harar's traditional consumerism and the city's regional and global commerce networks, the Egyptians failed to understand khat's commercial potential, and they expected that they would not derive economic benefit from it. Their "modern" policy and practices were expressed by their decision that this unknown species should be studied in depth, and until they discovered its unique characteristics they should be wary of it. The Egyptians did not accept the city inhabitants' explanations about the advantages of khat and, lacking scientific proof, saw the local explanations as a folktale.

However, there is also an ideological explanation. Khat, like the *mahlak*, the gates, and the walls, remained one of the symbols of Harar and its traditions. The prohibition against chewing khat was also an attempt to erase the unique characteristics of precolonial Harar in the process of transforming it into an Egyptian *hikimdariya*, an Egyptian modern city. Muhtar and Fauzi reported that the residents obeyed the decrees of the *ra'is*; but there are no additional testimonies beyond this note.[56]

The Egyptians were quite aware of the special characteristics of other agricultural produce growing in the fields around Harar. Through their botanic studies, they knew how to identify such species as wheat and sorghum seeds, peas, beans, black-eyed peas, sweet potatoes, sugarcane, onions and garlic, and all sorts of seed-producing plants (cotton, types of saffron, sesame, barley, poppy, and pumpkin), and they investigated and measured these plants.[57]

The main agricultural product in terms of its importance to trade was coffee, in the view of the Egyptians. They saw its significant economic potential within a general Egyptian and regional context as well.

> The agriculture in the city includes the good coffee bean, used to improve other types of coffee. Fine quality is unjustly attributed to Mocha [a city in Yemen] coffee. The traders of Aden and the Europeans prefer Harar coffee to Yemenite coffee. They buy Harar coffee at a higher price than Yemenite coffee. For the most part, the reason for the attribution of fine quality to Yemenite coffee is a result of the confusion between Yemenite coffee and Harar coffee, which is bought and sold in Aden. If all the Harar coffee were in Egypt, it would be possible to say that the best coffee is Egyptian coffee. When the *ra'is* became aware of the quality of the coffee in Harar and its

> abundance, and the prosperity and wealth in store for the khedive state, he encouraged the inhabitants to sow more, and they did so.[58]

The colonial exploitation of Harari coffee was immediately used to reject the precolonial past and the Egyptians negatively described the emirate's commercial monopoly patterns. It was also characterized as a "source of great benefit which will soon come to our homeland [*wattanuna* in Arabic] from this."[59]

There is no doubt that the term *watan* (homeland) was not yet understood by these writers in its full modern national meaning. But its appearance in Arabic in this context indicates the development of feelings of belonging and identities on the part of the agents of the khedival government in Harar. This can be seen by examining the report further. The reference at the beginning of the report was to the khedive; afterwards the "khedive state" was mentioned, and in the end "our homeland." Almost completely correlating with this, the description of Ra'uf Pasha develops from "commander" to "*hikimdar*" and then to *ra'is* (president). The development of the new Harar as an entity in itself was apparently, in the eyes of the officers there, a sort of imagining and building of a pioneer outpost of their Egyptian homeland—a stimulus to its advancement.

The Egyptian scientific research heralded novelty and revolution, but it showed a spirit of preservation and traditionalism as well. The Egyptians measured distance and height in their attempt to give their studies a modern character. Yet they based themselves on local traditions, and those traditions lived on. The geographic, topographic, and botanic reports of the Egyptians, together with modern maps, transformed Harar and its environs from an entity wrapped in mystery to an actual and concrete geographic area, upon which actual political measures could be applied. Egyptian research made use of information-gathering methods that had not been seen before in the city. This scientific approach was an innovation that reflected more on the Egyptians than on the inhabitants of Harar. The city did indeed surrender politically, but its heritage was not forgotten. The names of the gates of the city walls, for example, survived the Egyptian conquest. Even today, under Ethiopian rule, each gate bears its name in the Adari and Arabic languages.

Anthropological and Ethnographic Research

The Egyptians divided the societies in the Harar area into three categories: the Somali 'Issa, the Nole Oromo, and the people of Harar. The first section of their report was dedicated to the inhabitants of "'Issa land." The Egyptians divided the "Somali people of the 'Issa nation" into three different tribes: Ijal, Wardalan, and Dalul.[60] Each one of these tribes, they reported, was divided into clans with various branches, numbering some 130,000 in all. These tribes did not dwell in permanent housing but wandered between stations in the Somali coastal valley: Gildessa, Darabi, and the "Land of Danakil."[61] Gildessa was the western border of the 'Issa country and the eastern border of the Nole Oromo territory.[62] These stations and the dwelling place of the 'Issa people were noted by Fauzi and Muhtar in the maps they attached to the report.[63] They also emphasized that there were hostile relations between the Somali 'Issa and the Danakil ('Afar) and Gadabuursi clans.[64]

The Egyptians presented their findings about the occupations of the Somali 'Issa:

> Their occupation is limited to hiring out their camels. They are more involved in this than in agriculture. Industry is nearly nonexistent. These are their occupations. The 'Issa nomad is satisfied with hiring out a camel or two once or twice a year. The payment covers his needs and those of his family. He is in his village, raises his camels and shepherds his flock. He drinks their milk and eats their meat. The 'Issa own much livestock and many sheep. The number of camels is small, since they eat camel meat and keep the she-camels for breeding and to drink their milk.[65]

As the report continues, the civilizing mission of the Egyptians is mentioned in this section: "The *ra'is* forbade the 'Issa to slaughter the camels. He explained to them that hiring out their camels could bring them much silver and gold. They, for their part, are used to saying that riding on camels leads to the beasts' deaths. They have a common custom that a camel is given to a rider on the condition that he pays in advance. If he does not do so, he does not get the camel. Ra'uf Pasha wanted to lighten this difficulty when he rented camels from them, since they presented him with very difficult conditions."[66]

The Egyptian civilizing mission among the 'Issa also had a religious aspect. Fauzi and Muhtar described the 'Issa as "devout Muslims for the most part." The Egyptians describe the segmentary 'Issa political infrastructure, which lacked any real hierarchal order or any other type of institutionalized regime, and they pointed out the need to educate them in this aspect as well.

> The ignorance of the 'Issa in reading, writing and the basics of the Sharīʿa prevents them from distinguishing between good and evil. They have no strong and stable leader, except for the leader of the sheikhs of the 'Issa dignitaries, al-Awjas Radilah Farih. The government that they set up for themselves is a type of commonwealth. When they want to bring down the government, they undermine its authority. Their wise men and heads of clans assemble. They consult with one another, and sometimes this goes on for many weeks. When the majority opinion is accepted, the government carries it out. This is how the appointment or the dismissal of their dignitaries is carried out. But now, their political processes are to be carried out in coordination with the khedival government.[67]

The second part of the report relates to the Nole Oromo. It was relatively sparse due to the Egyptian colonial context. When the report was written in January 1876, the Oromo had not been totally defeated, and the report was limited to emphasizing their bravery and their fighting.

The third part of the report by Fauzi and Muhtar dealt with the people of Harar. As usual in their reports, the Egyptians excluded the precolonial past and mentioned the period of Emir 'Abdashakur, with the goal of casting aspersions on his name and rule. The report was "functional" and mentioned the people of the city only in relation to areas where the Egyptians could derive benefit—industry, trade, and the conduct of city residents. Muhtar and Fauzi described the wretched condition of the craftspeople in Harar and the good tidings that the conquerors brought with them:

> There are very few crafts in the city. It is very reminiscent of what can be seen in the Arab towns. There is not much besides an engraver of Hadrami origin. In the city, there are a few blacksmiths as well. But craftsmen have begun to develop and spread their crafts in this city. The *ra'is* noticed the business acumen of the young people of the city. He made a connection between them and the merchants and with other craftsmen as well: stonemasons, blacksmiths, tailors and saddle makers. He wished to awaken the desire of the residents to learn. His success in this was so great that competition arose for learning these crafts.[68]

From testimonies of the people of Harar in the twentieth century, we learn that their ancestors told them that "the Arabs [meaning the Egyptians] brought quality to the city."[69] Harari scholar Mahdi Gadid was, however, sharply critical of the economic behavior of the Egyptians in Harar. He presented his findings in 1979 in Addis Ababa, during the Marxist rule of Mengistu Haile Mariam. In this context, one should understand the criticism regarding class and economy that Gadid directs toward what he called the false progress presented by the Egyptians, whose entire purpose was inconsiderate economic exploitation of the lower class of the city, after mobilizing the ruling class.[70]

In any case, the Egyptians were the first to attempt to encourage economic and industrial enterprises in the city by creating working connections between the artisans there and the young people of Harar. Without a doubt, their intention was to promote their own colonial goals in the city by developing the almost nonexistent industrial and commercial entrepreneurship within the city.

The Egyptians identified economic potential in the textile industry of Harar. They envisioned the city's development into an industrial center. In this context as well, Fauzi and Muhtar emphasized modern education and the personal example set by the *ra'is*, Ra'uf Pasha:

> The textile craft in Harar is very advanced, in comparison with other regions in the Sudan. In Harar, many fine garments are woven. Therefore, the inhabitants should be encouraged to be involved in industry, in order to expand this field and derive benefit from it in the future. The *ra'is* prepared two garments for himself, and the number of those using

> this type of garment increased, since they imitated him. In this way, he wished to encourage the residents of Harar to be involved in this industry. This example that is sent from here is sufficient to show his good efforts in the matter. Our goal is to turn Harar into a city that is more industrial than agricultural in its character.[71]

The Egyptians presented and examined the character of trade activity in the city prior to their arrival, emphasizing the seemingly unbalanced and unfair trade between the city and its neighbors:

> There were trade relations between the Gala tribes and the other Ogden tribes, as well as developed trade with Zeila and Berbera. The khedival governments will preserve these ties. There is no doubt that these ties were possible due to the central geographical position of Harar. Harar was originally a trade city, except that the trade did not take place with money, but with exchange of goods. Most of the people of Zeila, Berbera, and Hadarmawt bought coffee from Harar. They took advantage of the people of Harar and paid with various types of merchandise, such as tobacco, kinds of pearls and copper dross from the Arab countries. In exchange for giving this merchandise to the people of the city, they received great quantities of its fine coffee, in addition to processed and unprocessed hides. They also sold foreign merchandise to the people of Harar; things that were not needed at all in the city. Among these were leopard skins, ostrich plumes and ivory.[72]

The Egyptians did not hide their intention to take advantage of the city's resources in favor of Egypt. In the manner of colonialists over the generations, they portrayed themselves as "saviors" from the economic standpoint as well. In this context, they continued to blacken the name of the past emirs of Harar and portray them as corrupt and responsible for the economic distress of the city in the present. This was another layer in the Egyptian attempt to undermine the legitimacy of the institution of the emirate, introducing it as a corrupt monopoly that deprived its subjects.

To overcome these "ills" of the past, the Egyptians presented their approach to economic policy in the city. This included, primarily, substituting Egyptian currency for the *mahlak*. Muhtar and Fauzi's report explained Ra'uf Pasha's actions with monetary logic. They presented the replacement of the local *mahlak* with the Egyptian *rial* as an economic necessity; not as a caprice or unplanned act, but as part of a wider economic vision:

> The *ra'is* decided to carry out economic activity in Harar in this manner: half through currency and half through exchange of goods. From the time of his entrance into the city, money changing actions were taken. These were taken because the people of Harar did not know the different currencies, and they did not want to use different coinage. They used a counterfeit coin that was minted in the city in other times. All of the coins are made of copper. They can be compared to the value of the well-known *rial* in name alone, at an exchange of 32 *mahlak*. The *ra'is* is aware of the ignorance of the inhabitants of the city in this respect. He ordered them to abandon all of the coins, and to use only the currency of the khedival state and that of the friendly countries. But when there was not one true silver coin, His Honor instructed that the exchange rate of the *rial* should be 320 *mahlak*, and the Egyptian *qirsh*, 26 *mahlak*.[73]

The claim was that not only did Ra'uf Pasha not force too rapid a change upon the residents of Harar, but that they themselves wanted to break with their past. The *mahlak* was depicted not as the coin of the emirate, but "the coin of the emirs."

New Harar, New Egypt

Muhtar and Fauzi expressed the self-concept of Egyptian identity and its translation into the "civilizing mission" of the city.

> Our love for our homeland and loyalty to service lead us to say that if the trade is directed exclusively toward Egypt [*Misr* in the original], great benefit will come from that. This will bring great benefit to the homeland. Its income will increase in this way. The government will derive three types of benefit: first, all the profits whose source is from buying and selling in Arab countries; second, additional monetary circulation. The benefit that the government can gain from civilizing its subjects

> is well known, and their real knowledge of the currency. Your Honor is aware of the advancement of Egypt, since the late Mohammad ʿAlī Pasha developed trade, and revealed the value of profit to the inhabitants [of Harar]. Third, extensive income enters Egypt from Suez and Zeila. In the same way, the income of Harar will increase. The residents of Harar will also benefit from this. The inhabitants will benefit from profits, welfare, comfort and progress, in contrast with what has been up until this point.[74]

The report of the Egyptian officers contains expressions of local and prenational Egyptian feelings. The link between Egypt's past and future is emphasized, together with mention of the legacy of Muhammad (Mehmet) ʿAlī Pasha and his contribution to the Egyptians. There is also reference to a civilizing mission emanating from Egypt as part of this legacy. Finally, the entire colonial enterprise is described as bringing blessings both to Egypt and local residents.

While it is apparent that Ra'uf Pasha, Muhtar, and Fauzi thought about the "homeland" as representing—for the most part—the khedive and his government, it is difficult to conclude from this expression that they were already motivated by clear Egyptian nationalism. Their words, however, definitely reflect a clear local and territorial attitude that relates to Egypt as a geopolitically separate homeland, and a sense of the locality through a prenational prism.

Referring to Harar's Muslim inhabitants, Muhtar and Fauzi wrote:

> The behavior of the people of Harar is praiseworthy. In terms of intelligence, they are motivated by pursuit of profit and love of the homeland. They are disposed toward learning. All the children read in the *katatib* (plural of *kuttab*, elementary Quranic schools) throughout the day. The older people continue to read at night as well. The others work at learning the Sharīʿa with the experienced among the *ʿulamā'*. This is for the purpose of becoming expert in Islamic law. Their greatest love is for the *madhhab* (school of legal thought) al-Shafiʿi. The older ones in the city rcceive Islamic education according to al-Shafiʿi school of thought. Islam is seen as the tie that binds, in addition to the colonial attachment. The al-Shafiʿi adherents in Egypt are proud of the people of Harar, who

> are very devoted to their school of thought, especially in light of the fact that they live in the heart of Africa.[75]

One can learn from the report that Ra'uf Pasha initiated the establishment of a modern educational system in Harar. The doctor and pharmacist of the Egyptian garrison in the city, whose names are not mentioned, were put in charge of education in the *madrassa* (establishment of learning where Islamic sciences are taught; a college for higher studies). It is not clear whether the conquerors set up a new madrassa in the city, or used an old, local madrassa, but it is clear that they added new subjects to the curriculum: grammar, arithmetic and penmanship.

Education in this form was understood as part of the colonialist project of modernization, with Egypt serving as the model for its development: "Our greatest efforts are aimed at raising the level of culture, progress, and well-being in Harar. This is so that Harar can be the foremost city in the east besides Egypt."[76]

The outlook of the writers of the report on the "east" and "Egypt" is important, and reflects some common Orientalist perspectives that were prevalent in the late nineteenth century Ottoman colonial context. What was "East" for the Egyptian officers was actually the area south of Egypt—Sudan and the Nile Valley. The "East" was not a concrete location, but more of an abstract idea that Harar, as a concrete location, could embody and represent. The concept of a "civilizing mission" and its role in the "East" found special expression here. The African "East" was the uncivilized element that required educating. Egypt was presented as a model of a high level of advancement, culture, and wealth. It seems that the Egyptians adopted the colonialist conceptions of the Europeans toward them.[77] According to Ra'uf's way of thinking, the renewed Harar would become intermingled with the "New Egypt." Once it attained the level of progress to which the Egyptians aspired, intermarriage would occur between the Egyptian soldiers and the daughters of the city.

An additional step was taken to bring tidings of "Western" wealth and progress to the people at the expense of their "uncivilized" culinary traditions, which became permanent due to the "the ignorance, wickedness and tyranny of [emir] 'Abdullah." The Egyptians surveyed the types of food in the city and announced that their program also included changes in dietary habits:

> The types of food in Harar are very good. But its people eat only dried beef and bread made from sorghum. They did not eat any type of vegetable. Sometimes people would make do with various kinds of food as a substitute for lunch. For dinner, they would eat a little butter left over from the rice. That is because their emir forbade them to eat rice. The emir forbade eating dates as well, because, he claimed, they were the food of reigning emirs alone. . . . For the same reason they were forbidden to eat sweets. The *ra'is* cancelled all those limitations. He did this for the satisfaction of the people of the city. He permitted them to eat fine food as part of his service to his homeland.[78]

Imagining new Harar in the "East" and imagining modern Egypt led to the idea of creating Egyptian-Harari families: "The people of Harar are good-tempered and have refined characters. The brotherhood between them and the Egyptian soldiers will be so great that most will hope to marry their daughters to soldiers . . . the *ra'is* has declared to the soldiers that he is interested in creating marital ties with the city's inhabitants. He gave the soldiers an incentive to treat the women of the city well, and to give them fine garments. This is so that each of the Harar people rejoices in his heart and wants to marry off his daughter to one of the soldiers."[79]

There are no written records of marriages between Egyptian soldiers and the daughters of Harar, but one can assume from what is written that different types of personal relations did occur between the Egyptians and the local women. It would seem that ties were institutionalized as a result. In the economic report submitted to the khedival government in 1878, Charles Gordon, governor of Sudan and the Red Sea at that time, mentioned offering economic incentives to encourage marriages between Egyptian soldiers and the women of Harar.[80]

The colonial scientific knowledge from Harar was publicized in the Egyptian press. The Egyptian newspaper *Al-Waqa'i'a al-Masriya* [Egyptian Affairs] published the following item in its "Internal Affairs" section, written by "Dr. Dor Bey, one of the members of the Khedive's Geographic

Society to Harar," who wrote about the city's characteristics and the condition of its inhabitants.[81] As in other colonial arenas in Africa and all over the world at that time, colonial knowledge from Harar was made accessible to the Egyptian public. It was an integral part of the contribution of the Royal Geography Society of Egypt to the establishment of what Omnia El Shakry has described as twentieth-century "Egyptian Knowledge."[82]

The Egyptian research in Harar was the foundation of the city's development during this decade of Egyptian colonial occupation. Despite the fact that the Egyptians' "civilizing mission" in Harar failed in the long run, as it did in other areas where they were present until the mid-1880s, the scholarly infrastructure of information that they set in place remains valuable. The maps, measures, and observations of the urban and tribal society all contributed to the European and Ethiopian studies of the Gulf of Aden Basin and the Somali coast and formed a basis for its colonial role later. The Egyptian study of Harar transformed the concept of the city from a mystical place to an actual concrete place. The Egyptians' studies were directed at emphasizing the scientific dimensions of the "civilizing mission" and preparing the city to be part of the new colonialist enterprise. They proclaimed that their intention was to advance the welfare of the people of Harar, but the *hikimdariya* was aimed primarily at serving Egypt.

Ra'uf Pasha's main efforts focused upon creating a new urban expanse accompanied by a building boom. Visitors to Harar today can see buildings that were constructed during the Egyptian period and remain, essentially, as the last remnant of their activity. Their other efforts in Harar—educational, economic, and political—all disappeared without a trace.

5

Activities and Institutions

Construction

The momentum of Egyptian construction in Harar during the period of Ra'uf Pasha advanced in two realms: building for military and security purposes, and building the public spheres. Both of these were top priorities for the Egyptians in creating a new political sphere—in the first stage inside the city, and in the second stage outside the city.

Within the framework of construction for security needs, the Egyptians built a fortress on the ridge of Mount Hakim, south of the city. They installed an artillery battery in order to deter the Oromo who resided around the city.[1] As part of carrying out the plan for securing the roads connecting Zeila and Berbera, the Egyptians also built military outposts in the territory of the Afran Qallo of the Oromo and the Somali 'Issa.

Within the framework of civilian construction, the khedival government displayed an interest in building institutions that would demonstrate and symbolize Egyptian sovereignty. For this reason, the khedival government requested that Ra'uf Pasha evaluate the existing public buildings in the city. These buildings were designated for use in setting up a council (*diwan*), a police station, and a hospital that would provide health services to the inhabitants of Harar. The government offered to rent or purchase the buildings that it intended to designate as public buildings.[2]

In October 1875, Ra'uf Pasha asked the khedival government to send building engineers, which the government promised to do at the beginning of November. The engineers arrived in Harar in March 1876 and began developing the city's infrastructure. The momentum of building in the city can be divided into two main periods. The first took place during the tenure of Ra'uf Pasha as governor of the city, which lasted until May 1878. This period was part of the "golden age" of Egyptian independence in the city. The second period was short, and took place during the tenure of Muhammad Nadi Pasha as governor of the city.

The main sources that document the pace of building during these two periods are European. When Philipp Paulitschke and Alfred Bardey were in Harar during the 1880s, they reported the impressive momentum of construction. They described the renovation of the city walls and the construction of ten new mosques across the city. These reports indicated that by 1881, the Egyptians had built more than thirty new municipal buildings. In addition, new private homes were built and old homes were renovated. Paulitschke and Bardey even cited numbers, reporting that the number of temporary structures in Harar went down from 2,000 to 1,500 by 1884, and the number of houses grew from 6,000 to 8,000.[3]

The development of municipal construction was accompanied by a revolution in sewage collection and sanitation, and these had the effect of eradicating the smallpox epidemics that had ravaged the city in previous centuries. Although the European sources did not cite statistics, it seems that the lifespan in Harar increased, and demographic growth was registered in the city. In 1875, they reported that there were some 30,000 people in Harar (there is a gap of some 50,000 people between this report and the report of Dor Bey; it is difficult to determine which of the versions is more accurate). In 1886, there were 42,000 people living in Harar.[4]

The European sources that described construction in the city were also used by Harari Ethiopian researchers during the twentieth century. Mohammed Hassen stated that "the Egyptians did much on behalf of the city."[5] On the other hand, Gadid described the Egyptian construction in the city as another link in the chain of feudal exploitation, which, in his opinion, was the purpose of the Egyptian building. As he understood it, the Egyptians learned to use the ruling class's abuse of the lower classes to their advantage for preserving and directing their building enterprise.[6]

To evaluate the Egyptian building and entrepreneurship in establishment of municipal infrastructure, it is necessary to focus on the architectural aspect as reflected in the research of anthropologists and sociologists.

Tim Carmichael pointed out that the Egyptians "implemented an extensive series of infrastructural, health, administrative and religious reforms."[7] Elisabeth-Dorothea Hecht analyzed the population of Harar's "new" and "old" quarters from a sociological point of view. Hecht saw the Egyptian period as a time of some change, but not as a revolutionary period. She based her conclusions largely upon examination of the architectural activities of the conquerors in the city. According to her, the Egyptians brought a measure of architectural change to Harar as they attempted to transform it into a modern city. But they did not dramatically change the structures between its city walls. The distinctive style of a typical Adari home, she states, can be traced back to the period of Emir Yusuf (r. 1754–56).[8] As to the city's mosques, the Egyptians renovated existing mosques but did not make any changes to their original design.[9] Nevertheless, Hecht agrees that Ra'uf Pasha built the large mosque in the central square of the city, Faras Magala, in 1876 to commemorate his rule over the city.[10] The name of the new mosque was "Ra'uf Mosque," and it was built in a style described as "Egyptian."[11]

The Egyptians preserved one of the most prominent symbols of Harar—the *jugal* (city wall). They did not change the route of the wall, but rather renewed and strengthened its gates.[12] Preserving the wall was a security necessity for them, despite the surrender of the Oromo, so the change they made was only symbolic. They changed the names of the five major gates from Adari to Arabic names, as discussed in chapter 4, and they preserved the routes of the five central paths that led from the gates of Harar to the central market square (*Suk Magala*). After 1887, the Ethiopian rulers moved the market outside of the city walls, thus damaging the architectural and commercial fabric of Harar. The new market was a symbol of the architectural and social change that Harar underwent during the Ethiopian conquest. According to Hecht, ten years of Egyptian occupation was, in retrospect, a sort of "dress rehearsal" for the large and dramatic revolution that the followers of Menilek and the Ethiopian Christians would carry out in the city. Camilla Gibb was also of the opinion that the real revolution in Harar began only in 1887. Her research touched only minimally on the Egyptian decade in the city, concentrating instead on the period of Ra'uf Pasha's tenure as governor of the city and its surroundings.[13]

The conclusions of Gibb and Hecht were reinforced by modern-day plans for preserving and restoring the old city of Harar, which were initiated during the 1980s and 1990s. The Egyptian period was hardly recalled during the restoration process, which emphasized the connection between construction and the social networks—such as *Afōča* and *Mugad*—within the city.[14] Construction during the independent emirate era before 1875, and the change that occurred after 1887, were central elements of the restoration plans.[15] The Egyptian construction was acknowledged in publications that surveyed the history of Harar in a very general way, mostly through mention of the mosque and the bank that the Egyptians erected in the city.[16]

Hecht and Gibb minimized the importance of the Egyptian period, and did not view Egyptian construction in the city as a significant stage in its history. They did not investigate the social and political ramifications of the Egyptian conquest. These were mentioned only generally, with a focus mainly on the contribution of the Egyptian rule to ending the hegemony of the Oromo, bringing security to the roads between Harar and the sea and preparing the foundation for the European presence on the eve of the Ethiopian conquest of the city.[17] In this way, these researchers ignored the innovative scientific and cartographic achievements of the Egyptian occupiers and presented the decade of their presence as merely a short interval that served as preparation for the Ethiopian occupation of the city.

Administration and Taxation

The construction boom was designed to reshape the face of the *hikimdariya* architecturally and to establish a foundation for change in the public sphere. The Egyptians purported to herald a vague "equality" alongside reliance on the Sharīʿa. Practically speaking, their actions were felt among the city's residents in two main areas: financial, with change of the *mahlak* to Egyptian currency, and in the realm of the tax authority.

In March 1876, the Egyptians inaugurated a council whose purpose was to report on "civil" matters. The Egyptians did not end the position of the local *qāḍī*. This remained in the hands of a city resident, who continued to be the adjudicator of Sharīʿa religious matters.[18] No documents or testimony from city residents have been found that can shed light on the council for civil matters under Egyptian rule, or on the function of the *qāḍī* in religious matters. It seems that the civil body that was created by the Egyptians did not have real influence on political life in the city, and all that is known about it is the appointment of ʿAbd al-Whahab Wahabi Bey as "council president of the *hikimdariya*."

There is no current information about the conduct of the Egyptian soldiers in Harar, except for the commercial relations discussed previously and general statements about interpersonal relations between the soldiers and families in the city. It is reasonable to assume that there were incidents of improper behavior, such as theft of property from private Harari houses or trees from private orchards, or general cases of mistreating the inhabitants of Harar. This is evidenced by the fact that Ra'uf found it necessary to reissue his instructions on these matters.[19]

The Egyptians implemented two tax systems in Harar beginning in February 1876.[20] They preserved the traditional *zakat* taxation system. In accordance with testimony handed down orally, the residents of Harar gave one-tenth of their produce during the harvest season to the emirs. The Egyptians now demanded that the *zakat* be transferred to the treasury of the *hikimdariya*.[21] City dignitaries visited the *diwan* building each month and gave over the money that was collected.[22] Despite their declarations, Ra'uf Pasha and his men did not change the social and political patterns that were attached to this taxation system, and they preserved the preferred status of the landowners in the city. Until 1875, the emir administered the economy and agriculture by means of a monopoly of landowners, who benefited from his protection. The Egyptians did not change the *zakat* system but rather its organization and collection by "officials" appointed from the city residents and the Oromo.[23] The titles of these officials were preserved through the period of the independent emirate: *oyna* and *herta*.[24] The job definition also remained as it was, except that the Egyptians gave it official status within their administration, and the number of "officials" grew significantly during their time.

At the same time, the Egyptians created a new taxation system in the city: the *miri* property tax, which was based on a survey and classification of the land. In this way, the Egyptians brought about a revolution in the city. They were the first to survey property and create an organized record of ownership. The Egyptian government collected *miri* from the owners of 11,000 agricultural properties across the city, ranging from six to eleven piasters per dunam, depending on the nature of the land. A city resident—the *zaka-ari*—was in charge of collecting the property tax. Each month, accompanied by soldiers, he appeared before the landowners for this purpose.[25]

The Egyptians encouraged agriculture within the walls of the city, especially the cultivation of coffee beans. After the economic potential became clear, the khedive's government required Ra'uf Pasha to compel the residents of Harar to grow this crop and took upon itself to send them manure to improve the ground in the city. The Egyptian government wished to train local "experts" in growing and cultivating coffee. It even mobilized British colonialism as a model for establishing groups of indigenous specialists to be trained in Egypt itself.[26] Reliance on the British colonial model in India was not incidental. The Egyptians, as we have seen, adopted much of the attitude that purported to "civilize" the other, viewing him as "backward." Similar to the British, they thought that it would be useful to cultivate an indigenous elite class that would serve as officials and experts in their service.

Evidence of the efficacy of the Egyptian taxation system and its function as a "model" for proper governance can be found in the replication of the registration method by the Ethiopian conquerors in 1887.[27]

Education

The khedival government promised the residents of Harar "the dissemination of knowledge and education" to bring them up to the level of "the civilized nations."[28] The Egyptian national narrative portrayed Ra'uf Pasha and his men as Egyptians who "spread the light of learning and knowledge among the people of Harar."[29] The Ethiopian historian Mohammed Hassen emphasized the Egyptian contribution to education in Harar. He claimed that the Egyptians did not actually establish new schools in the city itself, but they immeasurably improved the quality of teaching in the traditional religious schools in Harar. In Hassen's opinion, the Egyptians integrated secular content into these schools, and "also sent some promising students to Egypt for higher religious studies."[30]

There are no sources testifying to the sending of exceptional students to Cairo. Nor are there Egyptian testimonies on the activities of local inhabitants in the educational institutions in Harar at the time. However, it is evident from available sources that the Egyptians tried to advance the field of education. This notion is described in the testimonies of Europeans who were not particularly in favor of the Egyptian enterprise in the city.[31] As discussed in chapter 4, the doctor and pharmacist of the Egyptian force were in charge of disseminating knowledge in the subjects of grammar and arithmetic. The Egyptian testimonies emphasized the interest in spreading knowledge and culture in an attempt to expose the young people of Harar to educational opportunities, and to encourage them to become involved in economic and agricultural initiatives.

Local sources, however, rarely mention the subject of education per se. In a 1992 research paper on centers of traditional learning in the city, ʻAbd al-Nasr Edris, a resident of Harar, makes no mention of any Egyptian influence on the field of education or Islamic learning.[32]

It seems that the "education" of the inhabitants did not focus necessarily on study. It had as its vision creating a new Harari person—modern and hygienic in appearance, according to the Egyptian perception of "right" and "modern." After describing the style of dress in Harar, the Egyptians decided to change it:

> The clothing of the people of Harar is similar to that in Sudan. Youths wear a type of long cloak of cotton with stripes or checks like in other Arab countries. The dignitaries and sons of the emir wear a garment of the same sort of fabric over the robe. The larger the garment, the higher the status [of the wearer]. The men wear shoes. Among the women there are two classes. All are barefoot, except for the women in the emir's house. The men of the emir's house wear nothing on their heads, they always go bareheaded. When the *ra'is* saw this, he imposed his will on the inhabitants regarding dress. He informed them that not wearing the head-covering was seen as heresy in Islam. Every man must wear it, and if he does not do so, he will be punished.[33]

It seems that they were using religious justifications to achieve broader cultural and social changes, and that the emphasis on aesthetics was seen by the Egyptians as part of the educational process, beyond imparting knowledge. Other topics of reeducation included gardening, cleanliness, construction, and orderly and modern administration and urban daily life. Ra'uf Pasha's actions were explained as a need to educate the residents of Harar about a "healthier" urban life, but it was an integral part of the Egyptian colonial policy. For example, special clothing was cut for Haj Yusef Muhammad, the descendent of the emir, and for Yusef Ahmad, son of Emir Ahmad, and they were ordered to wear them.[34] The Egyptians thus used the new clothing of the Harari inhabitants to differentiate between political and social classes.

Summary

There is no doubt that the Egyptians heralded a change in many aspects of life in Harar. They exchanged the *mahlak* for Egyptian coinage, levied land taxes, built new buildings and presented a new type of education never seen in the city before their arrival.

After a short while, the Egyptians began to evoke resentment in Harar. When the residents recovered from the shock of the conquest and the subsequent murder of Harar's emir, they began to view the Egyptians as new exploiters, whose exploitation was replacing that of the last emir. Many residents of the city viewed the Egyptians' policies toward the Oromo as harsh cruelty. The phenomenon of soldiers stealing and the "marriage project" conceived of by Ra'uf, made them seem "immoral" in the eyes of the inhabitants.[35] The exploitation and rigidity of the Egyptians of the city is expressed in a poem in the Adari language that was popular among the people of Harar during the rule of Ra'uf Pasha: "We ate and drank for you/ we went and returned for you/we sat and filled the chair for you/we spoke, and spoke satisfactorily for you/we cut the trees that require group work/ there is nothing that we have not done for you."[36]

Paying careful attention to the proclamations of Ra'uf Pasha and his men regarding turning Harar into "Egypt of the East" while carrying out the "civilizing mission" reveals the ambivalence in these statements. On the one hand, one hears the euphoria of the conquerors regarding their unique military success in Harar, and their feeling—identified with their homeland, Egypt—that they do, indeed, represent progress, culture and power. On the other hand, it is difficult not to hear the hollowness of their declarations about re-education and revolutionary political and social reorganization of the locals for their own good. One example of this is the establishment of the *diwan*. There is no evidence, either in writing or handed down orally, regarding the activities of the *diwan* in civil matters among the residents of Harar. The *diwan*, and the attempt to create a "civil" sphere, which the conquerors presumed to represent, left no trace. Another example is the educational system. The conquerors did indeed presume to add secular content to the educational system, but it is doubtful that they enhanced education in any meaningful way.

Egyptian economic activity did leave its mark, but only in the short term. Organized taxation led to the efficient storage of crops that were harvested as part of the *zakat* tax. The produce was sold at a low, fair price, and it is nearly certain that the residents felt economic relief, as compared to the era of Emir Muhammad 'Abdashakur.[37] This relief in itself was obviously not the goal of the Egyptians. They exchanged the monopoly of Muhammad 'Abdashakur for central control and rigor, upon which they spread a cloak of multidimensional "modern vision." It is possible that this would have been the basis of meaningful change in Harar, had the Egyptians remained there longer.

6

The Environs of the Harar *Hikimdariya*

The Emirate and the Neighboring Afran Qallo Oromo

The Afran Qallo Oromo in the Harar region were divided into two main groups. One group lived near the city walls, and the other was concentrated in the Gara Mullata area, nearly forty miles south of Harar.[1] In order fully to understand the effect of the Turco-Egyptian conquest on the Afran Qallo Oromo, it is necessary to give a brief summary of their historical relationship with Harar.

The Afran Qallo who lived next to the city walls had a complex symbiotic relationship with the emirate. Until the middle of the nineteenth century, they were under the direct rule of the family of the Harar emirs.[2] The Harar emirate embraced the chosen leaders of the Oromo, who dwelled outside the city walls, clasping them to its political and economic bosom. In the center of this "embrace" was the dependence of the emirs on the leadership of the various populations outside the walls. This was a symbiotic relationship: the elected *bokku* of the Oromo clans were under the military and social sponsorship of the emirs, which helped them stabilize the emirs' rule. In exchange, the Oromo clans ensured the emirs' freedom of movement on the trade routes to and from the city, from the coast and from the Christian Ethiopian kingdom of Shewa.[3]

At the center of the relations between the emirate and its close neighbors were three prominent characteristics: blood ties between the emirs' family and the Oromo elite; the participation of the Oromo in the emirate economy and their ownership of the land outside the city; and the Islamization of the Oromo.

Regarding the first characteristic, the formation of marriage ties between the Oromo elite and the Harar emirs began in the seventeenth century as part of the establishment of the Ibn Da'ud's dynasty in Harar. These ties brought together two groups that viewed each other as the absolute "other," while forging a family bond and a path toward involvement in the political and social matters of the city.[4] It will be remembered that from the beginning of the nineteenth century, the Oromo began to progressively take over the institution of the emirate. This process reached its zenith when Emir Muhammad b. 'Abdashakur (who ruled between 1856 and 1875) became the protégé of the Nole Oromo.[5]

The second characteristic of the relations between the emirs and the Oromo found its expression in two central economic positions filled by the Afran Qallo in cooperation with the emirate. First, they took part in the administration of the economic household system of the emirs, a position called *amir garach* in the city's Adari language.[6] Second, they supplied food to the city in times of trouble, such as the eighteenth and nineteenth centuries, when the city's inhabitants were "poor and hungry and their control over the land surrounding the city was of a small radius."[7] The poverty that plagued the residents of the city was great, and there were those among the Somali and the Oromo who aided the population of the city by supplying agricultural produce.[8]

Regarding the third characteristic, Harar was considered, from the time of its founding, to be a regional center of Islamic learning.[9] It seems that marriage ties between the emirs and the Oromo elite outside the walls contributed to the conversion of a significant portion of this elite. Islamization stemmed mainly from political and practical motives of the emirate. Over the course of the eighteenth and nineteenth centuries, conversion to Islam succeeded in connecting the Oromo elite to the circles of religious and political identity in Harar.[10]

It was not only the emirate that derived political benefit from the Islamization of the Oromo. The Afran Qallo were also influenced by these social and political changes, as Islam was a political tool in the hands of the Oromo elite toward its subjects. Through Islam, the emirate became the political backer of the Oromo elite. The religious link between the emirate and the Oromo elite strengthened the latter's status among the

Oromo. Moreover, the Islamization of the Oromo elite helped this group strengthen its ties with Muslim and other ethnic groups on the southern Ethiopian plateau and the Somali coast.[11]

All of this notwithstanding, it seems that until the Turco-Egyptian conquest most of the Afran Qallo remained loyal to their traditional religion, *Waqqiya*.[12] This adds significance to the conversion of the elite to Islam in the days of the emirate. It seems that the repercussions were more political and economic than religious, and that the role of Islam was significant as an instrument of strengthening social and economic bonds among the Oromo themselves, not necessarily in strengthening religious institutions."[13]

Various sources point out that Islam was rooted among wide strata of Afran Qallo Oromo societies. Following a tour of the Oromo territories in 1876, Muhtar reported that he had encountered small Oromo children in the Bobasa region, east of Harar, who knew three-quarters of the Quran by heart.[14] Oral history from the Oromo describes the last emir of Harar, Muhammad b. 'Abdashakur, as "the herald and developer of modernization among them," through Islamization. According to these sources, the emir sent three religious preachers from Harar to the Oromo territories at the end of the 1860s. The three were Haj Omar, 'Abdullahi Saraj, and his brother Abbas Saraj. Their success was impressive: many of the Oromo, he reported, converted to Islam on the spot. Evidence of this success can be found in the construction of many mosques in the territory of the Nole Oromo clan. Most were named for Emir Muhammad.[15]

The three characteristics of relations between the emirate and close neighbors led to the establishment of the Afran Qallo Oromo elite that ruled outside the city walls. Even though this elite maintained traditional ties with the central political body of the Oromo in the Mulata region—the *Raba Dori*—it was even more connected to Harar.[16] An example of this can be found in Burton's 1856 report on Oromo agricultural groups that returned from the markets of Harar after selling butter and milk.[17]

There were significant repercussions to the deepening of ties between the city and the Oromo agricultural groups, for the city as well as for the Oromo. The process of settling groups of Afran Qallo Oromo farmers in permanent dwellings was accelerated in plots adjacent to the city wall.

This process began with the establishment of the Ibn Da'ud dynasty in the seventeenth century, and reached its peak at the end of the first half of the nineteenth century. The Oromo settlers became an essential part of the emirate's economy, and were integrated into its administration as well. In order to understand these mutual relations, it is necessary to present the main ranks in Harar up until 1875.

The administrative system of the emirate preserved the various administrative and taxation ranks that had originated in the Sultanate of 'Adal during the fifteenth century.[18] At that time, the city was divided into five sections or quarters for administration and tax collection. The emir appointed an official over each section. The official's title was *malaq*, a term created by joining two words in the Adari language: *mala*, meaning "roads" or "intentions," and *aqa*, meaning "knowledge."[19] The *malaq* was in charge of a defined and specified area within the city, as well as a defined area outside the walls. Within the city, he was responsible for enforcing the laws of the emirate and collecting taxes from owners of agricultural land. Under certain circumstances—such as when the emir's army set out on campaigns outside the city—the *malaq* was responsible for collecting special taxes to cover the costs of the campaign.[20] In addition, the *malaq* was responsible for distributing water for agricultural plots. In exchange for his services, he received a greater share of water than others in the city and was given 300 *gerib* of land in the agricultural region outside Harar.[21]

In the areas outside the city wall, the emirate created an additional rank: *garad*. The origin of the name is unclear, but in Somali it means a man who holds a high government office, sometimes parallel to a prince. The emirate appointed Oromo dignitaries who lived outside the walls to this position. The *garad* was a chief of a village or hamlet. His principal role was to collect taxes from the villagers and he was rewarded with 600 *gerib* of land by the emirate.[22]

The *garad*'s supervisor was the *dogin*—"governor of the outer areas" in the terminology of the Adari language.[23] The *dogin* was the "open eye of the emir" in the areas outside the city. This position was filled only by residents of Harar until the nineteenth century. The authority relationship between the *malaq* and *dogin* is not clear. It would seem that in periods when the emirs were strong, the *malaq* dealt only with internal matters, while the *dogin* was in charge of the areas outside Harar.[24]

The emirate made the *bokku* of the Afran Qallo populations subservient by apportioning tracts of land and giving out titles of official positions, thus becoming a significant element in their lives until the early nineteenth century. Apportioning land and bestowing other favors to members of the clan were tools in the hands of the emirs. These furnished social and political mobility among the clans surrounding Harar. An Oromo who had proven his loyalty to the emir and received land could achieve the rank of *bokku* and depose his predecessor.[25] In this way, the emirs turned into a major force that became involved in the internal politics of the clan. They succeeded in penetrating its inner political and social circles and using them for the benefit of the emirate. The process of bestowing positions and taxation privileges upon the Oromo dignitaries was effective for the emirs of Harar. They did not bring the Oromo into Harar; rather they created an indirect and concealed system of rule among their neighbors. This concealment did not hide the strength of the monopolies upon which the emirs' system rested. Sidney Waldron described it as "approximates a small-scale feudal system."[26]

Thus, until the beginning of the nineteenth century, the emirs succeeded in creating a barrier between the Oromo clans of the Afran Qallo surrounding Harar and the central ruling body of the Oromo in Mulata. In this way, they deepened the dependence of the Afran Qallo population clans on the city from a political and economic standpoint. The blood ties between the Harar elite and the Oromo dignitaries, and the bestowing of positions and land—alongside the growing involvement of the Oromo in the city's economy—all brought about the settlement of the Oromo in permanent dwellings outside the city walls. However, the weakening institution of the emirate and the growing dependence of the city residents on the trade routes between Harar and Zeila and Berbera on the one hand, and Shewa in Ethiopia on the other, disturbed this balance of power bit by bit over the course of the nineteenth century.

The growing dependence of the city on agriculture and the necessity of securing the trade routes to Berbera and Zeila led to the intensification of two major processes from the beginning of the nineteenth century: one demographic and political-economic, and the second, religious.

First, the demographic growth of the Oromo relative to their population size within the city, coupled with Harar's growing economic dependence on agriculture, strengthened the Oromo's might and disturbed the balance of power in the relationship between the city dwellers and their neighbors. The Oromo farmers closest to the city, called Quttu, and the Afran Qallo federation that lived in Mulata farther away, became a force that threatened to take over the emirate. The weakening of the institution of the emirate and the political tensions within the emirs' family regarding the attitude toward the Afran Qallo in Harar intensified this process.

Second, the process of settling the Quttu around Harar was accompanied by Islamization, which was the principal way of joining the political and economic circles of the city.[27] Islamization ate away at the barrier between the city and the rural spaces around it that the emirate had tried to erect prior to the beginning of the nineteenth century.

Richard Burton was the first to mention the Quttu. In his 1856 description of the agricultural districts surrounding Harar, he referred to the Oromo population as "the Kutti."[28] Burton incorrectly recorded the Oromo word Quttu, which means "workers of the land" in the Adari and Oromo languages. It seems that the occupations of Afran Qallo populations surrounding Harar can be divided into two: the Quttu (who are also called *argata*, meaning farmers) and Prontuma (meaning cattle raisers). The Oromo Quttu, were, in Muhtar's words, "a hardworking people with a reputation for good farming."[29] In addition, the *oyna* and *herta* officials, discussed in chapter 5, were an integral part of the economic and political circles in Harar.

Afran Qallo Military Downfalls

On 17 October 1875, Ra'uf Pasha received a letter (in Arabic) from *Garad* Adam Asihabiyye, one of the dignitaries of the Jarso people of the Oromo, who lived northeast of Harar.[30] The letter included a poem praising Ra'uf, and declared the surrender of the Jarso to Egypt. Beyond this, the letter was dedicated to a description of the historical ties of the Jarso Oromo to Harar, and explained that the Jarso were devout Muslims.[31]

In addition to the declaration of surrender that representatives of the Oromo presented to Ra'uf Pasha when he entered the city on 11 October 1875 (as mentioned in chapter 3, this declaration was signed by sixty-two representatives of the Afran Qallo), the letter contains an apparent expression of total loyalty. However, it seems the Egyptians felt that victory over the Oromo could not be achieved without humiliating them and destroying their power in a direct and final manner. Although we have no testimony from the Afran Qallo, it is reasonable to assume that there were some among them who did not agree to a real surrender.

The initial battles with the Afran Qallo's warriors on 8–10 October 1875 concerned the Egyptians. Ra'uf Pasha even added in his first report from Harar that his troops were insufficient to control the city and its surroundings. That was probably the context for his request that the khedival government send two companies and an artillery battery as reinforcements. In order to improve the morale of his troops, he requested a military band as well.[32]

In various European testimonies, there is evidence to back up the assumption that the Egyptian force was quite concerned about the Afran Qallo in the early months of its presence in the city. Alfred Bardey claims, for example, that the Egyptians knew that "the Oromo were, and remain, a constant threat to the rulers of Harar."[33] Philipp Paulitschke emphasized the threat that the conquerors felt from the Oromo—a threat that was removed only when the Egyptian force was strengthened at the beginning of 1876.[34] The British, in contrast, saw a direct connection between the military reinforcement in Harar and Ra'uf Pasha's "obsession" regarding the Oromo, rather than any real concern about a military threat.[35]

Ra'uf Pasha wanted to acquire the loyalty of the Afran Qallo elite as he had done with the tribes that surrendered to him on the way from Zeila to Harar. He requested from the khedival government two types of material for garments, one with red threads, as well as robes sewn with red threads to "give to the Gala dignitaries and their sheiks." He also asked for four gold watches "with one decorated with a diamond or two."[36] As a result, on 11 November 1875 the khedival government promised military reinforcements that would be comprised of regular soldiers and cannons.[37] This indicated that the khedival government wished to calm Ra'uf and support his intensive efforts in Harar and in the Afran Qallo regions. The commitment to send reinforcements was the government's first declaration of intent regarding its plans in Harar, and it seems that its purpose was to strengthen the spirit of the Egyptian force with the promise of a long-term Egyptian occupation of the city.

The Turco-Egyptian force was strengthened at the end of 1875 and during January 1876. The Egyptians built a military outpost at the top of mount Hakim, and from there they controlled the expanse stretching from the north and west of the city. Placement of an artillery battery there was meant to foil the advantage of the Afran Qallo cavalry. According to British reports, by the end of February 1876, the Egyptians had reinforced their army in Harar until it numbered a large regular infantry force, six hundred irregulars, two hundred cavalry, two batteries of Howitzer mountain cannons, and sixteen rocket launchers, as well as a unit of machine guns and a company kept ready at Berbera. An additional four hundred Egyptian infantrymen were spread out in key positions in the area of the Berbera and Zeila ports. Thus, the Egyptians succeeded in establishing their control over the urban centers and the coast, and in Harar.[38]

A string of new skirmishes between the Egyptians and the Afran Qallo took place around Harar during February and March 1876. There are a number of different versions. Oromo tradition claims that in the middle of February 1876 Ra'uf Pasha invited the senior Oromo leaders to a peacemaking meal at his office in Harar. They were sure that Ra'uf Pasha's invitation indicated a sincere desire to relieve the tension, or at least to give recognition to the Afran Qallo leaders. The Egyptians assembled the Afran Qallo delegation opposite the administration building and opened fire. Not one member of the delegation survived.[39]

Oromo tradition makes a connection between the Egyptians' slaughter of the Afran Qallo delegation and the new outbreak of fighting between the sides.[40] Immediately after the slaughter, the Egyptian forces rushed into the areas of the Nole people outside the city. They took advantage of the element of surprise and hoped that the state of shock induced by the murder of the Afran Qallo leaders would break the Afran Qallo more easily. According to Oromo tradition, the Egyptians took advantage of the presence of the Afran Qallo's leader, Orfo Jilo Biko, and the main Afran Qallo force in the Ogaden desert, where they had been involved for some time in scuffles with the Somali 'Issa people. However, the Oromo did not surrender easily. In the area known as Dire Gofile (which means "Valley of the Skulls" in Oromiffa, the Oromo people's language), located in the Nole territories east of Harar, a prolonged and bloody battle took place between the Egyptians and the Oromo. In the end, the Egyptians' heavy weaponry and modern military methods subdued the Afran Qallo.[41]

After the defeat in Dire Gofile, Orfo attempted to organize the remaining Afran Qallo's military forces and move toward Harar. The Oromo tradition portrays Orfo as a hero. Although he lost a foot in the battle with the Somali in Ogaden, he tried to lead the force that he had gathered to fight against the Egyptians in the Gara Mullata area, near Harar. The campaign ended in disaster for the Afran Qallo people. Orfo's son, Muhammad, related that his father was taken prisoner by the Egyptians, who humiliated him and forced him to convert to Islam.[42]

Afran Qallo tradition attributes great importance to the battle at Dire Gofile and the subsequent captivity of Orfo and his conversion to Islam. For the Afran Qallo, this was a military and political breaking point. The feeling of despair and humiliation spread to additional Oromo *gosa* of the Afran Qallo, such as the Jarso and Babillee. The elected political establishment of the *Raba Dori*, which will be discussed later, was crushed and never recovered.[43] From this point on, the Afran Qallo never dared to revolt against the Egyptians.[44]

Other versions did not mention the slaughter of the Afran Qallo leaders. In contrast with the Oromo tradition, they attributed no great importance to the battle at Dire Gofile. Most of the versions mention a chain of military skirmishes of uneven strength between the Egyptians and the Afran Qallo. Finally, at the end of March 1876, the Oromo were subdued. Apparently, they suffered heavy losses of life and property, since the Egyptian artillery destroyed their cavalry. However, no exact details of Egyptian casualties are available.[45]

The Egyptians officially reported an encounter with the Afran Qallo on 20 February 1876. The report indicated that a steamship of the Egyptian fleet, *Cairo*, unloaded military reinforcements at the Zeila port, including two companies of infantrymen and two artillery batteries. The goal of the force was to subdue the *fitna* of the Oromo tribes, which had decided to rebel against the Egyptians. The report mentions not even one battle. According to this, the reinforcements were sufficient to "return the Oromo to their senses," and convince them to pay taxes to the Egyptians and put down their weapons. The report mentioned that there was no need for such a large number of soldiers, and that three hundred returned from the Gildessa area to Harar itself.[46]

Apparently, the violent confrontation with the Afran Qallo Oromo had been provoked at Ra'uf Pasha's own initiative. The policy of the khedival government was markedly less militant toward the emir and residents of Harar. The khedival government provided the reinforcements Ra'uf had requested but did not press the defeat of the Oromo by force. It may be that the khedive was concerned about another crushing setback in Harar, and wished to lessen the conflict between the Egyptian force and the local elements—the emir and the Oromo. By contrast, Ra'uf Pasha and his men in Harar saw the Oromo as an existential threat.

This gap can be explained in a broader regional context. The khedival government was aware of the failures of McKillop Pasha and Munzinger Pasha on the Somali coast in December 1875. The conquest of Harar was carried out successfully and completely—certainly in contrast to the Egyptian debacle on the Somali coast. Nevertheless, the reports of the defeats on the Somali coast, together with vague reports of Ra'uf Pasha's arrival in Harar, created uncertainty in Cairo. The British knew of the emir's execution by the Egyptians and reckoned that the situation was dire, due to the Oromo attacks.[47] The British, on the one hand, were filled with admiration for the survival of the Egyptian force in Harar, after the failure in the area of other Egyptian forces that were meant to join and assist them in facing the Oromo.[48] On the other hand, they were skeptical about the ability of Ra'uf Pasha to stand firm in the city.[49] The uncertainty as to the fate of the Egyptian force in Harar reached its peak at the beginning of February 1876. The lack of communication between Harar and Zeila, and word of the severe battles between Ra'uf Pasha and the Afran Qallo, heightened the sense that the fate of the Egyptians in Harar was sealed. However, the

British reported on 12 February 1875 that Ra'uf Pasha had passed a message to the khedive saying "the situation in Harar is secure and stable."[50] It seems that Ra'uf Pasha understood early on that the nonarrival of Munzinger and McKillop, who were supposed to join him and reinforce his troops in Harar, was a bad sign. This left him isolated until the arrival of reinforcements from Zeila at the beginning of 1876. According to the estimation of the British, "the Egyptian officers were bitterly mistaken in their attempt to penetrate the land with troops that were unready for this, and without preserving lines of communication with their bases."[51] However, the successful campaign for Harar under the command of Ra'uf Pasha refuted this statement by the British.

During November 1875 the khedival government sent a list of detailed questions regarding the "Gala—their leadership, their political, social, and religious structures, their occupation, and their military abilities."[52] Some of these questions were answered by the report from Harar in January 1876, before the Oromo populations surrendered completely. The report noted that members of Nole were divided into four tribes, inhabiting delineated territories. Members of the "Gala Nole" were described as "warriors who attack in an organized fashion, arranging themselves neatly in rows. They are experts in fighting and do not fear death."[53]

In early April 1876, the khedival government learned of the Afran Qallo's riots around Harar and shared its thoughts with Ra'uf Pasha:

> Your report indicated that the Gala tribes have started a mutiny because their income has stopped and they no longer reap the benefits they were accustomed to in the time of the emir. It seems to us that if we could win their hearts by giving them, in full, that which they were used to and which caused them joy; we would have friendly cooperation with them. Perhaps we can even train several thousand of them as a fighting force. These fighters will not be given firearms, but will continue to carry the weapons they are accustomed to, such as spears and arrows. We could provide them with a salary or fabrics, as they were used to, and pay a monthly salary to their sheikhs as well. There is no doubt that when they understand that the government wants to make use of them by having them in its service, they will change their ways and their hearts will lean towards the government.[54]

It seems that the khedival government tried to determine a moderate and gentle policy toward the Oromo, and was offering to integrate them peacefully into the city administration, and even, critically, noted that military maneuvers conducted by the soldiers outside the city might have been the cause of the Oromo rebellion. The khedival government asked the *hikimdariya* to restrain the soldiers, and noted that those who do not act peacefully "should be sent back to Egypt to learn the basic rules."[55] However, the moderate attitude emanating from Cairo did not reflect the actual occurrences in Harar, and there was no coordination between the instructions of the government and what was happening in the city, at least until mid-1876.

The Destruction of Political Institutions

The Afran Qallo's military defeats led to multifaceted political and social destruction. Traditional analysis of the Afran Qallo's tragedy was used, almost immediately, to understand it as part of the mutual and reciprocal relationships between Harar and its neighbors. This trend was reflected in some historians' claims that the "arrival of Ra'uf Pasha brought to an end 300 years of reciprocal relations between the Oromo and the emirs of Harar" and that the "economic and political pact between the Oromo and Harar residents was violated by the Turco-Egyptian conquest."[56] Without any doubt, the Afran Qallo populations played a central role in the history of Harar's emirate until 1875 and they were deeply influenced by the political, religious, and economic reforms heralded by Turco-Egyptian colonialism. Reexamination of the historical events through the destruction of the Oromo military, political, and social sovereign institutions highlights even more the destructive effects of the Turco-Egyptian colonialism on the social and economic life of the Afran Qallo.

The *Raba Dori* was the central political and military institution of the Oromo living around Mulata, south of Harar. It was the "umbrella organization," a confederation, that brought the various clans of the Afran Qallo together. The *bokku* (heads of the different clans) were members of the *Raba*. The *Raba* was the elected political body and the *Dori* was its military branch.

The *Raba* was elected every eight years by Oromo men, members of the various clans. The last elections had taken place in 1872, three years before the arrival of the Egyptians. At the head of the *Raba Dori* sat the *abba fugug*, a sort of head of the Oromo federation of clans. Right before the arrival of the Egyptians, Orfo Jilo—the *bokku* of the Nole Oromo clan—served in this office. The *bokku* for the *Raba* were chosen mostly from among the elders of the various clans and were well-versed in the unwritten constitution of the Oromo clans. This constitution was called the *Hera Gosa* and it defined, through an oral tradition passed down from generation to generation within the clans, norms of government and law. The *bokku* of the clan was the unique authority regarding judgment and punishment. He was also in charge of disagreements in the clan, as well as consultation with the *bokku* of other clans when it came to disagreements among them. The *Hera Gosa* defined laws dealing with war and peace, dividing plunder according to blood ties within the clan, and providing compensation to the families of the warriors of the clans. The rules of electing the *Raba* were also defined in the constitution. In its social and economic aspects, the *Hera Gosa* was a codex of all the unwritten rules that encompassed the totality of subjects concerning the clans and their members. These rules emphasized mutual responsibility among the members of the clan. The obligation of the clan toward its members was expressed by economic aid in cases of poverty or payment for redeeming captives, among other ways.[57]

After the elections to the Raba were held, each clan sent its representative to Watar, a village twenty miles east of Dir Dawa. There, the representatives performed a series of ceremonies to appoint the *abba fugug* and the *abba dulla*, the deputy of the *abba fugug*, who served as head of the council of the various *bokku* in Mulata. The election ceremony for the two concluded with the planting of the sapling of the "governing tree," called *dala* in Mulata. Planting the sapling symbolized the establishment of the new *Raba* every eight years.[58]

In 1876, Muhammad Muhtar expressed his amazement at the Oromo systems of government and their values and called the *Raba* "an interesting democratic system, despite its primitive nature."[59] A more concrete reference to the Oromo political institutions was mentioned by Ra'uf Pasha in April 1877, when he noted their political unity:

> The residents of this region are different from the Sudan tribesmen, who are hostile to one another. Therefore, any official of the khedival government can make a treaty with anyone whom he wishes among the tribes, and act according to necessity, since the tribes are united. Their rule operates as following: each tribe has its own *majlis* [council] which is made up of 100 men. This body is elected for a year. The head of the council is called the *bokku* and is replaced each year. There is a council of 300 men that rules over the *majalis* [plural of *majlis*] of the tribes. The president of this body is called the "great *bokku*." If the councils decide on making peace or war, they inform him of this without delay.[60]

The final defeats of the *Dori* by the Egyptians in March 1876 led to the destruction of the Oromo institutions. For the members of the Afran Qallo populations, this was an incomparably difficult experience. As Father Cahagne, the head of the French Capuchin order in Harar, wrote in 1882: "The Gala feel like orphans whose rights have been cancelled from birth. They believe that the Egyptians have ruined their lives."[61]

The damage caused by Turco-Egyptian colonialism to the political and social fiber of the Afran Qallo surrounding Harar and Mulata was evident in a number of ways. First, the Egyptians destroyed the umbrella organization of the Oromo clans, and from 1876 it was not resurrected. Second, the destruction of the political and social institutions there put an end to the *gada* and *mooti* systems.

The *gada* was the division of the clan into age brackets of eight years.[62] The members of the third *gada*, ages sixteen to twenty-four, were the warriors; the members of the fourth *gada* were shepherds; the fifth *gada* members were the political leadership; and the sixth were the elders and counselors. This system contributed to tribal solidarity and stability and promised intergenerational mobility. The age groups functioned according to an order predetermined by the tribal leadership. This framework created institutionalized social and political structures among the Oromo in all of southern Ethiopia, as well as in the Harar region.[63]

Toward the end of the eighteenth century, the *gada* system became obsolete and was exchanged for the *mooti* system. The *mooti* was a type of copy of the sultanic system, similar to Islamic sultanic constructions that existed on the Ethiopian mountain plateau until the sixteenth century.[64] Instead of division into age brackets with specified roles within the tribe, "emirs" or "sultans" took over the Oromo clans and ruled over them in an authoritarian manner. The development of the slave trade in the area, and the transformation of Zanzibar Island to its center, changed the Oromo areas into principal trade routes from the Horn of Africa to the Arabian Peninsula. The Oromo "sultans" were involved in slave trade and ruled their tribes through the system of the ruling "court": the *mooti* court. The political and social change among the Oromo was expressed by the establishment of Oromo sultanates at the beginning of the nineteenth century, including the Jimma, Kafa, Sidamo, Guma, and Limmu-Ennarya.[65] These (with the exception of the Jimma) disappeared after the takeover of the Ethiopian mountain plateau by Menilek, the Ethiopian emperor, in 1889.

The Oromo scholar Asafa Jalata has blamed the people of Harar for making a treaty with the Egyptians, whose goal was to destroy the Oromo clans: "The *gada* system was attacked in eastern Oromia by the Turco-Egyptian and Adare alliance. The interethnic alliance and interdependence between the Adari and the eastern Oromo were shattered when the Adare invited the Turco-Egyptian power to colonize the Hararghe region in 1875. Under the Turco-Egyptian rule, between 1875 and 1885, the Adare consolidated their power and accumulated capital at the cost of the majority Oromo."[66] Jalata's main claim was that during the decade of Turco-Egyptian rule, the Adari solidified their power and grew wealthy at the expense of the Oromo majority. The Oromo who lived further east kept the *gada* system until this was destroyed by the Turco-Egyptian treaty with the Adari.

Jalata accepted as reliable the local oral histories regarding the Harari people's invitation to the Egyptians to occupy the city in 1875, and he stated that this invitation was a treasonous violation of the pact between the city residents and their neighbors. Thus, he ignored the suffering of the people of Harar and the growing strength of the Oromo at their expense from the beginning of the nineteenth century. He also ignored the suffering of the Harari residents under Egyptian rule, instead presenting the relations between the conquerors and the people of Harar as the relations between allies of equal status.

The term "Oromia," used in Ethiopia as the name of a state in the Ethiopian Federation since 1991, was not known to the Oromo themselves during the period under discussion. Its retroactive use is part of a current attempt to construct ethnic and national identities for the descendants of clan members of the past. This goal of Jalata's led him to reach sweeping conclusions. He hardly differentiated between the Quttu surrounding the city and the Oromo of the Mulata region. From his standpoint, all of the Oromo were subject to the *gada* system, which was less relevant to the Quttu. It was not at all relevant to the Mulata area, which was ruled by the *Raba Dori*.

Sidney Waldron has also pointed out that the Adari-Egyptian treaty was a means by which the people of Harar derived economic and political benefit at the expense of their Oromo neighbors. He claimed that the relations with the Egyptians allowed the people of Harar to revive their economic and political hegemony at the expense of the positions and land ownership of the Oromo dignitaries, even though they too were harmed by the Turco-Egyptian conquest.[67]

From 1876, the Oromo surrounding Harar did indeed lose their power. A number of their dignitaries were integrated into the administrative systems of the conquerors, but their status changed from that of officials appointed by the emirate and de facto rulers to that of officials appointed by the Egyptians, having no authority whatsoever. Jalata claimed that "the property of the Oromo was confiscated and they had to convert to Islam at gunpoint." This plot by the people of Harar against the Oromo, according to his version, was repeated later on "when the Ethiopians occupied Harar in 1887, the Adare allegiance shifted from Turco-Egyptians to Ethiopians."[68]

The Harar *hikimdariya* and the Afran Qallo

Ra'uf Pasha claimed that the opposition of the Oromo to the Egyptians stemmed, first and foremost, from the incitement of the last emir of Harar: "He said to them: 'The Turks will take your children and make them into soldiers and send them to Zeila.' I worked very hard among their families to put out the fire that the emir had lit."[69] Ra'uf Pasha's words might throw light on the rumors that the emir spread among the Oromo, and on his understanding of the colonial project of the Egyptians. It is notable that the emir saw the conquerors as "Turks," since, in the emir's eyes, they were Turco-Egyptians. It seems that the emir was aware of the behavior of the conquerors in Sudan, and of the forcible draft of the local population to its armed forces.

After the military defeat of the Oromo (the Quttu and the Oromo who lived together in the Mulata area) during March–April 1876, Ra'uf Pasha tried to create a new balance between the *hikimdariya* of Harar and its neighbors. He took a series of rigorous steps to "convince the Oromo that they were totally dependent on the new Egyptian administration in the city."[70]

Even after the defeats of the *Dori* and the disassembly of the *Raba*, the Egyptians did not completely control the area between Harar and the Somali coast.[71] The British reported in 1884 that after the occupation of the city, the Egyptians controlled only an area forty miles from the tilled fields outside the city.[72] Alfred Bardey claimed that, in the early 1880s, "the Egyptian rule could not guarantee the safety of Europeans in the city; even the distance of a ten minute walk from the walls."[73]

In contrast, Ra'uf Pasha outlined the borders of the Harar *hikimdariya* for Cairo in April 1887: "The original boundaries of the Harar emirate were as follows: from the coast—Gildessa; from the northeast—al-Awash River; from the southeast—the Ogaden tribes; and from the south—the Arusi tribes. I went out on an expedition 50 or 60 miles from Harar itself, and did not yet reach the boundaries of the *hikimdariya*." But the boundaries of the *hikimdariya* in Ra'uf's report did not indicate complete control by the conquerors. Ra'uf's 1877 report about tension between the Egyptian forces and the Ittu populations of the Oromo testified to the loose Egyptian control over the area between Zeila and Harar: "Until now, the route from the Ittu tribe was closed and trade with them was disrupted. But now, there is complete calm. The reason for this is a *sulha* (ceremony of forgiveness) that I arranged with the Ittu. I sent sixty men to settle the desolate areas. They set forth from Zeila. Due to ignorance, the Ittu thought that they were all soldiers who had been sent on military missions. This is because the irregular soldiers were sent at the same time to build an outpost there."[74]

Despite these descriptions, the Egyptians controlled the Oromo areas, since they were the strongest military force there. They succeeded in achieving political and religious changes among the Oromo. To understand the policies of the Egyptians, it is necessary to differentiate among the administrative, agricultural-economic, and religious aspects of these policies, which were interconnected as part of a comprehensive policy.

Administration

Despite subjugating the *Dori* and breaking the power of the *Raba*, the Egyptians' control over the Oromo was incomplete until they left in 1885.[75] From 1876, Ra'uf Pasha already understood that he would need to adopt the old method used by the emirs of the city: buying the loyalty of the Oromo elite by distributing administrative positions and providing economic incentives. According to Richard Caulk, the Oromo elite did not change its behavior: "Individual Oromo people survived the Egyptian slaughter, and strengthened their position by making connections with the new rulers of the city."[76]

One of the outstanding achievements of the Egyptians can be seen in the mobilization of Orfo Jilo Biko, the famed *bokku* warrior from the Nole Oromo. As previously mentioned, Orfo was the military officer of the Dori who fought along with the Egyptian forces when they were on their way to Harar. He also served in the position of *abba fugug* in the last *Raba*. Oral histories of the Oromo and Harar say that the Egyptians forced Orfo to convert to Islam in 1876, and made him a major "agent" for spreading Islam among the Oromo surrounding Harar. Orfo changed his name to Omar and forced many of the Oromo to convert to Islam. He punished those who refused and even confiscated their property. The fear that he inspired among his people was so great that there was a saying in the Oromiffa language around Harar: "I say *Allahu Akbar* because of Orfo."[77]

The defeat of the *Dori* and the destruction of the Raba caused the removal of the pre-1876 division between the Quttu and the more distant Oromo. In 1876, the Egyptians partitioned the Oromo lands outside the city into four new colonial administrative areas. The Egyptians called each of these areas a *mudiriya* (plural: *mudiriyat*), meaning administration or district. In this fashion, the conquerors tried to break the power of the traditional clans and to implement modern systems of administration and taxation among the Afran Qallo Oromo. The four *mudiriyat* in the Oromo areas were the Nole-Oromo, the Jarso-Giri, the Abado, and the Nunu.[78] The British report of 1884 on the Egyptians' rule from a distance of forty miles in the "areas of the cultivated hills" dealt with the *mudiriyat*. The Egyptian *mudiriyat* concentrated the sixty-two Afran Qallo tribes that had surrendered to Ra'uf Pasha in October 1875, and it seems that the main influence of the division was seen among the four main clans of the Nole Oromo.[79]

Each *mudiriya* was divided into a number of sub-*mudiriyat*, or branches, according to the number of Oromo populations. These branches were further divided into sub-clans. In this way, the Egyptians sought to oversee the various clans in the most effective way possible. The *mudiriya* of the Nole was divided into four branches, the Jarso-Giri *mudiriya* into ten branches, and the *mudiriyat* of the Abado and Nunu into seventeen branches.[80] Each *mudiriya* had its own administrative headquarters that supervised the Egyptian forces which ruled in the Oromo areas.

Muhtar reckoned that there were two million tribesmen, but this estimate seems exaggerated.[81] The British estimated in 1884 that the rural population of the Harar *hikimdariya* was 68,470 people, and the number of people living in the "area between Harar and the Somali border" was 454,770. They reached this estimate after surveying the population in the various *mudiriyat*, along with an attempt to estimate the numbers of the Somali ʻIssa and Gadabuursi populations. The two Somali tribes were not gathered into *mudiriyat* but were officially included in the region under the Egyptian occupation between Harar and the Somali coast:

Nole *mudiriya*—132,700 people
Abado *mudiriya*—68,270 people
Nunu *mudiriya*—57,800 people
Jarso *mudiriya*—70,000 people
ʻIssa Somal—80,000
Gadabuursi Somal—46,000
Total population: 454,770[82]

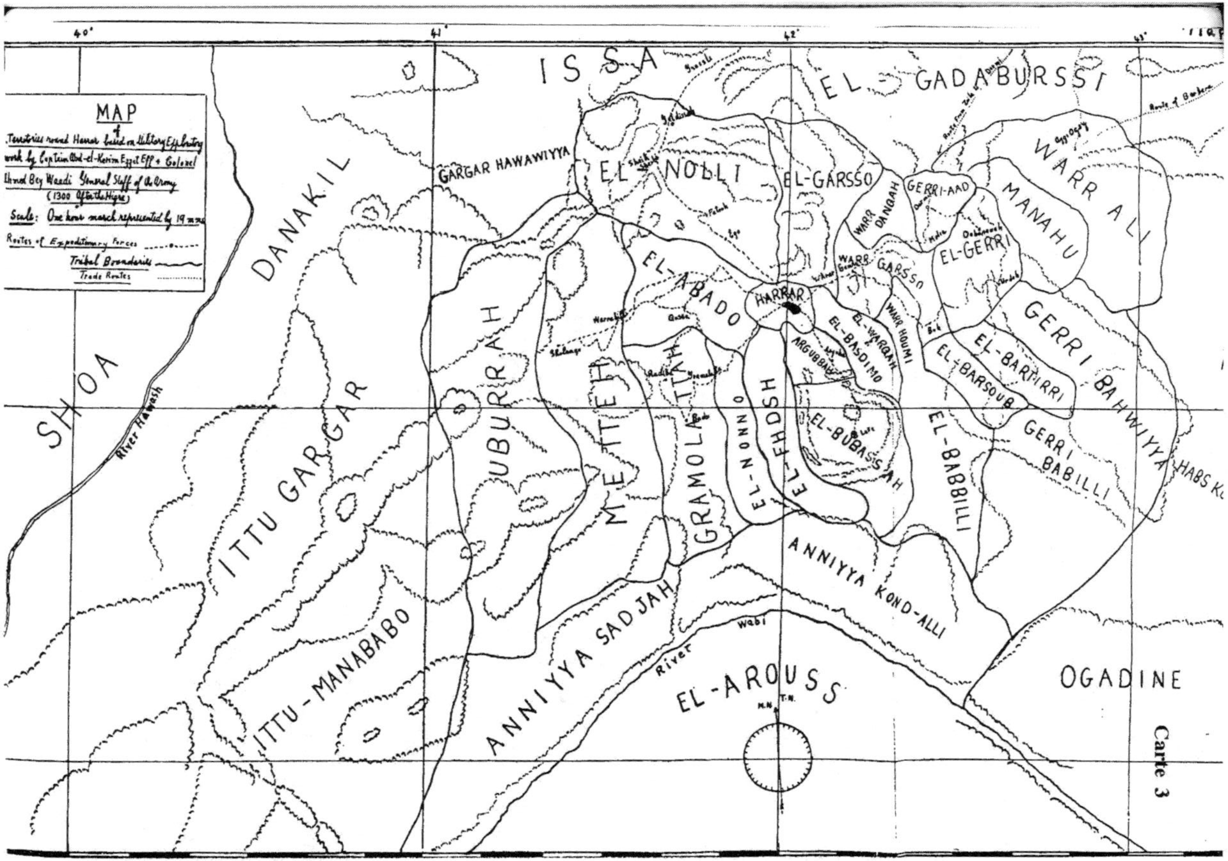

2. Map of the administrative and military division of Harar and surroundings, drawn by Al-Qarim Ezat Effendī in 1883. Source: M. Amer, “Some Unpublished Egyptian Maps of Harar,” *Bulletin de la Société Royale de Géographie d’Egypte* 19 (Cairo, 1937), 289–99.

The British surveyed the Egyptian military and administrative deployment in the territories of the *mudiriyat*. The main Egyptian outpost outside Harar was in Gildessa, in the territory of the Nole Oromo. The Egyptians turned it into the center of the *mudiriya* of the Nole Oromo. This is how the British described the Egyptian outpost there:

> Gildessa is located 13 miles northwest of Harar, on the road to Zeila. This is a high spot, overlooking the road. Gildessa is manned by 42 Egyptian infantrymen. An officer with the rank of captain is their commander. Gildessa is an important strategic spot for the placement of artillery force. The approach to Gildessa from the north is a wadi whose navigability is quite difficult. A hedge and a mud wall defend the Egyptian outpost, but these cannot prevent a forceful attack. Water is provided to the outpost by a river that passes nearby.[83]

The strategic Egyptian site that was second in importance was Warrabili:

> Warrabili is the center of the Abado Mudiriya. There is an outstanding presence of 105 Egyptian infantrymen and 19 artillerymen with rocket launchers, in addition to 10 irregulars of the *başhi bozuķ*. The road from Harar to this spot is quite good. It is comfortable by foot but difficult for artillery to navigate. The camp is located upon a hill, well-fortified against typical attacks of the Gala.[84]

The British reports on the *mudiriyat* of the Nunu and the Jarso included the following details:

> Gafra is the center of the Nunu mudiriya. Gafra is located 25 miles west of Harar. The forces there are made up of 97 infantrymen, 19 artillerymen with rocket launchers, and 10 irregulars of the *başhi bozuķ*. The approach to this spot is quite easy, the outpost is well-fortified. At the same time, the post office is not defensible from attack. Darimi is the center of the Jarso mudiriya. The site is located 30 miles northwest of Harar. The approach is quite difficult, since the stronghold is well fortified. The garrison includes 19 artillerymen with a large cannon and a rocket launcher, 25 *başhi bozuķ* irregulars and 207 infantrymen.[85]

The British reports show that the Egyptians preserved their military presence until the end of their conquest of the area to demonstrate to the Oromo that, even after their military and political surrender, the Egyptian army and administration were the sole rulers.[86] In this way, the Egyptians made continuous trade connections possible between Harar and the coast. They were the first to ensure complete security on the roads between Harar and Zeila and Berbera since the seventeenth century, the golden era of the early days of the Ibn Da'ud emirate dynasty. Philipp Paulitschke, the Austrian trader who lived in Harar during the 1880s, gives evidence for this: "In the time of the emirs, 70 caravans arrived in Harar and departed from the city in the course of a year. Under Egyptian rule, more than 400 caravans came into and went out of the city each year."[87]

In conclusion, it is possible to present two opposing interpretations of the implications of Egyptian reforms for the Afran Qallo Oromo territories. According to Richard Caulk, "the administrative changes that the Egyptians heralded in the rural areas and in Harar itself upset the balance between the city and its neighbors, since the Egyptians were the first to unite all the areas between Harar, Zeila and Berbera under one administration. They made the roads in this region safe for transit, and ensured stability and security there."[88] On the other hand, a British traveler of that time, Augustus Wylde, was critical of the behavior of the Egyptians toward the Oromo, and described "the destructive influence of the Egyptians, and the terrible cruelty that they demonstrated against the peaceable Nole and Argata agricultural tribes."[89]

Study of the Turco-Egyptian conquest of the Oromo in the Harar region presents a complex picture. The Egyptians kept the roads secure for a relatively long period, but the Oromo rebelled from time to time. The changes the Egyptians brought about among the Afran Qallo populations were indeed significant, since they paved the way for their subjugation and later assimilation by the Ethiopians.

One of the central goals of the Egyptians in dividing the Oromo territories into *mudiriyat* was to effect closer supervision over the city's neighbors and establish an effective taxation system in those territories. Evidence of the Egyptians' determination to subordinate the Oromo to the Harar *hikimdariya* can be found in the five study and supervisory expeditions led by Ra'uf Pasha himself in the territories during the short years of his rule.[90]

The first goal of the Egyptians was, as mentioned, to eliminate the traditional Oromo division of clans and gather the Oromo into "settlement blocs," similar to large, central villages.[91] Ra'uf Pasha reported that by April 1877, the Egyptians had set up 250 large and medium-sized towns that gathered the Quttu around the city.[92]

Alongside their revolutionary plans, the Egyptians preserved the Oromo elite's administrative ranks, just as they found them in 1875. As part of the attempt to co-opt this elite, Ra'uf Pasha retained the Oromo official system, including its ranks. But this time, the Harar *hikimdariya* was the direct sponsor of this official system.

Under the Turco-Egyptian rule, the office of *garad*, the Oromo administrative official, was retained, but now Ra'uf Pasha appointed the *garad*, who had responsibility for the most part over a small or medium-sized Oromo village. Oromo testimonies tell of the ceremony of the *garad*'s appointment by the Egyptians. The candidate for the appointment brought five oxen as a tax to the governor of the Harar *hikimdariya*, and in exchange received a turban, cloak, and hat, which served as a symbol of the position. Likewise, the *garad* received 1,000 *faddan* (4,200 square meters) of agricultural land.[93] In his report, Ra'uf Pasha described the delegation of authority to the Oromo dignitaries, in accordance with the khedival government's instructions.[94] The Egyptians changed the measure of land from the *gerib* to the *faddan* but preserved the principle of handing over of land for cultivation outside the Harar walls to officials. To emphasize the subordination of the *garad* to the *hikimdariya*, and at the same time to show that he had a high position among the Oromo, the Egyptians gave him prominent status symbols.

The Egyptians preserved the title of *malaq* but gave it different meaning. From 1876 on, the *malaq* was no longer a city resident responsible for one of its quarters. The Egyptians kept the urban title but now used it outside the city walls, changing it to a title to be given to the Oromo. The *malaq* was appointed to collect taxes in the small villages. In exchange, the *hikimdariya* granted the *malaq* 500 *faddan* of agricultural land to cultivate (the *malaq*, in contrast with the *garad*, did not receive any type of clothing from the Egyptians to emphasize his position).[95]

An additional administrative rank that the Egyptians used in the Oromo territories was *damin*. There are varying interpretations as to whether the Egyptians invented the title, or whether it was used in the period of the emirate. The Harari Mahdi Gadid claimed that *damin* is an Arabic term meaning "guarantor."[96] The Egyptians employed the *damin* during the decade they occupied Harar. The person in this position stood at the head of an entire tribe and was responsible, for the most part, for administrative matters in the tribe's territory.[97] Waldron has stated, in contrast, that the *damin* was a remnant of the days of the emirate and that he "was responsible for four or five *garad*. He was the direct agent of the emirate in villages of the Oromo. His main roles were judge and tax collector."[98]

Another title preserved by the conquerors was the *dogin*. The *malaq*, *garad*, and *damin* were subject to the individual with this rank, who was "responsible for the outer areas." The Egyptians left this role in the hands of the residents of Harar, with direct subjugation to Ra'uf Pasha.

The administrative rank of the Oromo under the Egyptians was responsible mainly for collecting the *zakat* and *miri* taxes (taxes on government lands) in the territories outside the walls.[99] Some Harari informants blamed the Egyptians for a change in the *zakat*, saying that "under their rule, the *zakat* changed from a religious tax meant for charity toward the unfortunate to a major channel of funding to strengthen their occupation."[100] From notes that survived the period of the emirate of 'Abdullahi (1885–87), it seems that all the Oromo farmers were required to pay 13 percent of their annual produce and the lands in their possession as *zakat* and *miri* taxes through the *malaq*, *garad*, and *damin*. These officials passed on the taxes and the agricultural produce to the *diwan* building in the city. After the Ethiopian conquest of Harar in 1887, the new Christian conquerors of the city preserved the model of tax collection that the Egyptians had established.[101]

Later land registration records in Harar make it possible to examine the pattern of Egyptian tax collection in the Oromo territories. Haj 'Alī 'Abdulahi Sadik served the Egyptians as *dogin* in the centralized Oromo areas—Maya Kalo, Adaile, and Dangago—which are located thirty miles from Harar. Sadik was so effective that the Ethiopians adopted him as their tax collector in the same areas, except that the Muslim-Egyptian *zakat* was changed to the Ethiopian Christian *kaleb*.[102]

The double *zakat* and *miri* tax payments worsened the Afran Qallo's economic situation and added to their dependency on the central government and its officials. The military defeat of the *Dori* prevented an armed uprising of the Oromo in the first years of the occupation.[103]

Although the Egyptians preserved the old administrative ranks, they made some changes. They employed the administrative ranks that had been used among the Quttu up until that point, on all territories of the *mudiriyat*, without any geographic or tribal differentiation. They tried to bring together all the Oromo not just as one administrative unit but to erase the division into clans, both near Harar and far from the city.

As long as Ra'uf Pasha ruled in Harar, the Egyptians succeeded in their plan to gather the Oromo surrounding Harar into "villages." This action was accomplished through threats and force, and most of the Oromo elite cooperated. More than sixty Oromo title-bearers from the period of the emirate were integrated into the Turco-Egyptian system and expressed their loyalty to the conquerors. In addition, the Egyptians appointed new officials who were not affiliated with the old system. In the "villages" they appointed approximately 11,829 *malaq* and *garad* officials among the Oromo. The conquerors appointed five hundred Oromo to the *damin* position. At the top of the ranking system, they appointed forty-five Harar residents as *dogin*.[104]

Even though the Egyptians apparently copied the traditional administrative ranking system almost in its entirety, they greatly damaged the political and social fabric of Oromo society. In the time of the emirate, the officials were *bokku*, or the traditional clan elite. A portion of the Oromo elite derived their power directly from their blood ties or political, economic, or military treaties with the emirate family. The conquerors destroyed these connections and exchanged blood ties and various treaties for political appointments.

The Egyptians abolished the *gosa* (clan) as an institution, thus influencing inter-Oromo politics as well as the relations between the Oromo and the city-dwellers. In contrast with the days of the emirate, the Oromo no longer chose their own *bokku*, and their leaders were appointed by the Egyptians. Mobility that was dependent on relations with the emirate up to 1875 was turned into appointments by the authorities with no consideration for inter-Oromo politics. From the Oromo standpoint, the Egyptian actions caused ongoing grief. The Egyptians rapidly replaced a political-tribal system that had functioned according to its own rules and internal political and social arrangements with a system of appointed officials, eradicating a centuries-old political and social system.

The damage and degradation to the Oromo was especially severe in light of the collapse of clans' hegemony in Harar's political and economic spheres immediately prior to the Turco-Egyptian occupation. Ra'uf Pasha changed their status from that of rulers of Harar under the last emir to a lower status subjugated under his rule. The demolition of Oromo political and social structures, together with their concentration into village blocs, represented the most significant impact of the Egyptians on the city's neighbors. These changes heralded the beginnings of transformation in the political and economic relationship between Harar and the Afran Qallo after the Egyptian conquest and during the Ethiopian conquest of the area, starting in 1887. Not only did these changes lead to the loss of Oromo sovereignty, but they also severely damaged the Oromo's unique identity in all of the southern Ethiopian plateau and paved the way for their assimilation through the Amhari-Christian "melting pot" policy.[105]

Agriculture and Economy

The Turco-Egyptian project to concentrate the Oromo into settlement blocs was accompanied by an attempt to introduce modern agricultural methods. Muhammad Muhtar described the goal of this policy as "encouraging the Oromo to settle and work the land."[106]

However, the Egyptians were not the first to gather the Afran Qallo in permanent settlements around Harar. The Quttu's interactions with Harar had actually been established during the first half of the nineteenth century. The Egyptians wished to present themselves as "civilizing" the Oromo through settlement and agricultural activity. In fact, the Egyptians were interested in deriving maximum advantage from the agricultural resources around Harar, especially through the cultivation of coffee beans.

On the one hand, the Egyptians preserved the monopolies that the city's emirs had maintained until the early nineteenth century. On the other hand, they allowed the Oromo farmers to continue holding onto their land. Before their arrival, the *garad* and *malaq* were the owners of the land, and the Quttu were their serfs. But when the Egyptians arrived in the area, they canceled the ownership of the *garad* and *malaq* over the land and promised the Oromo farmers material benefits and status symbols.

For the first time in the relations between the Quttu and Harar, the Egyptians changed the rules of inheritance. They promised transfer of property ownership to male heirs, or to married women in the absence of male heirs. In this way, the Egyptians impinged on the Afran Qallo tradition, which held that the land belonged to the *bokku* of the clan. In addition, the Oromo farmer was required to pay a tax on his produce, according to its estimation before threshing. In this way the conquerors heralded a real revolution among the Quttu.[107]

As mentioned, the Egyptian conquerors' interest in agricultural innovation derived from the economic potential of the coffee bean. Ra'uf Pasha was determined, in accordance with instructions he received from the khedive's government, to encourage the Oromo to grow coffee.[108] He reported that he saw the potential for economic advantages in the land of each tribe, which was agriculturally cultivated and abundant with water sources.[109]

In the agricultural areas outside the walls, in addition to growing coffee, the Egyptians planted all sorts of vegetables that were previously unknown in Harar and its surroundings. Among these were new grains, grapevines, tomatoes, and beets, as well as peach and lemon trees.[110] It seems that during the administration of Ra'uf Pasha, the Egyptian soldiers received land in the Oromo areas at the same time that the Oromo officials were given property.[111] These soldiers became agents for the propagation of new crops, both outside the walls and within them.[112]

Ra'uf Pasha's reports emphasized the integration of the Oromo dignitaries into the colonial agricultural administration:

> Each of the Galla dignitaries was given 1,000 *faddan* of uncultivated land to sow there. Sheikh *al-balad* brought two beasts as tax for us. He was arrayed in clothing made up of four pieces of coarse cloth. In addition, 500 *faddan* were apportioned to sheikh *al-balad* as well. This is our practice with them, since they also received land in a similar way. I can say with certitude that we received great benefit from giving them abandoned land. This is because most of the tribes, with the exception of the tribe of Alla [Oromo], have begun to plant coffee.[113]

One should note that Ra'uf Pasha made no distinction in his report between the *garad*, *dogin*, or *damin*. From his point of view, they were each equivalent to the term he was familiar with from Egypt—sheikh *al-balad*. It may be that he was referring to the *malaq*, who was responsible for tax collection in a certain village.[114] However, the Ethiopian equivalent to the Oromo *malaq* from 1887 and to the Egyptian sheikh *al-balad* was the Amharic title of *chiqashum* (*Č̣əqa Šum*, earth officer).[115]

Alongside activities to encourage agriculture among the Oromo, it seems that Ra'uf Pasha was very concerned about the patterns of commerce among them. He complained that there is no type of coinage among them: "The trader who has merchandise cannot arrive in Zeila, except after a period of a year and a half. The Muslim traders have found that bringing merchandise and buying and selling with payment is easier than barter."[116]

The Egyptians wished to change the traditional barter system—which was common in the area before the Egyptians arrived—to commerce based on the currency of the conquerors: the piaster and the guinea. As already mentioned, the conquerors abolished the *mahlak* and replaced it with their own currency. In Harar itself, they forced their policies upon the residents of the city as part of their attempt to uproot the symbols of the emirate, as well as to connect Harar to the economic spheres of Egyptian colonialism in Sudan and the Somali coast. In regard to the Afran Qallo populations, it would seem that their efforts at monetary change were not successful. The Egyptian military control of the territory of the four *mudiriyat* was only partial, and their inability to ensure safe transport of merchandise from Harar to Zeila and Berbera thwarted their plans in the Oromo territories and the Somali coast. Ra'uf Pasha complained that "the delay in commerce was caused by the lack of stations along the way. This is because the 'Issa are afraid of the Nole, and are always subjugated to the town of Gildessa. If there were a station in Gildessa, and a station in Darimi, and 500 men in each station, there would be security along the route, and commerce would be carried out in peace. Therefore, I request support for the suppression of those who are jealous of my efforts. I would also request the sending of 1,000 soldiers, even in stages, in order to develop Zeila."[117]

Ra'uf's claims emphasized the importance of military control over the roads connecting Harar and the coastal cities. He saw ensuring security on the roads, through intensive military presence in the Oromo territories, as the key to achieving economic goals and prosperity. Commerce did indeed develop as long as the military stations posed a threat to the Oromo and Somali populations. The Egyptians created conditions that enabled the arrival of European merchants to the city in the early 1880s, and the number of shops and the scope of commerce doubled in Harar's markets.[118]

Mohammed Hassen claimed that the "Egyptian decade was a golden age of prosperity and economic plenty in the city and the surrounding areas."[119] Influenced by Paulitschke's amazement about the conquerors' contribution to the wealth of the city residents, Hassen described, relying on local oral reports, that "there was a surplus of produce in Harar for the first time, since the Egyptian administration stored [crops] in silos. The produce was sold cheaply to the public."[120] However, Hassen's interest was the city itself, and not the Oromo. In contrast to Hassen, Gadid claimed that "the dominant colonialism of the Egyptians was significant not only to Ra'uf Pasha and his men. It also had tremendous significance for the deterioration of the Egyptian economy."[121] Gadid saw the *hikimdariya* as an important element in contributing to the depletion of the economy of the khedive's government.

There is no doubt that the expense of running the *hikimdariya* and the *mudiriyat* of the Oromo until May 1878 was great since, as Bardey reported, the Egyptians had to operate their *mudiriyat* both in the city and outside of it while they "relied upon 250 Egyptian officials, and hundreds of secretaries and functionaries that they had appointed." Still, the

Egyptians' profits were sufficient to "support between 4,000 and 5,000 soldiers and officials. Harar even sent surplus from its profits to Cairo."[122] Even if this testimony is inexact, it does show a general trend. It was not, however, the economy of the *hikimdariya* that was a failure, but rather what happened to the Egyptian economy during the second half of the 1870s that caused Ra'uf and his heirs to fail.

Islamization and Re-Islamization

The Afran Qallo populations in the vicinity of Harar had not been exposed to Islam or Christianity in a profound manner until the Egyptian conquest in 1875 and the Ethiopian conquest in 1887. The Oromo in this area remained faithful to *Waqqiya*, and their leadership partially adopted Islam for political and earthly reasons.[123] In contrast with the Oromo surrounding Harar, the Oromo who lived in the northern Ethiopian plateau began to convert to Islam over the course of the eighteenth century. The members of the Raya, Azobo, Wallo, and Yejju Oromo societies converted mainly to preserve their independent identity, since they were located in the heart of the imperial Ethiopian Christian plateau.[124] At this point, Harar and its vicinity had not yet come under Christian rule, and the push to convert to Islam was not yet viewed as a factor in defining identity and maintaining singularity. Rather, conversion to Islam was part of the fiber of relations between the city and its neighbors.[125] The Islamization of the Oromo was used by the emirate as a means of connecting them to the economic and political circles of the city, whereas the Islamization initiated in 1875 by the Egyptians was different in its goals, aim, and methods. The Oromo surrounding Harar were forced to convert to Islam by the Turco-Egyptian colonial forces between 1875 and 1885.[126]

There is nothing in the Egyptian reports or in the later Egyptian literature regarding the spread of Islam in the city or among the Oromo. If there is anything in the Egyptian reports that mentions the religious issue at all, it is in reference to Harar itself. This was seen as part of their ideology of spreading education in colonialist terms of reorganizing the area under its rule. However, the Egyptians took a tough stance on aspects of religion among the Afran Qallo, and this fits in with their destructive policy as it was expressed in its administrative and economic aspects. The most apt description of the new policy that began in 1875, in the religious sphere too, is "coercion." The forced Islamization was a further step, blunt and unequivocal, in Ra'uf Pasha's policy toward the Oromo. The destruction of their institutions and the erasure of their identity were meant to ensure their surrender to Egyptian rule. The religious aspect was part of comprehensive Egyptian behavior aimed at taking advantage of the resources of the conquered area under the cover of bringing the cultural, economic and Islamic progress of Egypt.

Thus, Islamization of the Oromo by the Egyptians was first and foremost a political act. While the *bokku* were being subjugated, "the long hair of the Oromo leaders was cut off and they were circumcised by the Egyptians." Afterwards, the leaders were sent to be their officials in the *mudiriyat*. Spencer Trimingham noted as well that some of the *bokku* preferred to die rather than go through that humiliating ceremony, but the Oromo had been defeated and were finally broken after two or three years under the Egyptian conquest.[127]

Islamization as a political instrument did not always express the hegemony of Harar over its neighbors. Even after the Oromo grew more powerful at the expense of the emirate in the first half of the nineteenth century, Islamization—or voluntary conversion—was part of the pattern of relations between the city and the Oromo. Apparently, the conquerors copied this pattern. But in actuality, they imposed its rules by force after destroying the economic strength of the Oromo and their political autonomy.

Before 1875, there was no attempt by the emirate to "civilize" or "reeducate" the Oromo. The Oromo were perceived as the "other," with whom there was a relationship of economic and political dependence. In contrast, the actions of the Egyptians, which included dismantling the clan structure, demolishing the institution of the *bokku*, and destroying the *Dori*, attempted to put an end to the Oromo "other" as a personal and separate element of identity in the *hikimdariya*, and to create a "new" and "modern" Oromo man.

It seems that the Egyptians opened a new chapter in spreading Islam among the Oromo, accelerating Islamization in the areas that had not come under the influence of the emirate before 1875.[128] The Egyptians Islamicized the Oromo in two main ways. The first was expressed by sending Egyptian preachers, accompanied by military forces, to the Oromo territories. They were part of a special unit that went along with the fighting forces of the conquerors. Oromo and Harar oral traditions say that the principal task of this unit was to circumcise Oromo men.[129] It should be noted that Emir Muhammad 'Abdashakur also sent preachers to the Oromo territories, and they were quite successful there. Harar's last emir did not invent this system. From the sixteenth century, the emirate had benefited from hegemony among its neighbors and spread Islam through *'ulamā'* (Islamic religious scholars) from Harar who set out on a mission from the city with the consent of the Oromo elite.

As mentioned earlier, the Egyptians sent their preachers accompanied by military forces. The *'ulamā'* that came from Riwaq al-Jabartiyya in the madrassa of al-Azahar in Cairo circumcised and converted the Oromo by force.[130] Unlike in the days of the emirate, the preachers were not from among the Adari but were Egyptians. The religious exhortation, like the physical humiliation and damage to the way of life of the Oromo, found expression in their circumcision. Circumcision was an act that deviated from the religious discourse that had gone on between the city and the Oromo up until that point. Like the military conquest and destruction of the traditional institutions, circumcision was part of the effort of the Egyptians to subjugate the Oromo without conditions, to create a new Oromo body and force their rule upon them.

The second means that the Egyptians utilized to Islamicize the Oromo began immediately after their military surrender in March–April of 1876. The Egyptians summoned the Oromo *bokku* and assembled them in the city square. There, the Egyptian aspired to turn them to "new" "hygienic" "modern" and "right" Muslims: The Afran Qallo's *bokku* were shaved and ordered to put on new clothing, and then were taken to the central mosque of Harar. The Egyptians told them that they were Muslims, and from this point they were responsible for disseminating Islam in the *mudiriyat*.[131] Confirmation of this story is provided by Alfred Bardey, who heard from the Oromo surrounding Harar that "the Egyptians assembled those who were not sufficiently Muslim in their eyes in the central mosque of Harar and informed them that now they belonged to the religion of Muhammad."[132]

Violent Islamization was unknown in the time of the emirate, but by 1875 it had become part of a comprehensive system. In addition to becoming "officials" of the new administration, the Oromo *bokku* became "agents" for Islamization. The conversion of Orfo Jilo Biko, discussed earlier, was not exceptional. The Egyptians changed his Oromo name to Omar, an expression of their effort to destroy the traditional Oromo identity from a religious and political standpoint and to create new Oromo identities in person and generally among the *gosas*. In accordance with his own rigid and dogmatic military attitude, Ra'uf Pasha saw the "redesigning" of the Oromo, including its administrative, political, economic, and religious aspects, as a necessary step toward establishing his political and economic rule over the area. The "religious measures" of the Egyptians were given a thin ideological coating that lacked real depth, in order to explain the harsh actions as part of "re-educating" the subjects of the *hikimdariya* for modern living.

The Islamization by force initiated by the Egyptians did not reflect the entire picture. Many of the Oromo had already converted to Islam as a result of processes that they had undergone in previous centuries. Their voluntary conversion was not damaged because of Egyptian coercion. After Christian Ethiopia took over the Oromo areas during the last two decades of the nineteenth century, the trend of Islamization among the Oromo increased in the various regions of the southern Ethiopian plateau. The Oromo of Arssi, Bale, Wallaga, and Illubabor converted to Islam as a religious and political protest against Ethiopian occupation.[133]

The Egyptian Islamization of the Oromo had political and agricultural implications, which mainly affected the traditional consumption patterns of the Afran Qallo. With the strengthening of the ties between the emirate and the Oromo elite in the middle of the nineteenth century, the use of khat spread among the Quttu, who adopted the custom of chewing the plant, common among the residents of Harar. The consumption of khat had social and religious significance, and its being chewed by the Quttu symbolized acceptance of the social as well as religious norms of Harar. The locals saw the chewing of khat as part of Islamic culture (and after

1887, the Ethiopian Christian rule saw it as a sign of religious heresy).[134] The Egyptians saw chewing khat as a bad habit that should be prohibited, since "chewing it confused the intelligence."[135] Ra'uf Pasha saw chewing khat as an "uncultured" activity that was not compatible with a modern religious vision. The prohibition that he declared against this popular cultural symbol of Islam and Harar was part of his attempt to create a "new" Harar and "new" Oromo, while mixing a modern order with orthodox Islam.

Summary

Discussion of the Egyptian policy in the Oromo territories up until 1878 leads to two different conclusions. One is that the Egyptian period was a golden age of prosperity and economic plenty, made possible by the security that the Egyptians ensured on trade routes connecting Harar and the Somali coast. According to this view, the Egyptians "liberated" the city from the Oromo threat and, in 1875, began a new chapter in which Harar—this time as an Egyptian *hikimdariya*—regained its hegemony in the tribal sphere. This view is lacking in that it sees the Oromo as one social and political mass, ignoring geographic, political, and social divisions within the various clans. Similarly, it treats the emirate as one monolithic and static unit that ruled over the Oromo until the beginning of the nineteenth century and from then on lost its hegemony over them.

The second conclusion presents the Egyptian conquest as a disaster for the people of Harar and its neighbors. This view relies on the perception that the Egyptians destroyed the "treaty" that existed between the emirate and the Oromo clans, and that they did so out of a colonialist interest in pronounced economic exploitation that destroyed the political, social, economic, and religious connections in the city and with its surroundings. Accordingly, one must regard the Oromo institutions as a complex system, having rich and varied economic, social, and religious frameworks, and must differentiate between the Quttu and the Oromo in the Mulata area. Another premise intrinsic to this conclusion sees the Oromo as an important element in the political and economic circles in Harar, and the Islamization of the *bokku* at the time of the emirate as a political statement rather than a religious one. The Afran Qallo populations, and the more distant institution of the *Raba Dori*, are portrayed as dynamic political and social bodies, having singularity despite their connections with the emirate. From this standpoint, it is clear that the Egyptians destroyed all of this and changed the relations between the city and the Oromo. These relations became one-directional when the *hikimdariya* dictated terms of economic exploitation, Islamization by force, social disgrace, and the destruction of traditional Oromo institutions. The Egyptians disturbed the balance between the city and its neighbors, and for the first time implemented a centralized government in Harar and its environs. The decade-long Egyptian effort brought great suffering upon the people of Harar, and especially upon their neighbors.

On the face of it, the Egyptians adopted a number of characteristics from the pattern of relations that had existed between the emirate and its neighbors prior to 1875. Among these were the preservation of the old administrative ranking system, distribution of land, and political "purchase" of the Oromo elite, which included their Islamization. However, the Egyptians wiped out the administrative divisions of the Quttu and the more distant Oromo and destroyed their institutions. The destruction of the *Raba* and the clans led to the paralysis of the independent social and political life among the Oromo, and ruined processes of internal social and political mobility among them. The picture that emerges from analyzing the implications of the Egyptian conquest on the Oromo territories is one of misery and destruction that ruined the fabric of their lives and reduced them to utter subjugation.

The Turco-Egyptians made a great contribution to the development of commerce in the city, mainly in connecting the economy of the Harar region to the Egyptian and European economies. They laid an infrastructure for the penetration of European economic elements into the *hikimdariya*, thus becoming the first to open up the city to Europeans. The economic growth that the Europeans brought to the city under the aegis of the Egyptians was short-lived. Actually, it brought Christian missionary activity and European colonialist interests to the area. In this way, the conquerors dug a pit for themselves, since their rule in Harar—as in Egypt—fell victim to a stronger colonialism: that of the Europeans.

PART THREE

The Colonial Transition

7

Decline, 1878–1882

Harar and Cairo: A Deteriorating Relationship

By the spring of 1876, following the Ottoman bankruptcy, Khedive Isma'īl declared the Egyptian treasury bankrupt. As a consequence of Isma'īl's declaration, direct European control of Egyptian finance began in 1876. He was now forced to put Egypt's economy under independent Anglo-French commissions—*Caisse de la Dette Public*—which assumed the task of consolidating and administering the Egyptian debt repayments.[1] In April 1877, Ra'uf Pasha complained that there were those in Cairo who were damaging his project in Harar because of jealousy. There was bitterness in his complaints: "The soldiers' salaries were sent from Cairo, but no cash. How will the money be sent? From the moment I was appointed over the Harar *hikimdariya*, I have acted only for its prosperity and development. I complained to no one about my thoughts. If I could assemble a military force from the local population, could the government take upon itself its expense? I am one of the sons of the homeland loyal to the government."[2]

The appointment of Charles Gordon as the governor of Sudan in 1877 seems to have contributed to Ra'uf's lack of confidence and bitterness in the *hikimdariya*. His concluding remarks in the letter that he sent to the khedival government may provide evidence of this: "I claim that most of the conquests in the region have borne fruit economically. It is the Harar *hikimdariya* that bears the costs, and soon great benefit will be derived from it. But all this will be impossible if a force is not maintained here. This is because the force deters the local people from beginning a war, and the soldiers here do their work faithfully."[3]

The khedival government's response to Ra'uf arrived two and a half months later, in July 1877. Alongside the many praises that were heaped upon the *hikimdar* for distributing land and encouraging the Oromo to plant coffee, the khedival government continued its policy of "progress and building." But it did not answer his request for reinforcements.[4] Furthermore, the khedival government ignored Ra'uf Pasha's request for aid, and answered:

> We understood from your previous report that the tribes under your control desire woven materials. Different types of cloth will be sent to you in a supervised manner, according to the quantity required. We can also send you samples of each kind of fabric. Afterwards, the fabric will be sent to you so that you can market them among the tribesmen through barter that will take place through exchanging the cloth for different kinds of coffee and other products of the tribesmen. These products will be sent to Cairo for marketing. The price of these products will be subtracted from the price of the items sent to you. Whatever remains from the profits will be sent to you, according to your needs and your request. The profit earned in future barter will also be used for the matter of the irregular soldiers [*bașhi bozuķ*].[5]

This exchange of words in the course of 1877 was the first sign of the end of the euphoria felt in the *hikimdariya*, of the increasing economic difficulties in Cairo, and the beginning of the worsening relations between the *hikimdar* and the khedival government and its representative; a process that ended with the dismissal of Ra'uf Pasha in May 1878.

Gordon and Ra'uf Pasha: A Chronicle of Personal Hostility

Khedive Isma'īl and his heir, Tawfiq, appointed the British Charles Gordon to two terms as the governor of Sudan.[6] His first tenure was from February 1877 to January 1880, and the second was from 1884 to 1885. Gordon held unprecedented widespread and independent authority during his first tenure under the rule of Khedive Isma'īl. He was defined as the "general governor of the Sudanese areas and the coasts of the Red Sea." The eight districts of Sudan—Dongola, Berber, Sennar, Kordofan, Darfur,

Fashoda, Bahr al-Ghazal, and Equatoria—were united into one administrative unit under his control, and he was subject directly to the khedive, and not to the khedival government.

Gordon frequently visited the areas under his authority. He wished to view the lifestyle and difficulties of the local population from close up and experience its functioning under his rule. These visits also enabled him to scrutinize the behavior of the Turco-Egyptian governors.[7] Gordon's visits frequently caused tension with the khedive on matters of appointments and dismissals, or punishing officials who transgressed. The khedive interfered in the appointment of governors in Sudan and did not always agree with the criteria that Gordon tried to establish in the professional work of the local officials. Even so, the considerations that motivated Gordon in his policies toward the Egyptian governors were not always relevant, and several times he appointed or fired officials who served in his government in Sudan and the Red Sea on a whim. Some were fired, for example, because he did not like their external appearance or their names.[8]

The letter of appointment that Khedive Isma'īl granted to Gordon in 1877 was published in Sudan, the Somali coastal cities, and Harar, and was intended for the officers and administrators there. The khedive appointed Gordon to the position of "*hikimdar* of Sudan, except for the areas of Zeila, Berbera and Harar." Even though the khedive regarded the Red Sea coast as part of the *hikimdariya* of Sudan, this was only as far as "Massawa and Sawakin, where the 'Ala'a al-Din Bey was the official representative."[9] This letter of appointment made no reference to the *hikimdariya* of Harar, but the separation between the Somali coastal cities and the new Sudanese governor's area of control did not last long. In early March 1877, the khedive requested that Gordon also annex the districts of the Red Sea and Harar to his administration: "Ra'uf Basha, one of the senior officers, is in Harar, and he is the city *hikimdar.* Governor Abu Bakr Pasha rules in the city of Zeila. Raduan Pasha, a maritime officer, is ruler in Berbera. The administration of the Zeila and Tadjoura region are also annexed to Berbera. It is proper that these administrations will also be under your authority."[10] The special regard of the khedival government for Ra'uf Pasha is very clear from the manner in which the governors and other authorities were presented to Gordon. In addition, Ra'uf was ranked the most senior of all position holders. However, Gordon already had an opinion of his own. On 17 April 1878, the eve of his arrival at the *hikimdariya*, he wrote: "I plan to leave tomorrow afternoon for Harar, where Ra'uf Pasha is. This man was in Equatoria with Baker and myself. I deposed him there exactly four years ago from yesterday. I plan to dismiss him again; it seems that he is being a tyrant, as he usually is."[11]

Gordon had served as governor for the khedive's government in Equatoria in Sudan between 1874 and 1876. The khedive chose him mainly in order to strengthen his own status among the Europeans as an enlightened ruler who was appointing a British citizen for the purpose of fighting slavery in the framework of a proper European-style administration.[12] Gordon's appointment to that position was at the expense of Ra'uf Pasha. Between 1869 and 1873, Samuel Baker, a British mercenary in the khedive's service, served as the governor of Equatoria. His failure to eradicate slave trading in the region, while strengthening the khedive's reign, brought his tenure to a close at the end of April 1873. Ra'uf Pasha, Baker's deputy, stepped into his shoes, but for a short period only.[13] Immediately upon Gordon's arrival in Equatoria in May 1874, Ra'uf Pasha was deposed. He returned to Egypt and remained idle until he was sent on his mission to Harar in the summer of 1875. Gordon, on the other hand, tried to change the character of the government in Equatoria. From the outset of his tenure as the governor of the region, he tried to give his staff an international flavor, and even tried to introduce himself not as an Egyptian, but rather as a "peacemaker" and representative of "world civilization." His success in Equatoria, until he submitted his resignation in 1876, was partial.[14] Despite this, the khedive was impressed with his war against slave trading and his frugal management of the district.[15]

There is no information as to why Gordon removed Ra'uf Pasha from Equatoria. It seems that Gordon had concerns regarding Ra'uf's personality, which was admired by his soldiers and excessively autonomous.[16] Gordon's perception of Ra'uf Pasha as a "dictator" was also the reason for Gordon's tour in April 1878 of the Zeila, Berbera and Harar regions. Gordon believed that it was correct to calm the atmosphere among the locals, following Ra'uf Pasha's pressure in early 1878 on the people of Zeila and its surroundings to pay the entire annual taxes in advance. The pasha's pressure was against the orders of Gordon, who believed in gradual taxation. In addition, Ra'uf Pasha's policy also caused unrest among some of his own soldiers, who objected to delays in the payment of their salaries. This unrest, it seems, did not reach a level of bloodshed, but was expressed only in the refusal of the local population to pay taxes, and in insubordination among some of the soldiers.[17] The level of tension in the area can be felt in the statement made by Ra'uf Pasha himself: "Until now, the road from the Ittu tribe was closed and trade there was inadequate. But things are completely quiet now. I sent 60 men from Zeila to settle the barren areas and the Ittu thought that the soldiers were sent on military missions. This is the reason for the outbreak of tensions. This is because the *başhi bozuķ* soldiers were sent there at the same time to build an outpost on that site. The soldiers did not build the outpost and were very angry at the delay in paying their salaries. I could not allow myself to delay salaries, even by one month."[18]

The second meeting between Gordon and Ra'uf Pasha in Harar was tied to broader affairs in the region, including internal Egyptian issues and European interests in Sudan and the Red Sea coasts. While the Egyptian conquerors of Harar were establishing their administration, several processes occurred in Cairo that actually weakened the level of Egypt's sovereignty from within. These processes directly affected the khedive's decision to appoint Gordon as the governor of Sudan and the Red Sea in 1877, and Gordon's decision to dismiss Ra'uf Pasha. The economic crisis that befell the khedival government in 1875 was one of the causes of Khedive Isma'īl's ousting in June 1879. The khedive did not succeed in paying his international debts and the interest that accrued on them. These growing debts, Isma'īl's failed journeys to the Somali coast, and the defeats in Ethiopia in 1875 and 1876 all forced the khedive to turn to Britain for help.[19] Britain's involvement, together with additional European forces, led to the establishment of the "Debt Fund" in 1876 and to Isma'īl's continued entanglement in the situation. In January 1878, a European investigation committee convened, with authorization to check all of Egypt's income and to read any related documents at will. The committee hinted at the fact that the khedive's authority in dealing with his country's economic crisis must be limited, and also recommended expropriation of the property of the khedive and his family. With no other choice, the khedive accepted the committee's recommendations and gave Nubar Pasha (1825–99), an Egyptian-Armenian politician and one of confidants of Khedive Isma'īl during the 1870s, the responsibility for convening the next government, in which many Europeans served as ministers.[20] By August 1878, Nubar Pasha's government, the Council of Appointees, had become the first independent government in Egypt. This government's main role was to apply the committee's recommendations. The khedive committed to accept this government's decisions, even though he did not support it or its moves. This political constellation actually prepared the ground for the growth of three movements that show the roots of Egyptian nationalism: the constitutional movement, the military movement, and the national movement.[21]

Gordon's appointment by the khedive as General Governor of Sudan and the districts of the Red Sea and Harar in March 1877 was made as part of the reorganization of the khedive's government. But this appointment was not separate from foreign interests, and especially British interests in the Red Sea and the Gulf of Aden. The port cities in Sudan and Somalia, which were under Egyptian control, were extremely important to the British, as they were used as stations along the maritime route to Aden, and from there to India. The British hope was to supervise activities at these ports, and they achieved their goal in an agreement signed with Egypt in June 1877.[22] One of the provisions in this agreement promised the British freedom of movement in their war against slave trading at the ports of the Red Sea and the Horn of Africa.[23]

Gordon's obligation and loyalty to the khedive and to Egypt's considerations must be examined in the context of this agreement. Gordon presented himself as an Egyptian officer and one "who does as he is told by the khedive."[24] Even so, it can be claimed that Gordon mainly served the interests of Britain in Sudan and the Red Sea, while serving as the emissary of the khedive. Accordingly, there is a possible connection between the 1877 agreement and Gordon's appointment as governor over Sudan and the Red Sea, reflected in the opinion of the German consul in Cairo, who claimed that Gordon received secret orders from the British government about its interests in Sudan.[25] There is no doubt that the British government supported Gordon's appointment in the hope that this would help British interests in the region. It is clear that the war against slave trade in Sudan was a concrete joint goal of both Gordon and the British government.[26]

The British foreign ministry consulted with Gordon on matters pertaining to the war against slave trading in the coastal cities of the Red Sea and in the development of British economic interests there. In 1877, Gordon recommended the opening of a British consulate in the port city of Sawakin in Sudan, which would be responsible for British interests in all Red Sea port cities.[27] The British foreign ministry attributed great significance to the events on the eastern coast of the Red Sea and, in the end, did not open any representation in the western coastal cities. Gordon operated as a "consultant" for the British government in regard to consular appointments in the coastal cities and western Sudan. He presented himself as the khedive's representative, but did not hide his disappointment with the British government's behavior in the Red Sea region.[28]

In July 1877, after the annexation of the districts on the coast of the Red Sea and Harar to the areas under control of the governor of Sudan in March of that year, Gordon submitted a financial report that summarized the expenses of the khedival government in Berbera, Zeila, Tadjoura, and Harar. He based the report on the account books that were submitted to him by the governors of the various cities, who reported at the khedive's request.[29] Gordon wrote that he considered Berbera to be "a city whose future is not bright, because Aden is located at the entrance to the Red Sea."[30] He defined Zeila as "a port with some importance."[31] Gordon regarded Tadjoura as an annex to Zeila. His attitude to Harar, on the other hand, was different: "Harar is one of the most important regions in Sudan. It is an important point on the connecting route to Zeila. This route is frightening and tiring. Therefore, I ordered to immediately allocate 200 Egyptian Lira to improve the place."[32] Gordon suggested improving the management of income and expenses at Zeila and Berbera, which he believed was the source of the financial deficits in the Red Sea cities.[33] He claimed that the excessive size of the garrison force there and the inefficiency of trade between Zeila and Aden were the main causes of these deficits.[34] Gordon criticized the inefficiency of the khedive's government and even the conduct of the British government: "The khedive's government wasted 70,000 pounds on a useless lighthouse, on providing water, a mosque, pier, etc. The income there was 170 pounds a year. The British government insists that Berbera is a free port, and will not allow us to charge taxes on 10,000 cows and 60,000 sheep which the khedive's government is transferring from Berbera to Aden."[35]

Gordon also determined that there was no financial necessity to maintain Bulhar as a port for export to Aden, and he recommended that Berbera be used as the only port in the region. Regarding Harar, Gordon claimed that "there were about 3,000 soldiers in the garrison force in Harar. Their accommodation and level of nutrition was good." He took upon himself the responsibility to pay the soldiers who had married women from the city and stated that such behavior would encourage other soldiers to marry local women, "making the situation of soldiers much better."[36] Gordon's statements indicate that marriage between the Egyptian soldiers and women from Harar was common during Ra'uf Pasha's term as city governor and that Ra'uf's vision on this matter, mentioned above, was in fact realized to some extent.[37]

Gordon presented the Harar budget as profitable. He claimed that the government's annual expenditure in Harar was about 13,000 Egyptian pounds and the annual income of the *hikimdariya* was about 17,500 Egyptian pounds, with an annual profit of 4,500 Egyptian pounds. Based on Gordon's criticism of the economic inefficiency in Berbera, the *hikimdariya* in Harar was described as efficient and profitable. Table 1 shows Gordon's summary of the financial balance of Berbera, Zeila, and Harar.

Table 1
Charles Gordon's report regarding *hikimdariya* of Harar, Zeila, and Berbera financial balances, July 1877

	Annual Deficit	*Annual Profit*
Berbera	8,000 Egyptian pounds	—
Zeila	—	1,800 Egyptian pounds
Harar	—	4,500 Egyptian pounds
Total	**8,000 Egyptian pounds**	**6,300 Egyptian pounds**

Source: Muhafez al- FO, Jul. 1877, in al-Jamal, *al-Wathā'iq al-ta'rikhiyya*, 320.

At the end of the report, Gordon committed "to pay additional amounts in order to strengthen these cities," and declared that "the *hikimdariya* of Sudan has guaranteed to eradicate the deficit created in Berbera's economic balance."[38]

Ra'uf Pasha's Dismissal

Gordon thought that Ra'uf Pasha's dismissal and a series of new appointments in Harar would calm the atmosphere. He regarded Ra'uf Pasha's behavior, to which accusations of fraud and corruption during his reign were also added, as the main cause of the unrest. Based on the atmosphere of the economic crisis that befell the khedive's government at that time, Gordon believed the situation in Berbera to be serious.[39]

At the end of March 1878, Gordon left Cairo for Suez, from which he sailed to Aden. After a short visit there, he crossed the Red Sea to Berbera on the Somali coast. On 17 April 1878, he traveled from Berbera to Zeila, and three days later he left Zeila, heading for Harar. A summary of Gordon's notes during his eight-day trip from Zeila to Harar shows that he suffered. He described this journey as "terrible, and comprised of a jumble of stones. The strip between the coast of Habash and the inner regions of the country is populated by fanatic Muslims. They engage in slave trade." Gordon's claims were tied to his pessimistic evaluation of his relationship with the khedive, the powerlessness of the British government on the Somali coast, and the failed economic management of the khedival government in the Berbera port. In his notes, he mentioned Ra'uf Pasha and Egyptian morality in general: "I found 2,000 pounds, profit from the sale of coffee, which my friend Ra'uf Pasha deposited in his private account in Aden. He planned to purchase retail merchandise and sell it at an exorbitant price to the soldiers in Harar. I confiscated the entire amount. This was my only way of punishing him. I could never do this to the khedive, who acts in the exact same way."[40]

Gordon ruled decisively that the money he found in Ra'uf's account was intended for profiteering, although it is doubtful that he could prove this. Did Ra'uf Pasha pay the price of Gordon's bad mood and anger due to the khedive's behavior? It seems that the motives for Ra'uf's dismissal can be split between the official and apparent ones, on the one hand, and the personal and concealed ones on the other.

Among the official motives Gordon mentioned for dismissing Ra'uf Pasha were his discovery of 2,000 pounds in Ra'uf's account in Aden, and the emphasis on Ra'uf's strict and centralized regime against the residents of Harar and the Oromo. Gordon regarded the pasha's reign as that of a tyrant who was enslaving and inflicting suffering upon the local population. He assumed that Ra'uf Pasha had accumulated too much independent power: "Ra'uf Pasha's power in Harar is so immense that only the khedive himself could fire him."[41]

Gordon's July 1877 report actually presented the normal maintenance of the *hikimdariya* and its economic profitability. Other than Gordon's statements, there is no proof of Ra'uf Pasha's account in Aden, or of any inappropriate behavior on his part. Why, then, did Gordon fire Ra'uf Pasha summarily? This question is intensified in light of the praise that Gordon gave to Ra'uf Pasha after his replacement in Equatoria in 1874, and Gordon's 1878 request from the khedive to treat Ra'uf Pasha with respect upon his return from Harar to Egypt, together with a recommendation to appoint him to another position.[42] In his message to the khedival government on the dismissal of Ra'uf Pasha, Gordon does not mention his accusations about Ra'uf's bank account in Aden or his tyrannical behavior.[43] Gordon's announcement of Ra'uf's dismissal was delivered to the government without any explanation. Another point to consider is the khedival government's silence and acceptance of Gordon's behavior.[44] It seems that answers must be sought in Gordon's complex relationship with Ra'uf Pasha, the independence of the *hikimdariya* and the weakness of the khedival government in 1878. Gordon was worried about the creation of a focus of power that would be too independent, under the control of Ra'uf Pasha.[45] He was worried about the development of a "new monarchy" in Harar and regarded Ra'uf Pasha as the driving force behind such a move.[46] Furthermore, claims about Ra'uf Pasha's tyranny appeared in the memoirs of some of the foreign traders who settled in Harar in the early 1880s. They regarded Ra'uf Pasha as a tyrant who masked his tyranny with an ideological veneer of modern culture and education, which was revealed to lack any content.[47] To conclude this point about the motives for Ra'uf Pasha's dismissal, there is no concrete evidence about specific reasons for Gordon's decision. On the one hand, one must assume that the only explanation for Gordon's behavior was "jealousy, political quarrel-mongering or clashes on personal differences."[48] On the other hand, Ra'uf Pasha was indeed a harsh governor who, using various arbitrary and violent methods, coerced Harari and Oromo men into conversion—cutting their hair, changing their names, forcing them to be circumcised, and so on.

On 26 April 1878, at a distance of two days' ride from Harar, Gordon met a group of *başhi bozuķ*. He told them that Ra'uf Pasha's soldiers had given him a letter in which Ra'uf stated that he knew Gordon was going to fire him.[49] In his letter the same day, Gordon explained his decision:

> The previous sultan, or the emir (as Burton described him in his book), oppressed his people in Harar three years ago. He preferred the Galla tribes, in order to exalt his name among the Muslim sectors of the population. City residents asked the khedive to come and take over the city, and he did so, sending Ra'uf to capture Harar. Ra'uf came and did not encounter any noticeable objection. Eight days later, he strangled the poor emir in an action that was not necessary on his part. The sultan's son went to Cairo and complained. He was told that the khedive was extremely angry, but took no action. Ra'uf imprisoned the head chief of the Galla in chains, but when he heard that I was coming to Harar, he released him.[50]

Gordon arrived in Harar on 28 April 1878, accompanied by two Egyptian officers who were meant to replace Ra'uf Pasha. These were Raduan Pasha, a navy officer and supervisor in Berbera, and Ahmad Rami Bey, an administrative officer in Berbera. They were joined by Yousef, the son of Emir Ahmad (r. March 1852–August 1856). Gordon wrote that on that day he was very tired and in a bad mood, and he was shocked to discover that the Egyptians had slaughtered cows in his honor at the city gate and central plaza. He added that Ra'uf was waiting for him at the *diwan* building and seemed very depressed because he knew about his impending dismissal. Gordon did not release any details about his conversation with Ra'uf Pasha, and there is no further information on this meeting from other sources. Gordon wrote dryly on 30 April 1878 that Ra'uf left Harar on that day and that he also planned to leave on the following day.

It seems that Gordon was interested in the history of the independent emirate in Harar. He derived most of his knowledge about the city from Burton's 1855 book *First Footsteps in East Africa, or an Exploration of Harar*. During his stay in Harar, Gordon noted that he was living in the same palace where Burton resided.[51] On 29 April 1878, during his stay in Harar, he sent a letter to Burton in which he referred to the history of the emirate until 1875, and gave a list of the names and periods of rule of the 'Alī b. Da'ud dynasty of emirs.[52] Gordon even wrote to Burton that he had erred when he thought that Emir Ahmad, the father of Yousef (who had accompanied Gordon on his visit to Harar), was the one executed at the end of October 1875. He emphasized to Burton that the Egyptians had strangled Emir Muhammad b. 'Alī b. 'Abdashakur, thus annihilating the emirate.[53]

Gordon's short visit to Harar brought Ra'uf Pasha's reign to an end, and a new period in the *hikimdariya* began in May 1878. This was the second time that Gordon had fired Ra'uf Pasha from his position as ruler and sent him back to Cairo (as mentioned above, the first was in 1874 in Equatoria). Ironically, Ra'uf Pasha would be the one to replace Gordon in the position of Governor General of Sudan from January 1880 to February 1882.[54]

Raduan Pasha, 1878–1880

In May 1878, Gordon informed the khedival government of Ra'uf's dismissal and of the new appointments in the Harar *hikimdariya*. Raduan Pasha was appointed director general of Harar and the coast, Ahmad Rami Bey was appointed as his *wakil* (authorized representative) in Harar, and Yousef, the son of Emir Ahmad, became "supervisor of the Harar administration." In this way, Gordon tied Harar to Berbera, and the former governor of Berbera also became the supervisor over Harar. Gordon noted that these appointments were temporary until they received khedival government approval. Gordon also mentioned that there was a sense of calm and security in Harar and on the Somali coast and assumed that, according to his plan, government expenses in Sudan and the Harar and coastal regions would reach about 10,000 Egyptian pounds per year. He determined that payments would be transferred by a steamboat sent to Berbera that would also carry provisions to the other regions on the Somali coast, such as Beilul and Ras Hafun.[55]

Raduan Pasha was an officer of Kurdish origin who served in the Egyptian navy and was responsible for the Egyptian forces in Berbera until his transfer to Harar. In comparison to the authoritative and centralizing personality of Ra'uf Pasha, Raduan Pasha was described as "short and thin. His nose is sharp for his face, his eyes are suspicious and his lips are thin. He looks like an arrogant and aggressive person."[56]

Gordon's examination of Raduan Pasha's service in Berbera showed failed performance, sharpening the questions around Gordon's true motives regarding appointments in the region. As stated, Gordon presented Berbera's lack of profitability during Muhammad Raduan Pasha's term there and even exposed an annual deficit of 8,000 Egyptian pounds in 1877.[57] Gordon also criticized Raduan's attempts to create a system of public works in Berbera, such as building granaries for storing and milling corn and wheat. In 1877, the Egyptian government earned only 200 Egyptian pounds from customs on its products that were sent from Berbera.[58] It seems that Gordon transferred Raduan Pasha to Harar not on the merits of his military or economic successes, but precisely because of his faults, as well as to damage—to a certain extent—the independence of the *hikimdariya* in Harar. He wanted to replace the centralization and independence of Ra'uf Pasha with a less prominent officer who would follow his orders. This was also the reason for the appointment of Yousef, son of Emir Ahmad, as the "supervisor of the Harar administration." With this double appointment, Gordon hoped to strengthen his own control over the *hikimdariya*, even at the cost of reviving Harar's past symbols of sovereignty. 'Abdullahi, son of Emir Muhammad b. 'Alī b. 'Abdashakur, was at that time, as mentioned, in Zeila, which was under the rule of Abu Bakr Pasha. Yousef's appointment to an official position in Harar was probably intended also to harm another strong and independent man in the region, Abu Bakr, the sponsor of 'Abdullahi.

Gordon's appointments greatly damaged Egyptian prestige and honor. Harar had economic ties with Berbera, and Raduan Pasha spent most of his time in Berbera during his tenure as governor of Harar. Ra'uf Pasha's strict policy in Harar was replaced with Raduan Pasha's cautious policy. Thus, Harar gradually lost its centrality in favor of Berbera and Zeila.

Control and Moderation

Raduan Pasha continued the development of infrastructure in Harar and Berbera, but at a more moderate pace, and even contributed to economic efficiency. It seems that the surge in research of the Harar region, and the construction and development of infrastructure in the city that characterized the term of Ra'uf Pasha, had slowed down during the term of Raduan Pasha. The enthusiasm of Egyptian pioneering was replaced with Gordon's careful considerations and funding, and the *hikimdariya* lost some of its independence. Even so, the *hikimdariya*'s economy under Raduan Pasha became more profitable, mainly due to the reduction of development enterprises.

By the end of 1879, Raduan Pasha submitted a report to Gordon summarizing the development of the *hikimdariya* while comparing the situation during his term to the situation prior to May 1878.[59] He proudly presented his economic achievements: profits of the Egyptian *hikimdariya* of Harar in 1876 were 18,636 Egyptian guineas, and by 1879 they had reached 37,408 guineas. He claimed that this data testified to "the success and prosperity achieved during his time." One of Raduan Pasha's main enterprises in Harar was the construction of the aqueduct. Raduan turned Ra'uf Pasha's dream into reality "and established the aqueduct with speed and talent, even though it had no drinking water until then, as he had done previously in Berbera for the comfort of the Harar residents."[60]

In social and political terms, Raduan Pasha did not leave any significant mark within the city. He invested great effort in preventing the trade and chewing of khat, as he regarded khat as "the source of different and bad influences on the nervous system."[61] Thus, one can conclude that Ra'uf Pasha's edicts did not influence the local traditions, and chewing of khat continued.

Raduan's economic policy corresponded with Gordon's strategy, which was intended to limit the khedival government's expenses, and it tended to limit any independent attempt of expression by the districts under Egyptian rule. In this regard, it seems that the khedive was subject to Gordon's influence and generally accepted his decisions.[62] In 1879, Gordon fulfilled the promise the khedive government had given two years earlier regarding the allocation of a budget for improving the route between Harar and Zeila. To maintain security provided by the Egyptians there, he offered to support the provision of military and government needs in Zeila by paying the soldiers their salaries and supplying wheat.[63] The governor of Zeila complained to the khedival government that he did not receive the financial allocation as promised, and this caused great resentment among the soldiers there. Gordon was furious with the governor, claiming that he had indeed transferred the money and food to Zeila. Harar was left out of this budget, but Gordon regarded the governors of Harar, Zeila, and Berbera as "one gang of subversives who tried to bypass him, tyrants and slave traders."[64]

Gordon could not have blamed Raduan Pasha for Ra'uf style "tyranny," not even in regard to the level of independence. Philipp Paulitschke claimed that "Raduan Pasha preserved the buildings that his predecessor left in Harar, and it is clear that they both worked in the same manner,"[65] but their behavior was different. In economics, Raduan preserved the framework of the *hikimdariya* and continued to develop Harar, but he did this with relative modesty in comparison to Ra'uf Pasha, and he was administratively subject to Gordon. However, with respect to the military, Raduan Pasha's term in office was different from that of Ra'uf Pasha, and was characterized by an undermining of the existing order, on the one hand, and a balanced and level-headed policy on the other.

The Somali Rebellions

During June and July 1878, the transition period between Raduan Pasha's term of office in Berbera and his term in Harar, the security situation in the region between Harar and the Somali coast deteriorated. The sense of unrest that was prevalent within the area prior to Ra'uf's dismissal did not die down after the new appointments, but became even stronger. The uprising of the Somali 'Issa populations that started in the area of Berbera spread to the Harar region. As stated, one of the reasons for Gordon's visit to the *hikimdariya* in 1878 was the Somali uprising and the bitter atmosphere among several of the Egyptian soldiers toward the end of Ra'uf Pasha's term.

It seems that Abu Bakr Pasha, the ruler in Zeila who was influential among the 'Afar and the Somali 'Issa, initiated—or at least encouraged—these Somali rebellions. Abu Bakr was offended by Gordon's moves and, in response, sabotaged his new appointments in the region by inciting the tribes in the area.[66] After the three years of quiet and security that the Egyptians had established in the region, the trade routes between Harar, Zeila, and Berbera had become dangerous, and trade and communication had suffered as a result.[67]

Raduan Pasha and his deputy, Ahmad Rami Bey, tried in July 1878 to overpower the rebels, who numbered no more than several hundred, but they underestimated the rebels' strength. The rebels surprised and struck down the small Egyptian force and escaped toward Zeila, fearing additional attacks.[68] In retaliation, the Egyptians invaded the abandoned villages and burned the homes of ten of the tribal leaders.[69]

Already, at the outset of his term, Raduan Pasha estimated that the garrison force in the city and its environs would not be able to cope with an overall rebellion of the 'Issa, and he warned the khedival government of the danger and need for military reinforcement for Harar. He demanded they bring back the Egyptian warship, which had been anchored in the Berbera area until early 1878 and left upon orders of the khedival government. The ship had two units on board whose responsibility was to support the forces in the area between the coastal cities and Harar.[70]

In July 1878, with the outbreak of the rebellions, the khedival government conveyed Raduan Pasha's request to Gordon, who replied that there was no need for additional soldiers to come to Harar, where, he claimed, there were more than three thousand soldiers. He determined that the problem was not with the number of soldiers but with poor military authority. Gordon suggested that the Council of Ministers appoint an American officer named Graffs, together with several other American officers, to "manage Harar."[71] Graffs was one of the American officers who had served as a teacher at the military college in Cairo (al-Jihadiya).

Gordon did not know that the American officers had already left Cairo in mid-1878 (except for General Stone).[72]

Gordon's policy, expressed through his dismissal of Ra'uf Pasha in Harar and damage to Abu Bakr Pasha's strength in Zeila, was what had contributed to the process of the Egyptian loss of control in the region between Harar and the Somali coast. The khedive's government, headed by Khiri Pasha, was now discussing the possibility of re-annexing the Red Sea coastal region and Harar to the *hikimdariya* of Sudan and returning Ra'uf Pasha to his position in Harar. In June 1878, the Egyptian government had, in fact, requested that Gordon reconsider reappointing Ra'uf because "the security situation requires this." Gordon responded that "if the Egyptian government believes that in order to achieve quiet and calm there is a need for eternal subservience and tyranny . . . then there is nothing preventing the return of Ra'uf Pasha to his previous position."[73] However, the government was careful to show respect to Gordon and responded that "any decision made by your Honor is acceptable to us."[74]

Gordon's refusal to send reinforcements left Raduan Pasha and his men abandoned in Harar and the region. In October 1878, Raduan Pasha tried to attack the Somali rebel strongholds in the Harar region and suffered another severe defeat. Twenty-six of his soldiers were killed, and the rebels succeeded in looting twenty-nine guns and thirty-eight horses from them. In November 1878, Raduan Pasha left Zeila for Harar at the head of a force of fifty soldiers and one cannon. He waited in Harar for the rebel leaders to meet him for negotiations, but when they failed to show up in the city, he traveled to their villages.[75]

Raduan's quiet and attentive behavior toward the tribes helped to calm the rebellion. At the end of a meeting at the rebels' stronghold outside Harar, Raduan Pasha agreed with their leaders on the payment of reduced and graded taxes. In return, they signed a ceasefire agreement in which they promised to allow transportation to the coast and even return the loot that they had plundered. Raduan informed Gordon of his achievements, and he reported to the khedive's government that order had been restored and there was no need for any military reinforcement whatsoever.[76] However, the ceasefire did not last long, and by early March 1879 transportation on the roads was once again unsafe. It is possible that the

Somali rebels understood Raduan's compromise as weakness, and the fact is that this time additional Somali tribes joined the rebellion. The rebels took control of the roads between Zeila and Harar, attacked and plundered convoys, damaged telegraph lines, and disconnected any communication with the coastal cities. Raduan Pasha demanded backup from the khedival government, and it arrived quickly by sea to Zeila. Now Raduan Pasha convened a heavy force of about 1,500 regular soldiers reinforced by tribes that opposed the rebels' coalition. On the other side were about 370 armed rebels, which were now easily defeated. From mid-March 1879 until the evacuation of Harar by the Egyptians in 1885, the Somali 'Issa did not raise their heads again.[77]

Raduan Pasha had succeeded, no doubt, in achieving his goal. He bravely warned the government in Cairo of the low quality force that was at his disposal and intelligently managed his ties with the Somalis.[78] The maritime officer from Berbera was found to be moderate and balanced, and mainly attentive to the developments in the Harar region, knowing what steps to take when it was necessary to use a tough approach. He continued to develop the city and managed its economy efficiently and profitably. By 1880, Raduan Pasha had succeeded in correctly maneuvering between Gordon's impulsive decisions and the unsure management of the khedival government. Ra'uf Pasha was regarded at that time as a strong person, a military leader, and a man of vision, who used his "iron hand" policy to realize the dreams of the Egyptian "homeland" in Harar. Raduan had to deal with Ra'uf's legacy, and he did this in a responsible and balanced way. Although he did not cultivate his own reputation or pursue a vision, he enabled the continuation of the *hikimdariya*, despite the decline in its level of sovereignty.

Raduan Pasha, like his predecessor Ra'uf Pasha, also fell victim to Gordon's impulsive behavior. Terminating Raduan's term in Harar and Berbera was one of the last moves made by the British colonel while serving as the Egyptian governor in Sudan. This time as well, it seemed that the instinctive and personal dimension greatly contributed to Gordon's decisions.

From March to October 1879, the political situation in Harar and its environs remained without any significant change, but this was not the case in Cairo. Economic and political developments in Egypt led to the ousting of Khedive Isma'īl on 26 June 1879 by the superpowers, and to the appointment of his son Tawfiq in his place. Gordon, Isma'īl's trustee, submitted his resignation in July 1879, was asked to continue serving, and remained in his position until January 1880. Throughout this time, he continued to bear a grudge against Raduan and Abu Bakr and blamed them for the 'Issa rebellion in 1878–79. He now worked to oust them both. Gordon decided that Raduan Pasha must return to Cairo, while suggesting that Abu Bakr Pasha be distanced from the Somali coast and exiled with his family to Hudaydah. In their place, Gordon recommended appointing Mustafa Pasha al-Tusiya, an officer whom Gordon regarded as "knowledgeable and wise," to the position of "general governor of Harar, Zeila and Berbera."[79]

Gordon's recommendation regarding Abu Bakr and his family was not put into action, as the khedival government did not want to publicly object to the local ruler. Khedive Tawfiq preferred to turn a blind eye to the slave trade and accumulation of power by the "strong man" of Zeila and the Somali tribes, as he feared their power and influence. Moreover, not only were Abu Bakr and his family not exiled to Hudaydah—they even continued to fulfill a central position in the weakening Egyptian system on the Somali coast. At the same time, Abu Bakr tightened his connections with the French and Italians, who were starting to show a growing interest in the region.[80]

Raduan Pasha's fate was different. The Council of Representatives in Cairo decided on 11 January 1880 to end his term as governor of Harar and the coastal cities.[81] Ten days later, on 22 January, the council appointed Muhammad Nadi Pasha to the position of "director general of Harar, Zeila, Berbera and Tadjoura,"[82] while appointing Muhammad Ra'uf Pasha to the position of "governor of all Sudanese areas and their annexes: Harar, Zeila, Berbera and Tadjoura."[83] Ra'uf Pasha's new appointment might have been caused by Egypt's policy toward Ethiopia, with the intention of toning down the dispute between the countries and possibly even reaching reconciliation.[84] But even if this decision was not at all connected to Harar and its environs, from the standpoint of this discussion, the situation had come full circle. Ra'uf inherited the position of Gordon, who had dismissed him, but did not succeed in renewing the vision that characterized his early days in Harar. The extent to which Ra'uf became a Turco-Egyptian "pasha" once again can be seen in nationalist al-Jamal's criticism: "Unfortunately, Ra'uf Pasha was the head judge of the military court that imposed the death sentence on Ahmad 'Urabi, after the 'Urabi national revolution."[85] Ra'uf, who imagined "the Egyptian homeland" in Harar, sentenced to death 'Urabi, who had proclaimed "Egypt to the Egyptians" in Cairo and plays a pivotal role in the Egyptian nationalist imagination to this day. The element of "Egyptian" identity, whose early buds blossomed in Harar, disappeared with the person who was one of its first heralds.

Nadi Pasha, 1880–1882

With his appointment as governor of Harar and the coastal cities, Muhammad Nadi Pasha was promoted to the rank of *liwa* (major general).[86] Opinions are divided regarding the two years of his reign. On the one hand, these years were characterized by a "policy of openness and tolerance," while avoiding actions involving Islamization, Ra'uf-style.[87] On the other hand, his term in office was characterized by a strengthening of military power. Nadi Pasha reconstructed Ra'uf Pasha's strict policy and returned the military initiative to the Egyptians by invading the lands of the Somali tribes, which were considered hostile. He fortified the outposts on the routes connecting Harar to the Somali coast and recruited a local force as militia in policing actions. The strengthening of the military force in his time was accompanied by an improvement of discipline and morals among the soldiers in Harar.[88]

Nadi Pasha was regarded as the leader who succeeded in bringing stability to the region. The military discipline, alongside growing cooperation with religious and commercial factors in the city, made him appear to the Europeans writers as an "enlightened despot" who was much more efficient than his predecessor. According to European testimonies from Harar during Nadi's regime, the garrison force had become smaller and remained imprisoned for months within the city. But all this changed on the day that Nadi Pasha was appointed head of the military force. His force included Sudanese soldiers, cavalry, and two fast-firing Krupp field cannons. He renewed communication with the coast and reduced dangers on the road leading to the coast.[89]

Nadi Pasha's arrival in Harar in June 1880, six months after his official appointment by the Council of Representatives, opened a new chapter in the annals of the *hikimdariya*. His regime can be regarded through two main aspects—administrative and European. The crux of the administrative aspect is a serious dispute between Nadi Pasha and Abu Bakr because of the accumulation of power by the governor of Zeila and his influence on the Somali tribes. The European aspect is characterized by the expansion of French tradesman Alfred Bardey's activity between the Somali coast and Harar, and the failed attempt of the Capuchin Catholic order to settle in Harar under the protection of the Egyptians.

With the arrival of Nadi Pasha in Harar, tensions with Abu Bakr increased. The khedival government blamed Abu Bakr for opportunism and disloyalty to Egyptian interests because of his support for the Somali rebellions during Raduan's term in office.[90] Abu Bakr maneuvered between the Egyptians and the Afran Qallo and Somali 'Issa populations, while simultaneously maintaining ties with the French and Italian representatives in the Obock region.[91] Contrary to Gordon's intention, the authority of the governor of Zeila increased after May 1877, and he became a double threat to the economic interests of the khedival government in the Somali coastal cities: he harmed the European tradesmen who refused to bow to his authority, and he incited, for his own advantage, the Somali tribes against the trade convoys.[92]

The tension between Abu Bakr and the tradesmen in Zeila peaked in 1879 during an open dispute between Abu Bakr and two French tradesmen, Henri Lucereau and Alfred Bardey. The two had settled in Zeila a year earlier, under Egyptian patronage, and were appointed to consular positions by the French government. They openly voiced their opposition to Abu Bakr and blamed him for plundering the trade convoys by using the Somali tribes in Zeila and the Tadjoura Bay.[93] Lucereau angrily rejected the concession Abu Bakr gave him in late 1879 to pave the road between Zeila and Harar. Instead, he went to Harar in September 1880 and, after spending several weeks in the city, continued westward to the

Oromo regions, where he and his servants were murdered in late September or early October 1880.[94] Bardey settled in Harar in late August 1880 and contributed greatly to the entrance of European trade to the city.

After settling in Harar, Nadi Pasha sent a stern report to the khedival government on the events in Zeila, in which he noted financial irregularities and corruption. He claimed that Abu Bakr had embezzled the money transferred to him by the khedival government and concealed profits from the taxes imposed on merchandise that was brought through the Zeila port. Nadi Pasha also accused Abu Bakr of nepotism and ignoring all rules of proper administration. As an example, he complained that Abu Bakr had appointed one of his own sons as customs officer in Tadjoura while promising him an inflated salary from the khedival government. Nadi also claimed that Tadjoura had become Abu Bakr's "private estate," as most of its residents belonged to his tribe. The governor of Harar warned against the lack of governmental power and claimed that the management of the fleet in Zeila port endangered human lives. He attributed this negligence to Abu Bakr's improper behavior. In light of this, he even appointed an Egyptian officer to supervise the situation in Zeila. Nadi Pasha claimed that Abu Bakr and his family had been promoted from officials in the Egyptian system to an independent source of power. Thus, for example, Abu Bakr gave his men official Egyptian ranks, even though they had never belonged to the Egyptian governmental system. He also distributed firearms that he received from the Egyptian garrison force to the 'Afar tribes, which incited struggles between them and the 'Issa tribes. Nadi Pasha believed that this intentional distribution of arms was the main cause of the decline in security on the roads between Zeila and Harar.[95]

Nadi Pasha, in fact, continued the tough line charted by Gordon toward Abu Bakr, and emphasized his disloyalty toward Egypt, without referring to the matter of the slave trade. Gordon, on the other hand, concentrated on Abu Bakr's slave trade and regarded it as a grave danger to the administration in the region, due to his political influence among the Somali tribes. Gordon's attempts prior to 1879 to limit Abu Bakr's family's power and damage its main occupation—slave trade—had failed. He could not prove that Abu Bakr was holding slaves illegally, and his attempts to do so provoked unrest among the tribes under Abu Bakr's influence in the Zeila region.[96]

Nadi Pasha also made his accusations to Captain Hunter, the first secretary of the British delegate in Aden, whom he met on 19 April 1880. Hunter reported that Nadi gave him a secret opinion, according to which Abu Bakr Pasha was a French agent in addition to being a slave trader, and that his presence in the region constituted a danger to British interests in the area of Obock Bay.[97]

Abu Bakr, for his part, fought back against Gordon and then against Nadi Pasha. After the new khedive, Tawfiq, was appointed, he complained to him in July 1879 that Gordon was harassing him. Khedive Tawfiq's response was that the involvement of the governor of Zeila in the slave trade was known in Cairo, and that he even knew that slaves were sent as a gift to his father, Isma'īl, but times had changed following his rise to the throne.[98]

In his battle against Nadi Pasha, Abu Bakr was more successful. He complained to the khedive that Nadi Pasha was motivated by envy and that he was the truly corrupt one. In 1881, Khedive Tawfiq decided to set up an inquiry committee headed by officer Hassan Sira Pasha. The committee set off to Harar and finally ruled that not only was there no basis for Abu Bakr's claims against Nadi Pasha, but his functioning as an honest and wise governor deserved special mention. Even so, despite the committee's conclusions, Abu Bakr emerged with the upper hand. Following the bitter dispute between the governors of Harar and Zeila, the new khedival government redefined the role of Nadi Pasha and decided, in late 1881, to separate the two districts. Harar's definition was now changed from a *hikimdariya* to an *idara* (administration).[99] Abu Bakr remained in his position in Zeila and continued to accrue power, even after Nadi Pasha left Harar at the end of 1882.

Egyptian Army and Administration

After the administrative separation between the Somali coastal cities and Harar, Nadi Pasha set himself a goal: to strengthen Egyptian rule in the city. He regarded the deterioration of morals and the loss of soldiers' fitness in Harar as the greatest danger threatening Egyptian rule in the city, and as a source of weakness.[100]

Like his predecessor Raduan Pasha, Nadi Pasha was also blamed for the failure to cope with the Somali revolutions due to the decline in his soldiers' abilities. However, Nadi Pasha believed that the key to improving the situation was cultivating the relationships between the Egyptians and the residents of Harar, and he set up a local police force comprised of locals. Evidence of this is given by the Italian traveler Antonio Cecchi, who visited Zeila port and, on his way into the depths of Ethiopia, spent six days in Harar from 28 November to 3 December 1881. Cecchi was deeply impressed by Nadi Pasha's attempt to strengthen cooperation between the Egyptian soldiers and Harar residents, and he noted the convening of the militia, "comprised of a unit of Turkish (Egyptian) policemen and another unit of native-born policemen."[101] Nadi Pasha separated the local police forces, in which Harar residents served and through which they achieved a certain level of autonomy, from the Egyptian forces, which protected the city from external dangers. He tried to remove his soldiers from the city, to the tribal regions, and thus to minimize friction with city residents.

In general, Nadi Pasha also succeeded in stabilizing the economic situation, as stated by Bardey: "During his term in office, the Egyptian garrison force returned to a situation where it was providing for its own needs: the customs was sufficient to uphold 4,000 to 5,000 soldiers and position holders and make payments for them. Harar often sent tax surpluses to Cairo."[102] But, as can be deduced from Philipp Paulitschke's critical testimony, this was not an uncorrupted enterprise: "Nadi Pasha made sure to fill his pockets. He appointed *dogins* that were close to him, for the purpose of collecting taxes. Several strange actions and extremely severe disciplinary measures incited violent protests against the governor by the Egyptian officers who were connected to Harar dignitaries."[103]

Several events occurred at the same time in Egypt that led to the British conquest in September 1882, including Ahmad 'Urabi Pasha's revolt of February 1881 and a series of events in Cairo and Alexandria.[104] There are no Egyptian sources on the influences of the rebellion in Egypt on events in Harar, but the European traders in the city found a connection.

Brothers Alfred and Pierre Bardey, who owned commercial agencies in Harar and Zeila, claimed that the ʻUrabi rebellion had a limited and minor effect on events in Harar. They claimed that the events in Egypt occurred because of the meeting between the Muslims in Egypt and the British conquerors, and it seems that the two were influenced by what they perceived as the hostile attitude of the Muslims in the city toward the foreigners. For this reason, they made a connection between the Muslims in Egypt and the Muslims of Harar: "the sounds of the revolution and the war of the Muslims in Egypt were spreading at a growing rate." On the other hand, Alfred Bardey claimed that "the uprisings in Egypt are expressed in a calmer manner than in Harar." Pierre Bardey stayed with his brother in the city for a short time during 1882. Pierre had a close relationship with Nadi Pasha, and it seemed that even he was impressed by the stability of the Turco-Egyptian government in the city, in light of the events in Egypt at that time.[105]

However, Gabriel Ferrand, a French trader who was in Harar around the same time, noted that there was an indirect connection between the end of Nadi Pasha's term in December 1882 and the ʻUrabi rebellion. He determined that "despite the fact that he was Egyptian, Nadi did not lack initiative. Unfortunately, his indirect participation in the rebellion distanced him from any position of command, even at the lowest rank possible."[106] There is no reference whatsoever to Nadi Pasha's involvement in the ʻUrabi rebellion, and it is not clear what sources Ferrand relied on. It seems reasonable to assume that the end of Nadi's term, and his departure from Harar on 11 January 1883, were connected to the redeployment in Egypt and to the beginning of the end of the colonial enterprise in Sudan and in the Horn of Africa.

The Turco-Egyptian garrison force was greatly affected by the new situation. The investments of the khedival government almost ended during 1881–82, and the plan for the economic rehabilitation of Egypt after 1882 did not allow the delivery of new soldiers, or the development of existing districts in Sudan and the Somali coast. Following the worsening of economic conditions, Nadi Pasha allowed his men to steal food and grain from the Afran Qallo Oromo. He paid salaries to his soldiers in cattle taken from the Oromo, while setting an exchange rate where each sheep was equal to five piasters.[107] In this way, Nadi Pasha had, in fact, calmed his soldiers' troubles, but he had also caused severe unrest among the Oromo outside the city.[108] From the moment of Egypt's downfall, the countdown to the collapse of the entire colonial enterprise began.

European Interests and Turco-Egyptian Transimperial Telegraph Projects

After stabilizing the security situation in the city in 1880–81, and later reestablishing its separation from the coastal cities, Nadi Pasha tried to reorganize Harar and its environs and worked to revive the *mudiriyat* of the Oromo.[109] He strengthened the existing systems and was determined to ensure a stronger and more efficient organization of the tribal realm. At the heart of his initiative was a population census upon which he reported in April 1883, five months after the end of his term in Harar. The census estimated the total number of Oromo and Somalis living under the Harar administration during Nadi Pasha's terms to be between half a million and one million people.[110] A British intelligence report in June 1884 estimated that the population reached close to half a million people in the *mudiriyat* around Harar.[111]

The keystone in Nadi Pasha's enterprise was the plan to connect Harar to Zeila and Berbera via telegraph lines. An engineer who came especially from Cairo was put in charge of the plan. The engineer (no information is found about him) found that 210 miles separated the two cities, and there was a need for eight thousand pillars to place the telegraph line between the two. In his vision, Nadi Pasha planned to continue the line from Zeila to Bulhar and from there to Berbera, and to connect the three areas under Egyptian control.[112] Thus, the Turco-Egyptians were the first colonial power to put down telegraph lines between Harar and the Somali coast during the first years of the 1880s. It was one of the technological climaxes introduced by the Turco-Egyptians in that area, and one of their strategies to portray themselves as empire builders in Africa, as well as builders of an intercontinental empire.[113] The Turco-Egyptians aspired to expand their telegraph network and to connect Harar's line to their other lines in the Nile Valley and along the Red Sea coastal outposts. The telegraph line of Sawakin (on Sudan's Red Sea coast) was already connected to the Egyptian telegraph network from 1865.[114] Similar to the Ottoman telegraph line projects between the Hijaz and Damascus, the Turco-Egyptian telegraph projects should be seen as transimperial projects; they certainly were an integral part of Istanbul's and Cairo's foreign policy during the 1880s.[115]

Nadi Pasha's project was reviewed in the Italian newspaper *L'Esploratore* in May 1883: "The Egyptian government allocated 200,000 lira to install a telegraph line from Zeila to Harar. The government invites European travelers and tradesmen to visit and explore the land of the Galla, where the climate is good and the land fertile. The activities and intelligence level of the residents seem to promise a good future for this land."[116]

This knowledge reflects, in the best way possible, the tendency for openness toward European officials that characterized Nadi Pasha's term in office. The telegraph enterprise was not conducted in the name of the euphoria of progress that was prevalent in the time of Ra'uf Pasha, and not even for the welfare of the city's residents as in the time of Raduan. Nadi Pasha wanted to develop an infrastructure that would facilitate the settlement of Europeans in Harar. It was particularly in light of the loss of internal sovereignty in 1882 that he had a vision for the economic and political future of the Harar administration as connected to European entities. At first, it seems, the future of Egyptian Harar was dependent not only on the khedival government, but also on the French and Italian tradesmen on the Somali coast and the British tradesmen in Aden.

Nadi Pasha left for Aden from Zeila during January 1883. In Aden he met with a British consul named Sealy and gave him a copy of the map of Harar and its environs. Sealy reported that Nadi Pasha besmirched Abu Bakr, the governor of Zeila, accused him of inciting the region of the Somali coast, and claimed that only the presence of the Egyptian warship off the Somali coast would maintain order there. Sealy himself received the impression during his meeting with Nadi Pasha that "there is a doubt about the level of Egyptian sovereignty on the Somali coast."[117] This meeting motivated the first British discussion on the question of evacuating Egyptian forces from the Somali coastal cities and from Harar.

The Egyptian historian al-Jamal portrayed Nadi Pasha as "a governor who fortified and strengthened the protection measures of the *hikimdariya* of Harar. He focused on the expansion of the circle of trade in the region and encouraged the residents to maximize use of their agricultural lands. Despite this, the incitements to defame him only increased and he was called to return to Egypt in December 1882."[118] It is not clear who were the individuals who spoke badly of Nadi Pasha, but it seems reasonable to assume that claims were made mainly by his bitter rival, Abu Bakr from Zeila. It is also possible that the connection between Nadi Pasha and 'Urabi's group, at which tradesman and traveler Ferrand hinted, gained Nadi additional enemies in Cairo. Either way, the end of Nadi's term in Harar was connected to the general downfall of the Egyptian colonial enterprise on the Somali coast and in Sudan.[119] Abu Bakr benefited most in the region in 1882 and he managed not only to maintain his status but also to strengthen his position and maneuver between the interests of the Italians and the Egyptians in the region, while relying on his great power among the Somali tribes.[120]

'Alī Riḍa Pasha: The Last Governor, 1882–1884

'Alī Riḍa was born in 1828 in Rethymnon in Crete. There is no information on his family background, only on the military path he took. In 1864, he underwent a military training session in France and specialized in artillery. In January 1881, he was appointed by the khedival government as governor of the Red Sea coast, from Suez to Ras Hafun.[121] This appointment sparked great interest among the British, who began to follow activities on the Somali coast more closely from their colony in Aden.[122]

Riḍa Pasha did, in fact, act as governor on behalf of the khedival government, but he no longer represented any real Egyptian authority. Immediately after his appointment, he sent the British an assessment of the situation regarding Italian aspirations in the Assab Bay, warning them that only an alliance between the Egyptian and British governments would prevent an Italian takeover that would endanger British interests in the region.[123] Riḍa Pasha has been besmirched within the modern national Egyptian narrative, which claims that he "helped the British and gave them reports on the situation of the tribes on the coast and around Harar, without understanding what was going on and without ever visiting there.

This is like a report that he would deliver to the British on the situation of the Indians in India before its conquest by Britain."[124]

The increasing British interest in Harar and the coast was also expressed in the appointment of a British "supervisor" on this matter. On 18 March 1881, the British government appointed Captain P. M. Hunter, who had served in Bombay and was the second secretary of the British representation in Aden at that time, to a special consular position. Hunter was appointed as the "British consul on the eastern coast of Africa, from Tadjoura to Ras Hafun," and within the framework of this role he was subject simultaneously to the chief British consul in Cairo and the Anglo-Indian government in Bombay. Hunter settled in Aden and later became responsible for the evacuation of the Egyptian forces from the Somali coast.[125]

In December 1882, immediately after Nadi Pasha left Harar, the khedival government appointed Riḍa Pasha as governor of Harar. He arrived in the city in November 1883 and held this position until December 1884.[126] 'Alī Riḍa Pasha tried to put orthodox Islamic values into action during his term of office in the city, to a greater extent than his predecessors, the Egyptian governors. He declared an all-out war against the traditional doctors in Harar, whom he regarded as witch doctors and heretics. In some cases, he burned their written works and destroyed the drugs and medications they concocted.[127]

It is possible that 'Alī Riḍa's religious fervor was also a reaction to the openness of his predecessor to the European tradesmen and missionaries, who drank wine in the city streets and walked among Harar's residents dressed in their Christian garb with crosses. In this way, the new governor insulted the traditional lifestyle of the Harar population and also a group that was regarded in the city as having medical abilities of all kinds. (There is written testimony, for example, that the local traditional doctors succeeded in developing a vaccination against smallpox.) Like his predecessors, 'Alī Riḍa also tried, unsuccessfully, to fight against the Harari traditional chewing of khat in the city by imposing taxes on trade with the plant, and fines on using it. To all his actions that were not favored by city residents, we can add the looting of the ancient forefathers' graves, close to the Argoba Bari/Bab-al-Rahmah gate in the southern city. He erroneously assumed that they were used for hiding treasures, but these were never found.[128]

ʿAlī Riḍa's actions in the name of Islam were somewhat similar, in their patronizing style over the locals, to Ra'uf Pasha's educational-cultural enterprise, but under different circumstances. ʿAlī Riḍa was the representative of a khedival government under British occupation, and he functioned also through cooperation with the British in the region. In contrast to Ra'uf Pasha, he did not enjoy freedom of action in an independent district. Harar was once again connected to the Somali coast, and from now on it would not have an independent government as it had in the past, including its unique administrative style. Thus, ʿAlī Riḍa Pasha is remembered as the leader who commenced preparations to evacuate the Egyptians from Harar.

8

Europeans in "Egyptian" Harar

Images and Colonial Reality

"There are several groups among the residents of Harar: merchants, thieves, corrupt people, fanatic Muslims and those who hate Europeans and Christians." So wrote Father Taurin Cahagne, the head of the Capuchin order in Harar, in August 1881, expressing his view of the local residents.[1] He explained the "character" of the people of Harar in these words: "The population of Harar, accustomed to being isolated behind its walls, demonstrates hostility toward any foreign element, likes human trafficking and regards us with displeasure. The presence of Christian monks here causes the minarets of their old mosques to tremble."[2]

Under the protection of Turco-Egyptian colonialism, Greek, French, and Italian merchants began to settle in the city in the early 1880s. In the wake of the French merchants, Catholic Capuchin missionaries arrived in the city, regarding Harar as a base for spreading Christianity among the Afran Qallo Oromo people who lived outside the city. The French and Italian merchants and the Capuchin missionaries wrote journal letters and reports, which, along with other documents, serve as important sources for understanding the historical processes that took place in the city during the Turco-Egyptian occupation.

According to Richard Pankhurst, the importance of such literature written in the city at the time lies in the fact that travelers were "important as observers; they recorded what they saw and in the majority of cases wrote with remarkable objectivity. Our knowledge of Ethiopian history inevitably rests heavily on the writings of observers."[3] Such "objective" knowledge fueled discourse over events in Ethiopia, as it did with discourse regarding other places where Europeans traveled among non-European societies, creating a "reality" that confirmed the conclusions on which the knowledge was based. Thus emerged a system of conceptions that was considered indisputable truth.[4]

The "objectivity" referred to by Pankhurst has been at the center of a heated debate over the past decades, with the emergence of the Orientalist approach in science, literature, and art, a debate that received a boost following the publication of Edward Said's *Orientalism* in 1978. Since then, academics have made wide use of Said's approach and arguments, whether out of agreement or in order to criticize. Timothy Mitchell, for instance, showed that Orientalist consciousness became ingrained in the minds of European travelers and researchers even before they came to the region, due to their exposure to existing research, literary works, and exhibitions.[5]

Besides their contribution as historical sources, however, these documents provide additional testimony to the ways in which the Europeans viewed Islam and Muslims—both the conquerors and the conquered—in Harar during the Egyptian occupation. The story of the encounter between Europeans and Muslims in Harar provides an additional historical contribution to the discussion of Orientalism and the portrayal of the Orient. The European attitude toward the Egyptian conquerors, the conquered people of Harar, and the neighboring peoples was replete with harsh expressions, sometimes quite vicious. In this, it was no different from European Orientalist writing in other places.[6]

European Traders, 1880–1884

The Egyptians invited the Europeans to Harar in the first half of the 1880s. Nadi Pasha understood that due to the loss of internal sovereignty in 1882, and the weakened state of Egyptian rule on the Somali coast and Harar, the political and economic future of the Turco-Egyptian regime in Harar was in the hands of the Europeans. Even the khedival government in Cairo understood that, due to political and economic circumstances, the future of its colonies on the Somali coast and in Harar was tied up with French and Italian traders on the Somali coast and with British merchants in Aden. That was the background to an initiative to lay a telegraph cable between Harar and the Somali coastal cities, with the goal of making it easier for traders to settle there. The Egyptian invitation bore fruit. After Nadi Pasha returned from Cairo, he claimed in March 1883 that "there are now in Harar 20 Greek grocers, French Jesuits, trade agents of a French company and of an Italian company. . . . We will be happy to welcome European travelers in Harar and help them as we helped their predecessors, merchants and clergy who settled in the city."[7]

In the summer of 1880, French traders and consuls Alfred Bardey and Henri Lucereau arrived in Harar from Zeila.[8] Bardey, who saw himself as "a scout with a keen eye, broad observation and sensitivity," described in his writings the sumptuous meals that his Turco-Egyptians hosts prepared for him in Harar: "They served me two bottles of Bordeaux wine and gave me time to eat according the customs of my country." Bardey was quite impressed by the Egyptian military orchestra in the city and its musicians who played Gounod's "Faust" and the French national anthem in his honor.[9] Bardey's descriptions centered on the attitude of the Egyptians toward him, and his reference to his surroundings in Harar related only to the economic potential that lay, in his opinion, in the markets of the city. He wrote in his only description about the city that "there are close to 5,000 Egyptian soldiers and more than 150 officials, secretaries and tax workers living in the city."[10] From Bardey's point of view, there were no local residents of Harar. In contrast, he described the Egyptian soldiers as having "flattened noses, thick lips and curly hair, topped with the red Egyptian tarbush."[11] Bardey described Nadi Pasha as "an impressive and well-built pasha, almost a head taller than his men."[12] Lucereau, like Bardey, also ignored the people of Harar and focused upon his reception by the Egyptian governor. He was especially impressed by the "orchestra that played the national tunes in the middle of Africa . . . what an unexpected occasion!"[13]

Bardey and Lucereau were the first Europeans to write from Harar during the Egyptian occupation, but they were not the first Europeans to visit it and write their impressions. Burton, in his 1866 book *First Footsteps in East Africa, or an Exploration of Harar,* described his ten-day visit to Harar and his impressions of the city's markets and buildings.[14] The people, he wrote, were "a wild and backward rabble," driven by a spirit of jihad in the legacy of Ahmad Gran. While he described the Muslims of the city as a faceless mass except for the religious fanaticism that characterized them, Burton wrote about the rulers of the city: "The Emir is the government in Harar. These little princes are accustomed to kill or arrest anyone who is suspected of aspiring to the crown." Even though Burton and Bardey made reference to rulers of Harar in different periods of time, Burton's "little princes" were substituted by Bardey with soldiers having "flattened noses and thick lips." The "masses," if they merited any reference at all, were characterized as featureless and driven by religious feelings alone.[15]

One of the merchants active in Harar in the 1880s was the well known French poet Arthur Rimbaud (1854–91). Rimbaud arrived in Harar in mid-December 1880, after being sent by Alfred Bardey to serve as his agent in the city. In accordance with the agreement with his employers, Rimbaud would earn nine shillings a day and fees for the merchandise he would purchase—coffee beans, rubber, ivory, and musk—through trade in cotton cloth with the people of Harar. Rimbaud, it seems, was enchanted by Bardey's stories about Harar and its residents, which were unknown to Europeans prior to 1855. He hoped to become rich there quickly.[16] Rimbaud's history in Harar is far from his image as "poet" in the East or in Africa. Rimbaud was an integral part of two colonial contexts—the Turco-Egyptian and the Ethiopian, which arrived in Harar in 1887. These contexts introduced Rimbaud not as a poet or humanist who traveled to Harar due to his inherent tendencies to the exotic "Orient," but as a white merchant and colonialist, who desired to become rich as a protégé within these colonial contexts. As opposed to his European colleagues, Rimbaud did not portray a binary reality of "civilized West" compared with "barbaric Orient," and his case demonstrates the travel writing genre as dynamic and varying, an integral part of its reciprocal relations with the indigenous sphere. Because of his reputation and uniqueness, Rimbaud was considered to have served as a memory agent of Harar, playing a key role in late-twentieth-century research in the region. The "museumization" of Rimbaud in Harar is another aspect of the "Orientalization" of his image, and the instrumentalization of the town as an "Oriental" stage for the "poet" character.[17]

Similar to other colonial cases around the globe, Christian missionaries settled in Harar in the footsteps of the merchants' commercial activities. This was the first time in the history of Harar that crosses were seen in the streets, and it was especially striking that this occurred under the protection of the Egyptian Muslim conquerors. If the traders who wrote dealt with the occupiers and the economic potential of Harar, and mainly ignored the local population, a study of the writings of the missionaries reveals a loaded religious and cultural encounter.

The Capuchin Mission in Harar

In 1867, French Capuchin missionary Taurin Cahagne established a mission station in the Oromo regions near the southern border of the Ethiopian Shewa kingdom. Cahagne, who spoke the Oromo language, aspired to cooperate with the Egyptian regime in Zeila, Berbera, and Harar to establish Capuchin mission stations among the Oromo people in the surrounding area. Due to Cahagne's connections with Bardey, the Capuchin missionary vision was to use Bardey's store in Harar as a base for missionary activities.[18]

The reasons for the connection between the Egyptians and the Capuchins are unclear. The Egyptians' decision to allow missionaries to settle in Harar appears illogical, since Egypt tried to establish its power upon, among other factors, spreading Islam among the residents of Harar and the Oromo. Perhaps the Egyptians understood their relative weakness compared to European elements. One of the testimonies supporting this theory is Bardey's claim that "establishing a mission in Harar is regarded by the Egyptians as necessary for the development of an Egyptian colony in Harar, since the future lies there."[19]

In early April 1881, Father Cahagne and his men set out from Zeila to Harar. As they prepared to enter the city, a fellow missionary in Cahagne's party wrote: "Harar spreads out on a high plateau, and over a lovely valley . . . agricultural terraces are built in the valley. It all looks like a garden. Above all these stand two or three minarets, and two or three large buildings that the Egyptians recently built. A wall surrounds it and is meant to defend them. We stand before the mysterious capital, which Europeans have not entered for hundreds of years."[20]

The mystification of Harar intensified when the missionaries first encountered the city's inhabitants, who gathered around the Capuchins upon their arrival in the city, and only scattered when the Egyptians intervened.[21] The missionaries immediately joined Bardey, who reported that the Capuchins' arrival was troubling to Harar's Muslim inhabitants, although the newcomers were greeted with "politeness and respect."[22] It seems that it was clear to the Capuchins that Harar would not serve as anything more than a mission base and point of departure for missionary journeys among the Oromo. They did not delude themselves about their activities in the city, which was a Muslim center.[23] Father Cahagne wrote about this in August 1881: "Harar is not the site of the activities of our mission, but rather a safe place that our Lord prepared for us under the protection of the Egyptian flag."[24]

Cahagne differentiated between the "Egyptians" and the "Muslims" of Harar. He tended to ignore the religion of the Egyptians, but he stressed that the city's inhabitants were Muslims. He saw the Egyptians in terms of their "function"; their role, in his eyes, was to provide protection from the "hostile" city-dwellers.[25] Cahagne stated that "five or six years ago in Harar, before the Egyptian conquest, we would have been immediately slaughtered upon arrival."[26]

For their part, it seems that the Egyptians saw their task as a "decorative" function that would show their supposed religious tolerance and their openness to foreigners in Harar. The khedival government passed on clear instructions to Abu Bakr and to Nadi Pasha regarding hosting the Capuchins properly.[27] Cahagne even claimed that the governor of Harar had received written instructions to treat his guests with respect and help them settle in the city.[28]

Despite their show of hospitality, it seems that the Egyptians were aware of the repercussions of the protection that they granted the Capuchins and understood that permitting freedom of the Catholic missionaries to act in the city would endanger their rule there.[29] Thus, for example, Selim Bey, the deputy governor of Harar, permitted the Capuchins to rent a house in the city in May 1881 with funding from Bardey, but he forbade any Christian religious activity outside of it. Selim Bey explained to the inhabitants of Harar that the house, bought in November 1881 by Cahagne, "serves as a simple civilian structure and as the home of a French citizen. It bears no outward Christian religious symbols, and it is not a mission where prayers are held inside."[30] The house that Bardey rented for the Capuchins was the home of Egyptian officer Mustafa Effendī. "The house looks like a small monastery, well-protected from the eyes of strangers," wrote Cahagne, "like every oriental structure, our new home looks like a small monastery."[31]

Emile Foucher completely adopted Father Cahagne's hostile assessment of Harar's residents from the previous century, and wrote in 1981: "The Capuchins felt great sadness and frustration because they were unable to save the hungry and the dying, and they also suffered from a hostile and fanatic Muslim population. The Capuchins were pioneers who struggled from day to day for water and bread because of local opposition toward them. They were forced to spend most of the day in their home. If they went out, it was in secret, and they walked silently on the edges of the narrow streets, while having to be polite to faces filled with hatred."[32]

It seems that the historical picture and the general colonial context are more complicated than the interpretation offered by the Capuchins. Despite the Egyptian attempt to moderate the protection given to "guests" and diminish the significance of the settling of Capuchins in Harar, the Capuchins were quite aware of their own achievements: establishing a Christian outpost for the first time in Harar's history and creating a base for ongoing missionary activities in the Afran Qallo Oromo areas outside the city. In spite of the limits imposed by the Egyptians on the activities in his house, Cahagne wrote with emotion: "For the first time, Christians are praying to Our Lord from this city! Until the hatred passes, we have been shut in our house when darkness falls for the past month. But our goal has been achieved: we have found a refuge as well as a base for spreading the gospel in the countryside."[33]

The Capuchins' seclusion in "a small monastery" secured against "strangers' eyes" was not, in more balanced historical perspective, necessarily caused by the exceptional "hatred" of the Muslims in Harar toward the missionaries. This hatred was expressed in the letter of Father Cahagne from Harar in August 1881:

> We must struggle against Islam that stretches like a cursed belt along the coasts of unfortunate Africa. Would it be that this accursed cult not conquer, each day, new conquests within the continent! However its progress is great, and the time has arrived for the Christians to rush to arise before the problem with the aim of setting up dikes in the face of this cursed invasion. It is forbidden for us to deny this. The religion of Muhammed is an expression of Satan's work. This is the dreaded monster spoken of in the Vision of the Apocalypse. Everything disappears under this poisoned rule. Not only are souls the principal victims of the destruction of the Muslims, but even the simplest tasks. The earth itself will soon be covered with destruction. Islam of today is to be considered organized barbarity![34]

The "fanaticism" ascribed to the people of Harar did not keep the Capuchins, according to their own testimony, from "walking around freely in the city streets, in their special garb and their crosses, without anyone daring to molest or harm them."[35] The "hatred" of the people of Harar did not prevent the Capuchins from holding a seminar on the principles of Christianity in their house, along with three separate study frameworks: studies for "freed slaves" (even though there is no evidence of slavery in Harar during the Turco-Egyptian conquest), French language classes (intended for the city people and Egyptians), and the study of the Oromo language and Arabic (for the missionaries themselves).[36]

The sale of the house to the Capuchins and the activities that went on within its walls were carried out with Egyptian approval. It was not without reason that the missionaries were seen by many of Harar's residents as part of the Egyptian colonialist exploitation and additional evidence of the "immorality" of the Egyptians and their "heresy." Thus, for example, many oral traditions from Harar attest that the Capuchins acquired a large garden in the city, whose area was around four acres, from an Egyptian officer named Omar. This fertile and tilled garden, with its seven hundred coffee plants, was confiscated from a Harar resident in 1875 by the Egyptian officers and sold at an overpriced sum to the Capuchins.

The Egyptians and the Capuchins were viewed, it seems, by the people of Harar as being the same. There are no testimonies from Harar's inhabitants regarding hostility toward the Capuchin missionaries, just as there are none regarding their attitude toward European traders.[37]

It could be theorized that the hostility of the Capuchins to the Muslims of Harar, and to Islam in general, grew in response to the difficult physical conditions in Harar. The hard rains and the oppressive heat overwhelmed them, and many soon became ill with malaria, as is recorded in their letters. In addition, they suffered from hunger and claimed that the hostile people of Harar intentionally refused to sell them good quality bread in the local markets, and that other types of food were sold to them at inflated prices.[38]

Part of the weakening of the Egyptian *hikimdariya* included the deterioration of the economic situation and famine in certain periods. In a broader context, what occurred in Harar was not unconnected to the process of the disintegration of the Egyptian hold over their territories in Sudan and the Somali coast at the end of the 1870s and the first half of the 1880s. However, the Capuchins ignored what was happening in general in Harar. They interpreted processes and various events as directed toward themselves—as part of the "hatred" and interreligious conflict that they perceived—and they interpreted the local inhabitants' suspicion and hostility toward colonialist Egyptian exploitation as hostility of Muslims toward Christians.

One of the most pronounced examples of putting a religious slant on what was happening in Harar is Father Cahagne's report on the revolt of Selim Bey in September 1881. Nadi Pasha was in Zeila at the time, and his deputy, Selim Bey, took advantage of his absence to seize control of the city, with the support of some of the Egyptian soldiers in the city and an unknown number of local residents. The rebellion failed after several days, since most of the Egyptian soldiers in the city supported Nadi Pasha. Egyptian sources claimed that the rebellion broke out over a personal quarrel between the governor and his deputy, and over the anger of the Egyptian soldiers in Harar about the months-long delay in paying their salaries. Cahagne viewed this internal Egyptian matter through his own fears: "We are witness to the attempt of Selim Bey to rebel. Several soldiers entered my house to complain about the behavior of the Bey. Should we fight? If a serious struggle were to take place between the governors, this would be a good opportunity for the fanatics of Harar to attack our house."[39]

The Muslims of Harar never attacked the Capuchins, either in their house or in the public sphere. Elements of a Christian lifestyle in Harar in the first half of the 1880s, including the appearance of crosses in the streets and public wine drinking during meals with the Egyptians, were unprecedented acts in Harar's history before that time. The local inhabitants and their neighbors had not had any real previous contact with Christian merchants and missionaries. Exhausted from Turco-Egyptian colonialist exploitation, they did not object more to the foreigners because they were Christian and European, just as they did not oppose their Muslim Egyptian conquerors. The colonial encounter that took place in Harar prior to 1885 was not colored by a religious or cultural war, in spite of the fears and biased opinions toward Islam and Muslims expressed in the Capuchin's writings. It seems that the Capuchin narrative of religious conflict does not accord with the historical context. The hostility toward Muslims in Harar and the prejudices of the Capuchins toward them receive additional weight when reexamining the encounter between the Europeans and the Oromo and Somali populations outside Harar.

Europeans in Harar's Environs

The Capuchins attempted to establish mission stations in the Oromo territories outside Harar between 1883 and 1885. The activities there were connected to the economic interests of Alfred Bardey and his representative in Harar, Arthur Rimbaud. The cooperation between Bardey and Father Cahagne, which made the settling of the Capuchins in Harar possible, continued in the areas outside of the city, and combined religious and commercial interests.

In July 1883, Rimbaud went out to the Oromo territories and the Somali area. Bardey sent him to investigate the markets of the Oromo outside Harar. Rimbaud stayed in the Capuchin mission station in the Oromo village of Bubasa, east of Harar, with Fathers Pierre and Julien.[40]

Father Cahagne had become known to Rimbaud in Harar, and his acquaintance with Bardey had made it possible for the Capuchins to settle in the city under Egyptian protection in the spring of 1881. Trade had opened the gates of Harar to the mission, and now the mission helped the trader. Rimbaud's friendship with the missionaries from his homeland intensified their mutual interests in Harar and outside the city. When Rimbaud returned from his excursion to Harar, he met Cahagne and told him of his experiences in the Oromo territories. He directed Cahagne and his men regarding the establishment of additional mission stations outside Harar, and even delivered a compass to them to that end.[41] It seems that Rimbaud contributed a great deal to the settlement of the missionaries in the Oromo territories, since "Rimbaud's journeys and enthusiasm encouraged Cahagne to establish mission stations in those areas."[42]

In contrast to the Capuchin's demonization of the people of Harar, they viewed the Oromo outside the city as "those who are used to meeting strangers and not regarding them as enemies."[43] This is the way, for example, that Capuchin Fathers Julien and Ernest treated the Oromo leaders whom they met in Bubasa in June 1883. The two Capuchins were very impressed by the openness of the Oromo leader there, "who gave a house to settle in Bubasa without hostility."[44] Despite their positive attitude toward the locals and their optimism about the locals' openness, Fathers Julien and Ernest did not succeed in spreading Christianity in the area of Bubasa, and Fathers Pierre and Andre came in their place. They wrote in frustration that "it is impossible to spread Christianity here, since Islam is implanted."[45] Father Pierre described the positive treatment that the Capuchins received from some of the Oromo in contrast with the less positive attitude of other Oromo: "The Galla here live in accordance with their old customs, free of any Muslim influence. Therefore, it is easier to spread Christianity among them."[46]

The Capuchins' attempt to present the Oromo and Somali peoples as "moderate" in comparison with the people of Harar does not fit with the historical events. Henri Lucereau described in his writings the sense of danger that lay in wait for foreigners outside of Harar: "The Gala mass around the gates of Harar. Any Muslim who goes a few miles from the walls of the city is in danger of being murdered or castrated without mercy, and whatever remains of him is hung, to one's horror, on the halter and reins of his horse."[47] Lucereau, it would seem, prophesied his own end. In autumn of 1880, he was murdered along with his servants by Oromo at a distance of six hours ride from Harar.[48] Another example of Europeans being murdered in the tribal territories, after no evil had befallen them in Harar, is the story of the Italian merchant, Pietro Sacconi. Sacconi arrived in Harar in June 1883 with the goal of setting up an Italian trading house for coffee and pelts within the city. Impressed with the security instituted by the Egyptians in Harar and its environs, he even compared them to the Romans and coined the phrase "Pax Egyptiana." He was murdered in July 1883 at the hands of Somalis in Ogaden. Another brother from the Sacconi family settled in the city several months later and continued his activities there after the Egyptians left.[49]

It is reasonable to assume that Cahagne and his men, within the city and outside of it, knew about the murder of traders in the tribal areas. Nevertheless, for the Capuchins, Harar was just a base for further missionary activity among the Oromo, whom they viewed as convenient "raw material" for conversion. "If they accepted Islam so easily, why should they not accept Christianity?" wrote Cahagne, referring to the Capuchin project among the Oromo.[50]

Major John Hunter, the British military consul in Aden who was in charge of evacuating the Egyptians from the Somali coast and Harar, fully embraced the conception of the Oromo people around Harar as a target for conversion to Christianity. After visiting Harar, Hunter wrote in November 1884: "The cross has not yet reached them, and they are unbelievers. It is easy to see that there are Gala who are called '*basha Muslimin*' meaning those who converted at the instruction of the Egyptian pashas. They are not very devout or fanatic. They are open to Christian influences."[51] Regarding the Muslims of Harar and the Turco-Egyptians, Hunter wrote: "The people of Harar have relatively high intelligence and are permeated with Muslim fanaticism, despite their submission and disarmament . . . the Egyptians are not viewed by them as pure from a religious standpoint. The pashas are lukewarm believers in the Prophet."[52]

9

The Egyptian Withdrawal

Historical Context

There was, indeed, a direct connection between the economic and political situation in Egypt from the time of its conquest by Great Britain in 1882 and the withdrawal of Egyptian forces from Sudan and the Horn of Africa.[1] However, examination of the process of loss of Egyptian control even earlier—from 1878—in Harar and the surrounding area reveals a parallel rise of the local African powers—the Ethiopian kingdom of Shewa and the 'Afar and Somali population and its leadership. Locals who observed this process were not surprised by the withdrawal. On the contrary, by the end of 1883 and the beginning of 1884 it seemed that the Egyptian era in the city and its surroundings was drawing to a close. Analysis of French, British, Ethiopian, and Egyptian sources from that time bears testimony that the "Harar question" was a major part of the issue of the future of the Somali coast after the British withdrawal, even with no connection to what was happening in Cairo and Alexandria at the time. Moreover, it is impossible to separate Egypt's evacuation of Harar from its withdrawal from the Somali coast. In the eyes of the global and local powers in the region at that time, the connection between the coast and Harar was unbreakable. After the Egyptians left in 1885, however, the historical development of Harar diverged from developments on the Somali coast.

A number of the twentieth-century Egyptian historians who studied the process of withdrawal accused the British of direct responsibility for the loss of Harar, Berbera, and Zeila, as part of the colonialist plot whose goal was to destroy Egyptian sovereignty and steal territories from the Egyptians.[2] In the broader Egyptian context, these claims were used to further the Egyptian national narrative that struggled against Western imperialism in the second half of the twentieth century. Nevertheless, continuing to occupy areas in Sudan and the Red Sea coast was an economic burden for Cairo, which had been in British hands since 1882. In addition, the Mahdī rebellion that took place in Sudan between 1881 and 1885 created difficulties for the Egyptian army and its British patrons from the economic and military standpoints, and hastened the decision to evacuate the outposts in Sudan and the Horn of Africa.[3] These factors added to previously mentioned causes of the economic crisis that had continued in Cairo from 1876, the dismissal of Khedive Isma'īl in 1879, the 'Urabi revolt, British interference in the summer and fall of 1882, and the conquest of Egypt in September that same year. All of these had a negative impact on the payment of salaries for the military garrison in Harar at the end of Nadi Pasha's rule as governor of the city.[4]

Menilek II and Harar, 1883–1884

Rimbaud and the Capuchins were the first to report Shewa military invasions toward Harar beginning in June 1883. Menilek's armies controlled the Afran Qallo regions up to Oborra, sixty miles east of Harar.[5] Other Capuchin testimonies, based on Rimbaud and Sacconi, reported that Menilek sent his officers Ras Gobbana and Ras Wolda-Gabriel to attack the Ittu population, and the Shewan army was close to two days' horse ride from Harar.[6] Rimbaud himself estimated that "Menilek will annex the Ittu territories by the beginning of 1884, but Harar is not on his plans."[7]

The Shewan army's entrance to the Ittu regions should be examined from a few aspects. First, it was one of the main indications of the Turco-Egyptian decline in the Harar environs and among the Afran Qallo. Menilek, king of Shewa, introduced himself by his actions among the Ittu as the regional African colonial power. Second, Menilek's policy in the Ittu and Harar areas derived from his inter-Ethiopian political and economic considerations. Menilek had to fortify his position in his struggle against the Ethiopian emperor Yohannes IV from the Tigray province, and expand to East and Southern Ethiopia during the 1880s.[8]

From an economic perspective, the Shewan plundering among the Ittu population was caused by Menilek's accelerated military arming and his need to pay European gun and ammunition traders for the firearms. Menilek's military regional aspirations were tightly connected to the firearms global markets, which spread from Europe to new potential markets such as the Balkans and the Red Sea basin during the 1860s to 1870s.[9]

Menilek perceived the firearms as a key element of the inter-Ethiopian political struggle, and the Oromo markets were for him a potentially fertile economic source.[10] Furthermore, the southern expeditions and occupations showed the kingdom of Shewa to be a significant political and military African power, an integral part of the "scramble for the Horn of Africa" during the late 1880s, and a base for negotiations with the king of Italy, for instance, in 1884.[11]

In Harar itself, there is no doubt that in the first half of 1884 there was a feeling that the Egyptian era was drawing to a close and that the Egyptians were no longer an element of power outside the city.[12] Even though the Egyptian forces were equipped with modern weaponry, their presence in the Oromo and Somali spheres was greatly reduced, and they remained closed within the city walls.[13]

It would seem that Menilek shared the feelings of Harar's residents, since even the campaigns of the Egyptians in the Oromo areas were seen as a weak reaction to the Ethiopian challenge east of Harar. Italian trader Sacconi reported that ʿAlī Riḍa Pasha instructed his soldiers to act forcefully in the Oromo areas in 1883 due to suspicion that the Oromo would aid Menilek in conquering the city from the Egyptians. Sacconi even claimed that the military invasions in the areas of the Oborra Oromo that were initiated by Nadi Pasha in spring 1882 should be understood in light of the Egyptians' concern about Ethiopian incursions into the Afran Qallo Oromo *mudiriyat* surrounding Harar.[14] Rimbaud also wrote in April 1884 that rumors about a war in Harar were growing stronger.[15] Both Sacconi and Rimbaud, who lived in Harar and traveled in the Oromo and Ogaden areas, reported their feelings that the Egyptians no longer controlled the region. The weakness of the Egyptians was apparent to both the Oromo on one side and Menilek from Ethiopian Shewa on the other.

Global Interests

In the eyes of the French and the British, the threat from Shewa to the Egyptians was more serious. French intelligence in January 1884 assessed that the Egyptians "are now dealing with a new front with Shoa, from the Awash River between Ankobar and Harar."[16] From 1882, the British had also followed the events unfolding in Harar with concern. They deduced that the Egyptians had lost their power of deterrence within the Somali and Oromo tribes, and that Zeila and Berbera had been under threat from the Somali tribes since the beginning of 1884. The British were also worried about the sudden loss of Egyptian control over the ports of Zeila and Berbera and about the possibility that they would need to rescue the Egyptians there. The general British assessment in January 1884 was that the immediate danger to Harar was not from Menilek's imminent conquest, but from the weakness of the Egyptians against the Oromo and the Somalis. They concluded that this weakness created a political and military vacuum in the region into which the Ethiopian forces were likely to penetrate.[17] Their nightmare scenario envisioned the conquest of the ports on the Red Sea coast by the tribes under the command of Abu Bakr of Zeila, in cooperation with Menilek, who would arrive from Shewa with his forces.[18]

The proximity of Harar to Shewa had interested the British before the Egyptian conquest in 1875. They followed the events there out of concern that the balance between Zeila and Berbera and Harar would be upset, which was likely to endanger their interests in the Red Sea.[19] With the weakening of the Egyptians' hold there in 1883, the British feared that the Capuchin monks in Harar would serve as French agents, leading to strengthened ties between France and Menilek and threatening British interests, principally in the port of Berbera. British reports indicate that Menilek's rising power in the area, along with the possibility of a treaty between him and France, was seen by the British as a real danger.[20]

In April 1884, British concern heightened since, according to their assessment, Abu Bakr's strength among the Somali tribes had caused him to urge Menilek to attack Harar.[21] This fear was not baseless, as Menilek did not conceal from the French his aspirations to rule over the areas

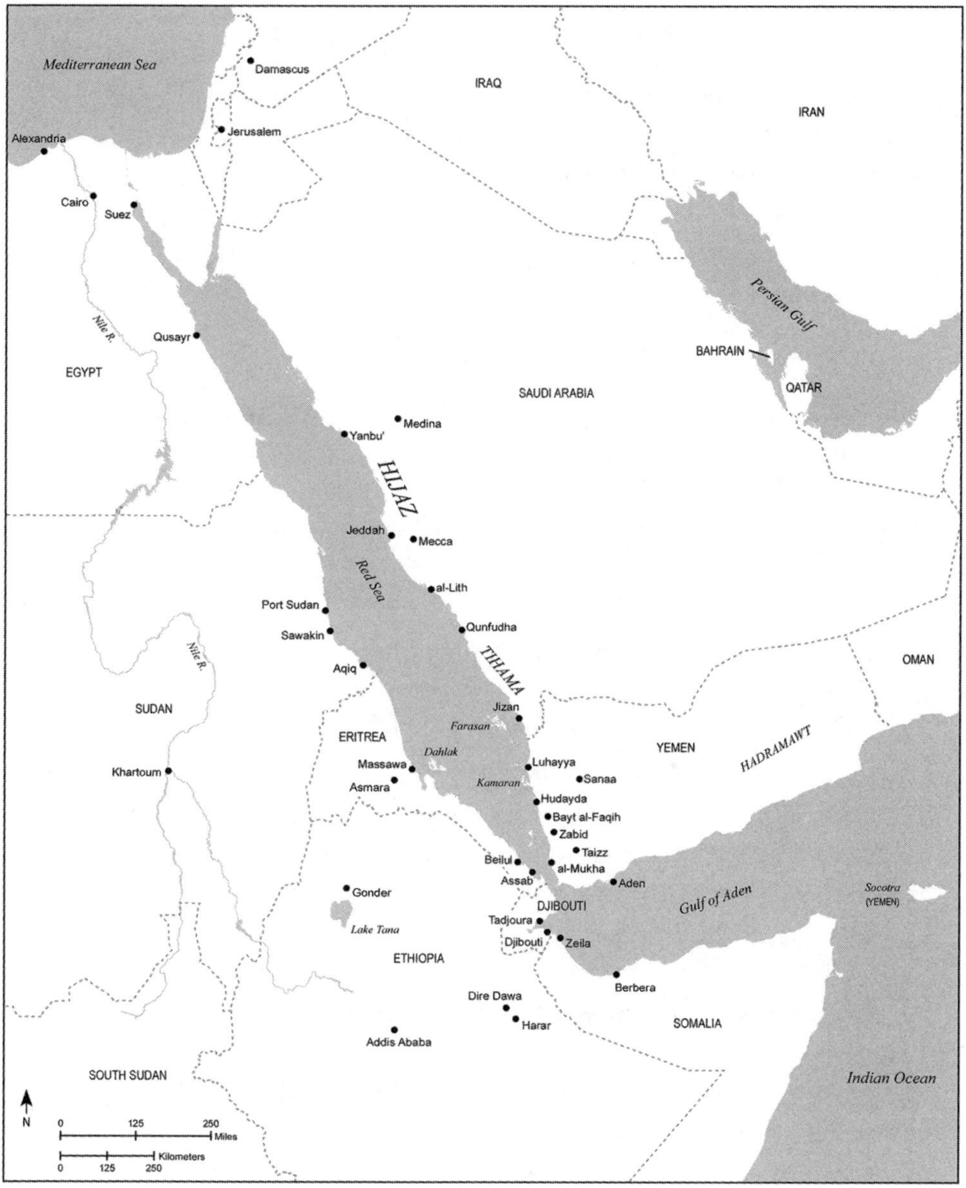

3. Map of the Red Sea Basin and the Gulf of Aden.

conquered by the Egyptians in the eastern Ethiopian plateau and Harar.[22] Considering the rising power of Abu Bakr and Menilek, the British perceived 'Alī Riḍa Pasha, the Egyptian governor of Harar, as incapable of taking care of Egyptian and British interests in the city, or even taking charge of the future withdrawal from Harar.[23]

Menilek was alert to the events transpiring on the Somali coast and Harar. He collected information regarding anything connected with the British conquest of Egypt in 1882 from European travelers who arrived at his court in Shewa, and he attempted to study the new Anglo-Egyptian policies in the area.[24] It is questionable whether Menilek was aware of the British intention to evacuate the Egyptian forces from Sudan and the Somali coast. He did know, however, that from April 1884 the British wished to appease Emperor Yohannes IV and to improve relations between him and the Egyptians, due to the collapse of Egyptian rule in Sudan as a result of the Mahdiyya revolt there.[25]

British Policy and Involvement in the Gulf of Aden

The increasing British interest regarding the events in the region led to the appointment on 18 March 1881 of "His Majesty's special consul for the Somali Coast," Major Hunter, who reported directly to the British consul in Cairo. His main role was to follow the activities of the Egyptian forces on the Somali coast from Aden and to trace the moves of other global powers such as the Ottomans, Italians, French, and Russians in the region.

At the beginning of 1884, British engagement in the Somali coast progressed from showing interest to real involvement. Hunter and the naval captain, Coffin, toured Berbera, Zeila, Sagallo, and Tadjoura to reassess Egyptian strength. On 4 February 1884, the two arrived from Aden at the port of Berbera and met there with the Egyptian governor 'Abd al-Rahman Bey. They learned from him that the situation in Berbera was calm, thanks to a garrison of 196 soldiers, of whom 126 were infantry, thirty-five artillery, and thirty-five armed cavalry. The two reported that the infantrymen were black-skinned and originated in Lower Egypt, and the rest were "Arabs from Egypt."[26] According to their assessment, the garrison in Berbera was in decline and untrained, and its ammunition was antiquated and ineffective, even though its weaponry was well maintained. They estimated that provisions for the Egyptian garrison were sufficient for eight months and that there was enough water for two months.[27]

When the British officers arrived in Zeila on 5 February 1884, Abu Bakr Pasha reported to them that the city and its surroundings were very calm. The garrison under his command numbered 120 infantrymen and forty artillerymen with a nine-liter canon loaded in one barrel, and two rocket launchers. Hunter and Coffin claimed that there was no professional officer to command the force. The two also presented information from Sagallo, where the Egyptian garrison numbered eighty soldiers and from Tadjoura where forty soldiers were deployed.[28] On 6 February, Coffin left Zeila and returned to Aden.[29] Hunter remained in Zeila and arrived in Harar for the first time in mid-March 1884.[30]

There is another version of the British officers' visit. Foucher claimed, in contrast, that Hunter and Coffin arrived in Harar on 24 February 1884. He seemingly based this on the writings of Bardey and Rimbaud (although there is no supporting evidence in the writings themselves): "All of the people of Harar came to see the British officers out of curiosity and not because they were especially popular. From the time that they were on their way to Harar, everyone was concerned with the questions of who they were and the purpose of their arrival."[31] From this version, it seems that Hunter lived in Rimbaud's house and, at the request of 'Alī Riḍa Pasha, he did not walk around in the city, so as not to draw the attention of the Muslim residents. Hunter even bought 500 Egyptian pounds worth of merchandise from Rimbaud to ease his difficult economic situation. According to Foucher, the English flag flew over Bardey's mercantile enterprise, which was administered by Rimbaud, and the cross at the center of the flag riled the residents.[32] There is no support for Foucher's version in Rimbaud's or Bardey's writing, nor in the letters of the Capuchins or Hunter's own report.

The next step of the British was to redefine their main objectives on the Somali coast.[33] They reckoned that the 1877 treaty that recognized the sovereignty of the khedival government on the Somali coast would not remain in force for very long and that it was now necessary to take positions on the coast and in its ports. In addition, they assessed the importance of the ports of Berbera, Zeila, Tadjoura, and Bulhar, as well as additional docking places, from an economic and strategic standpoint. They viewed the Berbera port as the most important resource for the export of cattle and sheep for their colony in Aden, according to data that Gordon presented while serving as governor of Sudan in 1887 regarding the number of heads of cattle exported from Berbera to Aden.[34] The 1884 British account of the balance of cattle exported to Aden during the years 1879 and 1880 is shown in Table 2.[35]

These data show the importance of Berbera and Bulhar to maintaining Aden, one of the linchpins of the British Empire. Until 1884, the British recognized Egyptian sovereignty on the Somali coast and followed the French presence in Obock and the attempt of the Italians to establish an outpost in the Gulf of Assab.[36] Like the French, the British intervened on the Somali coast until the second half of the 1870s by means of various treaties. For example, a defense treaty was signed in 1876 between the Sultan of Socotra, a small island in the area of Ras Hafun, and the British government. The sultan received a one-time grant of 3,000 dollars and an annual stipend of 360 dollars from the British envoy in Aden. In exchange, he was obligated not to hand over, sell, or loan his island to any power other than the British government.[37]

Table 2

British balance of cattle and sheep exported to Aden during the years 1879–1880

Export Source	*Cattle*	*Sheep*
Berbera and Bulhar	1,790	39,912
Gulf of Aden—Somali Ports	222	59,094
Zeila and Tadjoura	5	784
Gulf of Aden—Arabian Ports	15	3
Red Sea—African Ports	—	611
Red Sea—Arabian Ports	31	37
Total	**2,063**	**100,441**

Source: FO 78/3725: Memorandum of Egyptian Coast Territory South of the Red Sea (Admiralty, Foreign Intelligence Committee No. 28), 9 Feb. 1884, 10.

In 1879, representatives of the British government signed a treaty with the Somali Mijjerten population, who lived in the Ras Hafun area, approximately 140 miles west of Cape Guardafui. The Mijjerten leaders committed to "aid the British in all that is related to human life and property on the coast and to guard each harbor and lighthouse extant on the coast and any that will be built there." The sultan of the Mijjerten, who lived in the village of Alula, thirteen miles from Cape Guardafui, received an annual stipend of 360 dollars from the British representative in Aden in exchange for his commitment to "British law."[38] The British government ratified this treaty in July 1880, but it was violated during January and February 1883, when the leader of the Mijjerten took a portion of the booty from a British ship wrecked on the coast, in cooperation with other Somali leaders, and did not respond to the request of the British representative in Aden.[39] However, after the British officers visited the Mijjerten sultan in Alula and reprimanded him, the Somali dignitary made it clear that he was committed to the treaty with the British.[40] This treaty was ratified in February and May 1883.[41]

The British and the Question of Harar

On 29 March 1884, the khedival government recommended for the first time that its forces be withdrawn from Harar. The British saw this as a "wise step" and suggested that Hunter, as one "who is currently in the area and is familiar with the issue," become responsible for the evacuation.[42] The British suggestion from Cairo to appoint Hunter was approved immediately by the Foreign Office in London and received the approval of the Egyptian government.[43]

On 1 April 1884, under pressure from the British, the Council of Representatives in Cairo issued a notice regarding "withdrawal from Harar and turning it over to the closest heir of the late sultan. Giving the city to the new sultan is conditional on a future statement honoring trade in the city and ensuring freedom of commerce between Harar and Berbera and Zeila."[44] The khedival government also approved the appointment of Hunter as responsible for the evacuation of its soldiers from Harar and committed itself to bearing the costs of the withdrawal.[45]

Following the decision to withdraw from the city, the British policy in Harar and the Somali coastal area was characterized by duality. On the one hand, it seems that the British were concentrating not only on evacuating the Egyptians, but on attempting a colonialist takeover of areas adjoining Harar. At the end of February 1884, approximately two months before the first decision to evacuate the city, they contacted the Somali sheikh ʿAbdulla Shohaim al-Dankali, who expressed willingness to sell land under his control to the British government.[46] On the other hand, the British were quite careful not to violate the status quo with the French regarding their rule over Obock and in the Gulf of Aden Basin. Nevertheless, the British were concerned about the widening of French rule from Obock to Ogaden, and about the intensification of French influence over the Egyptians in the area.[47]

In mid-April 1884, the British emphasized the need for a British officer to take charge of the withdrawal. Their assessment was that "the Egyptian government is not capable of achieving the withdrawal of its soldiers from Harar, since its authority there—as in Egypt itself—is depleted of economic and human resources. This is similar to the difficulty in Sudan: carrying out the policy of evacuation in a practical way. Harar will not be evacuated unless an English officer is sent there to supervise. Major Hunter is suitable for this."[48] Another reason for the inability of the Egyptians to evacuate from Harar on their own was, according to the British assessment, that the Egyptian rule was viewed as "corrupt, unfair and rotten, just like in every other place."[49] This last British claim reflected their opinion of ʿAlī Riḍa Pasha as a "weak man, an old chatterbox, who considers himself of Turkish background. He has no idea of anything except the satisfaction of the British treasury and exploiting [Harar] for the good of the Egyptian government."[50]

The British deliberated about the proper time for the withdrawal from Harar and its implementation. The prime minister, as well as Lord Cromer, the consul general in Egypt, feared for the life of Hunter and considered whether to send him to the city in April 1884. They compared Hunter's dispatch to Harar to that of Gordon to Khartoum for the struggle with the Mahdiyya and the evacuation of Sudan. The British did not know how Gordon's mission to Khartoum would end, and they wished to wait before sending Hunter to Harar.[51] (The Mahdiyya rebels killed Gordon in Khartoum in 1885.) Nubar Pasha, who was at the head of the Egyptian government office for evacuating Sudan in 1884, was a full partner to the deliberations about the mission of the British officer.[52] He read the intelligence reports on Hunter from the beginning of 1884 and advised Cromer not to send Hunter to Harar until the consequences of Gordon's Khartoum mission were known.[53]

Major Hunter arrived in Harar in mid-March 1884 and sent two secret intelligence reports from there to Aden, where he surveyed the situation in the city and among the Oromo and Somalis. His surveys became the knowledge body that the British used in preparation for the evacuation of the city and its environs and the basis for actions taken by the Egyptian government, under British pressure, in advance of the withdrawal.[54]

Hunter estimated that there were 30,000 people in the city in 1884. He emphasized the high regard that remained toward the family of the emirs of the 'Alī b. Da'ud dynasty and raised the possibility that 'Abdullahi, son of Emir Muhammad b. 'Alī b. 'Abdashakur, who was murdered by the Egyptians, would return to rule after the Egyptian withdrawal and thus satisfy the residents of Harar.[55]

Regarding the tribal spheres, Hunter analyzed the Egyptian Islamization project among the Oromo as having succeeded and concluded that, "because of the Egyptians, many of the Gala have become Muslims." He noted that there were different estimates of the number of tribesmen, ranging from 250,000 to 2 million. Hunter stated that a premature and poorly planned Egyptian withdrawal from Harar was liable to cause anarchy in the region. He reported that the Egyptians officially ruled over the hills surrounding Harar, in the area of the *mudiriyat*—a radius of some forty miles around the city.[56] Hunter noted that the Somali 'Issa dwelled near the route connecting Harar and Zeila, and that even though they were apparently subjugated to Egyptian rule they were actually dangerous and numbered approximately 60,000. In contrast, the land of the Habar Awal could be found by the main road between Berbera and Harar, and they were quite friendly.[57]

Hunter's basic assumption was that the withdrawal from Harar must take place at the same time as the withdrawal from Zeila and Berbera, in order to prevent an all-out rebellion of the Oromo and Somalis against the evacuating Egyptian army. Hunter's concern was that after the beginning of the withdrawal, the tribal elements would attack the hated Egyptians from the rear, and that a "new" Mahdiyya rebellion similar to the one in Sudan would start due to the situation in the region.[58]

Regarding the condition of the Egyptians within the city, Hunter stated that the supplies at their disposal could last for five years and were stored well. The soldiers were relatively refreshed, and their number was sufficient for repelling any danger, thanks to their live weapons. He predicted that the Afran Qallo Oromo would not follow extreme Islam of the Mahdiyya version in Sudan, since Islam had been forced upon them and they found it repugnant.[59] Nevertheless, his concerns about the awakening of militant Islamic trends among the Oromo and Somali had not disappeared. In his view, the Mahdiyya rebellion remained a possible source of influence on the populations in the Harar region, but since the Mahdiyya had not been successful in achieving its goals in Sudan, he concluded that there was no immediate danger to Harar and its surroundings.[60]

Hunter anticipated that four obstacles would stand in the way of the evacuation. First, the withdrawal of 3,500 Egyptian forces could not be accomplished all at once but would need to be carried out in stages. Second, provision of camels to carry the force's equipment would depend on the Nole Oromo or the Somali 'Issa, both of whom were hostile to the Egyptians. Third, the departure of the Egyptians would leave a vacuum in Oromo and Somali political and economic systems once their sovereignty had been destroyed and they had been integrated into the Egyptian colonial system. And fourth, a military action by the Oromo against the withdrawing Egyptians and the British could potentially lead to Somali military involvement and a resulting military flare-up in Gildessa and Zeila. To overcome these difficulties, Hunter recommended the temporary appointment of a British officer as governor of Harar. He thought that this would be the only way to come to agreement with the Oromo and the Somalis during the withdrawal, and to evacuate the Egyptian forces safely in several stages of five hundred or six hundred soldiers each. In addition to overseeing the Egyptian withdrawal, Hunter recommended that the British governor oversee the return of autonomy to the

Afran Qallo and Somalis and the renewal of their independent political systems.[61]

Hunter's main concern was that the situation would worsen in Berbera, and not necessarily in Harar, since rumors had reached the port city of "disasters of the Egyptians in Sudan," in his words.[62] The situation in Berbera under the rule of 'Abd al-Rahman Bey worsened due to an incident in which the Somalis murdered an Egyptian sergeant in revenge for the death of a Somali who was killed while attempting to rob a trade caravan. Hunter stressed the feeling of insecurity in Berbera and his fears that the Somali 'Issa would conquer the city. He recommended that a British warship, under the command of a naval officer in Aden, be permanently anchored in the Berbera harbor to deter the Somalis until after the evacuation of Harar. In addition, Hunter mentioned two regional figures: Abu Bakr and Menilek. According to his assessment, Abu Bakr had a great deal of influence among the 'Issa and the 'Afar and was liable to amass power for himself with their help. Hunter claimed it was reasonable to assume that Menilek was planning to attack Harar with the help of the Oromo and that the Egyptian forces in the city were aware of this possibility.[63]

Hunter immediately rejected a suggestion to draft the Oromo and the Somalis into the Egyptian army in advance of the withdrawal, in order to ensure quiet in the region. He concluded that the Somalis were not capable of joining the Egyptian army, despite the fact that there was no question about their bravery and physical prowess.[64] He valued the Somalis more than the Oromo and regretted that they would not serve in the Egyptian army, since they would have been "allies who could be trusted." He viewed the Somalis as stronger in military terms, since the Egyptians had not succeeded in subduing them. At the same time, Hunter surmised that they could not be conscripted as "mercenaries to fight for a cause that has no direct connection to them."[65]

Hunter had only scant knowledge of the Oromo. He claimed that the Somalis and the Oromo shared a tremendous hatred for the Egyptian rule and therefore would not cooperate with the departing Egyptians.[66] Finally, he issued a warning about distributing weapons in the tribal area, since this would be a serious violation of the balance of power in the region. The Somalis and Oromo were afraid of live weapons and artillery, and so long as they did not possess them the Egyptians would maintain the military advantage, despite their weakness. The Somalis, said Hunter, did not know how to fire live weapons, and "even if the Somalis had weapons, no bullet would ever be shot from them."[67]

Hunter returned to Aden on 4 April 1884, and from there he attempted to establish his status as the only British officer who was fit for the position of temporary governor of Harar. He described his efforts to learn the different languages and ways of life in the Harar area and the contribution that he had made to Britain's glory among the Somalis and the Oromo. He again warned against a hasty withdrawal that would be interpreted by the Somalis and the Oromo as flight and claimed that it was necessary to act with deliberation and organization in the area to prevent anarchy in the Somali coastal towns. Emphasizing the dangerous situation in those cities and how much he and his position were needed, he warned that "the Bey of Berbera is an incautious ruler. He seems to be ready to listen to advice and accept it, but—like all his friends—his behavior is thuggish, rude and pressuring. In terms of integrity, he is no different than his friends." Regarding Abu Bakr in Zeila, Hunter stated that his rule in the city was absolute, but the slave trade should be supervised there.[68]

After surveying the various local and regional forces in the area, Hunter presented his recommendations to Lord Cromer. First and foremost, he recommended that the Egyptian government tighten its economic supervision by checking the account books of the governors of Zeila and Berbera. Second, he repeated his claim that only a British officer serving as the temporary governor of Harar could reach an agreement with the Somalis and Oromo. Therefore, 'Alī Riḍa Pasha should be dismissed from the office of governor. At the same time, he claimed that Harar should be separated administratively from Berbera, Zeila, and Tadjoura, and a British officer appointed over each area, with the responsibility for that area alone. In Hunter's opinion, it was necessary to accompany these two steps with a clear and uniform British policy regarding the degree to which the Oromo and Somalis should have autonomy following Egyptian withdrawal.[69]

Even though he was aware of the opposition of Her Majesty's Government, Hunter claimed that Great Britain should conquer Berbera and

Zeila and fly the Union Jack over these cities. He also saw cooperation with the Egyptians as lowering British prestige: "Cooperation with the Egyptian officers is bad for us, even if it is only formal. I recommend that we liberate Zeila and Berbera from the khedive's rule and ensure their independence, so that they do not fall to France or Italy. But I do not think that it is possible to bring about their sovereignty over the coastal cities."[70]

Hunter was concerned that official rule over the harbors would return to the Ottoman sultan, who would hand them over to the European powers for generous payment. He claimed that this scenario was the worst one possible for the British, since "it will be more difficult to oversee a Turkish coalition with the Somalis than the Egyptian rule there." Therefore, he recommended separating Berbera and Zeila, and keeping Berbera independent. Regarding the tribal area, Hunter stated that the British could act there while being less involved than was necessary in the case of the coast because "Great Britain is viewed by the Gala Somalis as a great power. Therefore, our involvement among them can only be as peacemakers or patrons."[71]

Hunter's visits to the coast and Harar in the first half of 1884 established his status as an ultimate authority among the Egyptians and Somalis. The governor of Berbera, ʿAbd al-Rahman Bey, released political prisoners from jail on Hunter's orders. Representatives of various Somali tribes arrived in the city and pledged their loyalty to Hunter. He created the impression that the Berbera port had come under British hegemony.[72]

Harar on the Eve of the Turco-Egyptian Evacuation

Hunter's report on events in Harar is one of the sole testimonies about the composition of the Egyptian forces in the city on the eve of the withdrawal in October 1884. He presented the following data: there were 3,370 Egyptian soldiers in Harar and its environs, including Harar residents who had been conscripted. Out of these, 288 were artillery soldiers, fifty-six regular cavalry, and 152 irregular *başhi bozuķ* cavalrymen. There were 2,819 infantrymen, fifty-five local militia members, and 806 black-skinned soldiers in and around Harar. In addition, there were 106 tradesmen—Egyptians and local people—working for the Egyptians.[73] Regarding the officers in Harar, Hunter wrote: "The Harar garrison is under the command of Lieutenant Colonel Ahmed Wahdi Bey, an intelligent but lazy officer. He speaks French quite well. The administration officer is Captain 'Abd Al-Qarim Effendī, who is under the direct command of Ahmed Wahdi Bey and is well versed in the turns of the road between Zeila and Harar. In addition, there are three medical officers with various specialties, who accompany the forces, along with four chaplains."[74] According to Hunter's report, the Egyptian artillery in Harar was formed of three batteries. Two of these were six-liter cannons and the third had seven rocket launchers and two German Krupp six-liter cannons. Several of the artillerymen carried Remington rifles and others carried pistols and other weapons. The uniforms of the artillerymen were identical to those of the regular soldiers: khaki trousers with white leggings. The officers, in contrast with the enlisted men, wore their ranks on their shoulders. Hunter reported that these forces had not undergone training or drills.[75]

The Egyptian cavalry in Harar was composed of regular and irregular soldiers. The irregular soldiers were occupied with administrative tasks, such as carrying postal packages and letters. They were armed with Remington rifles and cold weapons, characteristic of irregular soldiers. Hunter noted that the irregulars were mostly Turks from Anatolia. They did not wear standard uniforms, but their clothing was the same: a wide jacket decorated with a yellow ribbon, wide trousers, and high boots of no particular style.[76] The Egyptian infantry in Harar consisted of four battalions, equal in military prowess. Each was made up of six brigades, organized into 113 rear lines. At the head of each battalion stood a major, who had a captain and an administrative officer. Hunter was impressed by their organization, order, and training. Their uniforms consisted of khaki trousers, white leggings, and a white cape. They lived in stone quarters, each bloc housing twenty-two soldiers. Hunter mentioned that "the officers seemed intelligent and their uniforms are different, but of no distinguishing style. Most wear khaki, but some walk about in civilian dress."[77]

Hunter even tried to learn the mood and behavioral patterns of the soldiers. In his opinion, it seemed that "the soldiers were quite exhausted. The pasha's men include Egyptians, Turks, Sudanese and French. The difference between the members of this odd company can be found in their language. The orchestra of the company is made up of Sudanese and Abyssinians."[78] The soldiers complained to him that they had not received their salaries in an orderly fashion for several months, and as a result they were compelled to steal fruit, honey, fowl, and cattle from the Oromo surrounding Harar. They did not complain to the governor, since he would not listen to them and they knew that filing a formal complaint was liable to harm them.[79]

Hunter's work in June 1884 included a historical analysis of the independent emirate of Harar and a description of the process of the Egyptian takeover on the Somali coast. He described the people of Harar as "relatively intelligent and permeated with Islamic fanaticism, despite their surrender and that they do not bear arms."[80] Hunter's analysis related to the reciprocal relationship between the city and the Afran Qallo Oromo, and his finding was that trade relations and economy were of principal importance, rather than the religious element. In his opinion, the Egyptians were the ones who had damaged that relationship by trying to assert hegemony through forced Islamization—but they had failed because Egyptians were not regarded as "religiously pure by the Afran Qallo."[81] Hunter's assessment of this matter was that "the Turkish pashas were lukewarm believers in the Prophet. In contrast, the modern Egyptian officer does not define himself wholly by religion when he is far from Cairo."[82] Moreover, claimed Hunter, the British were wanted in the region, and the greatest danger in the long run was the possibility that Menilek would conquer Harar.[83]

The French, who followed the events in the area from their outpost in Obock, refrained from openly interfering for fear that this would lead to conflict with the British. The French ambassador in London showed interest in events on the Somali coast and expressed concern about the fate of French subjects on the Somali coast and in Harar. British activity in the area caused a small diplomatic incident with France in the wake of a remark of one of the members of Parliament in London. In early March 1884, Lord Edmond Fitzmaurice was quoted in the *Times* as saying that, "Her Majesty's Government is aware of the French claim to Obock, but the French would do well not to voice an additional claim in this matter." The French ambassador to London requested clarification on the matter, and the British response came swiftly: Obock was in the hands of the French, and Fitzmaurice erred in his use of the word "claim," since it was well known that the French had held Obock for a long time and there was no intention to change this situation.[84]

The reassuring messages of the British did not achieve their purpose. In April 1884, a French delegation visited Tadjoura, located in the area ruled over by Abu Bakr Pasha. This visit strengthened Menilek's assessment, echoed by the British, that the French were interested in expanding the area over which they ruled from the Obock Bay to the bay of Tadjoura, thus creating territorial contiguity between the two ports.[85] The British received a report about the French delegation from Abu Bakr Pasha himself, who was informed by Sheikh Hamid Muhammad, one of the Tadjoura dignitaries. The latter told Abu Bakr that a French ship had anchored in a natural dock in an area one hour from the city. Six Frenchmen arrived in the company of Ibrahim Muhammad, the Turco-Egyptian governor of Tadjoura, and "despite the fact that they saw the flag of the khedive government flying there, they declared that it was their possession from now on. In another six days, they would return there with French reinforcements." The British saw this as a sign of the struggle with the French over the inheritance of Egyptian property.[86]

Menilek's suspicions toward the French increased, and the suspicion that the French were planning to take over Harar reawakened in his court.[87] At the end of May 1884, he strengthened his ties with the Italians. For a time, the king of Shewa saw Italy as a force that was likely to support his expansion eastward at the expense of the Egyptian territories.[88] Indeed, this spoil was coveted by the Ethiopians, the British, the French, and the Italians. All of them were busy with the question of the future of Harar and the Somali port cities in the Gulf of Aden following the Egyptian evacuation.

London, Cairo, and Harar

The reports and recommendations of Hunter aided the formulation of British policy regarding the evacuation of Harar. Despite concern over the decline of the situation in the coastal cities and Berbera in particular, due to the rumors among the Oromo and Somalis of the impending Egyptian withdrawal, Nubar Pasha sought to delay the evacuation.[89] The British, who understood that preparation for the withdrawal would take several months, accepted Nubar's request while making two recommendations: replacing 'Alī Riḍa Pasha with Raduan Pasha (or any other agreed-upon Egyptian officer) in the coming months prior to evacuation from the city; and immediately deposing the governor of Berbera, 'Abd al-Rahman Bey.[90] In this way the British were able to postpone the permanent placement of an Egyptian destroyer or British ship in the port of Berbera, as well as the return of Hunter from Aden to Harar until July 1884. Despite the postponement, British concern for the Somali coastal cities grew.[91] The disintegration of Egyptian control and uncertainty about the behavior of the Somali populations awakened British concern that another power would take over the area if they did not do so.[92]

The concern about what was happening in Berbera increased with the receipt of a report from an Englishman named James, who was in Berbera with his brother and another friend during March 1884. James described acts of rape, murder, theft, and corruption by the Egyptian governor, including the imprisonment of opponents without trial and the treatment of the British and Italians in the city as "heretical dogs." 'Abd al-Rahman Bey had assumed his position after 1882, and James intimated that the governor of Berbera had bribed the governor of Harar, 'Alī Riḍa Pasha, after the latter was sent to investigate complaints regarding what was happening in Berbera. The relations between the governors of Harar and Berbera with the Massawa governor 'Alla'a al-Din Bey were described as "promiscuous and corrupt," and only Abu Bakr Pasha, governor of Zeila, was described as a man "whom one can rely on, but he deals with human trafficking." The harsh descriptions in James's report included acts of murder and blood vengeance between the Egyptian soldiers and the Somalis in Berbera and Bulhar.[93]

In Zeila, James and his friends met Father Cahagne, who introduced himself as the "bishop of the Galla areas." He told them that "the Egyptians are hated everywhere in this land" and described the destruction of the Oromo institutions, their oppression, and forced Islamization since the beginning of the Egyptian occupation of Harar. Beyond disparaging the Egyptians, James stressed that the British were seen as desirable by the Oromo and Somalis, more so than the other European powers, because of their illustrious legal system.[94] Hunter reported that he met James in Harar and got the impression from him that anarchy was rife in Berbera. Therefore, a British ship should be positioned there to deter both the Egyptians and the Somalis.[95]

The British pressure on Nubar Pasha bore fruit, and Khedive Tawfiq officially declared the deposal of Fa'iz 'Abd al-Rahman Bey from his position in Berbera and the appointment of Ibrahim Bey al-Saban in his place. This step was meant to appease the British and to signal the Egyptian government's seriousness in advance of withdrawing its forces from the Somali coast.[96] However, the deposal of the governor of Berbera was viewed by the British as an insufficient step, since "the Egyptians are unpredictable and they cannot rule over the Somali coast and in Harar."[97] Thus, in practical terms, the treaty of 1877 came to an end. With this treaty, the British government had recognized Egyptian sovereignty on the Somali coast. From the time that Egypt was conquered by the British in 1882, and especially after the increase of British pressure regarding the withdrawal from Sudan, the Somali coast, and Harar, this treaty lost more and more of its worth. Now, at the end of May 1884, the British decided to cancel it.[98]

The khedival government, for its own part, asked the British to postpone the evacuation from Harar and the coastal cities and to consider transferring the command of the withdrawal to the responsibility of the British governor in Bombay. The Egyptians claimed that a hasty withdrawal would endanger the soldiers, but the British deliberated on the matter because, according to Hunter's report, the situation in Harar was stable as of June 1884.[99] The British did not officially respond to the Egyptian request and continued to follow French activity in the area of Obock.[100] They also followed the strengthening of ties between the Italian agent Count Pietro Antonelli and Abu Bakr of Zeila, and the strengthening of ties between Antonelli and Sheikh 'Abd al-Rahman, one of the dignitaries of the 'Afar in the Zeila area.[101] British involvement hastened the European colonialist race on the Somali coast, which was dormant during the time when the khedive's government from Cairo ruled the port cities there.

To conclude this point, the concerns of the British sprang from various sources. First and foremost was the "Mahdiyya trauma" in Sudan and the concern that the Mahdī rebellion would spread and reach the Somali coast. Second, they were concerned about foreign takeover—European, Ethiopian, or by the Somali tribes—of the port cities on the heels of the collapse of Egyptian sovereignty. The main concern of the British was about the port cities, especially Berbera. Indeed, the single practical step taken by the khedival government was the deposal of the governor of Berbera and his replacement with another officer, which was proposed by the British. However, the British concern about the imminent collapse of Egypt there was exaggerated. In general, it may be said that Egyptian sovereignty was maintained in the port cities and Harar, and there is no evidence of violent outbreaks there until the conclusion of the Egyptian withdrawal from Harar in May 1885. In the midst of all this, Abu Bakr Pasha retained his power as the strong man in Zeila and its surroundings and continued with his sophisticated policies toward all the participants in the aforementioned area.

Abu Bakr tried to enlist Hunter as an ally, since he noticed increased British involvement in the area. During June 1884, he wrote to Hunter in an attempt to present himself as an Egyptian governor on the one hand, and a patron of the locals, a judge, and an arbitrator of monetary and legal matters on the other. He also tried to enlist Hunter's help after Italian merchants in Zeila threatened that he would be attacked by the Italian army if he did not improve his attitude toward them.[102] However, Hunter's superiors decided not to share their plans with Abu Bakr. They saw him as disloyal and unreliable; a slave trader who had connections to the Italians and the French.[103]

In general, the British did not establish a formal and uniform policy in dealing with the Somali tribes.[104] They settled for military deterrence on the coast, which relied on one Egyptian warship moored at Berbera and three ships at the ready in Aden.[105] Against the background of ambiguous British policy, Hunter took upon himself the mission of making contact with the Somalis in the Harar area, in the framework of advance preparations for the Egyptian evacuation.[106]

The British government was more interested in the moves of its European adversaries in the region. Primarily, the British were concerned about the influence of the French from Obock on the Somalis.[107] They knew of the recommendation to the French government by Lemet, the French consul in Khartoum, to annex Harar after the Egyptian withdrawal. In comparison, Italian intervention on the Somali coast was less cause for concern.[108]

Colonial Agreements and Treaties

The growing tensions among the imperial powers in the first half of July 1884 motivated the British to accelerate their preparations for evacuation from Berbera, Zeila, and Harar. They increased pressure on Nubar Pasha to approve the withdrawal, and to signal their intentions they dispatched Hunter once again to Berbera.[109] They assumed that, in addition to the pressure, the khedival government would demand monetary compensation for the public buildings that its forces had built in Harar and Berbera.[110]

When Hunter arrived in Berbera he apparently acted as though it belonged to him. Ibrahim Bey al-Saban, governor of Berbera, wrote about Hunter's tours of the city and his contact with the Somali tribal elders in advance of signing an agreement relating to their sovereignty after the Egyptian withdrawal. The Egyptian governor was impressed that the actual ruler of the city was Hunter and India's British government.[111]

At this point, the British sought to arrive at agreements and understandings with the Somali dignitaries through Hunter.[112] Hunter arrived at an agreement with the elders of the tribal coalition of Habar Awal in the middle of July 1884. They promised that peace would be preserved when the Egyptians withdrew from Berbera and Bulhar, and that they would welcome a British military presence to replace that of the Egyptians. In addition, the Somali delegates promised that the British would enjoy complete freedom of action in the Habar Awal territories and even committed themselves never to engage in the slave trade. Hunter, for his part, promised the Somali tribal representatives that the British would extend their protection to the tribes and not harm their way of life.[113] Twenty-nine of the Habar Awal elders signed the agreement and, on behalf of the British the document was signed by Hunter and his deputy, Lieutenant Peyton, who would go on to fulfill an important role in the evacuation of Harar. The agreement promised a British military presence in Berbera, which would thus become a British military and logistical beachhead from which they could supervise the Egyptian withdrawal and deter the other tribes in the area.[114]

After signing the agreement, Hunter turned to organizing the logistics of evacuating the coastal cities as a preliminary stage to withdrawing from Harar. He presented a report to the Bombay government in which he specified the required equipment for the British officers and the Indian soldiers who would replace the Egyptians. The cost reached tens of thousands of rupees, which the government had committed itself to pay.[115]

There were almost immediate repercussions to the agreement that Hunter had forged with the Somalis and the events in Harar. The understandings that were reached with the Somalis of Habar Awal deepened the rift between the Egyptians in Harar and the Somali ʻIssa, and Hunter was concerned about the possibility of Harar becoming cut off from the coast.[116] To prevent an ʻIssa revolt, Hunter recommended that the British rule over Zeila while the Egyptian forces were still there, by means of 150 local infantrymen reinforced with camels. Afterwards, from a state of military superiority, they would arrive at an agreement with the ʻIssa regarding the evacuation from Harar.[117]

The accord with the coalition of Somali tribes increased the pressure upon Nubar Pasha to approve an immediate evacuation from the coastal cities and Harar. Nubar did not change his basic position, however, and he replied in the name of the khedive that the Egyptians agreed to the evacuation of the coastal cities, but not immediately. As to Harar, he insisted on postponing the withdrawal. To show the British that immediate evacuation of Harar was unnecessary, Nubar Pasha presented economic data indicating the profitability of the city, in contrast with the unprofitability of Zeila and Berbera (Table 3).[118]

The British were not impressed with Nubar's data. They even considered returning Zeila and Berbera to Istanbul's control, on the assumption that a declaration of a supreme Muslim sovereignty would pacify Harar's residents and the Oromo and Somali populations and would also prevent

Table 3
Egyptian economic data for Harar, Zeila, and Berbera, July 1884

	Income	*Expenditure*	*Yearly Balance*
Harar	75,510 Egyptian pounds	60,229	15,281
Zeila	5,600 Egyptian pounds	9,105	-3,505
Berbera	6,047 Egyptian pounds	9,037	-2,963

Source: FO 403/82: Egerton to Granville, 26 July 1884, Alexandria.

possible conflict with France and Italy.[119] The Ottoman foreign minister offered to send forces to Zeila, Tadjoura, and even to Sawakin in Sudan if the British government would request it.[120] From the Ottoman standpoint, the Somali coast was substantially their historical property, and they requested further clarifications from the British.[121]

Hunter came out against the Ottoman alternative. He felt that the locals would despise the Ottomans no less than they loathed the Egyptians.[122] The British, who continued to maintain ambiguity, updated the Ottoman government on the impending Egyptian evacuation from the Somali coast and thanked it for its readiness to help by taking over the area, but they did not specify any role for Istanbul in the region.[123]

The rumors of the impending Turco-Egyptian withdrawal from outposts on the Somali coast arrived quickly in Harar. ʿAlī Riḍa wrote that the governor of Berbera reported to him at the beginning of August 1884 about intentions to evacuate Berbera by Hunter. The governor of Harar emphasized that the evacuation of Berbera must be accomplished at the same time as the evacuation of Harar, but that he and his men—officials and soldiers—were not set to do this yet.[124] He warned that the distance between Harar and Zeila was a four-day walk, that the road was difficult and lacked water sources in summer, and that it would be impossible to withdraw Egyptian forces without prior preparation. According to him, without material help from Cairo, he would not be able to control his men any more, since the profits from agricultural produce—mainly corn—were quite low.[125]

Nevertheless, rumors about the Egyptian evacuation of Harar increased daily. It is apparent that the governor of Harar did not believe there was truth to the rumors: "But if the rumor is true, and the evacuation of Harar has been raised for discussion, what steps should be taken in order to bring home such a large number of our soldiers and officials here, whose number reaches some 14,500 men? Besides this, what about all of the public buildings, lands, and property owned by the government here?"[126]

Moreover, wrote ʿAlī Riḍa Pasha, while the economic balance of Harar was profitable, he could not permit the evacuation of forces from the city on his own. He complained that the khedival government had not paid the salaries of its people in the city for the past three months and demanded an immediate transfer of 20,000 thaler silver coins to the city. He closed by expressing his opinion about the possible evacuation: the best time for withdrawal would be from October onward, due to the extreme heat and lack of water on the road. The forces should be evacuated from Harar to Gildessa and from there, after a certain stay, continue on to Zeila.[127] Nubar Pasha replied to the governor of Harar that Hunter, now residing in Zeila, was the representative of the khedival government and was responsible for taking all the steps that would enable a safe evacuation of the Egyptians from Harar.[128]

Waves of Egyptian Withdrawal from Harar, Summer–Fall 1884

In August 1884, the voice of the locals was heard: "the dignitaries, the *ʿulamāʾ*, the residents and merchants of Harar" sent a memo to ʿAlī Riḍa Pasha, to the Council of Representatives, and to the Interior Ministry and Ministry of War in Cairo.[129] The city dignitaries mentioned the "disturbing" rumors about the departure of the Egyptians and stated that, if they were correct, "the tears will flow and the soul will cease living." The memo expressed complete identification with the Egyptian government and great regard for its contribution to the security of the city and its economic prosperity during the previous nine years. The dignitaries wrote that the Egyptians had removed Harar from a situation of robbery and pillage and transformed it into a prosperous and safe urban and trade center, which it had never been before—a center that drew merchants from all over the world, for which they were grateful. It seems from the memo that the rumors about the withdrawal terrified the city dignitaries, who expressed fear for their lives and property if the Egyptians left: "We have no shelter except the khedival government. We ask the government's mercy. If the government's decision to withdraw is final, we will evacuate along with the soldiers to Egypt, and we will leave our property here for pillage."[130]

Less emotional, but still quite worried, the foreign merchants in the city presented their own memorandum to Harar's Egyptian governor. While the people of Harar asked the khedival government for mercy, the foreign merchants demanded from 'Alī Riḍa Pasha "clarification about the degree of truth of the rumors regarding the withdrawal."[131] The various merchants mentioned the period of time that they had spent in the city and their economic contribution to the city and to the Egyptian economy. They asked to know when the evacuation would take place, if at all, so that they could take care of their property in the city and if necessary, even evacuate with the Egyptians. The great concern of the foreign merchants was obvious from their demand that the Egyptians "guarantee the safety of foreigners, as is customary in the colonies of powers ruling in various places in the world." This document was signed by all the foreign merchants in the city at that time.[132] The foreign and local merchants sent a similar memo to Nubar Pasha as well. They claimed that "the decision of the khedival government to abandon the city will lead to anarchy and bloodshed. Fifty years ago, Harar was subject to the barbarity and rule of small kings; bloodshed and pillage were its fate. Nine years ago, the khedival government established its rule in Harar and brought order and security. The government turned Harar into a very important center of trade." Here, as well, the merchants—local and foreign alike—repeated their intention to leave together with the Egyptians and leave their property behind to be pillaged.[133]

The Capuchins, unlike other groups in the city, did not contact the Egyptian governor and the khedival government by formal memorandum. But the British were aware of the sensitive situation involving the presence of French Catholic missionaries in Harar and their connection to Bardey's agency in Zeila. They were concerned that the deepening rift between the governor of Harar and the Somali 'Issa dignitaries would lead to a violent outbreak on religious grounds and that the Egyptians would not be able to provide the missionaries of Cahagne with security, inside or outside of the city.[134] Evidence of the Capuchins' feelings toward the impending Egyptian withdrawal appears in the letter of Father Pierre from Harar from the end of August 1884: "Our mission in Harar stands before a crisis with many heavy consequences, to it and to me personally. The English have decided to evacuate the Egyptians, but they will not enter Harar in their place. Rumors say that the land will be left on its own and will become desolate and unfit for settling. The head of our order thinks that we must be careful and leave Harar."[135]

The British, who were afraid of the loss of contact between the Somali coast and Harar, continued to pressure the khedival government to accelerate the evacuation of its troops from Berbera, but they stressed that they would take no steps that were not coordinated with the Egyptians. The coordination was essential for the success of the withdrawal, and the British were concerned lest Nubar Pasha interpret their pressure as a British attempt to take the place of the Egyptians.[136] Indeed, a modern Egyptian national narrative saw the British plan as a plot to dispossess the Egyptians, for no reason, of their territories in the coastal cities and Harar.[137]

The importance that the British attributed to Hunter's mission on the Somali coast can be seen in the way senior advisors tied it to Gordon's mission in Sudan: "The two are agreed upon by the Egyptian government to evacuate Sudan, Harar and the Somali coast and to take all required measures to prevent chaos and bloodshed at the times of the evacuation of Egyptian forces and afterwards."[138] After signing the agreement with the Habar Awal and promising British presence in Berbera until the end of July 1884, the British focused on arrangements in advance of the evacuation from Zeila, to which Hunter had set out on 18 August from Aden.[139]

Due to the power of Abu Bakr among the Somali tribes, Hunter recommended that the British involvement in Zeila be less obvious than it was in Berbera and that a lower-ranking British officer be in charge of the evacuation on the route between Harar and Zeila, similar to the British move in the Massawa port in Sudan.[140] Major Heath was chosen for this task, since he "had lived amongst the Somalis and knew their language and way of life." Hunter even recommended providing Heath with 30,000 dollars to purchase the support of the Somali populations in the aforementioned area.[141]

The khedival government wished to keep the developments in Berbera and Zeila secret because of its concern about a violent reaction on the part of the Somali populations. It even emphasized to Abu Bakr that Hunter was its only agent in the area and stressed his authority as commander over the evacuation campaign as such.[142] On 25 August 1884, Hunter received approval from the British government to evacuate the Egyptians from Berbera.[143] After the government of Bombay was asked to send a ship to Suez for the evacuation of Egyptian forces, the withdrawal from Berbera was set for 25 September 1884.[144]

At the same time, Major Heath, along with another British officer and twenty-five soldiers who were based in Aden, set forth to Zeila to meet an authorized Egyptian officer who would help them evacuate Harar. The British planned that the Egyptian officer and Heath's force would depart from Harar together, after receiving approval and funding from Hunter and the Bombay government.[145] At this point, British pressure bore fruit. By the beginning of September 1884, Nubar Pasha understood that the fate of Harar had been decided. He accepted the British request and instructed Raduan Pasha to help him with the evacuation from the city. In addition, he recommended the appointment of an heir from the family of the ʿAlī b. Da'ud emirs to inherit the public buildings built by the Egyptians and assist with the administrative bureaucracy that they would leave in the city. Nubar expressed the commitment of the Egyptians to hand Harar over in an organized fashion to the chosen heir and to prevent chaos in the city and its environs at all costs, before and during the withdrawal.[146]

In early September 1884, a disagreement surfaced between Hunter in Zeila and Nubar Pasha and Edwin Henry Egerton, who was the British consul-general in Egypt and directly responsible for Hunter in Cairo. Nubar and Egerton stressed the need for a respectable evacuation of the Egyptians, with an orderly transfer of authority and government systems to the emirate heir. Hunter's main interest was the withdrawal of the Egyptian army and retaining British standing in the region; the Egyptians' considerations were not his chief concerns. It was quite obvious that he had contempt for the Egyptians and therefore saw cooperation with them as lessening the prestige of Her Majesty's Government. Hunter and those responsible for him were in disagreement regarding the arrangements with the Somalis and the new rule over Harar after the Egyptian departure.

Nubar Pasha's reaction to the issue of evacuating Harar made Hunter furious. He claimed that Nubar did not comprehend the complexity of the situation in Harar and the dangers involved in evacuating the city, since "it is impossible to arrive at an agreement with the tribes if any remnant of Egyptian rule remains in Harar." He even requested that 'Alī Riḍa Pasha leave Harar immediately and that his Egyptian substitute arrive in Harar as soon as possible.[147]

In Hunter's opinion, it would be impossible to carry out the withdrawal while trying to achieve popularity among the local elements. Rather, it was necessary to take unambiguously aggressive steps in order to prevent attacks on the withdrawing Egyptians and to foil the takeover of the city by the tribes while indiscriminate fighting broke out. At the same time, he repeated his demand to change the Egyptian rule in Harar immediately and requested that, in addition to an Egyptian officer, Heath should be sent to him as well.[148]

Egerton calmed Hunter down, praised his efforts and actions, and expressed complete faith in him. He stressed that the Egyptians were not trying to gain popularity among the locals but that they feared for their soldiers and property in the city. Nubar, according to Egerton, wanted "an honorable withdrawal with Egyptian assistance in this matter." Egerton promised that the Egyptian governor and senior officers in Harar would be deposed and a senior Egyptian officer would be sent in their place.[149] After he received Egerton's response, Hunter—completely ignoring the Egyptians—wrote, "My policy in Harar is to preserve the independence of the city under the son of the previous Emir. All of the Gala tribes and the Somalis will know the borders of their territories, as well as being aware of British superiority, which makes safety on the roads to the coast possible and prevents the slave trade."[150] In his reply to Hunter, Egerton asked whether a Harari notable named Ibrahim, one of the sons of Emir Muhammad 'Abdashakur, was the intended emir, and he added that the Egyptians were deliberating between Raduan Pasha and Ibrahim Roshdi for the senior position in Harar. Hunter replied immediately that he preferred Raduan, and his request was approved.[151]

Hunter was well aware of Raduan's deliberate and moderate conduct as governor of Harar toward the Somali tribes around the city when they had rebelled in the recent past, and considered him to be appropriate for the position. Immediately after his appointment was approved, Raduan was provided with 5,000 Egyptian pounds and the seal of the government of Khedive Tawfiq, and he set forth to Zeila. Hunter wrote at that time that "there is no substitute here for the seal of the khedive. There is no need for gold and it is possible to send rupees or dollars that are used in trade in this region."[152] He even expressed his hope that Raduan, as "the new governor of Harar," would contribute to dialogue with the Somali tribes outside the city.[153]

Hunter's superiors, however, thought otherwise. They worried that Hunter would deviate from the task of the evacuation and that he was liable to create a situation in the area that was not in the interest of Her Majesty's Government.[154] They granted him permission to arrive at agreements only with the neighboring Somalis dwelling in the coastal area but not with the Somalis living in the Harar area. They did not grant permission for him to take control of the city after the evacuation of the Egyptians. The government in London and its people in Cairo were concerned about complications of the direct control that Hunter was liable to initiate in Harar with the agreement of the Somalis. They were determined not to become directly involved in Ogaden or Harar.[155]

Hunter updated his superiors about shooting incidents between the French in Obock and the Somalis there, and about the hatred of the Somalis toward the Egyptians and the French in the area of Tadjoura as well. On these grounds, at the end of September 1884, he recommended the conquest of Tadjoura.[156] His enthusiasm for increased British involvement raised the concern that he would entangle Britain in a conflict with the Italians in the Assab area or with the French in Obock, after arriving at an agreement with the Somalis without the support of the government in London.[157]

Hunter displayed a lack of sensitivity toward the Egyptians and, as revealed by the documentation, he aspired to enhance the power and reputation of the British government in Harar. He asserted that British power in the area would be harmed if the Egyptian government approved a *firman* in the name of the khedive, appointing Raduan Pasha as governor of Harar under Egyptian auspices. In reply to Hunter, Lord Cromer clarified that it was the Egyptian government that would appoint the new governor with a *firman*, just as it would appoint the new emir after the Egyptian withdrawal. He instructed Hunter not to sign any agreements or commit orally to anything in the name of the British government, but to wait for instructions.[158]

Hunter even requested that an Anglo-Indian force from Aden escort him and his deputy, Heath, on their way to Harar. Lord Cromer replied that a direct British presence, which was liable to invite an attack, should not be demonstrated. Hunter's response to this was that he did not rely on the Egyptian forces and there was no fear of an attack on British forces made up of fifteen soldiers or more. He went so far as to say that he was not interested in an Egyptian escort that would leave Harar to meet him and his men on their way to the city.[159] Lord Cromer did not accept Hunter's arguments and did not approve an Anglo-Indian escort to Harar.[160]

The Egyptian Retreat from the Somali Coast

The evacuation of Berbera began on 25 September 1884 and was completed under Hunter's direction on 5 October 1884. Eight hundred soldiers and administrators left Berbera on the decks of the British-Indian ship *Abyssinia*.[161]

The Egyptian withdrawal awakened the imperial scramble for the Somali coast and the Gulf of Aden. The Ottomans and Italians were the only authorities who were updated by the British.[162] Following the evacuation of Berbera, the Italians increased weapons transports to their compound in Assab, along with their trade activities to and from it, updating the British on their part.[163] The French, who were not updated by the British, reacted by flying their flag in a defiant manner outside their compound in Obock.[164] The German consul in Cairo asked to clarify with Nubar Pasha whether Egypt allowed the British—or possibly gave them authorization—to take control over the Somali coast.[165]

Following the evacuation of Berbera, Hunter turned to evacuating the Egyptian forces from Sagallo and Zeila and set 29 October 1884 for beginning the evacuation. He even told his superiors that it would be possible to withdraw the Egyptian force from Tadjoura in mid-October.[166]

The evacuation from Zeila, Sagallo, and Tadjoura involved cooperation with Abu Bakr Pasha. The resourceful ruler of Zeila tried to gain favor in Hunter's eyes, providing him with his detailed economic balances from Zeila in 1883. Abu Bakr even admitted to Hunter that in the past he had traded in slaves but had ceased that activity since he had become a ruler for Egypt. Beyond this, he spoke to Hunter about the possibility of continuing his employment under any kind of new arrangement in the region after the Egyptian evacuation. He even requested pension arrangements for himself and his family in the event that he would not continue as the ruler of Zeila following the Egyptian evacuation. Hunter did not rule out the possibility, adding that part of Zeila's income could be used to fund the evacuation from Harar.[167] He even consulted with his superiors about Abu Bakr's retirement as ruler and beginning his pension payment in November 1884. In the opinion of Lord Cromer, Abu Bakr was entitled to a monthly pension, but Cromer wanted to discuss the issue with the British government in India and not to place the burden of payment on the Egyptian treasury.[168]

The Egyptians retreated from Sagallo on the night of 27–28 October 1884. Abu Bakr reported to the British that the French had flown their flag there immediately after the Egyptians left, and even sent some French officers to Tadjoura while the Egyptians were still there, in order to offer the local residents official French protection.[169] The British did not respond immediately to this move but considered sending a naval force to the straits of Tadjoura to signal that they would not tolerate any more extremely blatant violation of the status quo in the region.[170]

The Final Cut: Egyptian Evacuation of Harar

Hunter designated his two assistants, Heath and Peyton, along with Raduan Pasha, to carry out the evacuation. On 30 September 1884, at the height of the evacuation of Berbera, Hunter passed on instructions to Raduan Pasha, who had just arrived in Zeila, where he had met Peyton. Heath was also meant to join the two in Zeila. From Hunter's instructions, it is apparent that Raduan was given the job of "mission overseer" for the evacuation under Peyton's command. Hunter ordered Raduan to leave Zeila, seeing it only as a supply base for Harar, and to set off for Harar: "When you reach Harar, you must send 'Alī Riḍa Pasha and his men to the coast, together with 1,000 soldiers and administrators, including women and children. One camel will be provided to carry the baggage of every three men. In the event of oversized loads, the evacuees will be charged a special tax."[171] Hunter's words provide additional evidence that the Egyptian soldiers married Harari women and established families. Following the first stage of the evacuation, which encompassed the Egyptian citizens and families of soldiers, Hunter instructed Raduan to evacuate the Egyptian army from the city in the following manner: "First of all, each time, you should evacuate one artillery battery and 50 regular or irregular cavalry who will accompany it from Harar. Immediately following your arrival from Harar to Gildessa, you should send the irregular ones, each time assembling 50 men for accompaniment."[172]

Hunter ordered Raduan to free all the political prisoners from the Egyptian prison in the city, specifically a *garad* named Jibril, an Afran Qallo Oromo from the Gerhi clan. Contrary to the task that the British authorities and the khedival government had designated for Raduan, Hunter repeatedly emphasized, in Raduan's presence, that Peyton was the commander who had been designated for the evacuation by himself, Heath, and the khedive. From Hunter's point of view, Raduan's entire task consisted of carrying out Peyton's orders until Heath and Hunter reached Zeila from Aden at the beginning of October 1884.[173] Hunter instructed Peyton to take responsibility for renting camels for transportation from Harar to Zeila.[174] He even ordered him to meet, as his representative, with the dignitaries of the 'Issa and Gadabuursi, as well as with the Oromo and other Somali dignitaries, to listen to them and confer with them on arrangements for trade routes after the Egyptian departure. On this matter, too, Hunter strayed from the instructions he received from his superiors, which forbade him from conferring on future arrangements. Hunter even instructed Peyton to fly the British flag above his residence in Harar, and to turn his house into a British consulate that would provide assistance to European merchants as if they were British subjects.[175]

Hunter commanded Peyton to explain to the "chiefs" (as Hunter called the leaders) of the Oromo and Somali around Harar the "complexity of the new situation and the commitment of the British government to their well-being through noninvolvement in their trade. Britain will not conquer Harar, but will return the Emirate to power, as it was with the arrival of Egypt." He said that he would arrive in Harar shortly and would discuss with his deputies the imprisonment and expulsion of political opponents who were liable to endanger the Egyptian withdrawal, but he did not specify who they were at this point.[176]

Raduan Pasha and Peyton left Zeila for Harar on 12 October 1884, a week after the evacuation of Berbera. Raduan updated Hunter that the Egyptian forces in Harar had not received their salaries from the khedival government for five months and that at least 40,000 dollars should be budgeted for paying them, otherwise they would not retreat from the city.[177] The khedival government transferred 26,700 dollars and an additional 5,000 Egyptian pounds for the evacuation of Harar, and Hunter claimed that the entire sum would be earmarked for paying salaries in order to begin the retreat. Despite all of the difficulties, Hunter assumed that the retreat would proceed quietly because the Oromo and Somalis would not attack the retreating British and Egyptians, and that the presence of the British army in Zeila would deter them.[178]

Hunter even asked Heath to take 106,000 rupees to Harar, and from them to designate 40,000 rupees for renting camels for the evacuees, 40,000 rupees for transfer to Raduan to pay the salaries of soldiers in Harar, and 6,000 rupees for Abu Bakr in Zeila as a one-time grant. Heath was asked to transfer the balance to the British treasury in Zeila.[179] It seems that Heath transferred some of the money to Raduan Pasha, who noted that on 13 November 1884 Heath arrived with 3,200 Egyptian guineas for paying salaries to the Somali militia soldiers who served in Harar under the Egyptians.[180]

Correspondence among all the British and Egyptian authorities on the financial costs of the evacuation reveals their expectations and fears. It includes, among other things, a human viewpoint that might reflect the spirit of that period in Egypt. The khedival government estimated that additional funding would be required for the evacuation and decided to allow each soldier to take only two of his children who were the offspring of their intermarriage with local women, in order to reduce the number of evacuees to 11,500 at most.[181]

This created friction among the powers in the region. The Italians, who were following the final stages carried out in advance of the evacuation, demanded clarification about British intentions regarding the Gulf of Assab and Ras Beilul. The British calmed them by explaining that an evacuation would be carried out only from areas that had been captured by the Egyptians, and they had no intention of ruling over, or negotiating with, the tribal heads about any other areas.[182]

The British plan was that, parallel to the retreat of the Egyptian forces from Zeila on 29 October 1884, British artillery and infantry forces would be added to positions inside and outside the city.[183] There were two goals: first, creating a main outpost in advance of the evacuation of Harar and deterring the Somalis and Oromo in the area; and second, signaling to the French not to become involved. However, so as not to increase tensions with the French, the British considered replacing their artillery unit in Zeila with a camel unit armed with light ammunition.[184]

The British observed French activity in the Gulf of Tadjoura and considered sending armed forces there. In the middle of November 1884, the level of tension with the French increased. The Egyptian governor of Tadjoura informed that the French had revealed to the sultan of Danakil ('Afar) that the Egyptians were retreating from the region. Subsequently, the 'Afar leader in Tadjoura began to collect taxes in the city. The Egyptian governor asked Hunter for aid or permission to evacuate with his men to Zeila. After consulting with Nubar Pasha, it was decided that there was no reason to insist on remaining in Tadjoura, and if the governor there was interested, he could retreat with his men to Zeila.[185] One week later, the 'Afar forced the Egyptians to evacuate from Tadjoura to Zeila, after stopping the supply of water and other supplies to the Egyptian forces. Although the son of the local Egyptian-appointed Pasha remained there, the sultan of the 'Afar took over the port city. The retreaters from Tadjoura gathered in Zeila with their supplies, weapons, and family members on 19 November 1884.[186] At the end of November 1884 the French annexed Tadjoura to their ruling area by force of arms.[187] After the loss of Tadjoura to the French, Nubar Pasha attempted to revive the possibility of transferring the rule over the Somali coast to the Ottoman Empire.[188] But the British were already determined that the Ottomans not return to the region.[189]

Hunter arrived in Zeila on 4 November 1884 and reported from there that all was quiet in Harar and the routes leading to it. In the first stage, 1,036 Egyptians would be evacuated from the city. Its organization began at the end of October 1884 with the aim of reaching Zeila on 12 November and boarding two Egyptian ships bound for Egypt. The second wave of evacuees would be organized in Harar on 6 November and reach Zeila on 20 November 1884.[190] Hunter estimated that the number of evacuees from Harar would not exceed 10,000 people, and that no difficulties were expected on the routes, due to assistance provided by the Somali 'Issa populations. According to Hunter, even the expected cool weather would contribute to the quick and easy evacuation that "Peyton and Heath, who were in Harar, were planning in an effective and thrifty manner."[191]

On 4 November 1884, according to plan, two Egyptian ships, with 738 evacuees on the first and 257 on the second, left the Zeila port to cross the Suez.[192] Among the first wave of evacuees was Father Cahagne, who expressed his feelings in a letter to the head of the Capuchin order in Paris:

> The grave events that are taking place in Harar compel me to remain on the shore for a short while. You surely know that the Egyptian soldiers are evacuating Harar now. On October 30th I left with the first company, which was largely composed of the general staff of the Egyptians in the city. After twelve days, we reached Zeila. The Egyptian retreat was planned in such a way that by the end of January, or in February 1885, no Egyptian soldiers would remain in Harar. There is a local administration in Harar and autonomic governments ruling over different tribes. It is possible that serious difficulties will develop with a number of issues: Will the local authority in Harar be generous enough to protect us in our current situation? Will it be strong enough to protect us? Will the Gala tribes know how to preserve peace? Will they leave security in the hands of the residents of Harar?[193]

The questions Cahagne raised also disturbed the Italians, who feared a disruption of power in the area, due to the strengthening of Abu Bakr

Pasha following the evacuation and the end of British rule in Zeila.[194] The British, too, were worried by the possibility of the strengthening of Abu Bakr and Italian intervention there. They wanted to reach agreements with the Somalis in the Zeila region to neutralize the hegemony of Abu Bakr.[195]

Unlike the Italians, the French took practical steps. The French government appointed a civil engineer named Henri, who already lived in Harar, as consul there.[196] The French demanded that the British guarantee the security of the French subjects in Harar and see to the commercial interests of the French in Zeila, Berbera, and the routes that connected them to Harar.[197] They even took power over Tadjoura, although they did not declare official annexation.[198]

On 24 November 1884, Raduan Pasha, together with Peyton and Heath, arrived to supervise the evacuation of the Egyptians who remained in the city and the transfer of property from the ruling authority to the hands of the designated emir, ʻAbdullahi. They were escorted by twenty-two Indian soldiers who belonged to the British army in Bombay.[199] Rimbaud, who was in Aden at the time, voiced his opinion about what had taken place on the Somali coast and in Harar:

> The British, with their ridiculous politics, are now destroying the trade on all of the coasts. They wanted to change everything and achieved worse results than the Egyptians and the Turks, whom they destroyed as well. . . . Their Gordon is an idiot . . . and their actions are a ridiculous and senseless series of looting and destruction. France is also acting ridiculously here: One month ago, we seized the Gulf of Tadjoura in order to rule over the main routes to Harar and Ethiopia, but those coasts are completely desolate and the outlay here would be extraneous if we don't progress soon into the land (to Harar), where there are healthy and fertile lands.[200]

The final chapter in the saga of Egyptian Harar would end in May 1885 with joint British-Egyptian activity whose goal was, among other things, the withdrawal of Egyptian forces from the city and restoration of the emirate rule.

PART FOUR
Aftermath

10

Harar between Egypt and Ethiopia

The "Forgotten Emirate" of Harar, 1885–1887

The ʿAbdullahi emirate period occupies a place of relatively minor significance in historical research on Harar. The period from May 1885 to January 1887 is generally thought of as a brief interim between the Egyptian and the Ethiopian occupations of Harar in 1875 and 1887, respectively, and the emir's name often goes unmentioned.[1] When scholars do refer to ʿAbdullahi, they do so in mostly negative terms, for example, describing him as "weak," a "fanatic," or an "obsessive reactionary." The traits ascribed to ʿAbdullahi and his religious Muslim "fanaticism" were mostly based on a corpus of literature produced by European travelers—merchants and missionaries—who resided in Harar in the late nineteenth century. These documents might be considered as part of the Orientalist discourse in Western and Ethiopian Christian research, which was also brought to bear on Harar and the Muslim communities that resided in and around the city. Some of the studies that adopted this approach often couched encounters between the city's Muslims and Christians in strictly polarized religious and cultural terms, disregarding the actual events that took place in Harar at the time.[2]

The ʿAbdullahi episode took place when local and global imperial processes in the Horn of Africa and the Gulf of Aden collided in the history of Harar. ʿAbdullahi had to deal with the changes left by the decade of Turco-Egyptian colonial rule. It seems that he underestimated and misread the transformative power of the global European imperial interests and the regional interests of Menilek, king of Shewa, during the second half of the 1880s scramble for the Red Sea basin and the Gulf of Aden.

This, in turn, led to his rapid political fall and to the final destruction of the emirate's sovereignty in 1887.

'Abdullahi was the elder son of Muhammad b. 'Alī b. 'Abdashakur, the seventeenth emir of Harar, who was murdered by the Egyptians during October 1875.[3] After his father's murder, 'Abdullahi asked to be an Egyptian protégé, applying to Abu Bakr Ibrahim Shahim, the governor of Zeila at that time, to mediate between him and the khedival government in Cairo.[4] He asked for Egyptian protection for his family's occupied assets in Harar, and his request was answered positively.[5] The pasha of Zeila, the strongest local leader on the Somali coast of the Gulf of Aden, now became 'Abdullahi's new patron, paying him a monthly stipend and maintaining his servants during 1876.[6] The comparison between Abu Bakr and 'Abdullahi sheds new light on the global processes that began in the Red Sea, as well as on the various ways in which they impacted Zeila on the coastline and Harar further inland. Abu Bakr was the epitome of survival in the region from the early 1860s until his death in 1885.

Abu Bakr's status was earned not only by virtue of his political skill but also due to the nature of the city he ruled. Unlike the inland city of Harar, the port of Zeila became a transportation hub for the global political and economic forces drawn to the southern Red Sea and Gulf of Aden regions. Abu Bakr successfully mediated between political-imperial circles and local forces. He succeeded in adopting various aspects of the regional imperial discourse and its influences of flow of capital and the rapid maritime traffic revolution in the second half of the nineteenth century in the southern Red Sea. He did this without forsaking his local distinction as a tribal leader and slave trader. Thus, Abu Bakr's status as arbiter lent him power on both the local and global stages.[7]

'Abdullahi, on the other hand, embodied the exact opposite of Abu Bakr. As a scion of the emirs of Harar, he had to shoulder the independent political heritage of his city while dealing with an urban Muslim society that was still very much under the influence of the Turco-Egyptian occupation at the time of his appointment. He lacked any prior political experience and was essentially "parachuted" by the British into a position he was not qualified to fill. 'Abdullahi grew up in Harar, was not well-versed in the new discourses among late-nineteenth-century imperialist forces, and did not comprehend the regional processes. The sovereign dynasty of the Harar emirs built its political and economic strength over the centuries through interactions with the Afran Qallo Oromo and the Somalis on the Somali coastal plain and the Ogaden Desert, who controlled the trade routes between Harar and the coast. ʻAbdullahi was the first emir required, as a protégé of the British, to contend with the new geopolitical global dynamics in Harar and in the Somali coast of the Gulf of Aden, which dramatically changed the traditional local balance.

A Powerless Emir?

Hunter recommended that a scion of the dynasty of emirs that had been in power before the Turco-Egyptian occupation be appointed to rule after the Egyptians withdrew.[8] He suggested that the independence of the emirate in Harar be preserved "under the previous Ameer's son. Each Gala and Somali tribe should keep within his own limits, acknowledging British supremacy, and protect routes to the coast, denying passage to slavers."[9] Hunter saw Ibrahim and ʻAbdullahi, two of the sons of Emir Muhammad b. ʻAlī b. ʻAbdashakur, as potential candidates for the post of emir.[10] However, the British, who closely supervised the process through its conclusion in May 1884, expressed a desire that the new emir restore the emirate's hegemonic status vis-à-vis its neighbors, similar to the situation that existed until the early nineteenth century.[11] The British framed ʻAbdullahi's selection in such a way as to make the appointment seem like a reflection of the will of the locals.[12] They ensured that ʻAbdullahi would be the sole candidate. They banished two other nominees, whom they feared would receive the support of the people of Harar, to Zeila and to Aden, and they arrested prospective opponents of the appointment.[13] The first nominee was ʻAlī Abu Bakr, uncle of Emir Muhammad ʻAbdashakur and his bitter opponent. According to some local Harari traditions, ʻAlī Abu Bakr invited the Egyptians in 1875 to occupy Harar and incited them to murder the emir. The British perceived him as a dangerous opposition to ʻAbdullahi.[14] The second nominee was Haj Yusuf Barkely, a Harari slave trader.[15] Acting according to the "recommendation" of the British, an "elections committee" of fifty-five community luminaries—merchants, local *ʻulamā'*, and heads of the Oromo and Somali tribes around the Harar—was convened to "select" the new emir. The committee members also chose sixteen of their own to occupy key positions in the emirate's new administration. Twelve of these officials were selected to serve on a general council, the purpose of which was to assist the emir in matters pertaining to the judicial and law enforcement systems in Harar. Four additional committee members were appointed heads of police, treasury, customs, and a new local militia. The sixteen members of the committee unanimously selected 'Abdullahi as emir.[16]

The steps taken by the British implied that, although they were interested in officially restoring the emirate to Harar, in practice they wished to divest it of any true sovereignty. The emir was to become an utterly dependent ruler. Alongside the emir, the British also wished to appoint *qāḍīs*, *'ulamā'*, and deputies to serve as advisors. They even wanted to establish an army for the emir—made up of locals as well as Oromo and Somalis—that would take up the arms and ammunition left behind by the Egyptians. Hunter also suggested that the level of taxation levied on all goods entering or exiting Harar should be determined according to the rates instated in Zeila—4 percent on imports and 5 percent on exports. These he calculated according to the Indian rupee.[17] The decision reflected the British policy of preventing the resurgence of the *mahlak*, one of the historical symbols of the independent emirate, preferring instead to perpetuate Harar's reliance on regional and global economic forces in the southern parts of the Red Sea, the Gulf of Aden, and the southwestern parts of the Indian Ocean.

Religious Ideologies and Policies

On the eve of his official coronation, 'Abdullahi informed the British that the Sharī'a would be the sole law in Harar and the basis for the treatment of the city's residents, both Muslim and foreign. He affirmed his commitment to the wellbeing of foreigners and vowed to refrain from taxing them in manners that he deemed "superfluous," due to "their importance to commerce in the city."[18] The Egyptians, who officially handed over control of the city to 'Abdullahi, received promises to the effect that he would guarantee safety on the road from Harar to Zeila, shun the slave trade, include the *'ulamā'* in government, and adhere to Sharī'a law.[19]

The prospect of returning to Sharī'a rule was a source of profound anxiety for the city's European merchants, who had become accustomed to freedom of religious expression and special trade privileges during the Turco-Egyptian occupation. They saw the emir as a reactionary who "made it his goal to reintroduce Islam to the residents of Harar," dangerous because "he scorned any possibility of a European occupation of Harar."[20] The Capuchin missionaries saw in 'Abdullahi an "Islamic resurgence" that harmed their conversion enterprise and threatened their life in the city.[21] They even described the new emir as a variant of the Mahdiyya movement, which was imported from Sudan to Harar, and as a very dangerous figure.[22] The British also saw a direct connection between the Mahdiyya rebellion in Sudan and the situation in Harar—a perception that was not founded in fact. Hunter was informed about Gordon's murder in Khartoum in January 1885 and about the British defeat by Mahdist armies. The British were very concerned that Osman Digna, the Mahdist leader in the territories between the Kassala in Sudan and Massawa, would take over the Red Sea Egyptian territories and cooperate with the *'ulamā'* of Harar.[23]

'Abdullahi had no connection to the Mahdiyya or to Digna. He had never seen the Europeans in Harar as his religious enemies and never aspired to convert them to Islam. It seems he did not develop any organized religious ideology or hostile intentions toward the foreigners in Harar. It was British Major Hunter and some of the Capuchin missionaries who viewed the neighboring Afran Qallo Oromo as potential converts from Islam to Christianity, and preferred (each of them for his own reasons) to see Islam among the Oromo outside Harar as a temporary trend.[24]

Emir 'Abdullahi was decisive in restructuring Harar's public, economic, and religious spheres to its precolonial past. He had to contend with the Turco-Egyptian efforts to eliminate Harari traditional symbols and identities. It seems that the enlistment of Sharī'a rule was one of 'Abdullahi's political instruments to return Harar to its pre-Egyptian periods. The emir put himself in charge of Harar's city Sharī'a courts and commanded local women to dress modestly and wear veils. New mosques were built at his behest both inside and outside the city. 'Abdullahi also mandated the closure of cafés that had catered to the foreign residents and banned the consumption of alcohol in public spaces and in the home. All of Harar's residents were enjoined to pray in the mosques during the day and adhere to the edicts of Islam. These were the practical manifestations of what 'Abdullahi termed a "war against [the] wantonness" that he believed had characterized the Egyptian occupation.[25] It seems that the policy of 'Abdullahi was a reaction to what he perceived as modern trends, brought about by the Egyptians and their European protégés and not necessarily a direct result of a policy of religious allegiance.

Nevertheless, it is clear that the new policy marked a deterioration in the conditions of the Europeans, who had been accustomed to doing whatever they pleased in their religious and political activities. 'Abdullahi, however, did not directly target foreigners in the name of some religious or cultural motive. Rather, although he conceived of them as symptoms of the "ailments" of the Egyptian period, he had no intention of officially confronting them in the name of a religious jihad, at least not until the end of 1886.

Fiscal and Economic Aspects

The new emir's lack of political and diplomatic experience was soon reflected in his complicated political and commercial interaction with the European merchants in Harar. Three months after his coronation, 'Abdullahi was caught in the middle of a struggle between Greek merchants, who wished to obtain a monopoly on wheat trade in the city, and Italian ones. The Italians accused 'Abdullahi of showing favoritism toward the Greeks, who were considered his confidants, and complained about him to the British. The British rejected the complaints of the Italian merchants but nevertheless warned the emir "not to listen to stupid advice provided by interested parties in the city."[26]

'Abdullahi officially urged Harar's denizens to respect the European merchants, but actually he aspired to restrict their trade activities, declaring a 3 percent increase in customs duties on all imports and a 10 percent increase on all commodities stored in Gildessa, near Harar. One of the examples of this policy is reflected in the emir's demands of the Italian trader Sacconi to cease his large transactions. However, Sacconi totally ignored ʿAbdullahi's orders and continued with his large-scale commercial activities. He also moved the grain he bought from the Egyptians to Gildessa.[27]

Based on ʿAbdullahi's struggle with the merchants, modern scholars have portrayed him as "a weak and indecisive man, almost fully controlled by his advisors, who advocated a strict Islam."[28] This portrayal does not properly take account of actual events, and it ignores the regional and global factors that ʿAbdullahi had to contend with. One facet of the emir's strategy for restoring the precolonial emirate was to reduce the extent of foreign commerce in Harar. Ignoring the manner in which Harar's economy had become enmeshed in global circles, ʿAbdullahi changed the taxation and customs rates that had been set by the British. He decided that the *mahlak*—the traditional emirate's currency, which the Egyptians forbade using—that bore his name would be the only acceptable currency in the city, superseding the Egyptian and Indian currencies that were used extensively in regional trade. The foreigners, however, ignored his new policy and continued to use foreign currencies—rupees and dollars. In response, ʿAbdullahi clamped down on the merchants, citing Sharīʿa law to forbid loans with interest and imposing a steep tax on foreign currency used in the city.[29]

ʿAbdullahi's attempt to impose the Harari traditional currency can also be seen more as a part of his attempt to restore the emirate symbols than as a systematic policy aimed at harassing foreign merchants. It was only after the merchants flouted his new policy that he penalized them. The religious and cultural biases that cropped up in the writings of the merchants stemmed from their viewing the events in Harar through the lens of an interreligious struggle, but the facts appear to disprove them. The struggle between ʿAbdullahi and the city's Europeans should be looked upon as a political struggle and as an economic conflict rather than a religious and cultural confrontation. Furthermore, ʿAbdullahi's economic policy can be examined in the context of the tension of local market versus global market. ʿAbdullahi strictly insisted on full sovereignty and yet was unable to grasp that the changes, which were brought about when merchants settled in Harar and the city was intensively linked to the global economy and European imperial interests, precluded the possibility of such exclusive control.

Jihad and the Europeans

Some Harari informants testified that ʿAbdullahi aspired to revive the sixteenth century period of Imam Ahmad b. Ibrahim al-Gazi "Gragn" and his successor, Nur b. Mujahid, by emphasizing the rule of the Sharīʿa and reconstructing Islamic educational institutions inside Harar.[30] This hypothesis was almost automatically perceived as though ʿAbdullahi had restored the first half of the sixteenth century's "religious war" and jihad. However, Gragn and ʿAbdullahi lived and acted in completely different historical contexts.[31]

ʿAbdullahi's treatment of foreigners was not inspired by a systematic ideology, and the worsening of their conditions was the result of developments in the field rather than forethought. Not a single foreigner was murdered within the city's limits during the emir's time in power, and murders of foreign merchants at the hands of Oromo and Somalis also took place during the Egyptian occupation and the period leading up to the reestablishment of the emirate.

Throughout most of his time in power, ʿAbdullahi's approach toward the missionaries was moderate. Contrary to the "fanatic" label affixed to him, ʿAbdullahi did not expel them from the city after he rose to power. Nor did he incite against them or harm the mission stations they had established in the outlying Afran Qallo Oromo regions during the Egyptian occupation. Rather, ʿAbdullahi only acted indirectly against the Capuchin missionaries in the Afran Qallo Oromo territories by aspiring to intensify the presence and visibility of his new policy in the Afran Qallo spheres. That might be the explanation for the rapid construction of mosques in and around the city after his appointment, and the closing of mission stations among the Afran Qallo's regions around Harar. The Afran Qallo's elders around Harar preferred to cooperate with the emir and sever ties with the missionaries who had once received the Egyptians' blessing to be active in their territories. Missionary activity among the Oromo resumed with the start of Ethiopian Christian rule in Harar in January 1887.[32]

Inside Harar, however, the picture was more complicated, and the religious and cultural tensions between residents and Capuchins were more pronounced after May 1885. Various testimonies show that some of Harar's Muslims wished to compel foreigners to convert to Islam and harm them once the emirate was reestablished. ʻAbdullahi reined in the attempts at forced conversion and came out against harming foreigners in the city. He claimed that neither the Quran nor other Islamic judicial sources contained justification for such behavior.[33] However, according to the testimony of an Italian merchant, despite explaining to the residents of Harar that there was no justification for harming unarmed Christians who posed no danger, ʻAbdullahi did not respect the city's Capuchins.[34]

ʻAbdullahi's relations both with foreigners in the city and with Britain and Italy reached a nadir in April 1886. A deception that went wrong between ʻAbdullahi and an Italian merchant named Pietro Porro, who led a trade convoy to Zeila, resulted in the slaughter of the members of the convoy at the hands of armed Afran Qallo and Harari men and the looting of the merchandise they carried. In an attempt to dissuade the Somali tribes from raiding the convoy, Porro had circulated the rumor that it was a military convoy. The rumor reached ʻAbdullahi, who, afraid that the Italians were plotting to attack Harar, saw the convoy as "an expression of Italian aggression toward himself and toward the residents of Harar."[35] Nevertheless, ʻAbdullahi did not command his men to slaughter the members of the convoy. That decision was made by the Harari, Oromo, and Somali ʻIssa commanders in the field. ʻAbdullahi was shocked by the results of the incident. According to local and European testimonials, he ordered the execution of some twenty of his own soldiers, whom he considered responsible for the massacre, imprisoned some of his closest advisors, sank into depression, and fasted to mortify his body.[36]

The incident also had severe diplomatic repercussions that complicated the emir's position. In late April 1886, the foreign merchants became ʻAbdullahi's "hostages." Fearing an Italian reprisal, he reasoned that as long as Harar's foreigners remained in the city, Italian or other European forces would not dare to attack. During October 1886 the foreigners were allowed to leave, but not before they were made to sell their belongings to the emir.[37]

It seems that prior to April 1886 'Abdullahi tried to "recapture" Harar's public and religious spheres, and his policy was not necessarily a religious step aimed at the Europeans because of their Christianity or culture. The attempt to redefine the new-old emirate in the aftermath of the Egyptian effort to eradicate the old identities, as well as the European political and economic pressures that 'Abdullahi felt, were what led him to restructure Harar's public and religious space. This, I suggest, is the lens through which one should examine the erection of many mosques in and around the city during his reign, as well as the exclusion of women from public spaces, the closing of cafes that served the European merchants in the city's markets, and the ban on alcohol consumption in public areas and in the home.

Relations with the Oromo and the Somalis

In May 1885, under the protection of the British, 'Abdullahi and the elders of the Afran Qallo and the Somalis signed a treaty that promised mutual recognition and commercial cooperation with the tribes of the Nole, Nunu, Abadu, Mettah, Fidish, Bubasa, Babbile, Jarso Giri, and Manatayo. The leaders of the Oromo and the Somalis officially agreed to pay the traditional precolonial taxes to 'Abdullahi. By having the treaty signed under their colonial protégé, the British coerced some of the old variants of the economic and religious relationship that had existed until 1875 between Harar's emirs and the tribal elites, into a written agreement.[38]

Nevertheless, 'Abdullahi also adopted vigorous, reckless steps to eradicate all traces of the Egyptian administration within nearby Afran Qallo Oromo territories. He tried to consolidate his power there in early 1886 by deploying military force, and there are conflicting reports as to his success.[39] His military campaigns can be seen as part of a larger attempt to secure the new emirate's claim to the Oromo territories, which had been under its control before the Egyptian occupation, or at least until the beginning of the nineteenth century.

As opposed to the Afran Qallo Oromo, whose military and political institutions were severely damaged by the Egyptians, the Somalis were the strongest local factor in the regions between Harar and the coast after the Egyptian withdrawal. Apparently, as part of 'Abdullahi's policy to reestablish the emirate after the Egyptian occupation, he perceived the Afran Qallo Oromo as the "ultimate" enemy of the emirate, equal to the modern-global tradition of the Egyptian period.[40]

The British recognized the power of the Somali populations in the plain between Zeila, Berbera, and Harar and paradoxically contributed (as did the French) to strengthening these groups and fostering cooperation among them. The elders of the Somali Mijjerten, the Habar Awal, the 'Issa, and the Habar Toljaala signed with the British and the French, and it seems 'Abdullahi had no other political choice but to cooperate with the Somali tribal elders.[41] The British also coerced the establishment of a common Harari-Somali military force, which numbered three hundred warriors equipped with approximately five hundred rifles, over two million Remington bullets, and two cannons. According to some of the testimonies, the emir's militia was also strengthened by more than one hundred Egyptian soldiers who decided to stay in Harar due to their marriages to local Harari women.[42]

'Abdullahi was motivated neither solely by local objectives nor solely by any Harari historical tradition or religious dogmatic ideologies. He had to be pragmatic, and he reacted to changes that occurred in the area between Harar and the Somali coast around the time of his election. Abu Bakr's death in Zeila at the beginning of December 1885, and the involvement of Italy and France on the Somali coast, improved the status and military might of the Somali leaders. This development caused a gradual slackening of security along the trade routes.[43] The Somalis soon began to plunder and massacre European commercial convoys: 'Issa warriors murdered 103 Europeans and locals in the roads between Harar, Zeila and Berbera.[44] Simultaneously with these attacks, which were directed against foreigners, a bloody conflict broke out during November 1885 between the Somali 'Issa and the Gadabuursi about control of the trade routes between Harar and Zeila. Twenty were killed during the fighting, and the security condition on the routes was severely weakened.[45]

Thus, the emir did not control the regions near Harar. The Somalis were not 'Abdullahi's reliable allies, and soon they became a severe danger to his reign within Harar. Unlike the Egyptians, 'Abdullahi was unsuccessful in his bid to buy the loyalty of the Somali tribal leaders, and he did not possess the kind of military might required to bring them to heel.[46]

Emirate Collapse, January 1887

Despite 'Abdullahi's fear that the European superpowers would attack and remove him from power, his political demise was actually brought about by a Christian, African imperial force that came from the African inland. King Menilek of Shewa resolved to take control of Harar as soon as the Egyptians withdrew from the city.

After Egypt pulled out of Harar and the coastal cities, and Italy occupied Massawa in February 1885, Menilek tried to convince the Italians to sign a pact that would guarantee an Italian takeover of Berbera and Zeila along with the occupation of Harar by the Shewans. The Porro incident had highlighted the issue of Berbera and Zeila, and Menilek was afraid that the Italians would use the incident as a pretext to gain control of the coast. Therefore, as early as the summer of 1886, he acted to bolster his military presence in the Oromo regions outlying Harar, his final objective being the occupation of the city.[47]

'Abdullahi was aware of the concrete Shewa threat to his city. The Ethiopian Christian threat led the emir to abandon his moderate religious attitude. Testimonials of Harari residents show that it was not until December 1886 that 'Abdullahi began to employ religious rhetoric, calling for a holy war in an effort to rally the city to face the Ethiopians in battle. When his advisors entreated him to consider yielding to Menilek, 'Abdullahi replied, "Does the Quran permit us to surrender to the infidel?" Some of the Oromo from the areas surrounding Harar did not join the emir's army in the name of a holy war but rather out of mercenary motives, having been promised large portions of the loot that would be taken from the Ethiopians and due to their wish to capture Ethiopian soldiers and sell them into slavery.[48]

On 1 January 1887, 'Abdullahi massed his forces next to the town of Callanqo, some fifty miles west of Harar.[49] In a series of battles that began on 3 January and lasted until 7 January, the Shewan Ethiopian armies routed the emir's forces. The Ethiopians enjoyed an overwhelming numerical advantage. ʿAbdullahi's army numbered some four thousand men, only half of whom were armed with guns and properly trained. Menilek, on the other hand, commanded a force of between twenty and twenty-five thousand, eight thousand of whom carried firearms. The emir's hasty flight from the battlefield to the Ogaden Desert following the death of many of his troops, and the failure to rally groups of Oromo fighters that could make it to Callanqo in time, were among the factors that demoralized ʿAbdullahi's remaining soldiers. They finally surrendered on 6 January 1887.[50] The battle of Callanqo was a watershed event in the history of Harar, which had now become part of Menilek's expanding Shewa kingdom.[51]

The battle was a historic watershed not only in the process of the destruction of the Muslim emirate of Harar. It was also the first phase in the lengthy process of integrating of Harar's Muslims and the Afran Qallo Oromo into the Christian Ethiopian empire, conducted by Makonnen Walda-Mikael, the first Ethiopian governor of the town.[52] Menilek instructed Makonnen Walda-Mikael to let the Oromo and the Muslims live according their father's heritage.[53] These processes embodied both local phenomena of "Hararization" within the military and political Christian-Ethiopian establishments and simultaneous processes of "Ethiopianization" of the Harari elites.[54]

11

Afterword

Narratives in a Transitional Period

Since Ethiopia became a federal republic in 1994, Harar has been the capital of the state of the Harari people. Three years after the ousting of Marxist leader Mengistu Haile Mariam in 1991, the Federal State of Ethiopia recognized the existence of nine states, each representing a different ethnic group or confederation of ethnic groups. The new Harari regional state was home to two main ethnic groups—the city dwellers, who spoke Adari, and the Oromo. Today, smaller groups of the 'Afar, Somali, and Sidama people live in the state of Harar.

In 2004, Fuad Ibrahim, president of the Harari Regional State in the Republic of Ethiopia, wrote: "As Ethiopia's oldest living town, Harar is a historic town with a rich history and texture increasingly threatened by modern innervations and the loss of its traditional socio-economic bases. . . . Harar appears to be a town almost frozen in time."[1]

This book shows that Harar did not "freeze in time" but was—and still remains—a platform for a dynamic life of continuity and change. Harar has survived, among other things, a difficult and influential Egyptian colonial conquest, which, despite causing the loss of its political and economic sovereignty, did not trigger the loss of any of its religious and social characteristics. The period between 1875 and 1887 was significant to five different groups of people—five different "characters" whose paths crossed in the story of Harar and the Turco-Egyptian conquest: Harar, Egypt, the Somali people, the Oromo people, and Ethiopia. Each of these characters experienced a transitional period with repercussions that would affect its history, and each was influenced by the dynamics of relationships with the other elements that were present in the arena of the events.

At the start of this period, Harar was an independent emirate that had existed for centuries as a continuously local sovereignty with an urban and Islamic culture, unique in its language and religious practices, which combined orthodox attitudes with Sufi Islam. In 1875, Harar was conquered by the Turco-Egyptians and experienced colonial rule that brought a different culture and perception of Islam, along with new, modernist attitudes. At the end of this period, short-lived independence returned to Harar, but in January 1887, Harar fell to other conquerors, Ethiopian Christians.

Egypt entered this period at the height of its momentum as a regional power ruling over the Nile Valley and Sudan, spreading out toward the coasts of the Red Sea to expand and establish an empire in Africa. In the year Harar was captured (1875–76), there were already signs that this momentum was ending (a financial crisis at home and defeats in the conflict with Ethiopia in the area between the Red Sea and Sudan). The conquest of Harar and its environs promised renewal and strengthening.

The ensuing years heralded difficult changes, both throughout the "African Empire" and in Egypt itself. Egypt's economic debt and the pre-national revolt movement brought about the intervention of the European powers and the dismissal of the ruler, Khedive Isma'īl, in 1879. The outbreak of the Mahdiyya revolt in Sudan (1881) worsened the condition of the Egyptian empire in Africa, and Egypt itself was conquered by Britain in 1882. In this way, the conquerors of Harar become the conquered, and were forced to withdraw from the shores of the Red Sea and from Harar. Egypt would be freed from its British conquerors, but not until 1956.

As for the Oromo, the Turco-Egyptian decade profoundly affected their lives and was a disaster in the long term. The Oromo tried in vain to reconstruct their institutions after the Egyptians left in 1885. Together with Emir 'Abdullahi, who maintained the complex relationship between the city and the Oromo, they also fell into the hands of Ethiopian colonialism, beginning in January 1887.

Thus, the Turco-Egyptian conquest of Harar was a turning point in the history of the Afran Qallo. From an independent population that was part of the varied power plays of Harar and maintained a love-hate relationship with its emirs, the Oromo became subalterns. In defeating the Oromo and shattering their framework, the Turco-Egyptians essentially laid the groundwork for future conquests and the cultural, religious, and economic integration of Menilek II, the emperor of Ethiopia in the Oromo regions from the late nineteenth century.[2]

The Somali populations—with a more segmentary structure than that of the Oromo—entered this period while they, too, were sovereign over their lands. The members of the Somali tribes were mostly independent nomadic shepherds, as they had been for centuries in the area between the coastal cities and the Ogaden Desert and Harar. The conquering rulers established security on the roads connecting the Zeila-Harar-Berbera triangle, as well as centralized government. Unlike the Oromo, however, the Somali tribes succeeded in almost escaping the authority of Egyptian rule. Nevertheless, the short-lived Egyptian conquest heralded the arrival of other conquerors. Immediately after the withdrawal of Turco-Egyptian forces from the region, four other imperial elements took over the Somali area—Britain, Italy, France, and Ethiopia. The area seized by the Ethiopians at that time—the Ogaden Desert and its Somali inhabitants—is still part of Ethiopia today.

The book focuses less on Ethiopia, since its direct involvement with Harar began right at the conclusion of the period under discussion. However, Ethiopia was significantly present in the background of the events, and it is the only non-European victor in the story of the period. Christian Ethiopia entered 1875 as an entity spread over quite a small area—the mountainous territory between today's Addis Ababa and the present Eritrean border. Ethiopia was subject to the Egyptian threat mainly in its northern provinces, which were—in the eyes of Egyptian rulers—the area connecting the Red Sea and Sudan. Emperor Yohannes IV of the northern Tigray province succeeded in defeating the Egyptians in several battles, and afterwards defeated the Sudanese Mahdists and the pioneers of Italian imperialism on the Eritrean coast. Menilek, king of the southern Shewa province—and supposedly subordinate to Yohannes IV—set off at the same time on a campaign of conquest toward the south, thus demonstrating the power of the intensively armed Christian empire and its superiority in military organization compared to its neighbors.

In 1887, Menilek conquered Harar and territories in present-day Ethiopia. When Yohannes IV was killed in battle with the Mahdists in 1889, Menilek was crowned emperor of Ethiopia, becoming Menilek II. In 1896, he dealt the Italian imperialists a hard blow, and Ethiopia entered the twentieth century as a multinational empire, including, among others, the Oromo, Harar, and a large portion of the Somali tribes. The sovereignty of "greater Ethiopia" was recognized by Great Britain, France, and Italy—the powers that, from 1885, ruled over the territories surrounding Ethiopia: Eritrea, Sudan, Kenya, Italian Somalia, British Somaliland, and French Somalia.

Each of the five protagonists in the Harar story entered the city with its own internal tensions. These tensions influenced the characteristics of its behavior and its relationship with the other protagonists, as well as itself being influenced and reformulated by the events that took place.

At the onset of the conquest of Harar, Egypt was an almost-independent entity, where a power play took place with multiple players and various trends. The Harar story reflected one of Egypt's significant internal tensions. On one side stood the leading members of the khedive's rule, with its Ottoman-Egyptian culture and the dependency it had developed on the European powers. This system put the administration of the empire in Africa in the hands of a number of Europe's representatives. On the other side stood Turco-Egyptian army officers, who represented a stronger tie to Egypt itself and cultivated hostility toward the foreigners who were in charge of them. In Harar, especially during the rule of Ra'uf Pasha, these officers could express their ability to imagine and to build a kind of an extension of modern Egypt: dominant, powerful, and imperial. The general failure within Egypt and in Africa, and the collapse of the special project in Harar, made a significant contribution to the reformulation of this internal tension.

With the removal of Khedive Isma'īl came the end of the era of the khedivate's authoritarian rule, and the political culture that it represented was weakened. At the same time, the Egyptian failure in the Nile Valley and on the Red Sea coasts, and the British occupation of Egypt, solidified the new Egyptian command as a protest movement, which would become one of the heralds of modern Egyptian nationalism. Ahmad ʿUrabi, for example, had come from Massawa, another area in the Red Sea, but the episode of the conquest of Harar and the dismissal of Ra'uf by Colonel Gordon also contributed to the frustration and anger that nourished the roots of modern Egyptian nationalism.

The Afran Qallo Oromo populations came under the Egyptian yoke as well, as they experienced inner tension between tradition and modernity. A sizable proportion of their traditional institutions and frameworks (the *Raba Dori* and the *gada* systems, for instance) still remained, as well as their language, Oromiffa. In contrast, political innovations took place from the start of the nineteenth century, centering on the establishment of systems that were above the tribes and ruled by authoritative leaders (the *mooti*). The adoption of Islam was part of this establishment. The Oromo in the Harar area were conquered, their institutions were weakened or destroyed, Turco-Egyptian Islamization activities were propagated among them, and, at the same time, Christian missionary activities began.

In the end, the events led to a final collapse of the Oromo institutions and the fall of the Oromo into the hands of the Ethiopians. Under Ethiopian rule, the Oromo elites around Harar began to assimilate into the life of the empire, and with this, converted to Christianity or to Islam. The independence of the Oromo was never restored, and even their language was pushed out by Amharic, which took its place as the lingua franca official language of Ethiopia. Today, the Oromo people are the largest ethnic group in Ethiopia and the wider Horn of Africa. Some of the Oromo wish to secede from Ethiopia, establish an independent state, and return to their original culture and even to their former religion. Most of the Oromo aspire to a cultural and administrative revival, including a return to the Oromiffa tongue in the state of "Oromia" that was set up in 1993 as part of Ethiopia in its present configuration as a multiethnic federation. On 27 March 2018, the ruling Ethiopian People's Revolutionary Democratic Front elected Abiy Ahmed ʿAlī, an Ethiopian politician of Oromo origin, as its new chairman. He is the twelfth prime minister of Ethiopia.

Egyptian rule did not alter Somali ways. Even under the Harar *hikimdariya*, the Somalis remained free nomads with loose segmentary tribal structures. After the Egyptians withdrew, the Somalis fell to four European and African colonial powers: Great Britain, Italy, France, and Ethiopia. The European rule lasted until 1960, and Ethiopian rule over Ogaden has lasted until today. In these years, the lives of the Somalis have moved between extremes. On the one hand, they have accepted being conquered while continuing to maintain their autonomous traditional lives; on the other hand, at times they have clung to Islamic fervor, which has served as a supratribal bond in the anticolonialist struggle. Between 1899 and 1920, their national Muslim hero, Muhammad b. ʿAbdullah Hasan, led them in this spirit. Since achieving independence, the Somalis have fought to regain control of Ogaden from Ethiopia, and in 1977–78, they even laid siege to Harar and nearly conquered it in the name of Islam.

Ethiopia entered a period during which it was in tension between two conceptions of its government. Under the rule of Emperor Yohannes IV of the Tigray people, the country was ruled according to Tigray traditions, by principles of conservatism and isolationism combined with decentralization. King Menilek of Shewa represented an opposing approach that gave expression to the Amharic culture—openness toward the outside world, with political centralization and the domestic inculcation of Amharic language and culture. The struggle was won in the strategic arena. During the 1870s and 1880s, Yohannes IV was forced to fight severe defensive wars in the north (against the Egyptians, Mahdists and Italians) and thus, Menilek was able to fight wars of conquest, which gave him an advantage in the south. In this way, for example, in January 1887, while Menilek was conquering Harar, the army of Yohannes encountered the Italian army near Massawa; in the ensuing conflict, northern Ethiopia was emptied of all of its resources.

When Yohannes IV was killed in 1899, Menilek became the undisputed emperor. His forces continued their conquests in the south, and the residents became linguistically and culturally assimilated in the Amharic melting pot as the emperor's forces took over all their economic resources. Harar itself was a symbol of the building of Ethiopia in this spirit. Ras Makonnen Walda-Mikael, a relative of Menilek and his right-hand man, initiated annexation and modernization in Harar and its environs. Ras Makonnen allowed moderate and apolitical Islam in Harar and at the same time brought European missionaries back to the city.[3]

Harar soon became one of the centers of power in Ethiopia. Ras Makonnen recruited resources and power from the Oromo and Muslims as well, and promoted them to senior posts in the Ethiopian administration. His son, Ras Tafari, continued to rely upon Harar for everything throughout his lifetime, even after the coronation of Emperor Haile Selassie. He brought his firstborn son back to the city and bestowed upon him the title "Duke of Harar." Even Mengistu Haile Mariam, the chairman of the Derg, the military junta that deposed Haile Selassie in 1974, was one of the officers of the division located in Harar.

Since 1995, two cities have achieved the status of "state": Addis Ababa as the capital of the Ethiopian federation, and Harar. In its present formulation, Harar has thus achieved recognition of its historical uniqueness, and it has symbols of a sovereign entity de jure. Inside its walls and beyond them, a tempestuous ethnic and religious Adari-Oromo-Somali discourse continues. Nonetheless, it is clear that the days of the independent emirate have gone, never to return.

GLOSSARY

NOTES

BIBLIOGRAPHY

INDEX

Glossary

Abbreviations indicate the language in which the term is used:

Adari (Adr.)
Amharic (Amh.)
Arabic (Ar.)
Oromiffa (Or.)
Persian (Per.)
Somali (Som.)
Turkish (Tur.)

***abba dulla* (Or.):** the deputy of the *abba fugug*, who served as head of the council of the various *bokku* in Mulata

***abba fugug* (Or.):** the head of the *Raba Dori*, a sort of head of the Oromo federation of clans

***Afōča* (Adr.):** social networks comprised of Harari men who are experienced in economic and social mutual responsibility

***'arafa* (Ar.):** the holiest day in Islam that falls on the ninth day of Du al-Hijja of the lunar Islamic calendar. This happens to be approximately seventy days after the end of the month of Ramadan.

***'ashura* (Ar.):** tenth day of the Muslim month of Muharram

***ãw, ãwach* (pl.) (Adr.):** "father," refers to a respected sheikh, elder of the tribe, or holy man as well as a biological father

***bari* (Adr.):** quarter or gate

***başhi bozuķ* (Tur.):** irregular soldiers

bey (Tur.): civil and military title below Pasha

***bokku* (Or.):** tribal judge or leader of the Oromo *gosa*

***Ç̌əqa Šum* (Amh.):** earth officer

***damin* (Ar.):** guarantor. The Turco-Egyptians employed the *damin* during the decade they occupied Harar. The person in this position was responsible for administrative matters in the tribe's territory.

***diwan* (Ar.):** council, cabinet, board of advisers

***dogin* (Adr.):** the *garad*'s supervisor; governor of the outer areas

Effendī (Tur.)/ Afandī (Ar.): Mister (form of address), as well as honorary appellation given to members of learned professions

***faddan* (Ar.):** a square measure

***fariq* (Ar.):** military and naval rank equal to lieutenant general

***firman* (Ar.)/*ferman* (Tur.):** decree, order

***fitna* (Ar.):** seduction, enchantment; disorder resulting from seduction or enchantment; actions of opponents (in modern political contexts)

***gada* (Or.):** the division of the Oromo clan into age brackets of eight years

Galla (Amh.): outdated and offensive term, both Ethiopian and foreign, usually referring to the Oromo

***garad* (Som./Adr./Or.):** chief of a village or hamlet. The word's origin is unclear, but in Somali it means a man who holds a high government office, sometimes parallel to a prince.

***gerib* (Ar.):** a unit of land whose source is in Islamic law. Traditionally, the *gerib* in Harar was half of a square meter. The Turco-Egyptians changed the size of the *gerib* from 50 cm to 58 cm.

***gosa* (Or.):** clan, tribe, ethnic group

guinea (Ar.): Egyptian currency

haj (Ar.): pilgrimage, or a title for pilgrim

***herta* (Or.):** division

***Hera Gosa* (Or.):** the unwritten constitution of the Oromo clans

***hikimdar* (Tur./Ar.):** governor

***hikimdariya* (Tur./Ar.):** governor's office

imam (Ar.): one who stands in front; a role model for the Muslims in all its spiritual and secular undertakings

jihad (Ar.): from the Arabic root meaning "to strive," "to exert," "to fight"; exact meaning depends on context

***jugal* (Adr.):** Harar city's wall

***kaleb* (Amh.):** provision. The *kaleb* was a tax instituted in Harar and outside of the city immediately after its conquest by the kingdom of Shewa.

***kantar* (Tur.):** an Ottoman unit of measure weighing 125 pounds

khedive (Per.): "Lord" or "Ruler"; title used by the governor of Egypt officially since 1867 in the meaning of "Vice Sultan" or "Viceroy"

***kuttab, katatib* (pl.) (Ar.):** elementary Quranic School

***Laylat al-Qadr* (Ar.):** the great night of the twenty-seventh of the month of Ramadan; the night when Muhammad received the first revelation of the Quran

***liwa* (Ar.):** military rank equal to major general

***madhhab al-Shafi'i* (Ar.):** one of the four schools of legal thought of Islam, founded by Muhammad b. Idris b. al-Abbas b. Uthman b. Shafi'i in the eighth century; prominent in Egypt

madrassa (Ar.): establishment of learning where Islamic sciences are taught; a college for higher studies

Mahdī (Ar.): divinely guided one who will appear before the end of time to reestablish justice on earth

***mahlak* (Adr.):** Harar emirates' currency

***majlis, majalis* (pl.) (Ar.):** required local council, usually established in localities administered by the Egyptians in northeast Africa during the nineteenth century

***malaq* (Adr.):** an official responsible for enforcing the laws of the emirate and collecting taxes from owners of agricultural land. The term was created by joining two words in the Adari language: *mala*, meaning "roads" or "intentions," and *aqa*, meaning "knowledge."

***mecīdiye* (Tur.):** badge of courage; a ranking system named for the Ottoman Sultan Abdül Mejid (r. 1839–61)

***miri* (Ar.):** state lands held generally under tax-farming arrangements

***mooti* (Or.):** king, conqueror

***mooti adari* (Adr./Or.):** Adari king

***mudiriya, mudiriyat* (pl.) (Ar.):** administration or district

***muḥāfeẓ* (Ar.):** governor

***nā'īb* (Ar.):** deputy

***negus* (Amh.):** Ethiopian title equal to king

***ogaz* (Som.):** tribal leaders

***oyna* (Or.):** term referring to the division of land outside Harar in the days of the emirs. The Oromo chief in charge of transferring money to the emirs was called *oyna*.

pasha (Tur.), *bāshā* (Ar.): highest title in the Ottoman and the Egyptian court hierarchy

piaster (Ar.): Egyptian currency

***qāḍī* (Ar.):** judge

***qirsh* (Ar.):** Egyptian currency

Quttu (Or./Adr.): Oromo farmers closest to Harar; "workers of the land"

***Raba Dori* (Or.):** the central political and military institution of the Oromo living around Mulata, south of Harar; the "umbrella organization," a confederation, which brought the various clans of the Afran Gala Oromo together. The *Raba* was the elected political body and the *Dori* was its military branch.

***ra'is* (Ar.):** head, president

ras (Amh.): head, highest traditional title below *negus*

***rial* (Ar.):** Egyptian currency

Sharīʿa (Ar.): sacred, revealed law in Islam

sheikh (Ar.): old man, tribal chief, religious leader, or head of a Sufi brotherhood

sheikh *al-balad* (Ar.): "headman," an office held by Egypt's most influential bey beginning in the mid-eighteenth century; the Bedouin headman of an Egyptian village

***ʿulamā'* (Ar.):** learned men, religious scholars

***vilāyet* (Tur.), *wilāya* (Ar.):** an Ottoman administrative term for province

***wakil, wukula* (pl.) (Ar.):** authorized representative

***Waqa* (Or.):** traditional Oromo sky-god

***Waqqiya* (Or.):** Oromo traditional religion

***zakat* (Ar.):** required almsgiving that is one of the five pillars of Islam; Muslims with financial means are required to give 2.5 percent of their net worth annually.

***ziyāra* (Ar.):** visit; visitation to the tomb of a holy man

Notes

Introduction

1. I am grateful to Professor Heather J. Sharkey for her advice on framing the beginning of this book.

2. Ehud R. Toledano, *State and Society in Mid-Nineteenth Century Egypt* (New York: Cambridge Univ. Press, 1990), 92. About the discourse on identities in the Egyptian army during the first half of the nineteenth century, see Khaled Fahmy, *All the Pasha's Men: Mehmed Ali, His Army and the Making of Modern Egypt* (Cambridge: Cambridge Univ. Press, 1997), 239–77.

3. For further details, see Alice Moore-Harell, *Gordon and the Sudan: Prologue to the Mahdiyya 1877–1880* (London: Frank Cass, 2001), 4–5; Toledano, *State*, 68–93; Afaf Lutfi al-Sayyid Marsot, *Egypt in the Reign of Muhammad Ali* (New York: Cambridge Univ. Press, 1988), 6–7; J. R. I. Cole, *Colonialism and Revolution in the Middle East: Social and Cultural Origins of Egypt's Urabi Movement* (Princeton, NJ: Princeton Univ. Press, 1993), 31.

4. See, for example, the traditional Western studies on colonialism: Georges Balandier, "The Colonial Situation—A Theoretical Approach," in *Social Change: The Colonial Situation*, ed. Immanuel Wallerstein (New York: John Wiley & Sons, 1966), 34–61; Rupert Emerson, *From Empire to Nation* (Cambridge, MA: Harvard Univ. Press, 1968); Rupert Emerson, "The Problem of Identity, Selfhood and Image in the New Nations," *Comparative Politics* 1, no. 3 (Apr. 1969): 297–312; Thomas Hodgkin, *Nationalism in Colonial Africa* (New York: Frederick Muller, 1956); Ioan M. Lewis, ed., *Nationalism and Self-Determination in the Horn of Africa* (London: Ithaca Press, 1983).

5. Jürgen Osterhammel, *Colonialism: A Theoretical Review* (Princeton, NJ: Markus Wiener Publishers, 1997), 16–17; Edward W. Said, *Culture and Imperialism* (London: Vintage, 1993), 7.

6. Kenneth Ballhatchet, *Race, Class and Sex under Raj: Imperial Attitudes and Policies and their Critics, 1793–1905* (New York: St. Martin's Press, 1980); Helen Callaway, *Gender, Culture and Empire: European Women in Colonial Nigeria* (London: Macmillan Press, 1987); Nicholas B. Dirks, ed., *Colonialism and Culture* (Ann Arbor: Univ. of

Michigan Press, 1992); David Arnold, *Colonizing the Body: State Medicine and Epidemic Disease in Nineteenth-Century India* (Berkeley: Univ. of California Press, 1993).

7. Fredrick Cooper and Ann Laura Stoler, eds., *Tensions of Empire: Colonial Cultures in a Bourgeois World* (Berkeley; Los Angeles: Univ. of California Press, 1997).

8. For further details, see Marius B. Jansen, "The Meiji Restoration," in *The Cambridge History of Japan*, vol. 5, *The Nineteenth Century*, ed. Marius B. Jansen (New York: Cambridge Univ. Press, 1989), 308–66.

9. Haggai Erlich, "Muḥammad ʿAlī," in *Encyclopaedia Aethiopica*, ed. Siegbert Uhlig (Wiesbaden: Harrassowitz Verlag, 2003–14), 5:449–50; Omnia El Shakry, *The Great Social Laboratory: Subjects of Knowledge in Colonial and Postcolonial Egypt* (Stanford, CA: Stanford Univ. Press, 2007), 3; Timothy Mitchell, *Colonizing Egypt* (Cambridge: Cambridge Univ. Press, 1988), 34–40, 63–94.

10. For further details regarding Mehmet ʿAlī's rulers and the socioeconomic characteristics of the Ottoman-Egyptian elite in the middle of the nineteenth century and the social divide and the life of the lower strata, see Toledano, *State*, 39–148, 151–248.

11. Haggai Erlich, "Ismāʿīl," in Uhlig, *Encyclopaedia Aethiopica*, 3:216–17; El Shakry, *Great Social Laboratory*, 23–24; Cyntia Myntti, *Paris along the Nile: Architecture in Cairo from the Belle Epoque* (Cairo: American Univ. in Cairo Press, 1999), 9–15.

12. Eve M. Troutt Powell, *A Different Shade of Colonialism: Egypt, Great Britain and the Mastery of the Sudan* (Berkeley: Univ. of California Press, 2003), 66.

13. Erlich, "Ismāʿīl," 216; Troutt Powell, *Different Shade of Colonialism*, 67.

14. Troutt Powell, *Different Shade of Colonialism*, 68. For further details regarding the Mahdī, see Gabriel R. Warburg, *Islam, Sectarianism and Politics in Sudan since the Mahdiyya* (London: Hurst, 2003).

15. Erlich, "Ismāʿīl," 217; Troutt Powell, *Different Shade of Colonialism*, 68–69.

16. For further details regarding these Ottoman African and Arabian frontiers, see John Alexander, "Ottoman Frontiers Policies in North-East Africa," in *The Frontiers of the Ottoman World*, ed. A. C. S. Peacock (Oxford: Oxford Univ. Press, 2009), 225–34; Intisar Elzein, "Ottoman Archaeology of the Middle Nile Valley in the Sudan," in Peacock, *Frontiers*, 371–83; Paul Lane and Douglas Johnson, "The Archaeology and History of Slavery in South Sudan in the Nineteenth Century," in Peacock, *Frontiers*, 509–53; Michael Mallinson, Laurence Smith, Colin Bren, Wes Forsythe, and Jack Phillips, "Ottoman Suakin 1541–1865: Lost and Found," in Peacock, *Frontiers*, 469–92; Andrew Peterson, "The Ottoman Conquest of Arabia and the Syrian Hajj Route," in Peacock, *Frontiers*, 81–94.

17. For further details, see Mustafa Minawi, *The Ottoman Scramble for Africa: Empire and Diplomacy in the Sahara and the Hijaz* (Stanford, CA: Stanford Univ. Press, 2016); Selim Deringil, "'They Live in a State of Nomadism and Savagery': The Late Ottoman Empire and the Post-Colonial Debate," *Comparative Studies in Society and History* 45 (Apr. 2003): 311–42; Ussama Makdisi, "Ottoman Orientalism," *American Historical*

Review 107, no. 3 (Jun. 2002): 768–96; Yasemin Avçi, "The Application of Tanzimat in the Desert: The Bedouins and the Creation of a New Town in Southern Palestine (1860–1914)," *Middle Eastern Studies* 45, no. 6 (Nov. 2009): 969–83.

18. Troutt Powell, *Different Shade of Colonialism*, 5–8.

19. El Shakry, *Great Social Laboratory*, 23–25.

20. For theoretical approaches that focus mainly on traditional political, social, and economic systems of the occupied societies in Africa, see J. F. Ade Ajayi, "Colonialism: An Episode in African History," in *Colonialism in Africa*, ed. Lewis Gann and Peter Duignan (London: Cambridge Univ. Press, 1969), 1:497–509; J. F. Ade Ajayi, "Africa at the Beginning of the Nineteenth Century: Issues and Prospects," in *Africa in the Nineteenth Century until the 1880s*, ed. J. F. A. Ajayi, vol. 6 of *General History of Africa* (Paris: United Nations Educational, Scientific and Cultural Organization, 1989), 1–22.

21. See, for example, Homi K. Bhabha, *The Location of Culture* (London; New York: Routledge, 1994); Gayatry Chakravorty Spivak, "Subaltern Studies: Deconstructing Historiography," chap. 12 in *In Other Worlds: Essays in Cultural Politics* (New York: Routledge, 1988), 197–221.

22. On the dynamism of tradition and its "invention" for present purposes, see Eric Hobsbawm, *On History* (London: Weidenfeld & Nicolson, 1997), 17.

23. For extended reading on the *Afōča* and its significance in Adari society, see Elisabeth-Dorothea Hecht, "Afōča," in Uhlig, *Encyclopaedia Aethiopica*, 1:127–28; Peter Koehn and Sidney R. Waldron, *Afoca: A Link between Community and Administration in Harar, Ethiopia* (Syracuse, NY: Maxwell School of Citizenship and Public Affairs, Syracuse Univ., 1978); Yusuf Ahmed, "Afōča," *Journal of Ethiopian Studies* 3, no. 2 (1965): 125–32.

1. Harar and Its Environs Up to 1875

1. For further details, see Belle Asante, "Harär: Introduction," in Uhlig, *Encyclopaedia Aethiopica*, 2:1012–13.

2. Camilla C. T. Gibb, "Baraka without Borders: Integrating Communities in the City of Saints," *Journal of Religion in Africa* 29, no. 1 (1999): 104. For further details about Harari society today, see also Tim Carmichael, "Religion, Language and Nationalism: Harari Muslims in Christian Ethiopia," in *Islam in World Cultures Comparative Perspectives*, ed. Michael Feener (Santa Barbara, CA: ABC-CLIO Publishers, 2004), 217–52.

3. Gibb, "Baraka," 93. See also Simone Tarsitani, "Ḏikr in Harär: Zikri," in Uhlig, *Encyclopaedia Aethiopica*, 2:158–59; Ahmed Zekaria, "Harar: The Land of Ziyara, Pilgrimage," in *Institute of Ethiopian Studies: First Interdisciplinary Seminar of the IES*, 6–7 Jun. 1998 (Ethiopia: Nazareth, 1998), 1–9.

4. On the importance of khat and its role in Harari tradition, see Ezekiel Gebissa, *Leaf of Allah: Khat and Agricultural Transformation in Harerge Ethiopia 1875–1991*

(Athens, OH: Ohio Univ. Press, 2004); Elisabeth-Dorothea Hecht, "Çat in Harär," in Uhlig, *Encyclopaedia Aethiopica*, 1:698.

5. Spencer J. Trimingham, *Islam in Ethiopia* (London: Frank Cass, 1952), 93; Ewald Wagner, "Harär History till 1875," in Uhlig, *Encyclopaedia Aethiopica*, 2:1015–19.

6. Sidney R. Waldron, "The Political Economy of Harari-Oromo Relationship, 1559–1874," *Northeast African Studies* 6, no. 1–2 (1984): 32.

7. Nadia Ammi, "Awach, the Founding Fathers of Harar," in *Harar: A Muslim City of Ethiopia*, ed. Philippe Revault and Serge Santelli (Paris: Maisonneuve and Larose, 2004), 73–89; Sidney R. Waldron, "A Farewell to Bab Haji: City Symbolism and Harari Identity, 1887–1977," in *Working Papers in Society and History in Imperial Ethiopia: The Southern Periphery from the 1880's to 1974*, ed. Donald L. Donham and Wendy James (Cambridge: African Studies Center, 1980), 79.

8. Camilla C. T. Gibb, "Āw," in Uhlig, *Encyclopaedia Aethiopica*, 1:398–99.

9. Camilla C. T. Gibb, "In the City of the Saints: Religion, Politics and Gender in Harar, Ethiopia" (PhD diss., Oxford University, 1997), 94–96; for further details, see Sidney R. Waldron, "Harar: The Muslim City in Ethiopia," in *Proceedings of the Fifth International Conference of Ethiopian Studies, 13–16 April 1978*, ed. Robert L. Hess (Chicago: Office of Publications Services, Univ. of Illinois in Chicago Circle, 1979), 239–57.

10. Ibid., 99.

11. Patrick Desplat, "The Articulation of Religious Identities and Their Boundaries in Ethiopia: Labelling Difference and Processes of Contextualization of Islam," *Journal of Religion in Africa* 35, no. 4 (2005): 492; Gibb, "In the City of the Saints," 101; Ewald Wagner, "Abādir 'Umar ar-Riḍā," in Uhlig, *Encyclopaedia Aethiopica*, 1:4–5.

12. Richard A. Caulk, "Harar Town and Its Neighbors in the Nineteenth Century," *Journal of African History* 18, no. 3 (1977): 385.

13. Ibid. 372–73; Desplat, "Articulation of Religious Identities," 492.

14. Ewald Wagner, "Three Arabic Documents on the History of Harar," *Journal of Ethiopian Studies* 12, no. 1 (1974): 213–24.

15. Mordechai Abir, *Ethiopia: The Era of the Princes; the Challenge of Islam and the Reunification of the Christian Empire, 1769–1865*, (London: Longmans, 1968), 14; Abdunasir Edris, "Traditional Islamic Centers of Learning in Harar" (BA thesis, Addis Ababa University, 1992), 1–22.

16. Franz-Christoph Muth, "Aḥmad b. Ibrāhīm al-Ġāzī," in Uhlig, *Encyclopaedia Aethiopica*, 1:155–58.

17. For additional reading on the 'Afar and Gurage nations, see Didier Morin, "'Afar," in Uhlig, *Encyclopaedia Aethiopica*, 1:115–16; Gideon Goldenberg, "Gurage," in Uhlig, *Encyclopaedia Aethiopica*, 2:924–28.

18. Ahmed Ben Abd el-Qader Chihab ed-Din (Arab Faqih), *Futuh al-Habasha—Histoire de la Conquête de L'Abyssinie*, trans. and ed. R. Basset (Paris: E. Leroux, 1897); Haggai Erlich, *The Cross and the River: Ethiopia, Egypt and the Nile* (Colorado: Lynne

Rienner Publishers, 2002), 48–50; Haggai Erlich, *Ethiopia and the Middle East* (Colorado: Lynne Rienner Publishers, 1994), 29–33; J. Spencer Trimingham, *Islam in Ethiopia*, 2nd ed. (London: Frank Cass, 1965), 76–98.

19. Franz-Christoph Muth, "Nūr b. Muǧāhid," in Uhlig, *Encyclopaedia Aethiopica*, 3:1209–10.

20. Wagner, "Harär History till 1875."

21. Ibid. For additional information on the wall built by Nur and its long- and short-term implications, see Abdullahi Mohammed Ahmed, "A Survey of the Harar Djugel (Wall) and Its Gates," in *Proceedings of the First National Conference of Ethiopia Studies: Addis Ababa, April 11–12, 1990*, ed. Richard Pankhurst, Ahmed Zekaria, and Teddese Beyene (Addis Ababa: Institute of Ethiopian Studies, 1990), 321–34; Richard Pankhurst, *History of Ethiopian Towns*, vol. 2, *From the Mid-Nineteenth Century to 1935* (Wiesbaden: F. Steiner Verlag, 1985), 178–273. For the meanings of the wall for the Harari identities, see Sidney R. Waldron, "Within the Wall and Beyond: Harari Ethnic Identity and Its Future" (paper presented at the Harari Studies Conference, Addis Ababa University, Jun. 1975).

22. Ahmed Zekaria, "Harari Coins: A Preliminary Survey," *Journal of Ethiopian Studies* 24 (Nov. 1991): 23–46.

23. Richard Pankhurst, "Harar in the Old Days," in "Special Issue on Harar," ed. Sylvia E. Pankhurst, *Ethiopia Observer* 2, no. 2 (1958): 45.

24. Ewald Wagner, "'Alī b. Dā'ūd Dynasty," in Uhlig, *Encyclopaedia Aethiopica*, 1:199–200.

25. Abir, *Ethiopia*, 20; Caulk, "Harar Town," 376–79.

26. See Yusuf Ahmed, "An Inquiry into Some Aspects of the Economy of Harar and the Records of the Household Economy of the Amirs of Harar (1825–1875)," *Ethnological Society Bulletin* 1, no. 1–10, and 2, no. 1 (1954–1961), ed. Alula Pankhurst (Addis Ababa: Department of Sociology and Social Administration, Addis Ababa Univ., 1961), 375–419.

27. Wagner, "'Alī b. Dā'ūd."

28. Wagner, "Harär History," 1015–19; for more details, see Abdurahman Garad, *Harar: Wirtschaftsgeschichte eines Emirats im Horn von Afrika (1825–75)* (Frankfurt am Main: Peter Lang, 1990).

29. Mohammed Moktar, "Notes sur le Pays de Harrar," *Bulletin de la Société Khédiviale de Géographie* 1, no. 4 (1876): 391. For further details about Muhammad Muhtār, see Jonathan Miran, "Muḥammad Muḫtār," in Uhlig, *Encyclopaedia Aethiopica*, 3:1054.

30. Ewald Wagner, "Muḥammad b. 'Alī b. 'Abdaššakūr," in Uhlig, *Encyclopaedia Aethiopica*, 3:1049–51.

31. Mohammed Hassen, "Baarentuu," in Uhlig, *Encyclopaedia Aethiopica*, 1:426–27; Marco Bassi, "Boorana," in Uhlig, *Encyclopaedia Aethiopica*, 1:605–7.

32. Gebissa, *Leaf of Allah*, 33–34; Ulrich Braukämper, "Oromo Country of Origin: A Reconsideration of Hypotheses," in *Proceedings of the Sixth International Conference of*

Ethiopian Studies, Tel-Aviv, 14–17 April 1980, ed. Gideon Goldenberg (Cape Town: A. A. Balkema, 1986), 25–40.

33. Paul T. W. Baxter, "Gadaa," in Uhlig, *Encyclopaedia Aethiopica*, 2:633–38; Asmarom Legesse, *Gada: Three Approaches to the Study of an African Society* (New York: Free Press, 1973).

34. About the meaning of *gosa* and *bokku*, see Paul T. W. Baxter, "Gosa," in Uhlig, *Encyclopaedia Aethiopica*, 2:857–58; Andrea Nicolas, "Bokkuu," in Uhlig, *Encyclopaedia Aethiopica*, 1:602.

35. Thomas Zitelmann, "Qottuu," in Uhlig, *Encyclopaedia Aethiopica*, 4:301–3.

36. Muhammad Hassan, "The Relation between Harar and the Surrounding Oromo 1880–1887" (BA thesis, Haile Selassie I University, 1973), 6–22.

37. Caulk, "Harar Town," 373; Gebissa, *Leaf of Allah*, 34.

38. Giorgio Banti, "Somali Language," in Uhlig, *Encyclopaedia Aethiopica*, 4:693–96. On the origins of the Somalis, their homeland, division into tribes, and political institutions, see Ioan M. Lewis, *A Modern History of Somalia: Nation and State in the Horn of Africa* (London: Longmans, 1988), 4–5.

39. For additional information, see Thomas P. Ofcansky, "Dir ethnography," in Uhlig, *Encyclopaedia Aethiopica*, 2:166–67; Didier Morin, "Gadabuursi," in Uhlig, *Encyclopaedia Aethiopica*, 2:639–41; Didier Morin, "'Issa," in Uhlig, *Encyclopaedia Aethiopica*, 3:218–19. For older studies on the Somali 'Issa, see Enrico Cerulli, *Le Popolazioni della Somalia nella Tradizioni Storica Locl* (Rome: Dott. Giovanni Bardi, tipografo della R. Accademia nazionale dei Lincei, 1926); Philipp Paulitschke, *Ethnographie Nordost-Afrikas: Die Materielle Kultur der Danakil, Galla und Somal* (Berlin: Dietrich Reimer, 1893).

40. Lewis, *Modern History of Somalia*, 6–12.

41. Said S. Samatar, "Ogaden," in Uhlig, *Encyclopaedia Aethiopica*, 4:8–9.

42. Gebissa, *Leaf of Allah*, 36; Ioan M. Lewis, *A Pastoral Democracy* (London: Oxford Univ. Press, 1961), 7–14; Emilio Scarin, *Hararino: Ricerche e Studi Geografici* (Florence: G. C. Sansoni, 1942), 33–52.

43. Gebissa, *Leaf of Allah*, 36.

44. Ibid.; Peter D. Coats, "Factors of Intermediacy in Nineteenth Century Africa: The Case of the Issa of the Horn," in *Proceedings of the Second International Congress of Somali Studies*, ed. Thomas Labahn, 2:180–83. Hamburg: H. Buske, 1984.

45. Lewis, *Modern History of Somalia*, 15–17.

46. Ibid., 40–45.

47. Francesca Declich, "Habar Awal," in Uhlig, *Encyclopaedia Aethiopica*, 2:947–48.

2. The Egyptian Colonial Path to Harar

1. For additional information, see the following studies: Hervé Bleuchot, "Le Soudan au XXIème siecle," in *Le Soudan Contemporain*, ed. Marc Lavergne, 115–69 (Paris:

Karthala, 1989); Erlich, *Ethiopia*, 41–83; Erlich, *The Cross*, 59–79; Muhammad Sabry, *L'Empire égyptien sous Mohamed Ali et la question d'Orient (1811–1849)* (Paris: Lib. Orient, Paul Geuthner, 1930); Muhammad Sabry, *Le Soudan égyptien: 1821–1898* (Cairo: Imprimerie Nationale, 1947); A. Sammarco, *Précis de L'Histoire D'Egypte*, 4 vols. (Cairo: Imprimé par l'Imprimerie de l'Institut français d'archéologie orientale du Caire, 1933), 4:241; Heather Sharkey, *Living with Colonialism: Nationalism and Culture in the Anglo-Egyptian Sudan* (Berkeley: Univ. of California Press, 2003); Troutt Powell, *Different Shade of Colonialism*; Gabriel R. Warburg, *Historical Discord in the Nile Valley* (London: Hurst; Evanston, IL: Northwestern Univ. Press, 1992), 1–56; Warburg, *Islam, Sectarianism and Politics*, 6–12; Muhammad Ramadan, *Wad'a al-Sudan fi nitaq al-'alaqat bin Misr wa al-du'al al-Ottmaniya hata 1863* [The Position of Sudan in the Relations between Egypt and the Ottoman Provinces until 1863] (Cairo, 1955); Muhammad Fuad Shukry, *Al-Hukm al-Misri fi al-Sudan, 1820–1885* [The Egyptian Regime in Sudan, 1820–1885] (Cairo: dar al-fikr al-'arabi, 1947); Makki Shibayka, *Ta'rikh Shu'ub wadi al-nil* [The Nile Valley Peoples' History] (Beirut, 1965); Makki Shibayka, *Al-Sudan fi Qarn 1819–1919* [Sudan in 1819–1919] (Beirut: Dar al-Jil, 1991).

2. Erlich, "Ismā'īl."

3. David S. Landes, *Bankers and Pashas: International Finance and Economic Imperialism in Egypt* (Cambridge MA: Harvard Univ. Press, 1958), 150–51; Erlich, *The Cross*, 66–69.

4. Boutros Boutros-Ghali, "The Foreign Policy of Egypt (United Arab Republic)," in *Foreign Policy in a World of Change*, ed. Joseph E. Black and Kenneth W. Thompson (New York: Harper & Row, 1963), 319–48; Ghada H. Talhami, *Suakin and Massawa under Egyptian Rule, 1865–1885* (Washington, DC: Univ. Press of America), 232.

5. Jonathan Miran and Emeri van Donzel, "Nā'ib," in Uhlig, *Encyclopaedia Aethiopica*, 3:1116–18. For additional details, see Jonathan Miran, *Red Sea Citizens: Cosmopolitan Society and Cultural Change in Massawa* (Bloomington: Indiana Univ. Press, 2009), 33–65.

6. For additional information on the slave trade in the region, see Ehud R. Toledano, *The Ottoman Slave Trade and Its Suppression 1840–1890* (New Jersey: Princeton Univ. Press, 1982), 57, 219–28.

7. George Douin, *Histoire du Règne du Khédive Ismaïl*, vol. 3, part 2, *L'Empire africain (1869–1873)* (Cairo: L'Imprimerie de L'Institut Français d'Archéologie Orientale, for La Société Royale de Géographie d'Égypte, 1938), 171–72.

8. Ali Abdirahman Hersi, "Egyptian Administration in Somaliland 1874–1885" (paper presented at the International Symposium on the African Horn, 5–10 Jan. 1985, Institute of African Research and Studies, University of Cairo), 1–10.

9. Ghada H. Talhami, "Massawa under Khedive Ismaíl 1865–1879," in *Proceedings of the Fifth International Conference of Ethiopian Studies*, 13–16 Apr. 1978, ed. Robert Hess (Chicago: Office of Publications Services, Univ. of Illinois in Chicago Circle, 1979), 481–93; Talhami, *Suakin and Massawa*, 66–69.

10. FO 78/2632: Wylde to Foreign Office, 23 Apr. 1877, Jeddah.

11. R. Beachy, "The East African Ivory Trade in the 19th Century," *Journal of African History* 8, no. 2 (1967): 269–90.

12. Sven Rubenson, *The Survival of Ethiopian Independence* (London: Heinemann Educational Books, 1976), 294.

13. Werner Munzinger (1832–1875) was the son of the Swiss president. He served from 1864 to 1870 as the French Consul in Massawa and as the deputy consul of Britain there. In 1870, he began working in the service of Khedive Isma'īl, and he was appointed as governor of Massawa in 1871. In 1873, he also annexed the district of Sanhit to Egypt, causing military clashes between Egypt and Ethiopia in 1875–76. Munzinger and his family were murdered by the Somali 'Issa tribe in 1875. For further details, see C. Detlef G. Müller and Wolbert G. C. Smidt, "Munzinger, Werner," in Uhlig, *Encyclopaedia Aethiopica*, 3:1070–73.

14. Augustus B. Wylde, *Modern Abyssinia* (London: Methuen, 1901), 23.

15. Zewde Gabre-Sellassie, *Yohannes IV of Ethiopia* (Oxford: Clarendon Press, 1975), 63; FO 78/2632: Wylde to Foreign Office, 23 Apr. 1877, Jeddah; Bairu Tafla, "Yohannəs IV," in Uhlig, *Encyclopaedia Aethiopica*, 5:73–80.

16. Munzinger's ties with Kassai Mercha (known later as the Emperor Yohannes IV) are worthy of a separate discussion. Kassai Mercha claimed to be the Caesar of Dejazmach after the suicide of Emperor Tewodros in 1867, thus taking advantage of the internal Ethiopian rivalry in the Hamasen region in order to promote the possibility of an Egyptian invasion of Ethiopia. See William Dey McEntry, *Moslem Egypt and Christian Abyssinia* (1880; repr., New York: Atkin & Prout, 1969), 122; Douin, *Histoire du Régne*, 356–57; Talhami, *Suakin and Massawa*, 17; Wolbert Smidt, "Hamasen," in Uhlig, *Encyclopaedia Aethiopica*, 2:987–90; Wolbert Smidt, "Təgray," in Uhlig, *Encyclopaedia Aethiopica*, 4:888–95.

17. For further details, see Rubenson, *Survival of Ethiopian Independence*, 200.

18. Erlich, *The Cross*, 69–70; Gabre-Sellassie, *Yohannes IV*, 42; Stephan A. Longrigg, *A Short History of Eritrea* (New York: Oxford Univ. Press, 1945; repr. Westport, CT: Greenwood Press, 1974), 102 (page reference is to the Greenwood edition); Talhami, *Suakin and Massawa*, 203; Rubenson, *Survival of Ethiopian Independence*, 278; Haggai Erlich and Wolbert Smidt, "Märäb Malləš," in Uhlig, *Encyclopaedia Aethiopica*, 3:773–75.

19. Czeslaw Jesman, "Egyptian Invasion of Ethiopia," *African Affairs: Journal of the Royal African Society* 58, no. 230 (Jan. 1959): 75–82; Talhami, *Suakin and Massawa*, 203.

20. Gabre-Sellassie, *Yohannes IV*, 9, 18, 46–47; Talhami, *Suakin and Massawa*, 86–87, 132.

21. FO 1/28: Tremenheer to India Office, 7 Jul. 1872, London.

22. This is the Italian trading company Compagnia di Navigazione Rubattino. Egypt regarded the Italian conquest of Asaab as a blow to its sovereignty. In 1870, an Egyptian maritime force headed by Jamal Bey gained control over the city and removed the Italian

flag that was flying there. One can learn about the importance of the "Asaab incident" to Egyptian aspirations to strengthen the status of the Egyptian coastal cities from various correspondences; see FO 78/3187, FO 78/3188–3189: Vivian to Foreign Office, 22 Sep. 1873, Cairo. For additional information on the penetration of the superpowers to the Somali coast, see Ebreab Tesfai, "The Causes and Effects of the Dogali Encounter," in *The Centenary of Dogali: Proceedings of the International Symposium, Addis Ababa-Asmara, January 24–25, 1987*, ed. Taddesse Beyne, Taddesse Tamrat, and Richard Pankhurst, 91–102 (Addis Ababa: Institute of Ethiopian Studies, Addis Ababa Univ., 1988); Lewis, *Modern History of Somalia*, 41; Talhami, *Suakin and Massawa*, 391.

23. Haggai Erlich, "The Egyptian-Ethiopian War," in Uhlig, *Encyclopaedia Aethiopica*, 2:245–46; Thomas P. Ofcansky, "Gundät," in Uhlig, *Encyclopaedia Aethiopica*, 2:921–22; Wolbert Smidt and Denis Nosnitsin, "Gura‘," in Uhlig, *Encyclopaedia Aethiopica*, 2:922–24.

24. FO 78/2503: Stanton to Derby, 13 May 1876, Cairo; FO 78/2631: Vivian to Foreign Office, 23 Jan. 1877, Cairo; Dey McEntry, *Moslem Egypt*, 394; Douin, *Histoire du Règne*, 942–55.

25. Adhana Mengste-ab, "The Occupation of Keren by the Egyptians, 4 July 1872–10 April 1885," in *Proceedings of the First International Conference of Ethiopian Studies*, ed. Richard Pankhurst, 367–81 (Addis Ababa: Institute of Ethiopian Studies, Addis Ababa Univ., 1990).

26. John P. Dunn, *Khedive Ismail's Army* (New York: Routledge, 2005), 104–10.

27. The coast of south Somalia is also known as the Benadir region.

28. Mordechai Abir, "Caravan Trade and History in the Northern Parts of East Africa," *Paideuma, Mitteilungen zur Kulturkunde* (Wiesbaden: F. Steiner, 1968), 14:113–14; Muhammad Fuad Shukry, *The Khedive Ismail and Slavery in the Sudan: A History of the Sudan from the Egyptian Conquest of 1820 to the Outbreak of the Mahdiist Rebellion of 1881* (Cairo: Renaissance d'Egypte, 1938), 296–302.

29. Lewis, *Modern History of Somalia*, 42; Talhami, *Suakin and Massawa*, 199–202; Thomas E. Marston, *Britain's Imperial Role in the Red Sea Area 1800–1878* (Hamden: Shoe String Press, 1961), 388, 430–31.

30. E. A. Stanton, ed., "Secret Letters from Khedive Ismail in Connection with an Occupation of the East African Coast," *Journal of the Royal African Society* 34 (1935): 272–73; Douin, *Histoire du Régne*, 637; Lewis, *Modern History of Somalia*, 37–38.

31. Douin, *Histoire du Régne*, 634; Lewis, *Modern History of Somalia*, 36, 41–42.

32. FO 78/3187: India Office to Foreign Office, 17 Jan. 1875, London.

33. FO 78/3188: Stanton to Foreign Office, 11–14 Nov. 1875, London.

34. FO 141/91: Derby to Stanton, 3 Dec. 1875, London.

35. Rubenson, *Survival of Ethiopian Independence*, 313.

36. Christopher Clapham, "Mənilək II," in Uhlig, *Encyclopaedia Aethiopica*, 3:922–27.

37. For additional information, see Douin, *Histoire du Règne*, 721–26; Gabre-Sellassie, *Yohannes IV*, 57–58; Rubenson, *Survival of Ethiopian Independence*, 368–77; Talhami, *Suakin and Massawa*, 150–51.

38. Mesfin Wolde-Mariam, *An Introductory Geography of Ethiopia* (Addis Ababa: Berhanena Selam H.S.I. Printing Press, 1972), 49.

39. Douin, *Histoire du Régne*, 111; Gabre-Sellassie, *Yohannes IV*, 63.

40. FO 881/3058: Stanton to Derby, 22 Nov. 1875; Hunter to Foreign Office, 25 Nov. 1875, Aden.

41. FO 78/3188: Telegram from the Governor of Bombay, 26 Nov. 1875; Dunn, *Khedive Ismail's Army*, 112; Talhami, *Suakin and Massawa*, 150.

42. FO 78/3189: Drafts (Mar. 1877 and Jun. 1877), Agreement between the British and the Egyptian Governments respecting the Jurisdiction of his Highness the Khedive over the Somali Coast.

3. The Conquest of Harar

1. Jonathan Miran, "Muḥammad Ra'ūf," in Uhlig, *Encyclopaedia Aethiopica*, 3:1056–57.

2. Hassan, "Relation between Harar and Oromo," 20. This local version also appeared in the diary of Charles Gordon, governor of Turco-Egyptian Sudan during 1877–80. For further details, see George B. Hill, *Colonel Gordon in Central Africa 1874–1879* (England, 1881; repr. New York: Macmillan, 1969), 312–13.

3. Ethiopian scholar Mohammed Hassen collected testimonies in 1972–73 from a number of Harari elders: Haj Ahmed Mohamed, Mume Bashir, and Sheikh Yassin Mohamed. These are his sources on this topic. See Hassan, "Relation between Harar and Oromo", 19–20. Another scholar who discussed this tradition in Harar was the Ethiopian Mahdi Gadid. In 1979, he met with several Harari elders and quoted them in his research. According to them, the Egyptians were invited to the city to save it from the tyranny of Emir 'Abdashakur and his allies, the Oromo. See Mahdi A. Gadid, "Feudalism in the Emirate of Harar up to 1887" (BA thesis, Addis Ababa University, Jul. 1979), 48.

4. See, for example, Richard A. Caulk, "The Occupation of Harar, January 1887," *Journal of Ethiopian Studies* 9 (Jul. 1971), 2; Gabriel Ferrand, "Notes sur la situation politique, commerciale et religieuse du pachalik de Harar et de ses dépendences," *Bulletin de la Société de Géographie de l'Est*, part 1, vol. 8 (Nancy, 1886): 4–6; Gabre-Sellassie, *Yohannes IV*, 289; Sidney R. Waldron, "Social Organization and Social Control in the Walled City of Harar, Ethiopia" (PhD diss., Columbia University, 1974), ii, v; Gadid, "Feudalism," 49.

5. Marc Fontrier, "Abū Bakr Ibrāhīm Šaḥim," in Uhlig, *Encyclopaedia Aethiopica*, 1:52. For a comprehensive political biography of Abu Bakr Ibrahim, see Marc Fontrier, *Abou-Baker Ibrahim: Pacha de Zeyla—Marchand d'Esclaves* (Paris: L'Harmattan, 2003).

6. Fontrier, *Abou-Baker Ibrahim*, 87–113.

7. Ibid., 135–38.

8. Toledano, *Ottoman Slave Trade*, 57–58. For correspondence of Abu Bakr with outside elements, see the following examples in Sven Rubenson, ed., *Acta Ethiopica*, vol. 3, *Internal Rivalries and Foreign Threats 1869–1879* (Addis Ababa: Addis Ababa Univ. Press, 2000): Abu-Bakr Ibrahim to Minilik, Mar. 1871, 82–83; Abu-Bakr Ibrahim to C. W. Tremenheere, 28 Aug. 1871, 97; Abu-Bakr Ibrahim to Isma'īl Ibrahim, 27 Nov. 1872, 130–31; Abu-Bakr Ibrahim to Khairi, 27 Aug. 1876, 255.

9. FO 78/3187: India Office to Foreign Office, 17 Jan. 1874.

10. FO 78/3188: Schinder to the Government of Bombay, 23 Dec. 1874, Aden; FO 78/3187: Stanton to Derby, 26 Dec. 1874, Alexandria.

11. Dunn, *Khedive Ismail's Army*, 88–93; Peter M. Holt and M. W. Daly, eds., *A History of the Sudan*, 4th ed. (London: Weidenfeld & Nicolson, 1988), 76–77).

12. Fontrier, *Abou-Baker Ibrahim*, 63–105. Fontrier's research emphasized the relations between France and Abu Bakr. He portrayed the governor of Zeila as a gifted politician who was able to maneuver between the European powers and maintain, to a degree, his autonomy.

13. Douin, *Histoire du Règne*, 602–3.

14. Jonathan Miran, *L'Occupation Egyptienne de Harar (1875–1885)*, Mémoire de Diplôme de Recherche et d'Etudes Appliquées Est-Africaines et Malagaches (Paris: Institut National des Langues et Civilisations Orientales, 1993), 40–41.

15. 'Amr qarim ila Ra'uf basha muḥāfeẓ Zayla, 25 Rajab 1292, wathiqa raqam 204, daftar 2, awamir Arabi 101 [A Decree to Ra'uf Pasha, the Governor of Zayla, 27 Aug. 1875, paper no. 204, notebook no. 2, commendes in Arabic 101], in 'Abdallah al-Bayumi, *Al-Ta'arikh al-'askari al-Misri fi al-'asr al-hadith: al-kitab al-thalit: al-ta'arikh al-'askari li-alǧayš al-Misri fi 'asr hulaffa' Muhammad 'Alī* [The Egyptian Military History in the Modern Period: The Third Book: The Military History of the Egyptian Army at the Time of Muhammad 'Alī's Successors] (Cairo, 1993), 103.

16. Shawqī 'Atā'Allāh al-Jamal, *Siyasat Misr fi al-bahr al-achmar fi al-nisf al-thani min al-qarn al-tsi' 'ashar* [The Egyptian Policy in the Red Sea in the Second Part of the Nineteenth Century] (Cairo: Wizarat al-Takafa, al-Maktaba al-'Arabia, 1974), 346.

17. Miran, "Muḥammad Ra'ūf."

18. Gustav Bayerle, *Pashas, Begs and Effendis: A Historical Dictionary of Titles and Terms in the Ottoman Empire* (Istanbul: The Isis Press, 1997), 17.

19. Douin, *Histoire du Règne*, vol. 3, part 3, *Fascicules A and B: L'Empire Africain (1874–1876)* (Rome: Istituto poligrafico dello stato and L'Imprimerie de L'Institut Français d'Archéologie Orientale, for La Société Royale de Géographie d'Égypte, 1941), 695; Philipp Paulitschke, "Le Harar sous l'administration égyptienne (1875–1885)," *Bulletin de la Société Khédiviale de Géographie du Caire* 10, no. 2 (Mar. 1887): 575–76; Philipp Paulitschke, *Harar: Forschungsreise nach den Somal und Gallaländern Ostafrikas* (Leipzig:

F. A. Brockhaus, 1888), 229–30; Muhammad Sabry, *L'Empire égyptien sous Ismail et l'íngérence anglo-française (1863–1879)* (Paris: Paul Geuthner, 1933), 418–19.

20. The British received a comprehensive report from the Egyptians regarding the Harar campaign. See FO 881/3058: Nubar to Stanton, 8 Nov. 1875, Cairo.

21. FO 881/3058: Stanton to Derby, 22 Nov. 1875.

22. Alfred Bardey, "Notes sur le Harar," *Bulletin de Géographie Historique et Descriptive* 12 (1897), 150; Richard Burton, *First Footsteps in East Africa, or an Exploration of Harar*, vols. 1 and 2 (London, 1856; repr., New York: Dover Publications, 1987), 1:31–33 (page reference is to the Dover edition).

23. Muhammad Ra'uf basha ila maharadar Khedevi, al-wathiqa 'arabia raqam 2/3/3 ward 'Abdeen fi 18 Ramadan 1292 [Muhammad Ra'uf Pasha to the Khedive, paper in Arabic no. 2/3/3 'Abdeen, 19 Oct. 1875] in Shawqī 'Atā'Allāh al-Jamal, *Al-Wathā'iq al-ta'rikhiyya li-siyāsat Misr fī al-bahr al-achmar, 1863–1879* [Historical Documents of the Egyptian Policy in the Red Sea, 1863–1879] (Cairo: Matba'at lajnat al-bayan al-'arabi, 1959), 271.

24. al-Jamal, *Al-Wathā'iq al-ta'rikhiyya*, 272.

25. Douin, *Histoire du Règne*, 607.

26. Moktar, "Notes sur le Pays de Harrar," 360.

27. al-Jamal, *Al-Wathā'iq al-ta'rikhiyya*, 271.

28. Paulitschke, "Le Harar sous l'administration égyptienne," 576.

29. Moḥammad 'Alī 'Abd al-Shakūr to Muḥammad Ra'uf, 6 Oct. 1876, in Rubenson, *Acta Ethiopica*, 188–89.

30. Douin, *Histoire du Règne*, 612; Salvatore Tedeschi, "L'emirato di Harar secondo un documento inedito," *IV Congresso Internazionale di Studi Etiopici* (Rome: Accademia Nazionale dei Lincei, 1974), 497–98.

31. There is a problem validating the third letter, since it, as well as the preceding letter, bears the same date, 6 October 1875. The content of the third letter deals with occurrences in Harar regarding the surrender to the Egyptians. This makes no sense. Rubenson suggests a solution of his own to the problem. The seventh of Ramadan 1292 fell on 7 October according to the Gregorian calendar. This congruency is the source of the problem. Although 7 October was on a Thursday, the third letter, according to his claim, was written in Harar on Wednesday evening, 7 October. Apparently, it only reached Ra'uf Pasha the next day, on 7 October. See Rubenson, *Acta Ethiopica*, 189.

32. Abdaššakūr to Mohammad Raúf, 6 Oct. 1876, in Rubenson, *Acta Ethiopica*, 190.

33. Muhammad Ra'uf basha ila maharadar Khedevi, in al-Jamal, *Al-Wathā'iq al-ta'rikhiyya*, 273.

34. Rubenson, *Acta Ethiopica*, 190.

35. Muhammad Ra'uf basha ila maharadar Khedevi, in al-Jamal, *Al-Wathā'iq al-ta'rikhiyya*, 273.

36. al-Jamal, *Al-Wathā'iq al-ta'rikhiyya*, 273–74.

37. Miran, *L'Occupation Egyptienne*, 43–44.

38. For further details, see Sylvia E. Pankhurst, "Harar under Egyptian Rule," in "Special Issue on Harar," ed. Sylvia E. Pankhurst, *Ethiopia Observer* 2, no. 2 (1958): 56; Bardey, "Notes sur le Harar," 155; James Frank Linsly, *The Unknown Horn of Africa: an exploration from Berbera to the Leopard River* (London: George Philip, 1888), 333.

39. Dunn, *Khedive Ismail's Army*, 108.

40. al-Jamal, *Al-Wathā'iq al-ta'rikhiyya*, 273.

41. Hassan, "Relation between Harar and Oromo," 19–20.

42. MS no. 300: Manuscript in Arabic from Harar (Addis Ababa: Addis Ababa University Institute of Ethiopian Studies).

43. Moktar, "Notes sur le Pays de Harrar," 388.

44. Ibid., 386–87. For further details about Muhammad Muhtār, see Jonathan Miran, "Mohammed Mokhtar, officer égyptien et explorateur," in *Les orientalistes sont des aventuriers: guirlande offerte à Joseph Tubiana par ses élèves et ses amis*, ed. Alain Rouaud, 130–35 (Paris: Sépia, 1999); Miran, "Muḥammad Muḫtār."

45. Moktar, "Notes sur le Pays de Harrar," 388.

46. Caulk, "Harar Town," 371, 383–84; Lewis, *Modern History of Somalia*, 43; Paulitschke, *Harar: Forschungsreise nach den Somal*, 576; Sabry, *L'Empire égyptien sous Ismail*, 419.

47. al-Jamal, *Al-Wathā'iq al-ta'rikhiyya*, 273.

48. Ibid. We have no reports from the residents of Harar or the Oromo regarding the Egyptian entrance into the city on 12 October 1875.

49. Ibid.

50. Ibid., 274.

51. Moktar, "Notes sur le Pays de Harrar," 377–79.

52. Douin, *Histoire du Règne*, 607; IES 1771: Letter from Major F. M. Hunter, Officiating Political Resident, Aden, to the Chief Secretary to Government Political Department, Bombay, No. 219–1414, dated Aden Residency, 30 Jun. 1884, 2–3.

53. Moktar, "Notes sur le Pays de Harrar," 377–79.

54. In his 1973 thesis at Haile Sellasie I University, Hassen presented the collection of documents of ʿAbd Al-Rahman Abugan, who had personally presented these stories and documents to Hassen between 1971 and 1972. This informant was connected, on his mother's side, to the family of the emirs of Harar. His father was a senior official in the city at the time of the Ethiopian rule of Ras Makonnen in Harar (1887–1906). See Hassan, "Relation between Harar and Oromo," 20.

55. *Al-Waqa'iʿa al-Misriya* [Egyptian Official Gazette] 631 (16 Shaʿaban 1292; 1875), in al-Bayumi, *Al-Ta'arikh al-ʿaskari*, 105.

56. Miran, *L'Occupation Egyptienne*, 57.

57. al-Jamal, *Al-Wathā'iq al-ta'rikhiyya*, 275.

58. Rubenson, *Acta Ethiopica*, 188–91.

59. al-Jamal, *Al-Wathā'iq al-ta'rikhiyya*, 274–75.

60. Hassan, "Relation between Harar and Oromo," 21; Tedeschi, "L'emirato di Harar," 498.

61. Emile Foucher, "Harar au temps d'Artur Rimbaud, 1880–1891," in *Proceedings of the 8th International Conference of Ethiopian Studies*, ed. Taddese Beyene (Addis Ababa: Univ. of Addis Ababa Press, 1988), 1:367.

62. Bardey, "Notes sur le Harar," 167.

63. Hassan, "Relation between Harar and Oromo," 21.

64. Hill, *Colonel Gordon*, 313; Paulitschke, "Le Harar sous l'administration égyptienne," 579.

65. Ila hikimdar Harar wa-mulhaqātihā: firman li ahali Harar ba'ad futuh'ha, daftar 10, awamir 'arabi raqam 1 fi 12 Šhawal 1292 [To *hikimdar* Harar and Its Dependencies: An Order to the People of Harar after the City's Conquest, notebook no. 10, decrees in Arabic no. 1, 11 Nov. 1875], in al-Jamal, *Al-Wathā'iq al-ta'rikhiyya*, 283.

66. al-Jamal, *Al-Wathā'iq al-ta'rikhiyya*, 274.

67. Ibid.

68. Ibid.

69. Ibid., 274–75.

70. Ibid., 275.

71. 'Amr ila Muhammad b. 'Alī b. 'Abdashakur, daftar 10, awamir Arabi 21 raqam 54 fi 12 Šhawal 1292 [Decree to Muhammad b. 'Alī b. 'Abdashakur, notebook no. 10, decrees in Arabic 21 no. 54, 11 Nov. 1875], in al-Jamal, *Al-Wathā'iq al-ta'rikhiyya*, 279.

72. Ibid., 280.

73. Ibid., 288.

74. 'Amr ila hikimdar Harar wa-mulhaqātihā, daftar 10, awamir 'arabi 23 no. 1 fi 12 Šhawal 1292 [Decree to *hikimdar* Harar and Its Dependencies, decrees in Arabic 23 no. 1, 11 Nov. 1875], in al-Jamal, *Al-Wathā'iq al-ta'rikhiyya*, 284.

75. al-Jamal, *Al-Wathā'iq al-ta'rikhiyya*, 279. This was al-Jamal's explanation for the emir's "death," but al-Jamal did not note the circumstances.

76. al-Bayumi, *Al-Ta'arikh al-'askari*, 108.

77. al-Jamal, *Siyasat Misr*, 214.

78. Min muhafazat Zayla, daftar 17, muaya 'arabi—ward al-ifadat raqam 323 min jihat al-aqalim wa al-muhafazat fi 19 rabi'a al-awal 1293 [From the Administration's Province of Zeila, notebook 17 simultaneity in Arabic to all the provinces, 13 Apr. 1876], in al-Jamal, *Al-Wathā'iq al-ta'rikhiyya*, 307.

79. al-Jamal, *Siyasat Misr*, 214.

80. 'Amr ila hikimdar Harar wa-mulhaqātiha, daftar 105, mukatba raqam 6 fi 16 Rajab 1293 [Decree to *hikimdar* Harar and Its Dependencies, notebook 105, correspondence no. 6, 8 Aug. 1876], in al-Jamal, *Al-Wathā'iq al-ta'rikhiyya*, 314.

81. Min Muhammad Ra'uf basha ila maharadar Hadiva, al-wathiqa al-'arabia raqam 2/3/3 warad 'Abdeen, fi 18 Ramadan 1292 [From Muhammad Ra'uf Pasha to the Khedive,

paper in Arabic no. 2/3/3, posted to 'Abdeen palace, 18 Oct. 1875], in al-Jamal, *Al-Wathā'iq al-ta'rikhiyya*, 276.

82. 'Amr ila hikimdar Harar wa-mulhaqātihā, daftar 10, awamir 'arabi 23 no. 1 fi 12 Šhawal 1292 [Decree to *hikimdariya* Harar and Its Dependencies, decrees in Arabic 23 no. 1, 11 Nov. 1875], in al-Jamal, *Al-Wathā'iq al-ta'rikhiyya*, 284.

83. al-Jamal, *Siyasat Misr*, 212.

84. al-Jamal, *Al-Wathā'iq al-ta'rikhiyya*, 276.

85. Douin, *Histoire du Règne*, 620–21. About the *Mecīdiye*, see Bayerle, *Pashas, Begs and Effendis*, 105.

86. Douin, *Histoire du Règne*, 620–21.

87. 'Amr ila hikimdar Harar wa-mulhaqātihā, daftar 10, awamir 'arabi 23 no. 1 fi 12 Šhawal 1292 [Decree to *hikimdariya* Harar and Its Dependencies, decrees in Arabic 23 no. 1, 11 Nov. 1875], in al-Jamal, *Al-Wathā'iq al-ta'rikhiyya*, 284.

88. Ibid., 287.

89. 'Amr ila hikimdariyat Harar wa-mulhaqātihā, daftar 10, awamir 'arabi 23 no. 1 fi 12 Šhawal 1292 [Decree to *hikimdariyat* Harar and Its Dependencies, decrees in Arabic 23 no. 1, 11 Nov. 1875], in al-Jamal, *Al-Wathā'iq al-ta'rikhiyya*, 285.

90. Talhami, *Suakin and Massawa*, 67–96.

91. 'Amr ila hikimdar Harar wa-mulhaqātihā, daftar 10, awamir 'arabi 23 no. 1 fi 12 Šhawal 1292 [Decree to *hikimdariya* Harar and Its Dependencies, decrees in Arabic 23 no. 1, 11 Nov. 1875], in al-Jamal, *Al-Wathā'iq al-ta'rikhiyya*, 286.

92. Correspondence Respecting Egyptian Proceedings on the Somali Coast, British Library, BP 24/21 (1): Cookson to the Earl of Derby, 11 Jul. 1876, Alexandria, 185–88, Correspondence Respecting Egyptian Proceedings on the Somali Coast, British Library, London.

93. BP 24/21 (1): Hunter to Salisbury, 13–19 Jan. 1876, Aden, 165–68, Correspondence Respecting Egyptian Proceedings on the Somali Coast, 1870–1877 (printed for the use of the Foreign Office, Apr. 1878), British Library, London.

94. BP 24/21 (1): Schneider to Salisbury, 24 Feb.–1 Mar. 1876, Aden, 178–83. Correspondence Respecting Egyptian Proceedings on the Somali Coast, British Library, London.

4. Creating "Egyptian" Harar

1. 'Amr ila hikimdar Harar wa-mulhaqātihā, daftar raqam 10, awamir 'arabi 26 raqam 2 no. 1 fi 12 Šhawal 1292 [Decree to *hikimdar* Harar and Its Dependencies, notebook 10, decrees in Arabic 26 no. 2, 11 Nov. 1875], in al-Jamal, *Al-Wathā'iq al-ta'rikhiyya*, 281.

2. Ibid.

3. 'Amr ila hikimdar Harar wa-mulhaqātihā, daftar 10, awamir 'arabi 23 no. 1 fi 12 Šhawal 1292 [Decree to *hikimdariya* Harar and Its Dependencies, decrees in Arabic 23 no. 1, 11 Nov. 1875], in al-Jamal, *Al-Wathā'iq al-ta'rikhiyya*, 286. Regarding the importance

of the coal mines on the Shewa border and the Egyptian economic considerations, see also Douin, *Histoire du Règne*, 625–26.

4. Jlal Yahya, *Misr al-ifriqiya wa al-itma'a al—isti'mariya fi al-Qarn al-Tasi''Ashar* [African Egypt and the Colonial Aspirations in the Nineteenth Century] (Cairo, 1967), 167–68.

5. Muhammad Ra'uf basha ila maharadar Khedevi, in al-Jamal, *Al-Wathā'iq al-ta'rikhiyya*, 275.

6. 'Amr ila hikimdar Harar wa-mulhaqātihā, daftar 10, awamir 'arabi 23 no. 1 fi 12 Šhawal 1292 [Decree to *hikimdariya* Harar and Its Dependencies, decrees in Arabic 23 no. 1, 11 Nov. 1875], in al-Jamal, *Al-Wathā'iq al-ta'rikhiyya*, 284.

7. al-Jamal, *Al-Wathā'iq al-ta'rikhiyya*, 287.

8. Bayerle, *Pashas, Begs and Effendis*, 91.

9. al-Jamal, *Al-Wathā'iq al-ta'rikhiyya*, 287.

10. El Shakry, *Great Social Laboratory*, 23–25.

11. Ibid., 25–26.

12. al-Jamal, *Al-Wathā'iq al-ta'rikhiyya*, 288.

13. Jeffrey Weeks, "Foucault for Historians," *History Workshop Journal* 14, no. 1 (Oct. 1982): 106–19.

14. For a comparative examination, see Paul A. Ericson and Lian D. Murphy, *A History of Anthropological Theory* (Toronto: Univ. of Toronto Press, 2008), 130–34; Bernard S. Cohen, *Colonialism and Its Forms of Knowledge: The British in India* (Princeton: Princeton Univ. Press, 1996), 1–15. For a comparative perspective on the late-nineteenth-century Ottoman colonial scientific projects, see Mehmet Hacisalihoglu, "Border, Maps and Censuses: The Politicization of Geography and Statistics in the Multi-Ethnic Ottoman Empire," in *Comparing Empires: Encounters and Transfers in the Long Nineteenth Century*, ed. Jörn Leonhard and Ulrike von Hirschhausen (Göttingen: Vandenhoeck & Ruprecht, 2011), 171–210.

15. William C. Harris, *Highlands of Ethiopia*, 3 vols. (London: Longman Brown, 1844), map in vol. 1; Richard Pankhurst, "Harris, William Cornwallis," in Uhlig, *Encyclopaedia Aethiopica*, 2:1036–37. Harris was a British member of the mission that went on a journey to Shewa in Ethiopia, but it is not clear whether that mission visited Harar. It seems that the first sketch of Harar and its environs is found in his book.

16. Burton, *First Footsteps*, 1; G. J. Abbink, "Burton, Richard Francis," in Uhlig, *Encyclopaedia Aethiopica*, 1:649–50.

17. Burton's scientific instruments were a pocket compass, a watch, and a thermometer. See Burton, *First Footsteps*, 209–14.

18. El Shakry, *Great Social Laboratory*, 25–30.

19. Mustafa Amer, "Some Unpublished Egyptian Maps of Harär," *Bulletin de la Société Royale de Géographie d'Egypte* 19 (1937): 289–90. Amer's article is a paean to

Egyptian nationalism and its agents in Harar, as well as to the Egyptian royal house and its "civilizing mission" in Africa in the second half of the nineteenth century. The article should be examined in the historical context in which it was written: as part of the scientific project advanced by the Egyptian royal house in the 1930s. Nonetheless, the facts presented are important, and according to this, the Europeans ignored the Egyptian scientific attainments (as well as other achievements) in Harar and later appropriated them for themselves.

20. Wolbert Smidt, "Cartography from the 18th Century Onward," in Uhlig, *Encyclopaedia Aethiopica*, 1:688–90.

21. Amer, "Some Unpublished Egyptian Maps," 291; Federico Bonola Bey, *L'Égypte et la Géographie* (Cairo: Imprimerie Nationale, 1889).

22. Dor Bey, "Werner Munzinger Pacha," *Bulletin de la Société Khédiviale de Géographie du Caire*, vol. 1 (1876), no. 1: 124–27; no. 8: 38; nos. 9–10: 43–76.

23. Bonola Bey, *L'Égypte et la Géographie*, 74.

24. *Bulletin de l'Etat-Major Général de l'Armée Egyptienne* 1, no. 1 (Cairo, 1876): 29–35.

25. *Bulletin de la Société Khédiviale de Géographie du Caire* 2, no. 7 (Cairo, 1881): 349.

26. Sabry, *L'Empire égyptien sous Ismail*, 397–98.

27. *Bulletin de la Société Khédiviale de Géographie du Caire* 1, no. 8 (Cairo, 1881): 29–42; *Bulletin de la Société Khédiviale de Géographie du Caire* 10 (Cairo, 1887); Bonola Bey, *L'Egypte et la Géographie*, 72.

28. Min arqan harb mamoriyat Harar, muhafaza 3 'Abdeen no. 4, fi 3 Muharram 1293 [From Harar's Headquarters, 'Abdeen Palace no. 4, 30 Jan. 1876], in al-Jamal, *Al-Wathā'iq al-ta'rikhiyya*, 302.

29. *Bulletin de l'Etat-Major Général de l'Armée Egyptienne* 1, no. 5 (Cairo, 1877): 385–400; no. 6: 462–79. Miran's work includes photos of the maps mentioned here. See Miran, *L'Occupation Egyptienne*, Annexes A: Annexes Cartographiques.

30. This map can be found today in the Royal Geographic Society in London. It was taken from the Egyptians in Harar by the British, almost certainly by 1884. The map is drawn on one sheet, without mention of scale. Its designation in the British archive is RGS/BG Djibouti S.6.

31. Amer, "Some Unpublished Egyptian Maps," 294.

32. *Bulletin de la Société Khédiviale de Géographie du Caire* 1, no. 4 (Cairo, 1877). This map was also taken by the British in advance of the Egyptian evacuation from Harar. It is divided into four sheets and can be found today in the Royal Geographic Society in London. Its designation is RGS/BG Ethiopia s/s 24.

33. Philipp Paulitschke drew a map nearly identical to the Egyptian map of 1876 for the British in June 1885, one month after the Egyptians left. See RGS/BG LBR Somalia

s/s 24, Royal Geographical Society Archive, London. Regarding Paulitschke, see Herman Amborn, "Paulitschke, Philipp Victor," in Uhlig, *Encyclopaedia Aethiopica*, 4:124.

34. Reiserote des Majors Heath und des Lieuts. Peyton von Harar nach Berbera [The Itinerary of Major Heath and Lieut. Peyton from Harar to Berbera], (Jun. 1885), RGS/BG LBR (Royal Geographical Society Archive, London): PP 3946 (maps room).

35. Jonathan Miran, "Muḥammad Nādī," in Uhlig, *Encyclopaedia Aethiopica*, 3:1054–55.

36. *Bulletin de la Société Khédiviale de Géographie du Caire* 2, no. 10 (Cairo, 1887): 575–91; Bonola Bey, *L'Egypte et la Géographie*, 74; Paulitschke, "Le Harar sous l'administration égyptienne."

37. Amer, "Some Unpublished Egyptian Maps," 290.

38. For further theoretic analysis regarding cartography, see J. B. Harley and David Woodward, eds., *Cartography in the Traditional Islamic and South Asian Societies*, vol. 2.1 of *The History of Cartography* (Chicago: Univ. of Chicago Press, 1992); J. B. Harley and David Woodward, eds., *Cartography in the Traditional African, American, Arctic, Australian, and Pacific Societies*, vol. 2.3 of *The History of Cartography* (Chicago: Univ. of Chicago Press, 1998); Denis Wood, *The Power of Maps* (London: Guilford Press, 1992).

39. For further details regarding Isma'īl's modern constructions and architectural vision (especially by creating Cairo as a modern French metropolis), see Myntti, *Paris along the Nile*, 9–15.

40. Muhammad Ra'uf basha ila maharadar Khedevi, in al-Jamal, *Al-Wathā'iq al-ta'rikhiyya*, 272. About Ğildessa, see Ewald Wagner, "Ğildessa," in Uhlig, *Encyclopaedia Aethiopica*, 2:797–98.

41. 'Amr ila hikimdariyat Harar wa-mulhaqātihā, daftar 10, awamir 'arabi 23 no. 1 fi 12 Šhawal 1292 [Decree to *hikimdariya* Harar and Its Dependencies, decrees in Arabic 23 no. 1, 11 Nov. 1875], in al-Jamal, *Al-Wathā'iq al-ta'rikhiyya*, 285.

42. 'Amr ila hikimdariyat Harar wa-mulhaqātih, daftar sader maiya 'arabi bidun numra safha 34 fi 12 Šhawal 1292 [Decree to *hikimdariya* Harar and Its Dependencies, notebook in Arabic without number, page 34, 11 Nov. 1875], in al-Jamal, *Al-Wathā'iq al-ta'rikhiyya*, 291.

43. Min arqan harb mamoriyat Harar, muhafaza 3 'Abdeen no. 4, fi 3 Muharram 1293 [From Harar's Headquarters, 'Abdeen Palace no. 4, 30 Jan. 1876], in al-Jamal, *Al-Wathā'iq al-ta'rikhiyya*, 293.

44. Ibid., 294.

45. 'Amr ila hikimdariyat Harar wa-mulhaqātih, daftar sader maiya 'arabi bidun numra safha 34 fi 12 Šhawal 1292 [Decree to *hikimdariya* Harar and Its Dependencies, notebook in Arabic without number, page 34, 11 Nov. 1875], ibid., 291–92.

46. Min arqan harb mamoriyat Harar, muhafaza 3 'Abdeen no. 4, fi 3 Muharram 1293 [From Harar's Headquarters, 'Abdeen Palace no. 4, 30 Jan. 1876], in al-Jamal, *Al-Wathā'iq al-ta'rikhiyya*, 295.

47. Ibid., 296

48. Ibid.

49. See map of the walls and mosques of Harar in Philippe Revault and Serge Santelli, eds., *Harar: A Muslim City of Ethiopia* (Paris: Maisonneuve and Larose, 2004), 40; Ewald Wagner, "Harär City Structure and Buildings," in Uhlig, *Encyclopaedia Aethiopica*, 2:1013–15. For the names of Harar's gates, see Kabir Abdulmuhaimin Abdunasir, "Different Names of Jugol 5 Gates," *Everything Harar*, accessed 27 Apr. 2018, http://www.everythingharar.com/e-reading/articles/225-different-names-of-jugol-5-gates.

50. Min arqan harb mamoriyat Harar, muhafaza 3 'Abdeen no. 4, fi 3 Muharram 1293 [From Harar's Headquarters, 'Abdeen Palace no. 4, 30 Jan. 1876], in al-Jamal, *Al-Wathā'iq al-ta'rikhiyya*, 296.

51. Ibid., 297.

52. Ibid.

53. Ibid., 298.

54. On the importance of khat and its role in Harar tradition, see Gebissa, *Leaf of Allah*; Hecht, "Çat in Harär."

55. Min arqan harb mamoriyat Harar, muhafaza 3 'Abdeen no. 4, fi 3 Muharram 1293 [From Harar's Headquarters, 'Abdeen Palace no. 4, 30 Jan. 1876], in al-Jamal, *Al-Wathā'iq al-ta'rikhiyya*, 299.

56. Ibid.

57. Ibid., 298.

58. Ibid.

59. Min arqan harb mamoriyat Harar, muhafaza 3 'Abdeen no. 4, fi 3 Muharram 1293 [From Harar's Headquarters, 'Abdeen Palace no. 4, 30 Jan. 1876], in al-Jamal, *Al-Wathā'iq al-ta'rikhiyya*, 298.

60. Ibid., 294.

61. Ibid. The 'Afar people (also known by the name *Danakil* in Arabic) live in the desert regions of Ethiopia, Eritrea, and Djibouti, from the Buri peninsula to Tajura gulf and the Ethiopian plateau. Some of the 'Afar people live in the areas around Massawa and Assab, neighboring the Oromo peoples. For further details, see Didier Morin, "Dankáli," in Uhlig, *Encyclopaedia Aethiopica*, 2:89–90; and Morin, "'Afar."

62. al-Jamal, *Al-Wathā'iq al-ta'rikhiyya*, 295.

63. In this context see the map RGS/BG LBR Djibouti S.6, Royal Geographical Society Archive, London.

64. al-Jamal, *Al-Wathā'iq al-ta'rikhiyya*, 294.

65. Min arqan harb mamoriyat Harar, muhafaza 3 'Abdeen no. 4, fi 3 Muharram 1293 [From Harar's Headquarters, 'Abdeen Palace no. 4, 30 Jan. 1876], in al-Jamal, *Al-Wathā'iq al-ta'rikhiyya*, 294.

66. Ibid., 294–95.

67. Ibid., 295–96.

68. Ibid., 299.

69. See Gadid, "Feudalism," for the testimony of the following informants in Harar in 1979: Ali Nafisa Kalo, Ali Maimuna Saed, and Shiekh Ahmed Abdulahi.

70. Gadid, "Feudalism," 54.

71. Min arqan harb mamoriyat Harar, muhafaza 3 'Abdeen no. 4, fi 3 Muharram 1293 [From Harar's Headquarters, 'Abdeen Palace no. 4, 30 Jan. 1876], in al-Jamal, *Al-Wathā'iq al-ta'rikhiyya*, 299–300.

72. Ibid., 300.

73. Ibid.

74. Ibid., 300–301.

75. Ibid., 301.

76. Ibid., 302.

77. El Shakry, *Great Social Laboratory*, 2–3.

78. Min arqan harb mamoriyat Harar, muhafaza 3 'Abdeen no. 4, fi 3 Muharram 1293 [From Harar's Headquarters, 'Abdeen Palace no. 4, 30 Jan. 1876], in al-Jamal, *Al-Wathā'iq al-ta'rikhiyya*, 302.

79. Ibid.

80. Muhafez al- FO, Jul. 1877, in al-Jamal, *Al-Wathā'iq al-ta'rikhiyya*, 320.

81. *Al-Waqa'i'a al-Masriya* [Egyptian Affairs] 655 (28 Rabia' al-aw'al 1293; 23 Apr. 1876), in al-Jamal, *Al-Wathā'iq al-ta'rikhiyya*, 308.

82. El Shakry, *Great Social Laboratory*, 29.

5. Activities and Institutions

1. Dunn, *Khedive Ismail's Army*, 107.

2. 'Amr ila hikimdariyat Harar wa-mulhaqātihā, daftar 10, awamir Arabi 23 no. 1 fi 12 Šhawal 1292 [Decree to *hikimdariyat* Harar and Its Dependencies, decrees in Arabic 23 no. 1, 11 Nov. 1875], in al-Jamal, *Al-Wathā'iq al-ta'rikhiyya*, 283.

3. Paulitschke, "Le Harar sous l'administration égyptienne," 586–87; Bardey, "Notes sur le Harar," 31–32.

4. Paulitschke, "Le Harar sous l'administration égyptienne," 587.

5. Hassan, "Relation between Harar and Oromo," 28.

6. Gadid, "Feudalism," 51–52.

7. Carmichael, "Religion, Language and Nationalism," 222.

8. Elisabeth-Dorothea Hecht, "The City of Harar and the Traditional Harar House," *Journal of Ethiopian Studies* 15 (1982): 57.

9. Paulitschke, "Le Harar sous l'administration égyptienne," 578; Antonio Cecchi, *Da Zeila alle Frontiere della Caffa* (Rome: E. Loescher, 1886–87), 2:619. Antonio Cecchi (1849–1896) was an Italian traveler and scientist, who stayed in Harar from 28 November

to 3 December 3. For additional reading, see Marco Lenci, "Cecchi, Antonio," in Uhlig, *Encyclopaedia Aethiopica*, 1:704.

10. Paulitschke, "Le Harar sous l'administration égyptienne," 578; Moktar, "Notes sur le Pays de Harrar," 364–65.

11. Abdullahi Mohammed Ahmed, "Survey of the Harar Djugel."

12. Hecht, "The City of Harar," 57–58.

13. Gibb, "In the City of the Saints," 2.

14. For extended reading on the *Afōča* and its significance in Adari society, see Hecht, "Afōča"; Koehn and Waldron, *Afoca*; and Yusuf Ahmed, "Aföča." For further details about the Mugād, the term for associations of young people in Harar, see Ewald Wagner, "Mugād," in Uhlig, *Encyclopaedia Aethiopica*, 3:1038.

15. Jara Haile Maryam, "An Approach to the Conservation of the Historical Town of Harar," in *Proceedings of the First National Conference of Ethiopian Studies, Addis Ababa, April 11–12, 1990*, ed. Richard Pankhurst, Ahmed Zekaria, and Teddese Beyene (Addis Ababa: Institute of Ethiopian Studies, Addis Ababa University), 403–40; IES 19/D/6: Jara Haile Maryam, "Historic Town of Harar: An Approach to Its Conservation" (master's thesis, Institute of Advanced Architectural Studies, University of New York, 1989).

16. Sylvia E. Pankhurst, "Harar under Egyptian Rule," 58–59; Revault and Santelli, eds., *Harar*, 42–44, 46–48.

17. Richard A. Caulk, "Harar in the 19th Century and the Loss of Its Independence" (paper prepared for the Interdisciplinary Seminar of the Faculties of Arts and Education, Addis Ababa University, 1967–1968), 5–6.

18. Moktar, "Notes sur le Pays de Harrar," 373.

19. Min hikimdar 'umum al-Gala wa al-Somal wa Harari ila Urta hikimdariyat Harar, daftar 245 hikimdariyat Harar—raqam 202 musalasal, fi 17 Muharam 1293 [From the Governer of General Gala, Somali and Harar to Battalion the Governancy of Harar, 12 Feb. 1876], in al-Jamal, *Al-Wathā'iq al-ta'rikhiyya*, 303.

20. Hassan, "Relation between Harar and Oromo," 29.

21. Hassen interviewed the Harari Mume Bashir in 1973, when Bashir was 107 years old. Bashir held some senior positions during the Turco-Egyptian period, during the short period of 'Abdullahi's emirate (1885–87), and after the Ethiopian rule in Harar in 1887. Hassen called Bashir "the book of the history of Harar during the nineteenth and twentieth centuries." Hassan, "Relation between Harar and Oromo," 29.

22. FO 403/82: F. M. Hunter, "Report on the Province of Harär," 30 Jun. 1884, Aden.

23. Gadid, "Feudalism," 52; Hassan, "Relation between Harar and Oromo," 30.

24. These terms are in the Oromiffa language. Their origins are in the period when the Oromo were connected to the emirate and to the monopoly policy that was forced upon them. *Oyna* was the term referring to the division of land outside the city in the days of the emirs. The Oromo chief in charge of transferring money to the emirs was called

oyna. The meaning of the term *herta* is division. See Gadid, "Feudalism," 42. For further details about the *oyna* and the *herta*, see Waldron, "Political Economy of Harari-Oromo," 36; Yusuf Ahmed, "An Inquiry into Some Aspects of the Economy of Harar," *Ethnological Society Bulletin*, 387–88.

25. Gadid, "Feudalism," 42.

26. 'Amr ila hikimdariyat Harar, daftar 10, awamir 'arabi 27 no. 4 wa-mulhaqātihā fi 12 Šhawal 1292 [Decree to *hikimdariya* of Harar and Its Dependencies, decrees in Arabic 27 no. 4, 11 Nov. 1875], in al-Jamal, *Al-Wathā'iq al-ta'rikhiyya*, 290.

27. Alula Abate, "Studien zur Jungeren Entwicklung der Kulturlandschaft im Hochland von Harar" (PhD diss., K. Friedrich-Wilhelms Universität, 1969), 76–77.

28. 'Amr ila hikimdariyat Harar wa-mulhaqātihā, daftar 10, awamir 'arabi 23 no. 1 fi 12 Šhawal 1292 [Decree to the *hikimdariya* of Harar and Its Dependencies, decrees in Arabic 23 no. 1, 11 Nov. 1875], in al-Jamal, *Al-Wathā'iq al-ta'rikhiyya*, 290.

29. al-Jamal, *Siyasat Misr*, 214.

30. Hassan, "Relation between Harar and Oromo," 28.

31. Bardey, "Notes sur le Harar," 32.

32. Edris, "Traditional Islamic Centers."

33. Min arqan harb mamoriyat Harar, muhafaza 3 'Abdeen no. 4, fi 3 Muharram 1293 [From Harar's Headquarters, 'Abdeen Palace no. 4, 30 Jan. 1876], in al-Jamal, *Al-Wathā'iq al-ta'rikhiyya*, 301.

34. Ibid.

35. Gadid, "Feudalism," 55.

36. From the testimony of Abd Al-muhaimin Abd-Nasair in Gadid, "Feudalism," 55.

37. For handed-down testimony from Mume Bashir, see Hassan, "Relation between Harar and Oromo," 31.

6. The Environs of the Harar *Hikimdariya*

1. Alain Gascon, "Gara Mulläta," in Uhlig, *Encyclopaedia Aethiopica*, 2:695–96.

2. Hassan, "Relation between Harar and Oromo," 24.

3. Waldron, "Political Economy of Harari-Oromo," 23–39.

4. Richard A. Caulk, "Harar Town"; Enrico Cerulli, "Documenti arabi per la storia dell'Etiopia," *Rendiconti della Reale Accademia dei Lincei* 6, no. 4 (1931): 37–101.

5. Caulk, "Harar Town," 379.

6. Waldron, "Political Economy of Harari-Oromo," 31.

7. Volker Stitz, "Arabic Town Records and the Economic and Population History of Harar during the 19th Century" (paper presented to a conference of the History Society of Ethiopia, Addis Ababa, Jun. 1975), 5.

8. Ibid., 9–11.

9. Trimingham, *Islam in Ethiopia*, 2nd ed. (1965), 93.

10. Waldron, "Political Economy of Harari-Oromo," 32.

11. Ulrich Braukämper, "Notes on the Islamization and the Muslim Shrines of the Harar Plateau," in *Islamic History and Culture in Southern Ethiopia—Collected Essays*, ed. Ulrich Braukämper (Hamburg: Lit Verlag Münster, 2002), 106–23.

12. Oromo traditional religion cannot be considered as uniform or monolithic. The pantheon of Oromo religion was dominated by *Waqa*, the male divinity of the sky, and *Lafa*, the female chthonic divinity. See Dirk Bustorf, "Oromo Religion," in Uhlig, *Encyclopaedia Aethiopica*, 4:64–65. For further details about the Oromo religious faiths and practices, see Lambert Bartels, *Oromo Religion* (Berlin: Dietrich Reimer, 1983), 15–16; Mohammed Hassen, *The Oromo of Ethiopia: A History* (Cambridge: Cambridge Univ. Press, 1990), 6–9; Asafa Jalata, *Oromia and Ethiopia: State Formation and Ethno-national Conflict 1868–1992* (Boulder, CO: Lynne Rienner, 1993), 25.

13. Waldron, "Political Economy of Harari-Oromo," 32.

14. Moktar, "Notes sur le Pays de Harrar," 388.

15. Hassan, "Relation between Harar and Oromo," 16–17.

16. Waldron, "Political Economy of Harari-Oromo," 32–33.

17. Burton, *First Footsteps*, 170.

18. Gadid, "Feudalism," 51; Waldron, "Political Economy of Harari Oromo," 34.

19. Gadid, "Feudalism," 35; Waldron, "Political Economy of Harari-Oromo," 34.

20. Waldron, "Political Economy of Harari-Oromo," 36.

21. Gadid, "Feudalism," 36.

22. Ibid.; Alessandro Gori, "Gärad," in Uhlig, *Encyclopaedia Aethiopica*, 2:696–97.

23. Yusuf Ahmed, "An Inquiry into Some Aspects of the Economy of Harar and the Records of the Household Economy of the Amirs of Harar," *University College of Addis Ababa Ethnographic Bulletin* No. 5 (Addis Ababa, 1961), 24.

24. Ibid., 25–26.

25. Ibid., 23.

26. Waldron, "Political Economy of Harari-Oromo," 34.

27. Ibid., 32.

28. Burton, *First Footsteps*, 155.

29. Moktar, "Notes sur le Pays de Harrar," 381.

30. Gadid, "Feudalism," 36.

31. Adam Asihabiyyë to Muhammad Raúf, 17 Oct. 1875, in Rubenson, *Acta Ethiopica*, doc. 135, 192–93.

32. al-Jamal, *Siyasat Misr*, 277.

33. Bardey, "Notes sur le Harar," 156.

34. Paulitschke, "Le Harar sous l'administration égyptienne," 577; Sabry, *L'Empire égyptien sous Ismail*, 415.

35. FO 78/3189: India Office to Foreign Office, 11 Apr. 1876, London, with enclosures: News report from Aden (7–19 Jan. and 14 Feb.—1 Mar. 1876).

36. al-Jamal, *Siyasat Misr,* 275.

37. Ibid., 285.

38. Dunn, *Khedive Ismail's Army,* 108–9.

39. Hassan, "Relation between Harar and Oromo," 22.

40. Carlo Conti-Rossini, "Testi in Lingue Harari," *Miscellanea* 2 (1921): 413–14.

41. Hassan, "Relation between Harar and Oromo," 22. Hassen brought testimony from Oromo elders in the early 1970s. He wrote down the story of the battle as he heard it from Sayed Abu Bakr and Haj Ahmad Mohammad.

42. Ibid., 23.

43. Ibid., 22.

44. Paulitschke, "Le Harar sous l'administration égyptienne," 577.

45. Bardey, "Notes sur le Harar," 156; Caulk, "Harar Town," 382–84; Paulitschke, *Harar: Forschungsreise nach den Somal,* 230; Paulitschke, "Le Harar sous l'administration égyptienne," 578; Marston, *Britain's Imperial Role,* 490.

46. *Al-Waqa'i'a al-Misriya* [Egyptian Official Gazette] 645 (25 Muharam 1293; 1876), in al-Jamal, *Al-Wathā'iq al-ta'rikhiyya,* 304.

47. FO 881/3058: News report from Aden, No. 47 of 1875 (25 Nov.–2 Dec. 1875).

48. FO 881/3058: Schneider to Gonne, 14 Dec. 1875, Aden.

49. FO 881/3058: News report from Aden (9–15 Dec. 1875).

50. FO 881/3058: Stanton to Derby, 12 Feb. 1876, Cairo: News report from Aden (26 Jan.–2 Feb. 1876).

51. FO 881/3058: News report from Aden (25 Nov.–2 Dec. 1875).

52. 'Amr ila hikimdariyat Harar wa-mulhaqātihā, daftar sader ma'iya 'arabi bidun numra safcha 34 105 fi 12 Šhawal 1292 [Decree to *hikimdariya* of Harar and Its Dependencies, decrees in Arabic without number, page 34, 11 Nov. 1875], in al-Jamal, *Al-Wathā'iq al-ta'rikhiyya,* 291–92.

53. Min arqan harb mamoriyat Harar, muhafaza 3 'Abdeen ward ma'iya no. 4, fi 3 Muharram 1293 [From Harar's Headquarters, 'Abdeen Palace no. 4, 30 Jan. 1876], in al-Jamal, *Al-Wathā'iq al-ta'rikhiyya,* 295.

54. 'Amr ila hikimdar Harar wa-mulhaqātihā, daftar 10, awamir 'arabi 33 no. 1 fi 9 Rabi'a al-awal 1293 [Decree to *hikimdar* Harar and Its Dependencies, decrees in Arabic 23 no. 1, 4 Apr. 1876], in al-Jamal, *Al-Wathā'iq al-ta'rikhiyya,* 305–6.

55. al-Jamal, *Al-Wathā'iq al-ta'rikhiyya,* 305–6.

56. Jalata, *Oromia and Ethiopia,* 24–25; Waldron, "Political Economy of Harari-Oromo," 31.

57. Hassan, "Relation between Harar and Oromo," 24.

58. Hassen relied on Oromo oral histories that described the political institutions of previous generations. He collected these versions in the framework of the paper he wrote in 1973. Hassan, "Relation between Harar and Oromo," 24–25.

59. Moktar, "Notes sur le Pays de Harrar," 382.

60. Min Muhammad Ra'uf basha hikimdar Harar wa ma yatabaha'ha, daftar 17 wared ma'iya 'arabi wathiqa 65, 2 Rabi'a al-Thani 1293 [From Muhammad Ra'uf Pasha, *hikimdar* Harar and Its Environs, notebook 17 in Arabic, document 65, 16 Apr. 1877], in al-Jamal, *Al-Wathā'iq al-ta'rikhiyya*, 310.

61. Archives des Capucins, Reg. 960, 28: Lettre manuscrite de Mgr. Taurin Cahagne au T.R.P. Provincial de Paris, 20 May 1881, Harar.

62. Paul T. W. Baxter, "Gadaa."

63. Hassen, *Oromo of Ethiopia*, 9–17.

64. Herbert S. Lewis and Dirk Bustorf, "Mooti," in Uhlig, *Encyclopaedia Aethiopica*, 3:1015–16.

65. For further details, see Jalata, *Oromia and Ethiopia*, 24–25; Paul T. W. Baxter, "The Problem of the Oromo or the Problem for the Oromo?" in *Nationalism and Self-Determination in the Horn of Africa*, ed. Ioan. M. Lewis (London: Ithaca, 1983), 129–49; Erlich, *Ethiopia*, 43–46; Gada Melbaa, *Oromia: A Brief Introduction* (Finfine, Oromia: Gada Melbaa, 1980).

66. Jalata, *Oromia and Ethiopia*, 24–25.

67. Sidney R. Waldron, *Ethnicity as Epiphenomenon: Foundation of Harar-Oromo Relations under the Empire* (New York: State Univ. of New York, Cortland, n.d.), 19–20.

68. Jalata, *Oromia and Ethiopia*, 25.

69. Min Muhammad Ra'uf basha hikimdar Harar wa ma yatabaha'ha, daftar 17 wared ma'iya 'arabi wathiqa 65, Rabi'a al-Thani 1293 [From Muhammad Ra'uf Pasha, *hikimdar* Harar and Its Environs, notebook 17 in Arabic, document 65, 16 Apr. 1877], in al-Jamal, *Al-Wathā'iq al-ta'rikhiyya*, 309.

70. Abate, "Studien zur jüngeren," 76.

71. Gadid, "Feudalism," 55.

72. FO 403/89: F. M. Hunter, "The State of Affairs at Harar," 20 Jan. 1887, Aden, enclosure No. 100, p. 1, in "Report on the Province of Harar," 30 Jun. 1884, Aden.

73. Bardey, "Notes sur le Harar," 132.

74. Min Muhammad Ra'uf basha hikimdar Harar wa ma yatabaha'ha, daftar 17 wared ma'iya 'arabi wathiqa 65, Rabi'a al-Thani 1293 [From Muhammad Ra'uf Pasha, *hikimdar* Harar and Its Environs, notebook 17 in Arabic, document 65, 16 Apr. 1877], in al-Jamal, *Al-Wathā'iq al-ta'rikhiyya*, 309–10.

75. Gadid, "Feudalism," 36.

76. Caulk, "Harar in the 19th Century," 11.

77. Oral history transmitted by Mohamed Orfo, Mume Bashir, and Abd al-rahman Abogn. The three gave their testimonies to Hassen in 1973. Muhammed Orfo was the son of Orfo Jilo, and after his conversion to Islam was called "Omar." Hassan, "Relation between Harar and Oromo," 48.

78. Moktar, "Notes sur le Pays de Harrar," 378.

79. FO 403/89: F. M. Hunter, "The State of Affairs at Harar," 20 Jan. 1887, Aden, enclosure No. 100, p. 1, in "Report on the Province of Harar," 30 Jun. 1884, Aden.

80. Moktar, "Notes sur le Pays de Harrar," 378–79.

81. Ibid.

82. IES 1771: Letter from Major F. M. Hunter, Officiating Political Resident, Aden, to the Chief Secretary to Government Political Department, Bombay, No. 219–1414, dated Aden Residency, 30 Jun. 1884, 2.

83. Ibid., 11.

84. Ibid., 2–3.

85. Ibid. 12. Hunter's military reports greatly reflected the perspective of the British imperial apparatus. His reports were very similar to other British reports from Sudan and other parts of Africa at that time. See Daniel R. Headrick, *The Tools of Empire: Technology and European Imperialism in the Nineteenth Century* (New York: Oxford Univ. Press, 1981), 105–14.

86. Hassan, "Relation between Harar and Oromo," 26.

87. Paulitschke, *Harar: Forschungsreise nach den Somal*, 238.

88. Caulk, "Harar in the 19th Century," 5.

89. Wylde, *Modern Abyssinia*, 143.

90. Min Muhammad Ra'uf basha hikimdar Harar wa ma yatabaha'ha, daftar 17 wared ma'iya 'arabi wathiqa 65, Rabi'a al-Thani 1293 [From Muhammad Ra'uf Pasha, *hikimdar* Harar and Its Environs, notebook 17 in Arabic, document 65, 16 Apr. 1877], in al-Jamal, *Al-Wathā'iq al-ta'rikhiyya*, 309.

91. Hassan, "Relation between Harar and Oromo," 29.

92. Min Muhammad Ra'uf basha hikimdar Harar wa ma yatabaha'ha, daftar 17 wared ma'iya 'arabi wathiqa 65, Rabi'a al-Thani 1293 [From Muhammad Ra'uf Pasha, *hikimdar* Harar and Its Environs, notebook 17 in Arabic, document 65, 16 Apr. 1877], in al-Jamal, *Al-Wathā'iq al-ta'rikhiyya*, 309–10.

93. Ibid. In reference to the *faddān*, see Hans Wehr, *A Dictionary of Modern Written Arabic* (Wiesbaden: Otto Harrassowitz, 1974), 700.

94. Min Muhammad Ra'uf basha hikimdar Harar wa ma yatabaha'ha, daftar 17 wared ma'iya 'arabi wathiqa 65, Rabi'a al-Thani 1293 [From Muhammad Ra'uf Pasha, *hikimdar* Harar and Its Environs, notebook 17 in Arabic, document 65, 16 Apr. 1877], in al-Jamal, *Al-Wathā'iq al-ta'rikhiyya*, 309–10; 'Amr ila hikimdar Harar wa-mulhaqātihā, daftar 10, awamir 'arabi 33 no. 1 fi 9 Rabi'a al-awal 1293 [Decree to *hikimdar* Harar and Its Dependencies, decrees in Arabic 23 no. 1, 4 Apr. 1876], in al-Jamal, *Al-Wathā'iq al-ta'rikhiyya*, 305.

95. Min Muhammad Ra'uf basha hikimdar Harar wa ma yatabaha'ha, daftar 17 wared ma'iya 'arabi wathiqa 65, Rabi'a al-Thani 1293 [From Muhammad Ra'uf Pasha, *hikimdar* Harar and Its Environs, notebook 17 in Arabic, document 65, 16 Apr. 1877], in al-Jamal, *Al-Wathā'iq al-ta'rikhiyya*, 309.

96. The Arabic word is *ḍamin*. See Wehr, *Dictionary of Modern Written Arabic*, 54.

97. Gadid, "Feudalism," 37.

98. Waldron, *Ethnicity as Epiphenomenon*, 19–20.

99. Wehr, *Dictionary of Modern Written Arabic*, 933.

100. Gadid, "Feudalism," 57.

101. IES: Harar Land Records: Town's Men Tax Registers (Farm Land) by Gates (1895–1898), Institute of Ethiopian Studies, MS no. 3, reel no. 8 (microfilm), Addis Ababa University; Abate, "Studien zur jüngeren," 77.

102. IES: Harar Land Records: Town's Men Tax Registers (Farm Land) by Gates (1895–1898), Institute of Ethiopian Studies, MS no. 3, reel no. 8 (microfilm), Addis Ababa University. The *kaleb* is an Amharic term meaning "provision." The *kaleb* was instituted in Harar and outside of the city immediately after its conquest by Shewa. See Gadid, "Feudalism," 75.

103. Ibid., 57.

104. Hassan, "Relation between Harar and Oromo," 29; IES 1771: Letter from Major F. M. Hunter, Officiating Political Resident, Aden, to the Chief Secretary to Government Political Department, Bombay, No. 219–1414, dated Aden Residency, 30 Jun. 1884, 12.

105. For greater elaboration on the various changes among the Oromo after the Egyptian conquest, see Clarke Harding Brooke Jr., "Settlements of the Eastern Galla, Hararge Province, Ethiopia" (PhD diss., University of Nebraska, 1956).

106. Moktar, "Notes sur le Pays de Harrar," 382.

107. Gebissa, *Leaf of Allah*, 42.

108. Sabry, *L'Empire égyptien sous Ismail*, 422. Paulitschke, "Le Harar sous l'administration égyptienne," 579; Paulitschke, *Harar: Forschungsreise nach den Somal*, 238.

109. Min Muhammad Ra'uf basha hikimdar Harar wa ma yatabaha'ha, daftar 17 wared ma'iya 'arabi wathiqa 65, Rabi'a al-Thani 1293 [From Muhammad Ra'uf Pasha, *hikimdar* Harar and Its Environs, notebook 17 in Arabic, document 65, 16 Apr. 1877], in al-Jamal, *Al-Wathā'iq al-ta'rikhiyya*, 309.

110. Paulitschke, "Le Harar sous l'administration égyptienne," 588.

111. Sylvia E. Pankhurst, "Harar under Egyptian Rule," 56.

112. Hassan, "Relation between Harar and Oromo," 30–31.

113. Min Muhammad Ra'uf basha hikimdar Harar wa ma yatabaha'ha, daftar 17 wared ma'iya 'arabi wathiqa 65, Rabi'a al-Thani 1293 [From Muhammad Ra'uf Pasha, *hikimdar* Harar and Its Environs, notebook 17 in Arabic, document 65, 16 Apr. 1877], in al-Jamal, *Al-Wathā'iq al-ta'rikhiyya*, 309.

114. Gadid, "Feudalism," 56.

115. Caulk, "Harar in the 19th Century," 2. For further details on the Ethiopian title, see Richard Pankhurst, "Çəqa Šum," in Uhlig, *Encyclopaedia Aethiopica*, 1:707–8.

116. Min Muhammad Ra'uf basha hikimdar Harar wa ma yatabaha'ha, daftar 17 wared ma'iya 'arabi wathiqa 65, 2 Rabi'a al-Thani 1293 [From Muhammad Ra'uf Pasha

hikimdar Harar and Its Environs, notebook 17 in Arabic, document 65, 16 Apr. 1877], in al-Jamal, *Al-Wathā'iq al-ta'rikhiyya*, 310.

117. al-Jamal, *Al-Wathā'iq al-ta'rikhiyya*, 310.

118. Paulitschke, "Le Harar sous l'administration égyptienne," 586–88.

119. Hassan, "Relation between Harar and Oromo," 31; Paulitschke, *Harar: Forschungsreise nach den Somal*, 238.

120. Hassan, "Relation between Harar and Oromo," 31.

121. Gadid, "Feudalism," 58.

122. Bardey, "Notes sur le Harar," 31.

123. Jalata, *Oromia and Ethiopia*, 25.

124. For further study, see Hussein Ahmed, *Islam in Nineteenth-Century Wallo, Ethiopia: Revival, Reform and Reaction* (Leiden: Brill, 2001); Ulrich Braukämper, *Islamic History and Culture in Southern Ethiopia—Collected Essays* (Hamburg: LIT Verlag Münster, 2002); Braukämper, "Oromo Country"; Hassan, *Oromo of Ethiopia*, 31.

125. Ulrich Braukämper, "Notes on the Islamization and Muslim Shrines of the Harar Plateau," in *Proceedings of the Second International Congress of Somali Studies, Hamburg, 1–6 August 1983*, ed. Thomas Labahn, 2:145–74 (Hamburg: H. Buske, 1984).

126. Jalata, *Oromia and Ethiopia*, 24.

127. Trimingham, *Islam in Ethiopia*, 2nd ed. (1965), 121.

128. Hassan, "Relation between Harar and Oromo," 26–27.

129. Hassen especially relies upon the testimony of Mume Bashir, who was 107 in 1973. Bashir served in a number of administrative positions at the time of the Egyptian conquest, during the emirate of 'Abdullahi (1885–87), and from the time that Ethiopian rule was established in the city. See Hassan, "Relation between Harar and Oromo," 27, 48.

130. Erlich, *The Cross*, 68.

131. Hassan, "Relation between Harar and Oromo," 28.

132. Bardey, "Notes sur le Harar," 32.

133. Abas Haji, "The History of Arssi: 1880–1935" (BA thesis, Addis Ababa University, 1982), 63–75.

134. Gebissa, *Leaf of Allah*, 5.

135. Min arqan harb mamoriyat Harar, muhafaza 3 'Abdeen no. 4, fi 3 Muharram 1293 [From Harar's Headquarters, 'Abdeen Palace no. 4, 30 Jan. 1876], in al-Jamal, *Al-Wathā'iq al-ta'rikhiyya*, 299.

7. Decline, 1878–1882

1. Troutt Powell, *Different Shade of Colonialism*, 66.

2. Min Muhammad Ra'uf basha hikimdar Harar wa ma yatabaha'ha, daftar 17 wared ma'iya 'arabi wathiqa 65, Rabi'a al-Thani 1293) [From Muhammad Ra'uf Pasha,

hikimdar Harar and Its Environs, notebook 17 in Arabic, document 65, 16 Apr. 1877], in al-Jamal, *Al-Wathā'iq al-ta'rikhiyya*, 311.

3. Ibid.

4. 'Amr ila hikimdar Harar, Wathiqa 'arabia 8/76, daftar 10 awamir 'arabi 76 no. 8 fi 18 jumādā al-thaniya 1293 [Decree to *hikimdar* Harar, paper in Arabic 8/76 notebook 10 decrees in Arabic 76 no. 8, 1 Jul. 1877], in al-Jamal, *Al-Wathā'iq al-ta'rikhiyya*, 312.

5. Ibid., 312–13.

6. Haggai Erlich, "Gordon, Charles George," in Uhlig, *Encyclopaedia Aethiopica*, 2:851–52.

7. Hill, *Colonel Gordon*, 111.

8. For further details about Gordon in Sudan, see Moore-Harell, *Gordon and the Sudan*.

9. 'Amr ila Gordon basha, daftar no. 18, awamir 'arabi, 8, no. 19 fi 4 Safar 1294 [Decree to Gordon Pasha, notebook no. 18, decrees on Arabi, no. 19, 19 Feb. 1877], in al-Jamal, *Al-Wathā'iq al-ta'rikhiyya*, 315.

10. 'Amr ila Gordon basha, hikimdar al-aqalim al-Sudaniya, daftar no. 18, awamir 'arabi, Wathiqa no 3/8 fi 16 Safar 1294 [Decree to Gordon Pasha the Governer of the Districts of Sudan, notebook no. 18, decrees on Arabi, paper 3/8, 19 Feb. 1877], in al-Jamal, *Al-Wathā'iq al-ta'rikhiyya*, 316.

11. Hill, *Colonel Gordon*, 310.

12. Pierre Crabitès, *Gordon: The Sudan and Slavery* (London: G. Routledge and Sons, 1933), 17; Richard Grey, *History of the Southern Sudan 1839–1899* (London: Oxford Univ. Press, 1961), 105.

13. For further details, see John H. Waller, *Gordon of Khartoum: The Saga of a Victorian Hero* (New York: Atheneum Books/Macmillan, 1988), 149; Crabitès, *Gordon*, 12–13.

14. Moore-Harell, *Gordon and the Sudan*, 45–80.

15. Na'um Shuqayr, *Ta'rikh al-Sudan* [The History of Sudan] (Beirut: dar al-thaqafa, 1981), 283; Percy F. Martin, *The Sudan in Evolution: A Study of the Economic, Financial and Administrative Conditions of the Anglo-Egyptian Sudan* (London: Constable and Company Ltd., 1921), 208.

16. Miran, *L'Óccupation Egyptienne*, 69.

17. Moore-Harell, *Gordon and the Sudan*, 45–80.

18. Min Muhammad Ra'uf basha hikimdar Harar wa ma yatabaha'ha, daftar 17 wared ma'iya 'arabi wathiqa 65, Rabi'a al-Thani 1293 [From Muhammad Ra'uf Pasha, *hikimdar* Harar and Its Environs, notebook 17 in Arabic, document 65, 16 Apr. 1877], in al-Jamal, *Al-Wathā'iq al-ta'rikhiyya*, 310.

19. For additional information, see Erlich, "Egyptian-Ethiopian War"; Haggai Erlich, *Ras Alula and the Scramble for Africa* (Asmara: Red Sea Press, 1996), 9–42; Erlich, *Ethiopia*, 53–63; Erlich, *The Cross*, 66–77.

20. About Nubar Pasha (1825–99), see Moore-Harell, *Gordon and the Sudan*, 263. Nubar Pasha introduced the khedive to Gordon.

21. For additional reading on the abovementioned processes in political terms and their influence on Egyptian society, see the Earl of Cromer, *Modern Egypt* (London: Macmillan, 1911), 1:34–72; Peter M. Holt, *Egypt and the Fertile Crescent, 1516–1922* (Ithaca, NY: Cornell Univ. Press, 1966), 212; John Marlow, *Cromer in Egypt* (New York: Praeger, 1971), 56–61; Panayiotis J. Vatikiotis, *History of Modern Egypt*, 2nd. ed. (London: Johns Hopkins Univ. Press, 1980), 128–40; Malcolm E. Yapp, *The Making of the Modern Near East* (London: Routledge, 1987), 157.

22. FO 141/105: Agreement between the British and the Egyptian Governments Respecting the Jurisdiction of His Highness the Khedive over the Somali Coast (Jun. 1877); FO 78/3138: Malet to Foreign Office, 16 Jan. 1880.

23. Toledano, *Ottoman Slave Trade*, 224–28.

24. FO 141/109: Vivian to Derby, 19 Mar. 1877.

25. ʻAbd al-Jalil al-Shtir al-Busayli, *Maʻalim Ta'rikh Sudan wa Wadi al-Nil min al-Qarn al-ʻAshr ila al-Qarn al-Tasi' ʻAshar al-Milady* [The Outlines of the History of Sudan and the Nile Valley from the Tenth Century to the Nineteenth Century] (Cairo: Maktabat al-ʻArab, 1955), 163; al-Jamal, *Siyasat Misr*, 231–33.

26. Moore-Harell, *Gordon and the Sudan*, 22–38.

27. FO 84/1472: Derby to Vivian, 19 Mar. 1877.

28. Moore-Harell, *Gordon and the Sudan*, 22–38.

29. ʻAmr ila Gordon basha, daftar no. 18, awamir ʻarabi, 8, no. 19 fi 4 Safar 1294 [Decree to Gordon Pasha, notebook no. 18, decrees on Arabi, no. 19, 19 Feb. 1877], in al-Jamal, *Al-Wathā'iq al-ta'rikhiyya*, 315; ʻAmr ila Gordon basha, hikimdar al-aqalim al-Sudaniya, daftar no. 18, awamir in Arabi, wathiqa no 3/8 fi 16 Safar 1294 [Decree to Gordon Pasha the Governer of the Districts of Sudan, notebook no. 18, decrees on Arabi, paper 3/8, 19 Feb. 1877], in al-Jamal, *Al-Wathā'iq al-ta'rikhiyya*, 316.

30. Muhafez al- FO, Jul. 1877, in al-Jamal, *Al-Wathā'iq al-ta'rikhiyya*, 318.

31. Ibid., 319.

32. Ibid., 320.

33. al-Jamal, *Al-Wathā'iq al-ta'rikhiyya*, 318–19; Miran, *L'Occupation Egyptienne*, 67.

34. al-Jamal, *Al-Wathā'iq al-ta'rikhiyya*, 319.

35. Hill, *Colonel Gordon*, 312.

36. al-Jamal, *Al-Wathā'iq al-ta'rikhiyya*, 319.

37. Paulitschke, "Le Harar sous l'administration égyptienne," 584.

38. al-Jamal, *Al-Wathā'iq al-ta'rikhiyya*, 320.

39. Miran, *L'Occupation Egyptienne*, 68.

40. Hill, *Colonel Gordon*, 310–12.

41. Ibid., 312.

42. Min Gordon basha ila Khieri basha, daftar 4 'Abdeen telegraph al-'arabi al-shafra 710, jumādā al-awal 1295 [From Gordon Pasha to Khieri Pasha, notebook 4 'Abdeen Palace, telegraph in Arabic 710, 12 May 1787], in al-Jamal, *Al-Wathā'iq al-ta'rikhiyya*, 321.

43. al-Jamal, *Al-Wathā'iq al-ta'rikhiyya*, 321–22.

44. al-Jamal, *Siyasat Misr*, 233–34.

45. Henri Labrousse, "Rivalité entre L' Égypte et L'Éthiopie dans la Mer Rouge à la fin du XIXe siècle," in *Proceedings of the Seventh International Conference of Ethiopian Studies* (Addis Ababa: Institute of Ethiopian Studies; Uppsala: Scandinavian Institute of African Studies, 1984), 291; Sabry, *L'Empire égyptien sous Ismail*, 423–24.

46. Paulitschke, "Le Harar sous l'administration égyptienne," 579.

47. Paulitschke, "Le Harar sous l'administration égyptienne," 580; Luigi Robecchi-Bricchetti, *Nell'Harar* (Milan: Galli, 1896), 119.

48. Dunn, *Khedive Ismail's Army*, 109.

49. Hill, *Colonel Gordon*, 312.

50. Ibid., 312–13.

51. Ibid., 313.

52. C. G. Gordon to Burton, 29 Apr. 1878, Harar, RGS/BG LBR MS. 1, Royal Geographical Society Archive, London.

53. Ibid.

54. al-Jamal, *Siyasat Misr*, 235

55. Min Gordon basha ila Khieri basha, daftar 4 'Abdeen telegraph al-'arabi al-shafra 710, jumādā al-awal 1295 [From Gordon Pasha to Khieri Pasha, notebook 4 'Abdeen Palace, telegraph in Arabic 710, 12 May 1787], in al-Jamal, *Al-Wathā'iq al-ta'rikhiyya*, 321–22.

56. Cecchi, *Da Zeila alle Frontiere*, 1:7.

57. al-Jamal, *Al-Wathā'iq al-ta'rikhiyya*, 318–19.

58. Ibid., 319.

59. al-Jamal, *Siyasat Misr*, 238.

60. Miran, *L'Occupation Egyptienne*, 72.

61. Paulitschke, "Le Harar sous l'administration égyptienne," 590.

62. Al-Jamal, *Siyasat Misr*, 238.

63. Gordon to Khieri Basha, 6 Jumādā al-awla 1296, 28 Feb. 1879, in Moore-Harell, *Gordon and the Sudan*, 185–86.

64. Khiery Basha to Gordon, 26 Rajab 1296, 16 Jul. 1879, and Gordon to Khiery Basha, 4 Jumādā al-Thania, 26 Apr. 1879, in Moore-Harell, *Gordon and the Sudan*, 185–86.

65. Paulitschke, "Le Harar sous l'administration égyptienne," 580.

66. Alfred Bardey, *Barr Adjam—Souvenirs d'Afrique Orientale 1880–1887* (Paris: ed. du SNRS, 1981), 69; Fontrier, *Abou-Baker Ibrahim*, 162–63.

67. Mudir Zaila to Cabinet Secretariat, 3 Rajab 1295, 3 Jul. 1875, in Moore-Harell, *Gordon and the Sudan*, 186–87.

68. Mohammad Raduan Pasha to Cabinet Secretariat, 8 Rajab 1295, 8 Jul. 1878, in Moore-Harell, *Gordon and the Sudan*, 186–87.

69. Mohammad Raduan Pasha to Cabinet Secretariat, 13 Rajab 1295, 13 Jul. 1878, in Moore-Harell, *Gordon and the Sudan*, 186–87.

70. Mudir Harar to Cabinet Secretariat, Jamādā al-A'achira 1295, 12 Jun. 1878, in Moore-Harell, *Gordon and the Sudan*, 186.

71. Gordon to Khieri Pasha, Rajab 1295, 24 Jul. 1878, Khartoum, in al-Jamal, *Al-Wathā'iq al-ta'rikhiyya*, 324.

72. Ibid., 324–25; al-Jamal, *Siyasat Misr*, 235.

73. al-Jamal, *Siyasat Misr*, 234.

74. Ibid., 236.

75. Mudir Zaila to Cabinet Secretariat, 10 Rabia al-awal 1296, 4 Mar. 1879, in Moore-Harell, *Gordon and the Sudan*, 187–88.

76. Gordon to Khieri Pasha, 30 Muharram 1296, 24 Jan. 1879, in Moore-Harell, *Gordon and the Sudan*, 188.

77. Ibid.

78. Mudir Zaila to Cabinet Secretariat, 22 Rabia al-awal 1296, 16 Mar. 1879, in Moore-Harell, *Gordon and the Sudan*, 188.

79. Gordon basha to Khiery basha, Ḍu al-hija 1296, 7 Oct. 1879, in al-Jamal, *Al-Wathā'iq al-ta'rikhiyya*, 326; al-Jamal, *Siyasat Misr*, 236. There are no biographical details about Mustafa Basha al-Tusiya.

80. Fontrier, *Abou-Baker Ibrahim*, 177–212.

81. al-Jamal, *Siyasat Misr*, 238.

82. 'Amr ila Muhammad Nadi basha, 10 Safar 1297, 22 Jan. 1880, in al-Jamal, *Al-Wathā'iq al-ta'rikhiyya*, 327.

83. al-Jamal, *Siyasat Misr*, 238.

84. FO 881/4249X: Malet to Salisbury, 23 Mar. 1880, Cairo.

85. al-Jamal, *Siyasat Misr*, 235.

86. 'Amr ila Muhammad Nadi basha, 10 Safar 1297, 22 Jan. 1880, in al-Jamal, *Al-Wathā'iq al-ta'rikhiyya*, 327; Miran, "Muḥammad Nādī."

87. Miran, *L'Occupation Egyptienne*, 74.

88. Bardey, "Notes sur le Harar," 156; Dunn, *Khedive Ismail's Army*, 129; Paulitschke, "Le Harar sous l'administration égyptienne," 579.

89. Bardey, *Barr Adjam*, 68.

90. Miran, *L'Occupation Egyptienne*, 74. See also the British evaluation of Abu Bakr in FO 403/81A: Heron to the Political Resident at Aden, 5 Jun. 1880, Aden.

91. Fontrier, *Abou-Baker Ibrahim*, 158–81.

92. Bardey, *Barr Adjam*, 4; Fontrier, *Abou-Baker Ibrahim*, 189–91; Miran, *L'Occupation Egyptienne*, 74–75.

93. Miran, *L'Occupation Egyptienne*, 75; M. Perret, "Voyage sans Retour: Henri Lucereau en Ethiopie, 1879–1880," in *L'Africa ai tempi di Daniele Camboni*, Atti del Congresso Internazionale di Studi Africani, Roma, 19–21 Nov. 1981 (Rome: Istituto italo-africano), 194–201.

94. Perret, "Voyage sans Retour."

95. Eleven-page report from Mohammad Nadi Pasha (undated) in al-Jamal, *Siyasat Misr*, 239–40.

96. Moore-Harell, *Gordon and the Sudan*, 188–90.

97. FO 78/3725: Memorandum of Egyptian Coast Territory South of the Red Sea (Admiralty, Foreign Intelligence Committee, No. 28, 9 Feb. 1884), 19.

98. FO 141/124: Gordon, Notes on Abyssinia 1877–1879, 23 Sep. 1879.

99. Eleven-page report (undated) from Mohammad Nadi Pasha in al-Jamal, *Siyasat Misr*, 240.

100. al-Jamal, *Siyasat Misr*, 240.

101. Cecchi, *Da Zeila alle Frontiere*, 2:622.

102. Bardey, "Notes sur le Harar," 32.

103. Paulitschke, "Le Harar sous l'administration égyptienne," 580–82.

104. For more details and a critical discussion about the roots of Egyptian nationalism and the characteristics of the ʿUrabi phenomenon, see Cole, *Colonialism and Revolution*.

105. Bardey, *Barr Adjam*, 321–23; Miran, *L'Occupation Egyptienne*, 84.

106. Ferrand, "Notes sur la situation politique," 3.

107. Dunn, *Khedive Ismail's Army*, 109; Paulitschke, "Le Harar sous l'administration égyptienne," 579.

108. Dunn, *Khedive Ismail's Army*, 109.

109. al-Jamal, *Siyasat Misr*, 241.

110. Ibid.

111. IES 1771: Letter from Major F. M. Hunter, Officiating Political Resident, Aden, to the Chief Secretary to Government Political Department, Bombay, No. 219–1414, dated Aden Residency, 30 Jun. 1884, 2.

112. Three-page report from Muhammad Nadi Pasha (Rabiʿa al-awal 1300, Jan. 1880), in al-Jamal, *Siyasat Misr*, 241.

113. Headrick, *Tools of Empire*, 150–56, 209–10.

114. Cole, *Colonialism and Revolution*, 112; Talhami, *Suakin and Massawa*, 97–124.

115. Minawi, *Ottoman Scramble*, 100–111.

116. *L'Esploratore* 7 (Milan, 1883): 432; Miran, *L'Occupation Egyptienne*, 85.

117. FO 403/81D: Sealy to Malet, 31 Jan. 1883, Aden.

118. al-Jamal, *Siyasat Misr*, 241.

119. Caulk, "Occupation of Harar," 2–3; Ferrand, "Notes sur la situation politique," 2–3; Paulitschke, "Le Harar sous l'administration égyptienne," 583.

120. Fontrier, *Abou-Baker Ibrahim*, 192–96, 203–7.

121. Miran, *L'Occupation Egyptienne*, 86.

122. FO 403/81B: Malet to Granville, 22 Jan. 1881, Cairo; FO 403/81A: Malet to Granville, 17 Jan. 1881, Cairo.

123. FO 403/81B: Malet to Granville, 25 Jun. 1881, London; FO 403/81B: Report by Aly Pasha Ridah, 21 Jan. 1881.

124. al-Jamal, *Siyasat Misr*, 246.

125. FO 403/81C: Cookson to Granville, 6 Mar. 1882, Cairo.

126. Emile Foucher, "Une Page de L'Histoire de Harar ou Arthur Rimbaud sous L'Administration Egyptienne," in *Quaderni di Stadi Etiopicu* (Asmara: Centro studi etiopici, 1980), 479; Miran, *L'Occupation Egyptienne*, 87.

127. Paulitschke, "Le Harar sous l'administration égyptienne," 582; Paulitschke, *Harar: Forschungsreise nach den Somal*, 235.

128. Paulitschke, *Harar: Forschungsreise nach den Somal*, 235.

8. Europeans in "Egyptian" Harar

1. Archives des Capucins, Reg. 185, 21: Lettre de Mgr. Taurin Cahagne, 8 Aug. 1881.

2. Ibid.

3. Richard Pankhurst, *Travelers in Ethiopia* (London: Oxford Univ. Press, 1965), vii.

4. Edward W. Said, *Orientalism* (London: Vintage, 1978), 21–23.

5. Timothy Mitchell, "Orientalism and the Exhibitionary Order," in *Colonialism and Culture*, ed. Nicholas B. Dirks (Ann Arbor: Univ. of Michigan Press, 1992), 309–14.

6. For further discussion of various aspects of the critique on Said's interpretation of the concept "Orientalism," see Bhabha, *Location of Culture*; and Denis Porter, "Orientalism and Its Problems," in *Colonial Discourse and Post-Colonial Theory*, ed. P. Williams and L. Chrisman (New York: Columbia Univ. Press, 1994), 150–61. For the critical discourse on Said's conceptions that is relevant to this article, see Nicholas Harrison, "A Roomy Place Full of Possibilities: Said's *Orientalism* and the Literary," in *Edward Said and the Literary, Social and Political World*, ed. Ranjan Ghosh (New York: Routledge 2009), 3–18; William D. Hart, *Edward Said and the Religious Effects of Culture* (Cambridge: Cambridge Univ. Press, 2000), 62–87.

7. "Exposé de Nadi Pacha à la séance du 23 Mars 1883," *Bulletin de la Société Khédiviale de Géographie du Caire* 2, no. 8 (Cairo, 1886): 464.

8. Alfred Bardey (1854–1934) was a merchant in Lyon, France. In the early 1880s he established companies to import coffee in Zeila and Aden. Henri Lucereau was the French consul in Zeila from 1879. He arrived in Harar in September 1880, and after his visit in the city he went to the Oromo areas, where he was murdered in early October 1880. For further reading on Bardey and Lucereau, see Jonathan Miran, "Bardey, Xavier Alfred," in Uhlig, *Encyclopaedia Aethiopica*, 1:476; Perret, "Voyage sans Retour."

9. J. Tubiana, "Le Patron de Rimbaud," preface to *Barr Adjam—Souvenirs d'Afrique Orientale 1880–1887*, by Alfred Bardey (Paris: ed. du SNRS, 1981), vi–ix.

10. Bardey, "Notes sur le Harar," 31.

11. Bardey, *Barr Adjam*, 129–30.

12. Ibid., 140.

13. "Lettre de Lucereau au Président de la Société de Géographie Commerciale de Paris, Harar, le 12 août 1880(?)," *Bulletin de la Société de Géographie Commerciale de Paris* 3 (Oct. 1880–Oct. 1881): 47.

14. Burton, *First Footsteps*, 1:204–9, 2:1–41.

15. Ibid., 20.

16. Enid Starkie, *Arthur Rimbaud* (London: Faber and Faber, 1961), 352.

17. For an alternative reading of Rimbaud's history in Harar, see Avishai Ben-Dror, "Arthur Rimbaud in Harär: Images, Reality, Memory," *Northeast African Studies* 14, no. 2 (2014): 159–82.

18. Eloi Ficquet, "Cahagne, Taurin," in Uhlig, *Encyclopaedia Aethiopica*, 1:664–65. For more on the Capuchin order and its activities in Ethiopia, see Antonios Alberto and Andreu Martinez, "Capuchins," in Uhlig, *Encyclopaedia Aethiopica*, 1: 682–83.

19. Bardey, *Barr Adjam*, 243–44.

20. Archives des Capucins, Ms. 1242 et 2795, 79: Lettre manuscrite de Père Julien de Mamers au T.R.P. Provincial de Paris, 25 Apr. 1882, Harar.

21. Archives des Capucins, Reg. 185, 21: Lettre manuscrite de Mgr. Taurin Cahagne au T.R.P. Provincial de Paris, 8 Aug. 1881, Harar.

22. Bardey, *Barr Adjam*, 266.

23. Aleme Eshete, "The Establishment of the Capuchin Catholic Mission Among the Qottu of Harar: 1881–1889" (paper prepared for the conference on Harari Studies by the Historical Society of Ethiopia, Addis Ababa University, Jun. 1975), 2.

24. Archives des Capucins, Reg. 185, 21: Lettre manuscrite de Mgr. Taurin Cahagne au T.R.P. Provincial de Paris, 8 Aug. 1881, Harar.

25. "100 Years, The Harar Mission," fascicule non publié préparé par la Mission des Capucins à Harar en 1981 célébrant le centenaire de la Mission (1881–1981), IES HAR 250, 12.

26. Archives des Capucins, Reg. 185, 21: Lettre de Mgr. Taurin Cahagne, 8 Aug. 1881.

27. Eshete, "Establishment of the Capuchin Catholic Mission," 3.

28. Archives des Capucins, Ms. 1242 et 2795, 87: Lettre manuscrite de Mgr. Taurin Cahagne au T.R.P. Provincial de Paris, 7 Mar. 1882, Zeila.

29. Eshete, "Establishment of the Capuchin Catholic Mission," 5.

30. Archives des Capucins, Ms. 1242 et 2795, 75: Lettre manuscrite de Mgr. Taurin Cahagne au T.R.P. Provincial de Paris, 7 Mar. 1882, Zeila.

31. Archives des Capucins, Reg. 960, 28: Lettre manuscrite de Mgr. Taurin Cahagne au T.R.P. Provincial de Paris, 20 May 1881, Harar.

32. Emile Foucher, "First Impressions," in "100 Years Harar Mission," Institute of Ethiopian Studies, IES HAR 250, 12, Addis Ababa: Addis Ababa University.

33. Archives des Capucins, Reg. 960, 28: Lettre manuscrite de Mgr. Taurin Cahagne au T.R.P. Provincial de Paris, 20 May 1881, Harar.

34. Archives des Capucins, Reg. 185,21: Lettre de Mgr. Taurin Cahagne, 8 Aug. 1881.

35. Eshete, "Establishment of the Capuchin Catholic Mission," 6.

36. Ibid., 7.

37. Ibid.; Hassan, "Relation between Harar and Oromo," 33.

38. Archives des Capucins, Ms. 1242 et 2795, 87: Lettre manuscrite de Père Julien de Mamers au T.R.P. Provincial de Paris, 25 Apr. 1882, Harar; Archives des Capucins, Reg. 960, 28: Lettre manuscrite de Mgr. Taurin Cahagne au T.R.P. Provincial de Paris, 20 May 1881, Harar.

39. Archives des Capucins, Ms. 1242 et 2795, 75, 63: Lettre manuscrite de Mgr. Taurin Cahagne au T.R.P. Provincial de Paris, 20 Jan. 1883, Aden; Foucher, "Harar au temps d'Artur Rimbaud," 1:368.

40. Bardey, *Barr Adjam*, 358.

41. Bardey, *Barr Adjam*, 274, 287.

42. Foucher, "Une Page de L'Histoire," 81.

43. Archives des Capucins, Ms. 1242 et 2795, 75, 63: Lettre manuscrite de Mgr. Taurin Cahagne au T.R.P. Provincial de Paris, 20 Jan. 1883, Aden.

44. Ibid.

45. Eshete, "Establishment of the Capuchin Catholic Mission," 7.

46. Archives des Capucins, Ms. 1242 et 2795, 75, 137: Lettre manuscrite de Père Pierre De Locminé au T.R.P. Provincial de Paris, 15 Jul. 1883, Harar.

47. "Lettre de Lucereau au Président de la Société de Géographie Commerciale de Paris, Harar, le 12 août 1880(?)" *Bulletin de la Société de Géographie Commerciale de Paris* 3 (Paris: Oct. 1880–Oct. 1881): 47.

48. Perret, "Voyage sans Retour."

49. Manlio Bonati, "Sacconi, Pietro," in Uhlig, *Encyclopaedia Aethiopica*, 4:439; Pietro Sacconi, "Il Governo Egiziano e le tribu Galla e Somali," *L'Esploratore* 7 (Milan, 14 Feb. 1883), 169–73; Foucher, "Une Page de L'Histoire," 480.

50. Archives des Capucins, Ms. 1242 and 2795, 75, 63: Lettre manuscrite de Mgr. Taurin Cahagne au T.R.P. Provincial de Paris, 20 Jan. 1883, Aden.

51. FO 403/82: Hunter to Baring, 24 Nov. 1884, Aden.

52. FO 403/82: Hunter to the Earl of Kimberley, 5 Jun. 1884, Aden.

9. The Egyptian Withdrawal

1. Miran, *L'Occupation Egyptienne*, 102; Paulitschke, "Le Harar sous l'administration égyptienne," 583.

2. See, for example, modern national Egyptian historiography: Yahya, *Misr al-ifriqiya*, 644–61, 664–79; Rajab Haraz, *Ifriqiya al-sharqia wa al-Isti'imar al-Urubi* [East Africa and European Imperialism] (Cairo, 1968); Mohammad Sabry, *Al-Imbarraturiya al-Sudaniya fi al-Qarn al-Tasi''Ashar* [Imperial Sudan in the Nineteenth Century] (Cairo, 1948), 40–49.

3. Regarding the causes of the Mahdī rebellion and the Mahdī policies in Sudan during the years 1881–99, see Warburg, *Islam, Sectarianism and Politics*, 6–57. For a discussion on Mahdī historiography, see Warburg, *Historical Discord*, 13–61.

4. Miran, *L'Occupation Egyptienne*, 102–3; Paulitschke, "Le Harar sous l'administration Egyptienne," 581–82.

5. Archives des Capucins, Reg. 960, 60: Lettre manuscrite de Mgr. Taurin Cahagne au T.R.P. Provincial de Paris, 15 Jun. 1883, Harar.

6. Archives des Capucins, Reg. 960: Lettre manuscrite de Père Ferdinand au T.R.P. Provincial de Paris, 25 Jun. 1883, Harar.

7. Rimbaud's letter from Harar (23 Sep. 1883) in Arthur Rimbaud, *Oeuvres Complètes*, ed. André Guyaux (Paris: Gallimard, 2009), 534–35.

8. For more details, see Donald Donham and Wendy James, eds., *The Southern Marches of Imperial Ethiopia: Essays in History and Social Anthropology* (Oxford: James Curry, 2002).

9. Jonathan A. Grant, *Rulers, Guns and Money: The Global Arms Trade in the Age of Imperialism* (Cambridge, MA: Harvard Univ. Press, 2007), 37–65.

10. Abir, *Ethiopia*, 13–14, 172–73; Richard A. Caulk, "Firearms and Princely Power in 19th Century Ethiopia" (paper prepared for the Interdisciplinary Seminar of the Faculties of Arts and Education, Haile Selassie I University, Addis Ababa, 1969–70), 14–16; Richard A. Caulk, "Firearms and Princely Power in Ethiopia in the Nineteenth Century," *Journal of African History* 8, no. 4 (1972): 620–21.

11. Ministero degli Affari Esteri, Comitato per la Documentazione dell'Opera dell'Italia in Africa, Historical Series, vol. 1, in Carlo Giglio, *Ethiopia-Mar Rosso* (Rome: Poligrafico dello Stato, 1958–1966), tome 3 (1960), 65.

12. Caulk, "Occupation of Harar," 3.

13. FO 633/55: Egypt No. 14 (1885): Hunter to Baring, "Correspondence Respecting Ports of the Red Sea and the Gulf of Aden and the Province of Harar," 5 Apr. 1884, Aden.

14. Sacconi, "Il Governo Egiziano," 169–73.

15. Rimbaud, letter from Harar, 24 Apr. 1885, in Rimbaud, *Oeuvres Complètes*, 544.

16. Caulk, "Occupation of Harar," 2.

17. FO 633/55: Baring to Granville, 1 Jan. 1884, Cairo; Pauncefote to the Secretary of Admiralty (Foreign Office), 3 Jan. 1884; Godley to Pauncefote (India Office), 7 Jan. 1884.

18. FO 403/82: Hewett to the Secretary to the Admiralty, 7–10 Jan. 1884.

19. Marston, *Britain's Imperial Role*, 481–83.

20. Ibid.; FO 633/55: Godley to Pauncefote (India Office), 7 Jan. 1884.

21. Caulk, "Occupation of Harar," 3; FO 633/55: Hunter to Baring, 5 Apr. 1884, Aden.

22. Henry Audon, "Voyages au Choa (1884–1888)," *Le Tour du Monde* 58 (Paris, 1889), 144.

23. FO 633/55: Blair to Egerton, 25 Apr. 1884, Aden; FO 403/82: Blair to Egerton, 25 Apr. 1884, Aden.

24. Caulk, "Occupation of Harar," 3.

25. Ibid.; IES No. 73: "Ya Galla Tarik," Unpublished manuscript compiled in 1905; Sven Rubenson, "The Adwa Peace Treaty of 1884," *Proceedings of the Third International Conference of Ethiopian Studies* (Addis Ababa: Institute of Ethiopian Studies, Haile Selassie I Univ., 1969), 1:225–36.

26. FO 633/55: Coffin to the Secretary of the Admiralty, 7 Feb. 1884, Aden.

27. Ibid.

28. Ibid.

29. Ibid.

30. FO 403/82: Hunter to Baring, 7 Apr. 1884, Aden.

31. Foucher, "Harar au temps d'Arthur Rimbaud," 1:370.

32. Ibid.

33. FO 78/3725: Memorandum of Egyptian Coast Territory South of the Red Sea (Admiralty, Foreign Intelligence Committee No. 28, 9 Feb. 1884), 6.

34. FO 78/3725: Stopford to the Secretary to the Admiralty, 12 Jul. 1884, Berbera.

35. FO 78/3725: Memorandum of Egyptian Coast Territory South of the Red Sea (Admiralty, Foreign Intelligence Committee No. 28, 9 Feb. 1884), 10.

36. Ibid, 1–3.

37. Ibid., 4.

38. Ibid., 2–3.

39. Ibid.

40. FO 633/55: Gonne to Grant, 7 Feb. 1884, Bombay Castle: Extract from a report dated 23 January 1883, by Brigadier-General Blair, on his visit to Ras Alula and Bunder Muraiyah, Ridgeway to Gonne, 21 Mar. 1884, Fort William.

41. FO 633/55: Sultan Othman bin Muhammad, Mijjertayn, to Brigadier-General Blair, 19 Feb. 1883; Blair to Gonne, 5 May 1883, Aden.

42. FO 633/55: Baring to Granville, 29 Mar. 1884, Cairo.

43. FO 633/55: Granville to Baring (Foreign Office), 29 Mar. 1884; Granville to Baring (Foreign Office), 5 Apr. 1884; FO 403/82: Granville to Baring (Foreign Office), 29 Mar. 1884.

44. The Decision of the Representative Council on the Evacuation of Harar (1 Apr. 1884), in al-Jamal, *Siyasat Misr*, 246.

45. FO 403/82: Granville to Baring (Foreign Office), 5 Apr. 1884.

46. FO 403/82: Godley to Pauncefote (India Office), 3 Apr. 1884.

47. FO 403/82: Egerton to Granville, 22 Apr. 1884, Cairo; Lyons to Granville, 25 Apr. 1884, Paris.

48. FO 633/55: Baring to Granville, 17 Apr. 1884, Cairo.

49. FO 402/82: Baring to Granville, 17 Apr. 1884, Cairo.

50. FO 403/82: Hunter to Baring, Memorandum Regarding the Proposed Restoration of Harrar to a Member of the Old Ruling Family, 5 Apr. 1884, Aden.

51. Ibid.

52. Regarding Nubar Pasha (1825–99), see Moore-Harell, *Gordon and the Sudan*, 263.

53. FO 402/82: Baring to Granville, 17 Apr. 1884, Cairo.

54. FO 403/82: Hunter to Baring, Memorandum Regarding the Proposed Restoration of Harrar to a Member of the Old Ruling Family, 5 Apr. 1884, Aden.

55. Ibid.; Ahmed Zekaria, "ʿAbdullāhi b. Muḥammad," in Uhlig, *Encyclopaedia Aethiopica*, 1:38–39.

56. FO 403/82: Hunter to Baring, Memorandum Regarding the Proposed Restoration of Harrar to a Member of the Old Ruling Family, 5 Apr. 1884, Aden.

57. Ibid.

58. Ibid.

59. FO 403/82: Hunter to Baring, Memorandum Regarding the Proposed Restoration of Harrar to a Member of the Old Ruling Family, 5 Apr. 1884, Aden.

60. Ibid.

61. Ibid.

62. FO 633/55: Hunter to Baring, Memorandum Regarding the Proposed Restoration of Harrar to a Member of the Old Ruling Family, 5 Apr. 1884, Aden.

63. Ibid.

64. FO 403/82: Hunter to Baring, Memorandum Regarding the Possibility of Enlisting Somalis and Gallas in Aden, or Opposite African Coast, for the Egyptian Army under English Officers, 5 Apr. 1884, Aden.

65. Ibid.

66. Ibid.

67. FO 403/82: Hunter to Baring, Memorandum Regarding the Possibility of Enlisting Somalis and Gallas in Aden, or Opposite African Coast, for the Egyptian Army under English Officers, 5 Apr. 1884, Aden.

68. FO 403/82: Hunter to Baring, 7 Apr. 1884, Aden.

69. Ibid.

70. Ibid.

71. Ibid.

72. Ibid.

73. IES 771: Major F. M. Hunter, Officiating Political Resident, Aden, to the Chief Secretary to Government Political Department, Bombay, No. 219–1414 (dated Aden Residency, 30 Jun. 1884), 5.

74. Ibid., 8–9.

75. Ibid., 6.

76. Ibid., 7.

77. Ibid.

78. Ibid, 8.

79. Ibid.

80. FO 403/82: Hunter to the Earl of Kimberley, 5 Jun. 1884, Aden.

81. Ibid.

82. Ibid.

83. Ibid.

84. FO 633/55: Waddington to Granville, 5 Mar. 1884, London; Granville to Waddington (Foreign Office), 10 Mar. 1884; Granville to Baring (Foreign Office), 10 Mar. 1884.

85. Caulk, "Occupation of Harar," 4.

86. FO 633/55: The Governor of Zeyla to Nubar Pasha (n.p., 1 May 1884); FO 403/82: Egerton to Granville, 18 May 1884, Cairo; Lyons to Granville, 24 May 1884, Paris; Dufferin to Granville, 24 May 1884, Constantinople.

87. A. Brockett, "Anglo-French Rivalry on the Somali Coast in the 1880s," in *Proceedings of the 1968 Conference of the Historical Association of Kenya* (Nairobi: East African Publishing House, 1970), 127–56.

88. Caulk, "Occupation of Harar," 4.

89. FO 633/55: Egerton to Granville, 28 Apr. 1884, Cairo.

90. FO 403/82: Egerton to Granville, 28 Apr. 1884, Cairo.

91. FO 403/82: Granville to Egerton (Foreign Office), 2 May 1884; FO 633/55: Blair to Hewett (Political Department), 7 Apr. 1884, Aden; Blair to Egerton, 25 Apr. 1884, Aden; the Secretary to the Admiralty to Pauncefote (Admiralty), 10 May 1884.

92. FO 403/82: Blair to Hewett, 7 Apr. 1884, Aden.

93. FO 403/82: James to Baring, 21 Apr. 1884, Cairo.

94. Ibid.

95. FO 633/55: Blair to Hewett, Extract from a Report Regarding to the Proposed Retrocession of Harrar, 7 Apr. 1884, Aden.

96. FO 633/55: Egerton to Granville, 6 May 1884, Cairo; Egerton to Granville, Extract from the "Moniteur Egyptien," 10 May 1884, Cairo; Assim Pasha to Musurus Pasha, 25 May 1884, Constantinople.

97. FO 403/82: The Viceroy of India to the Earl of Kimberley, 10 May 1884, Simla.

98. FO 633/55: Granville to Dufferin (Foreign Office), 29 May 1884.

99. FO 633/55: Egerton to Granville, 2 Jun. 1884, Cairo; Godley to Pauncefote (India Office), 17 Jun. 1884; FO 403/82: Egerton to Hunter, 29 May 1884, Cairo.

100. FO 403/82: Stopford to Blair, 12 May 1884, Aden; Lyons to Granville, 11 Jun. 1884, Paris; Godley to Currie (India Office), 12 Jun. 1884.

101. FO 633/55: Egerton to Granville, 2 Jun. 1884, Cairo; FO 403/82: Egerton to Granville, 5 Jun. 1884, Cairo; Egerton to Hunter, 5 Jun. 1884, Cairo; Nubar Pasha to Hunter, 5

Jun. 1884, Cairo; Stopford to the Secretary to the Admiralty, 14 Jun. 1884, Aden; Marco Lenci, "Antonelli, Pietro," in Uhlig, *Encyclopaedia Aethiopica*, 1:283.

102. FO 403/82: Abu Bekr Pasha to Hunter, 20 Jun. 1884, n.d.; Khwajah Menahim Messa to Hunter, 23 Jun. 1884, Aden; Abu Bekr Pasha to Hunter, 21 Jun. 1884, n.d.

103. FO 403/82: Lumley to Granville, 16 Jul. 1884, Rome.

104. FO 633/55: The Viceroy of India to Kimberley, 2 Jul. 1884, Simla; Kimberley to the Viceroy of India (India Office), 3 Jul. 1884; Granville to Dufferin (Foreign Office), 17 Jul. 1884; Granville to Egerton (Foreign Office), 17 Jul. 1884; Egerton to Granville, 18 Jul. 1884, Cairo.

105. FO 403/82: Hunter to Kimberley, 15 Jul. 1884, Aden; FO 633/55: Hunter to Fergusson, 5 Jul. 1884, Aden.

106. FO 403/82: Hunter to Kimberley, 5 Jul. 1884, Aden.

107. FO 403/82: Lyons to Granville, 26 Jun. 1884, Paris; Egerton to Granville, 21 Jun. 1884, Cairo; Godley to Pauncefote (India Office), 3 Jul. 1884.

108. FO 403/82: Hunter to Kimberley, 9 Jul. 1884, Aden.

109. FO 403/82: Granville to Egerton (Foreign Office), 17 Jul. 1884; Egerton to Granville, 18 Jul. 1884, Cairo.

110. FO 403/82: Egerton to Granville, 18 Jul. 1884, Cairo.

111. FO 403/82: The Governor of Berbera to Nubar Pasha, 15 Jul. 1884, Berbera; the Governor of Berbera to Nubar Pasha, 16 Jul. 1884, Berbera.

112. FO 403/82: Pauncefote to Godley (Foreign Office), 19 Jul. 1884); Godley to Pauncefote (India Office), 23 Jul. 1884; FO 633/55: Pauncefote to Godley (Foreign Office), 25 Jul. 1884.

113. FO 633/55: Hunter to Kimberley, 15 Jul. 1884, Aden; Agreement between Major Hunter and the Elders of the Habar Awal, 14 Jul. 1884.

114. FO 403/82: Wood to Hunter, 21 Jul. 1884, Cairo.

115. FO 403/82: Hunter to the Chief Secretary to Government, Bombay, 6 Aug. 1884, Aden.

116. FO 403/82: Granville to Egerton (Foreign Office), 4 Aug. 1884.

117. FO 633/55: Hunter to Kimberley, 30 Jul. 1884, Aden; Hunter to Kimberley, 31 Jul. 1884, Aden; FO 403/82: Godley to Pauncefote (India Office), 30 Jul. 1884.

118. FO 403/82: Egerton to Granville, 26 Jul. 1884, Alexandria.

119. FO 633/55: Granville to Egerton (Foreign Office), 4 Aug. 1884; Godley to Pauncefote (India Office), 5 Aug. 1884; Hunter to Kimberley, 5 Aug. 1884, Aden); Granville to Egerton (Foreign Office), 7 Aug. 1884; Dufferin to Granville, 8 Aug. 1884, Constantinople.

120. FO 633/55: Dufferin to Granville, 3 Aug. 1884, Theraphia; Dufferin to Granville, 13 Aug. 1884, Constantinople.

121. FO 633/55: Assim Pasha to Musurus Pasha, 7 Sep. 1884 Constantinople.

122. FO 403/82: Hunter to Kimberley, 2 Aug. 1884, Aden.

123. FO 403/82: Granville to Musurus Pasha (Foreign Office), 22 Aug. 1884; Musurus Pasha to Granville (Imperial Ottoman Embassy), 8 Sep. 1884, London; FO 403/82: Granville to Dufferin (Foreign Office), 2 Sep. 1884.

124. FO 403/82: Governor of Harrar to Nubar Pasha, 11 Chwal 1301, 3 Aug. 1884, Harrar.

125. Ibid.

126. FO 633/55: Governor-General of Harrar to Nubar Pasha, 11 Aug. 1884, Harar.

127. Ibid.

128. FO 633/55: Nubar Pasha to the Governor of Harrar, 18 Aug. 1884, Cairo.

129. From Harar's Dignitaries, Erudits, Citizens and Merchants to the General Governor of Harar and Its Environs (Šhawal 1301, 6 Aug. 1884), in al-Jamal, *Al-Wathā'iq al-ta'rikhiyya*, 329–30.

130. Ibid.

131. From the Foreign Merchants to the General Governor of Harar and Its Environs (Šhawal 1301, 6 Aug. 1884), in al-Jamal, *Al-Wathā'iq al-ta'rikhiyya*, 328–29.

132. Ibid.

133. FO 633/55: The European and Native Merchants of Harar to Nubar Pasha, 10 Aug. 1884, Harar.

134. FO 633/55: Hunter to Kimberley, 30 Jul. 1884, Aden.

135. Archives des Capucins, Reg. 1241, 157: Lettre manuscrite du Père Pierre au T.R.P. Provincial de Paris, 28 Aug. 1884, Harar.

136. FO 633/55: Granville to Egerton (Foreign Office), 15 Aug. 1884.

137. al-Jamal, *Siyasat Misr*, 247–48.

138. FO 403/82: Egerton to Granville, 9 Aug. 1884, Cairo; FO 633/55: Granville to Egerton (Foreign Office), 11 Aug. 1884; Egerton to Granville, 12 Aug. 1884, Cairo.

139. FO 633/55: Granville to Egerton (Foreign Office), 18 Aug. 1884.

140. FO 633/55: Hunter to Kimberley, 4 Aug. 1884, Aden.

141. Ibid.

142. FO 633/55: Nubar Pasha to the Governor of Zyala, 15 Aug. 1884, Cairo.

143. FO 403/82: Walpole to Pauncefote (India Office), 25 Aug. 1884; Kimberley to Hunter (India Office), 25 Aug. 1884.

144. FO 633/55: Granville to Egerton (Foreign Office), 30 Aug. 1884; Hunter to Kimberley, 10 Sep. 1884, Aden.

145. FO 633/55: Hunter to Kimberley, 4 Sep. 1884, Aden; Hunter to Kimberley, 8 Sep. 1884, Aden.

146. FO 403/82: Egerton to Hunter, 1 Sep. 1884, Cairo.

147. FO 403/82: Hunter to Egerton, 2 Sep. 1884, Aden.

148. FO 403/82: Hunter to Egerton, 3 Sep. 1884, Aden.

149. FO 403/82: Egerton to Hunter, 2 Sep. 1884, Cairo; Egerton to Hunter, 3 Sep. 1884, Cairo.

150. FO 403/82: Hunter to Egerton, 4 Sep. 1884, Aden.

151. FO 403/82: Egerton to Hunter, 4 Sep. 1884, Cairo; Hunter to Egerton, 5 Sep. 1884, Aden; Egerton to Hunter, 6 Sep. 1884, Cairo; Egerton to Granville, 7 Sep. 1884, Cairo.

152. FO 403/82: Hunter to Egerton, 7 Sep. 1884, Aden.

153. FO 633/55: Baring to Hunter, 20 Sep. 1884, Cairo; Baring to Granville, 21 Sep. 1884, Cairo; Granville to Baring (Foreign Office), 24 Sep. 1884; Baring to Hunter, 25 Sep. 1884, Cairo.

154. FO 403/82: Baring to Hunter, 20 Sep. 1884, Cairo; Baring to Granville, 21 Sep. 1884, Cairo.

155. FO 633/55: Granville to Baring (Foreign Office), 24 Sep. 1884; Baring to Granville, 25 Sep. 1884, Cairo; Baring to Hunter, 25 Sep. 1884, Cairo.

156. FO 403/82: Baring to Granville, 22 Sep. 1884, Cairo.

157. Ibid.; Currie to Walpole (Foreign Office), 8 Oct. 1884.

158. FO 403/82: Hunter to Baring, 23 Sep. 1884, Aden; Baring to Hunter, 24 Sep. 1884, Cairo.

159. FO 403/82: Hunter to Baring, 25 Sep. 1884, Aden; Baring to Hunter, 25 Sep. 1884, Cairo.

160. FO 403/82: Baring to Hunter, 25 Sep. 1884, Cairo; Baring to Hunter, 27 Sep. 1884, Cairo.

161. FO 633/55: The Resident of Aden to Kimberley, 5 Oct. 1884, Aden; Baring to Granville, 16 Oct. 1884, Cairo; Hunter to Baring, n.d.

162. FO 633/55: Granville to Musurus Pasha (Foreign Office), 3 Oct. 1883; Granville to Baring (Foreign Office), 8 Oct. 1884; Currie to Walpole (Foreign Office), 10 Oct. 1884.

163. FO 403/82: Nigra to Granville, 13 Oct. 1884, London; Nigra to Granville, 20 Oct. 1884, London.

164. FO 403/82: Baring to Granville, 5 Oct. 1884, Cairo; Godley to Currie (India Office), 10 Oct. 1884.

165. FO 403/82: Baring to Granville, 18 Oct. 1884, Cairo.

166. FO 633/55: Hunter to Baring, 15 Oct. 1884, Aden.

167. Ibid.; Fontrier, *Abou-Baker Ibrahim*, 216–18.

168. FO 633/55: Hunter to Baring, 22 Oct. 1884, Aden; Baring to Hunter, 27 Oct. 1884, Cairo.

169. 633/55: Baring to Granville, 28 Oct. 1884, Cairo.

170. FO 403/82: Kimberley to the Viceroy of India (India Office), 7 Nov. 1884.

171. FO 403/82: Major Hunter's Instructions to Redwan Pasha, Harar, Berbera, 30 Sep. 1884, Aden.

172. Ibid.

173. Ibid.

174. FO 633/55: Instructions to Lieutenant Peyton, 8 Oct. 1884, Aden.

175. Ibid.

176. Ibid.

177. FO 403/82: Hunter to Baring, 15 Oct. 1884, Aden.

178. FO 403/82: Hunter to Baring, 15 Oct. 1884, Aden.

179. FO 633/55: Hunter to Heath, 23 Oct. 1884, Aden.

180. Report on Šhawal 1306, 15 Jul. 1885, in al-Jamal, *Al-Wathā'iq al-ta'rikhiyya*, 333.

181. Ibid.

182. FO 633/55: Mancini to Nigra, 29 Oct. 1884, Rome; FO 403/82: Granville to Lumley (Foreign Office), 5 Nov. 1884; Granville to Lumley (Foreign Office), 6 Nov. 1884; Baring to Granville, 11 Nov. 1884, Cairo; Granville to Baring (Foreign Office), 11 Nov. 1884; Granville to Lumley (Foreign Office), 13 Nov. 1884.

183. FO 633/55: Hunter to Blair, 19 Oct. 1884, Aden.

184. FO 633/55: Hunter to Blair, 22 Oct. 1884, Aden.

185. FO 633/55: Baring to Granville, 17 Nov. 1884, Cairo.

186. FO 633/55: Baring to Granville, 25 Nov. 1884, Cairo; Hewett to the Secretary of Admiralty, 19 Dec. 1884, n.p.

187. FO 633/55: Baring to Granville, 26 Nov. 1884, Cairo.

188. FO 403/82: Baring to Granville, Draft of Proposed Note from Nubar Pasha to Sublime Porte, 17 Nov. 1884, Cairo.

189. FO 403/82: Baring to Granville, 3 Nov. 1884, Cairo; Granville to Baring (Foreign Office), 12 Nov. 1884.

190. FO 633/55: Hunter to Baring, 7 Nov. 1884, Zeyla.

191. FO 633/55: Baring to Granville, 12 Nov. 1884, Cairo; Granville to Baring (Foreign Office), 13 Nov. 1884; FO 403/82: Baring to Granville, 17 Nov. 1884, Cairo.

192. FO 633/55: Hunter to Baring, 17 Nov. 1884, Aden.

193. Archives des Capucins, Ms. 1242 and 2795, 161–62: Lettre manuscrite de Mgr. Taurin Cahagne au T.R.P. Provincial de Paris, 26 Nov. 1884, Obock.

194. FO 403/82: Nigra to Granville (Italian Embassy), 21 Nov. 1884, London; FO 633/55: Granville to Lumley (Foreign Office), 11 Dec. 1884); Granville to Lumley (Foreign Office), 22 Dec. 1884.

195. FO 633/55: Baring to Granville, 8 Dec. 1884, Cairo; Granville to Baring (Foreign Office), 8 Dec. 1884; Granville to Lumley (Foreign Office), 11 Dec. 1884; Baring to Granville, 13 Dec. 1884, Cairo.

196. FO 633/55: Baring to Granville, 24 Nov. 1884, Cairo.

197. FO 633/55: Raffray to Hunter, 28 Nov. 1884, Aden.

198. FO 633/55: The Viceroy of India to Kimberley, 11 Dec. 1884, Calcutta.

199. Foucher, "Harar au temps d'Arthur Rimbaud," 1:370; Miran, *L'Occupation Egyptienne*, 104–5; Report on Šhawal, 1306, 15 Jul. 1885, in al-Jamal, *Al-Wathā'iq al-ta'rikhiyya*, 333.

200. Jérôme Vérain, ed., *Arthur Rimbaud—Lettres du Harar* (Paris: Mille et Une Nuits, 2001), 45–46.

10. Harar between Egypt and Ethiopia

1. For instance, see Revault and Santelli, eds., *Harar*, 17, for a review of major periods in the history of the city in an album published in the last decade.

2. See, for instance (and in the order of the quotes), Caulk, "Harar in the 19th Century," 6; Foucher, "Harar au temps d'Artur Rimbaud," 1:370–71; Hassan, "Relation between Harar and Oromo," 33–35. A more balanced approach is taken by Ahmed Zekaria, who portrays ʿAbdullahi as "someone who tried to revert to Harar's old system of government, which relied on a closed-door policy by limiting the presence and influence of foreigners in the city." See Zekaria, "ʿAbdullāhi b. Muḥammad."

3. Wagner, "Muḥammad b. ʿAlī b. ʿAbdaššakūr."

4. For further details, see Fontrier, "Abū Bakr Ibrāhīm Šaḥim."

5. al-Jamal, *Siyasat Misr*, 214; ʿAmr ila hikimdariyat Harar wa mulhaqātihā, daftar 105 77 mukataba raqam 6 fi 16 Rajab 1293 [Decree to *hikimdariyat* Harar and Its Dependencies, notebook 107 55 no. 6, 8 Aug. 1876], in al-Jamal, *Al-Wathāʾiq al-taʾrikhiyya*, 314.

6. Min muhafazat Zayla, daftar 17 Arabic—wared al-ifadat 65 raqam 323 min Jihat al-Aqalim wa al-Muhafazat fi 19 Rabia al-Awal 1293 [From the Administration's Province of Zeila, notebook 17 simultaneity in Arabic to all the provinces, 13 Apr. 1876], in al-Jamal, *Al-Wathāʾiq al-taʾrikhiyya*, 307.

7. For more on merchants as "mediators" between occupiers and occupied, see Abner Cohen, "Cultural Strategies in the Organization of Trading Diasporas," in *The Development of Indigenous Trade and Markets in West Africa*, ed. Claude Meillassoux (London: Oxford Univ. Press, 1971), 266–81. Regarding mediation and cosmopolitan spheres in the Red Sea Basin, see Miran, *Red Sea Citizens*.

8. FO 403/82: Hunter to Baring: Memorandum Regarding the Proposed Restoration of Harar to a Member of the Old Ruling Family, 5 Apr. 1884, Aden.

9. FO 403/82: Hunter to Egerton, 4 Sep. 1884, Aden.

10. FO 403/82: Egerton to Hunter, 4 Sep. 1884, Cairo; Hunter to Egerton, 5 Sep. 1884, Aden.

11. FO 403/82: Hunter to Baring, 24 Nov. 1884, Aden.

12. Bardey, *Barr Adjam*, 333–34; Foucher, "Harar au temps d'Arthur Rimbaud," 1:371.

13. Hassan, "Relation between Harar and Oromo," 33; FO 403/83: Baring to Granville, 29 Dec. 1884, Cairo; Bardey, "Notes sur le Harar," 147–48.

14. FO 403/83: Baring to Granville, 29 Dec. 1884, Cairo.

15. Bardey, "Notes sur le Harar," 147–48.

16. Report on Šhawal, 1306, 15 Jul. 1885, in al-Jamal, *Al-Wathāʾiq al-taʾrikhiyya*, 331.

17. FO 403/82: Hunter to Baring, 24 Nov. 1884.

18. FO 403/83: Haj Abdillahi (son of the late Ameer Mohamed bin Ali bin Nasr Abd Shakor) to Hunter, 5 Jemadi II 1302, 22 Mar. 1885, Harar.

19. al-Jamal, *Siyasat Misr*, 249.

20. Paulitschke, *Harar: Forschungsreise nach den Somal*, 192–93; Bardey, *Barr Adjam*, 335.

21. Eshete, "Establishment of the Capuchin Catholic Mission," 9.

22. Archives des Capucins, Reg. 185, 173: Lettre manuscrite de Mgr. Taurin Cahagne au T.R.P. Provincial de Paris, 19 Feb. 1886, Harar.

23. FO 403/83: Hunter to Baring, 4 Mar. 1885, Aden; FO 403/83: Baring to Granville, 17 Mar. 1885, Cairo; Blair to Kimberley, 17 Mar. 1885, Aden; Granville to Baring (Foreign Office), 20 Mar. 1885. On 23 September 1885, in the battle of Kūfit, the Ethiopian military leader Ras Alula routed Digna, and the Mahdiyya presence in the northeastern parts of Ethiopia and the Red Sea was eliminated. For more details, see Erlich, *Ethiopia*, 66–70.

24. FO 403/82: Hunter to Baring, 24 Nov. 1884, Aden; Archives des Capucins, Ms. 1242 and 2795, 161–62: Lettre manuscrite de Mgr. Taurin Cahagne au T.R.P. Provincial de Paris, 26 Nov. 1884, Obock.

25. Undated Arabic manuscript, page 1, in Hassan, "Relation between Harar and Oromo," 52.

26. FO 403/84: Egerton to the Marquis of Salisbury, Précis of a Dispatch from Captain Sealy to Egerton, 1 Sep. 1885, Cairo.

27. Bardey, "Notes sur le Harar," 54; Paulitschke, *Harar: Forschungsreise nach den Somal*, 404.

28. Caulk, "Harar in the 19th Century," 6.

29. Hassan, "Relation between Harar and Oromo," 52; Paulitschke, *Harar: Forschungsreise nach den Somal*, 390.

30. Testimonies of Mumē Bashir and Haj Yusuf Abdl-Rahman in Hassan, "Relation between Harar and Oromo," 34.

31. For further details about images of sixteenth-century religious wars of Ethiopia, see Jon Abbink, "A Historical-Anthropological Approach to Islam in Ethiopia: Issues of Identity and Politics," *Journal of African Cultural Studies* 11, no. 2 (1998): 114.

32. Eshete, "Establishment of the Capuchin Catholic Mission," 9.

33. Hassan, "Relation between Harar and Oromo," 34. See also Arabic manuscript in Hassan, 52.

34. Carlo Giglio, ed. *L'Italia in Africa*, vol. 1 (Rome: Istituto poligrafico dello Stato, 1958), 2223.

35. Matteo Salvadore, "Porro expedition," in Uhlig, *Encyclopaedia Aethiopica*, 4:178–79. For more on the Porro incident and its aftermath, see Ario M. Amodeo, "I Reporti tra Italia e Abissinia nel 1886 e nel 1889 in un Carteggio inedito di Ottorino Rosa con Porro, Guasconi, Sacconi e Cecchi," *Gli Annali dell'Africa Italiana* 4, no. 3 (1941): 905–22; E. De Leone, "Le Prime Ricerche de Una Colonia e La Esplorazione Geografica, Politica ed Economica," Minister degli Affari Esteri, Comitato per la Documentazione dell'Opera dell'Italia in Africa, *L'Italia in Africa*, vol. 2 (Rome: Istituto poligrafico dello Stato, 1955);

Carlo Giglio, *Ethiopia—Mar Rosso*, vol. 1, tome 5: Documenti 1885–1886 (Roma: Poligrafico dello Stato, 1958–73); Paulitschke, *Harar: Forschungsreise nach den Somal*, 388.

36. Paulitschke, *Harar: Forschungsreise nach den Somal*, 388; Arabic manuscript pages 2–3 in Hassan, "Relation between Harar and Oromo," 52–53. The Capuchins also testified that the emir had not given the order to murder the members of the convoy and that the decision was made by the commanders in the field. See Foucher, "Harar au temps d'Arthur Rimbaud," 1:371.

37. Archives des Capucins: Père Jarosseau Microfilm (Bobine I) (n.d.) 92.

38. FO 403/83: Hunter to Baring, Agreement, 3 Apr. 1885, Aden.

39. Arabic manuscript pages 2–3 in Hassan, "Relation between Harar and Oromo," 53–54.

40. For further details about Harari-Adari identities relevant to this period, see Waldron, "A Farewell to Bab Haji," 248–49.

41. FO 403/84: Egerton to the Marquis of Salisbury, 9 Dec. 1885, Cairo.

42. Eshete, "Establishment of the Capuchin Catholic Mission," 8; Hassan, "Relation between Harar and Oromo," 33–34; Paulitschke, *Harar: Forschungsreise nach den Somal*, 386.

43. Lewis, *Modern History of Somalia*, 45–49; FO 403/84: Egerton to the Marquis of Salisbury, 9 Dec. 1885, Cairo.

44. Paulitschke, *Harar: Forschungsreise nach den Somal*, 404.

45. FO 403/84: Hunter to Egerton, 24 Nov. 1885, Aden.

46. Hassan, "Relation between Harar and Oromo," 37–38; Paulitschke, *Harar: Forschungsreise nach den Somal*, 397–404.

47. Caulk, "Occupation of Harar," 6–8.

48. See testimonials of Hararis and Oromos regarding ʻAbdullahi's efforts to recruit soldiers for a war against Menilek: Caulk, "Occupation of Harar," 13; Hassan, "Relation between Harar and Oromo," 42–43.

49. Sevir Chernetsov, "Ç̣ällänqo," in Uhlig, *Encyclopaedia Aethiopica*, 1:676–77.

50. For more on the battle of Čällänqo and its progression, see Caulk, "Occupation of Harar," 14–17; Hassan, "Relation between Harar and Oromo," 43–44.

51. For more on the cooperation between the Harari elites and Makonnen at the outset of the Ethiopian occupation, see Richard A. Caulk, "Menilek's Conquest and Local Leaders in Harar," *History Society of Ethiopia: The History and Culture of the People of Harar Province* (Addis Ababa: Addis Ababa Univ., Jun. 1975), 1–15.

52. Tim Carmichael, "Mäkʷännən Wäldä Mika'el," in Uhlig, *Encyclopaedia Aethiopica*, 3:686–87; Caulk, "Menilek's Conquest," 1–15.

53. Carlo Conti-Rossini, "Testi in Lingua Harari: Cronica di Harar," *Rivista Degli Studi Orientali* 8 (Nov. 1919): 425.

54. Tim Carmichael, "Harär from the late 19th to the 20th Century," in Uhlig, *Encyclopaedia Aethiopica*, 2:1020–21; Enrico Cerulli, "La Fine dell'Emirate di Harar in Nuovi

Documenti Storici," *Annali dell'Instituto Universitario Orientale di Napoli*, annoli nuova series 14 (1964): 75–82.

11. Afterword: Narratives in a Transitional Period

1. Revault and Santelli, eds., *Harar*, preface, 5.

2. For additional reading, see Brooke, "Settlements of the Eastern Galla." For further details about the Ethiopian expansions during the latter part of the nineteenth century, see Donham and James, eds., *Southern Marches*.

3. Carmichael, "Mäk^{w}ännən Wäldä Mika'el"; Carmichael, "Harär from the Late 19th to the 20th Century."

Bibliography

Archives

Ethiopia

Institute of Ethiopian Studies (IES), Addis Ababa University

France

Archives des Capucins, Paris: Correspondance entre les missionnaires à Harar et la R.P. Provincial de Paris, 1881–1885

Bibliothèque Nationale de France, Paris

Great Britain

Correspondence Respecting Egyptian Proceedings on the Somali Coast (BP), British Library, London

Foreign Office Archive (FO), National Archives (formerly Public Record Office), London

Royal Geographical Society Archive (RGS/BG LBR), London

Italy

Istituto Italiano per L'Africa e L'Oriente, Rome

Società Geografica Italiana, Rome

Books, Articles, and Other Published or Secondary Sources

Abate, Alula. "Studien zur jüngeren Entwicklung der Kulturlandschaft im Hochland von Harar." PhD diss., K. Friedrich-Wilhelms Universität, 1969.

Abbink, G. J. "Burton, Richard Francis." In Uhlig, *Encyclopaedia Aethiopica*, 1:649–50.

———. "A Historical-Anthropological Approach to Islam in Ethiopia: Issues of Identity and Politics." *Journal of African Cultural Studies* 11, no. 2 (1998): 109–24.

Abdunasir, Kabir Abdulmuhaimin. "Different Names of Jugal 5 Gates." *Everything Harar.* Accessed 27 Apr. 2018. http://www.everythingharar.com/e-reading/articles/225-different-names-of-jugol-5-gates.

Abir, Mordechai. "Caravan Trade and History in the Northern Parts of East Africa." *Paideuma, Mitteilungen zur Kulturkunde*, 14:113–14. Wiesbaden: F. Steiner, 1968.

———. *Ethiopia: The Era of the Princes; the Challenge of Islam and the Re-unification of the Christian Empire, 1769–1855.* London: Longmans, 1968.

Ahmed, Abdullahi Mohammed. "A Survey of the Harar Djugel (Wall) and Its Gates." In *Proceedings of the First National Conference of Ethiopia Studies: Addis Ababa, April 11–12, 1990*, edited by Richard Pankhurst, Ahmed Zekaria, and Teddese Beyene, 321–34. Addis Ababa: Institute of Ethiopian Studies, Addis Ababa University, 1990.

Ahmed, Hussein. *Islam in Nineteenth-Century Wallo, Ethiopia: Revival, Reform and Reaction*. Leiden: Brill, 2001.

Ahmed, Yusuf. "Aföča." *Journal of Ethiopian Studies* 3, no. 2 (1965): 125–32.

———. "An Inquiry into Some Aspects of the Economy of Harar and the Records of the Household Economy of the Amirs of Harar (1825–1875)." *Ethnological Society Bulletin* 1, no. 1–10, and 2, no. 1 (1954–1961), edited by Alula Pankhurst, 375–419. Addis Ababa: Department of Sociology and Social Administration, Addis Ababa Univ., 1961.

———. "An Inquiry into Some Aspects of the Economy of Harar and the Records of the Household Economy of the Amirs of Harar (1825–1875)." *University College of Addis Ababa Ethnographic Bulletin* No. 5, 7–41. Addis Ababa, 1961.

Ajayi, J. F. Ade. "Africa at the Beginning of the Nineteenth Century: Issues and Prospects." In *Africa in the Nineteenth Century until the 1880s*, edited by J. F. Ade Ajayi, 1–22. Vol. 6 of *General History of Africa*. Paris: United Nations Educational, Scientific and Cultural Organization, 1989.

———. "Colonialism: An Episode in African History." In *Colonialism in Africa*, edited by Lewis Gann and Peter Duignan, 1:497–509. London: Cambridge Univ. Press, 1969.

Alberto, Antonios, and Andreu Martinez. "Capuchins." In Uhlig, *Encyclopaedia Aethiopica*, 1:682–83.

Alexander, John. "Ottoman Frontiers Policies in North-East Africa." In Peacock, *Frontiers of the Ottoman World*, 225–34.

Amborn, Hermann. "Paulitschke, Philipp Victor," in Uhlig, *Encyclopaedia Aethiopica*, 4:124.

Amer, Mustafa. "Some Unpublished Egyptian Maps of Harär," *Bulletin de la Société Royale de Géographie d'Egypte* 19 (1937): 289–90 + six maps.

Ammi, Nadia. "Awach, the Founding Fathers of Harar." In *Harar: A Muslim City of Ethiopia*, edited by Philippe Revault and Serge Santelli, 73–89. Paris: Maisonneuve and Larose, 2004.

Amodeo, Ario M. "I Reporti tra Italia e Abissinia nel 1886 e nel 1889 in un Carteggio inedito di Ottorino Rosa con Porro, Guasconi, Sacconi e Cecchi," *Gli Annali dell'Africa Italiana* 4, no. 3 (1941): 905–22.

Arnold, David. *Colonizing the Body: State Medicine and Epidemic Disease in Nineteenth-Century India*. Berkeley: Univ. of California Press, 1993.

Asante, Belle. "Harär: Introduction." In Uhlig, *Encyclopaedia Aethiopica*, 2:1012–13.

Audon, Henry. "Voyages au Choa (1884–1888)." *Le Tour du Monde* 58 (Paris, 1889).

Avçi, Yasemin. "The Application of Tanzimat in the Desert: The Bedouins and the Creation of a New Town in Southern Palestine (1860–1914)." *Middle Eastern Studies* 45, no. 6 (Nov. 2009): 969–83.

Balandier, Georges. "The Colonial Situation—A Theoretical Approach," in *Social Change: The Colonial Situation*, edited by Immanuel Wallerstein, 34–61. New York: John Wiley & Sons, 1966.

Ballhatchet, Kenneth. *Race, Class and Sex under Raj: Imperial Attitudes and Policies and their Critics, 1793–1905*. New York: St. Martin's Press, 1980.

Banti, Giorgio. "Somali Language." In Uhlig, *Encyclopaedia Aethiopica*, 4:693–96.

Bardey, Alfred. *Barr Adjam—Souvenirs d'Afrique Orientale 1880–1887*. Paris: ed. du SNRS, 1981.

———. "Notes sur le Harar." *Bulletin de Géographie Historique et Descriptive* 12 (1897): 130–80.

Bartels, Lambert. *Oromo Religion*. Berlin: Dietrich Reimer, 1983.

Bassi, Marco. "Boorana." In Uhlig, *Encyclopaedia Aethiopica*, 1:605–7.

Baxter, Paul T. W. "Gadaa." In Uhlig, *Encyclopaedia Aethiopica*, 2:633–38.

———. "Gosa." In Uhlig, *Encyclopaedia Aethiopica*, 2:857–58.

———. "The Problem of the Oromo or the Problem for the Oromo?" In *Nationalism and Self-Determination in the Horn of Africa*, edited by Ioan M. Lewis, 129–49. London: Ithaca, 1983.

Bayerle, Gustav. *Pashas, Begs and Effendis: A Historical Dictionary of Titles and Terms in the Ottoman Empire*. Istanbul: Isis Press, 1997.

Bayumi, ʿAbdallah al-. *Al-Taʾarikh al-ʿaskari al-Misri fi al-ʿasr al-hadith: al-kitab al-thalit: al-taʾarikh al-ʿaskari li-alǧayš al-Misri fi ʿasr hulaffaʾ Muhammad ʿAlī* [The Egyptian Military History in the Modern Period: The Third Book: The Military History of the Egyptian Army at the Time of Muhammad ʿAlī's Successors]. Cairo, 1993.

Beachy, R. "The East African Ivory Trade in the 19th Century." *Journal of African History* 8, no. 2 (1967): 269–90.

Ben-Dror, Avishai. "Arthur Rimbaud in Harär: Images, Reality, Memory." *Northeast African Studies* 14, no. 2 (2014): 159–82.

Bey, Dor. "Werner Munzinger Pacha." *Bulletin de la Société Khédiviale de Géographie du Caire*, vol. 1 (1876) no. 1: 124–27; no. 8: 38; nos. 9–10: 43–76.

Bhabha, Homi K. *The Location of Culture*. London; New York: Routledge, 1994.

Bleuchot, Hervé. "Le Sudan au XXIème siècle." In *Le Sudan Contemporain*, edited by Marc Lavergne, 115–69. Paris: Karthala, 1989.

Bonati, Manlio. "Sacconi, Pietro." In Uhlig, *Encyclopaedia Aethiopica*, 4:439.

Bonola Bey, Federico. *L'Egypte et la Géographie*. Cairo: Imprimerie Nationale, 1889.

Boutros-Ghali, Boutros. "The Foreign Policy of Egypt (United Arab Republic)." In *Foreign Policy in a World of Change*, edited by Joseph E. Black and Kenneth W. Thompson, 319–48. New York: Harper & Row, 1963.

Braukämper, Ulrich. *Islamic History and Culture in Southern Ethiopia—Collected Essays*. Hamburg: Lit Verlag Münster, 2002.

———. "Notes on the Islamization and the Muslim Shrine of the Harar Plateau." In *Islamic History and Culture in Southern Ethiopia—Collected Essays*, edited by Ulrich Braukämper, 106–23. Hamburg: Lit Verlag Münster, 2002.

———. "Notes on the Islamization and Muslim Shrines of the Harar Plateau." In *Proceedings of the Second International Congress of Somali Studies, Hamburg, 1–6 August 1983*, edited by Thomas Labahn, 2:145–74. Hamburg: H. Buske, 1984.

———. "Oromo Country of Origin: A Reconsideration of Hypotheses." In *Proceedings of the Sixth International Conference of Ethiopian Studies, Tel-Aviv,*

14–17 April 1980, edited by Gideon Goldenberg, 25–40. Cape Town: A. A. Balkema, 1986.

Brockett, A. “Anglo-French Rivalry on the Somali Coast in the 1880s.” In *Proceedings of the 1968 Conference of the Historical Association of Kenya*, 127–56. Nairobi: East African Publishing House, 1970.

Brooke, Clarke Harding, Jr. “Settlements of the Eastern Galla, Hararge Province, Ethiopia.” PhD diss., University of Nebraska, 1956.

Bulletin de la Société Khédiviale de Géographie du Caire (Cairo) 1, no. 4 (1877); no. 8 (1881): 29–42; nos. 9–10 (1881); 2, no. 7 (1881): 349; 10 (1887): 575–91.

Bulletin de l'Etat-Major Général de l'Armée Egyptienne (Cairo) 1, no. 1 (1876): 29–35; no. 5 (1877): 385–400; no. 6 (1877): 462–79.

Burton, Richard. *First Footsteps in East Africa, or an Exploration of Harar.* Vols. 1 and 2. New York: Dover Publications, 1987. First published in London, 1856. Page references are to the Dover edition.

Busayli Shatir, ʿAbd al-Jalil al-. *Maʿalim Ta'rikh Sudan wa Wadi al-Nil min al-Qarn al-ʿAshr ila al-Qarn al-Tasi' ʿAshar al-Milady* [The Outlines of the History of Sudan and the Nile Valley from the Tenth Century to the Nineteenth Century]. Cairo: Makatabat al-ʿArab, 1955.

Bustorf, Dirk. “Oromo Religion.” In Uhlig, *Encyclopaedia Aethiopica*, 4:64–65.

Callaway, Helen. *Gender, Culture and Empire: European Women in Colonial Nigeria*. London Macmillan Press, 1987.

Carmichael, Tim. “Harär from the late 19th to the 20th Century.” In Uhlig, *Encyclopaedia Aethiopica*, 2:1020–21.

———. “Mäkʷännən Wäldä Mika'el.” In Uhlig, *Encyclopaedia Aethiopica*, 3:686–87.

———. “Religion, Language and Nationalism: Harari Muslims in Christian Ethiopia.” In *Islam in World Cultures Comparative Perspectives*, edited by Michael Feener, 217–52. Santa Barbara, CA: ABC-CLIO Publishers, 2004.

Caulk, Richard A. “Firearms and Princely Power in 19th Century Ethiopia.” Paper prepared for the Interdisciplinary Seminar of the Faculties of Arts and Education, Haile Selassie I University, Addis Ababa, 1969–70.

———. “Firearms and Princely Power in Ethiopia in the Nineteenth Century.” *Journal of African History* 8, no. 4 (1972): 609–30.

———. “Harar in the 19th Century and the Loss of Its Independence.” Paper prepared for the Interdisciplinary Seminar of the Faculties of Arts and Education, Addis Ababa University, 1967–68.

———. "Harar Town and Its Neighbors in the Nineteenth Century." *Journal of African History* 18, no. 3 (1977): 369–86.

———. "Menilek's Conquest and Local Leaders in Harar," *History Society of Ethiopia: The History and Culture of the People of Harar Province*, 1–15. Addis Ababa: Addis Ababa Univ., Jun. 1975.

———. "The Occupation of Harar: January 1887." *Journal of Ethiopian Studies* 9 (Jul. 1971): 1–20.

Cecchi, Antonio. *Da Zeila alle Frontiere del Caffa*, 3 vols. Rome: E. Loescher, 1886–87.

Cerulli, Enrico. "Documenti arabi per la storia dell'Etiopia." *Rendiconti della Reale Accademia dei Lincei* 6, no. 4 (1931): 37–101.

———. "La Fine dell'Emirate di Harar in Nuovi Documenti Storici." *Annali dell'Instituto Universitario Orientale di Napoli*, annoli nuova series 14 (1964): 75–82.

———. *Le Popolazioni della Somalia nella Tradizioni Storica Locl.* Rome: Dott. Giovanni Bardi, tipografo della R. Accademia nazionale dei Lincei, 1926.

Chernetsov, Sevir. "Čällänqo." In Uhlig, *Encyclopaedia Aethiopica*, 1:676–77.

Chihab ed-Din, Ahmed Ben Abd el-Qader (Arab Faqih). *Futuh al-Habasha—Histoire de la Conquète de L'Abyssinie*. Translated and edited by R. Basset. Paris: E. Leroux, 1897.

Clapham, Christopher. "Mənilək II." In Uhlig, *Encyclopaedia Aethiopica*, 3:922–27.

Coats, Peter D. "Factors of Intermediacy in Nineteenth Century Africa: The Case of the Issa of the Horn." In *Proceedings of the Second International Congress of Somali Studies*, edited by Thomas Labahn, 2:180–83. Hamburg: H. Buske, 1984.

Cohen, Abner. "Cultural Strategies in the Organization of Trading Diasporas." In *The Development of Indigenous Trade and Markets in West Africa*, edited by Claude Meillassoux, 266–81. London: Oxford Univ. Press, 1971.

Cohen, Bernard S. *Colonialism and Its Forms of Knowledge: The British in India.* Princeton: Princeton Univ. Press, 1996.

Cole, J. R. I. *Colonialism and Revolution in the Middle East: Social and Cultural Origins of Egypt's Urabi Movement.* Princeton, NJ: Princeton Univ. Press, 1993.

Conti-Rossini, Carlo. "Testi in Lingua Harari: Cronica di Harar." *Rivista Degli Studi Orientali* 8 (Nov. 1919): 401–25.

———. "Testi in Lingue Harari." *Miscellanea* 2 (1921), 413–14.

Cooper, Frederick, and Ann Laura Stoler, eds. *Tensions of Empire: Colonial Cultures in a Bourgeois World*. Berkeley and Los Angeles: Univ. of California Press., 1997.

Crabitès, Pierre. *Gordon: The Sudan and Slavery*. London: G. Routledge and Sons, 1933.

Declich, Francesca. "Habar Awal." In Uhlig, *Encyclopaedia Aethiopica*, 2:947–48.

De Leone, E. "La Prime Ricerche di Una Colonia e La Esplorazione Geografica, Politica ed Economica." Minister degli Affari Esteri, Comitato per la Documentazione dell'Opera dell'Italia in Africa. *L'Italia in Africa*, Vol. 2. Rome: Istituto poligrafico dello Stato, 1955.

Deringil, Selim. "'They Live in a State of Nomadism and Savagery': The Late Ottoman Empire and the Post-Colonial Debate." *Comparative Studies in Society and History* 45 (Apr. 2003): 311–42.

Desplat, Patrick. "The Articulation of Religious Identities and Their Boundaries in Ethiopia: Labelling Difference and Processes of Contextualization of Islam." *Journal of Religion in Africa* 35, no. 4 (2005): 482–505.

Dey McEntry, William. *Moslem Egypt and Christian Abyssinia*. New York: Atkin & Prout, 1969. First published in 1880.

Dirks, Nicholas B., ed. *Colonialism and Culture*. Ann Arbor: Univ. of Michigan Press, 1992.

Donham, Donald, and Wendy James, eds. *The Southern Marches of Imperial Ethiopia: Essays in History and Social Anthropology*. Oxford: James Curry, 2002.

Douin, Georges. *Histoire du Règne du Khédive Ismail*, 3 vols. Cairo: Impr. Del'Innst. Français d'Archéologie Orientale du Caire; Rome: Istituto poligrafico dello stato and L'Imprimerie de L'Institut Français d'Archéologie Orientale; for La Société Royale de Géographie d'Égypte, 1936–41.

Dunn, John P. *Khedive Ismail's Army*. New York: Routledge, 2005.

Earl of Cromer. *Modern Egypt*, 2 vols. London: Macmillan, 1911.

Edris, Abdunasir. "Traditional Islamic Centers of Learning in Harar." BA thesis, Addis Ababa University, 1992.

El Shakry, Omnia. *The Great Social Laboratory: Subjects of Knowledge in Colonial and Postcolonial Egypt*. Stanford, CA: Stanford Univ. Press, 2007.

Elzein, Intisar. "Ottoman Archaeology of the Middle Nile Valley in the Sudan." In Peacock, *Frontiers of the Ottoman World*, 371–83.

Emerson, Rupert. *From Empire to Nation*. Cambridge, MA: Harvard Univ. Press, 1968.

———. "The Problem of Identity, Selfhood and Image of New Nation," *Comparative Politics* 1, no. 3 (Apr. 1969), 297–312.

Ericson, Paul A., and Lian D. Murphy. *A History of Anthropological Theory.* Toronto: Univ. of Toronto Press, 2008.

Erlich, Haggai. *The Cross and the River: Ethiopia, Egypt and the Nile.* Colorado: Lynne Rienner Publishers, 2002.

———. "The Egyptian-Ethiopian War." In Uhlig, *Encyclopaedia Aethiopica,* 2:245–46.

———. *Ethiopia and the Middle East.* Colorado: Lynne Rienner Publishers, 1994.

———. "Gordon, Charles George." In Uhlig, *Encyclopaedia Aethiopica,* 2:851–52.

———. "Ismā'īl." In Uhlig, *Encyclopaedia Aethiopica,* 3:216–17.

———. "Muḥammad 'Alī." In Uhlig, *Encyclopaedia Aethiopica,* 5:449–50.

———. *Ras Alula and the Scramble for Africa.* Asmara: Red Sea Press, 1996.

Erlich, Haggai, and Wolbert Smidt. "Märäb Malləš." In Uhlig, *Encyclopaedia Aethiopica,* 3:773–75.

Eshete, Aleme. "The Establishment of the Capuchin Catholic Mission Among the Qottu of Harar: 1881–1889." Paper prepared for the conference on Harari Studies by the Historical Society of Ethiopia, Addis Ababa University, Jun. 1975.

"Exposé de Nadi Pacha à la séance du 23 Mars 1883." *Bulletin de la Société Khédiviale de Géographie du Caire* 2, no. 8 (Cairo, 1886): 464.

Fahmy, Khaled. *All the Pasha's Men: Mehmed Ali, His Army and the Making of Modern Egypt.* Cambridge: Cambridge Univ. Press, 1997.

Ferrand, Gabriel. "Notes sur la situation politique, commerciale et religieuse du pachalik de Harar et ses dépendances." *Bulletin de la Société de Géographie de l'Est,* part 1, vol. 8 (Nancy, 1886): 1–17, 231–44.

Ficquet, Eloi. "Cahagne Taurin." In Uhlig, *Encyclopaedia Aethiopica,* 1:664–65.

Fontrier, Marc. *Abou-Baker Ibrahim: Pacha de Zeyla—Marchand d'Esclaves.* Paris: L'Harmattan, 2003.

———. "Abū Bakr Ibrāhīm Šaḥim." In Uhlig, *Encyclopaedia Aethiopica,* 1:52.

Foucher, Emile. "Harar au temps d'Arthur Rimbaud, 1880–1891." In *Proceedings of the 8th International Conference of Ethiopian Studies,* edited by Taddese Beyene, 1:367–73. Addis Ababa: Addis Ababa Univ. Press, 1988.

———. "Une Page de L'Histoire de Harar ou Arthur Rimbaud sous L'Administration Egyptienne." In *Quaderni di Stadi Etiopicu,* 479–85. Asmara: Centro studi etiopici, 1980.

Gabre-Sellassie, Zewde. *Yohannes IV of Ethiopia.* Oxford: Clarendon Press, 1975.

Gadid, Mahdi A. "Feudalism in the Emirate of Harar up to 1887." BA thesis, Addis Ababa University, Jul. 1979.

Garad, Abdurahman. *Harar: Wirtschaftsgeschichte eines Emirats im Horn von Afrika (1825–75)*. Frankfurt am Main: Peter Lang, 1990.

Gascon, Alain. "Gara Mulläta." In Uhlig, *Encyclopaedia Aethiopica*, 2:695–96.

Gebissa, Ezekiel. *Leaf of Allah: Khat and Agricultural Transformation in Harerge Ethiopia 1875–1991*. Athens, OH: Ohio Univ. Press, 2004.

Gibb, C. T. Camilla. "Āw." In Uhlig, *Encyclopaedia Aethiopica*, 1:398–99.

———. "Baraka without Borders: Integrating Communities in the City of Saints," *Journal of Religion in Africa* 29, no. 1 (1999): 88–108.

———. "In the City of the Saints: Religion, Politics and Gender in Harar, Ethiopia." PhD diss., University of Oxford, 1997.

Giglio, Carlo. *Ethiopia—Mar Rosso*, 5 vols. Rome: Istituto Poligrafico dello Stato, 1955–72.

———, ed. *L'Italia in Africa*, Vol. 1. Rome: Istituto Poligrafico dello Stato, 1958.

Goldenberg, Gideon. "Gurage." In Uhlig, *Encyclopaedia Aethiopica*, 2:924–28.

Gori, Alessandro. "Gärad." In Uhlig, *Encyclopaedia Aethiopica*, 2:696–97.

Grant, Jonathan A. *Rulers, Guns and Money: The Global Arms Trade in the Age of Imperialism*. Cambridge, MA: Harvard Univ. Press, 2007.

Grey, Richard. *History of the Southern Sudan 1839–1899*. London: Oxford Univ. Press, 1961.

Hacisalihoglu, Mehmet. "Border, Maps and Censuses: The Politicization of Geography and Statistics in the Multi-Ethnic Ottoman Empire." In *Comparing Empires: Encounters and Transfers in the Long Nineteenth Century*, edited by Jörn Leonhard and Ulrike von Hirschhausen, 171–210. Göttingen: Vandenhoeck & Ruprecht, 2011.

Haji, Abas. "The History of Arssi: 1880–1935." BA thesis, Addis Ababa University, 1982.

Haraz, Rajab. *Ifriqiya al-sharqia wa al-Isti'imar al-Urubi* [East Africa and European Imperialism]. Cairo, 1968.

Harley, J. B., and David Woodward, eds. *Cartography in the Traditional African, American, Arctic, Australian, and Pacific Societies*. Vol. 2.3 of *The History of Cartography*. Chicago: Univ. of Chicago Press, 1998.

———, eds. *Cartography in the Traditional Islamic and South Asian Societies*. Vol. 2.1 of *The History of Cartography*. Chicago: Univ. of Chicago Press, 1992.

Harris, William Cornwallis. *Highlands of Ethiopia*, 3 vols. London: Longman Brown, 1844.

Harrison, Nicholas. "A Roomy Place Full of Possibilities: Said's *Orientalism* and the Literary." In *Edward Said and the Literary, Social and Political World*, edited by Ranjan Ghosh, 3–18. New York: Routledge, 2009.

Hart, William D. *Edward Said and the Religious Effects of Culture*. Cambridge: Cambridge Univ. Press, 2000.

Hassen, Mohammed. "Baarentuu." In Uhlig, *Encyclopaedia Aethiopica*, 1:426–27.

———. *The Oromo of Ethiopia: A History*. Cambridge: Cambridge Univ. Press, 1990.

Hassan, Muhammad. "The Relation between Harar and the Surrounding Oromo 1800–1887." BA thesis, Haile Sellasie I University, 1973.

Headrick, Daniel R. *The Tools of Empire: Technology and European Imperialism in the Nineteenth Century*. New York: Oxford Univ. Press, 1981.

Hecht, Elisabeth-Dorothea. "Afōča." In Uhlig, *Encyclopaedia Aethiopica*, 1:127–28.

———. "Ç̣at in Harär." In Uhlig, *Encyclopaedia Aethiopica*, 1:698.

———. "The City of Harar and the Traditional Harar House." *Journal of Ethiopian Studies* 15 (1982): 57–78.

Hersi, Abdirahman Ali. "Egyptian Administration in Somaliland 1874–1885." Paper presented at the International Symposium on the African Horn, 5–10 Jan. 1985, Institute of African Research and Studies, University of Cairo.

Hill, George B. *Colonel Gordon in Central Africa 1874–1879*. New York: Macmillan, 1969. First published in England, 1881.

Hobsbawm, Eric. *On History*. London: Weidenfeld & Nicolson, 1997.

Hodgkin, Thomas. *Nationalism in Colonial Africa*. New York: Frederick Muller, 1956.

Holt, Peter M. *Egypt and the Fertile Crescent, 1516–1922*. Ithaca, NY: Cornell Univ. Press, 1966.

Holt, Peter M., and M. W. Daly, eds. *A History of the Sudan*, 4th ed. London: Weidenfeld & Nicolson, 1988.

Jalata, Asafa. *Oromia and Ethiopia: State Formation and Ethno-national Conflict 1868–1992*. Boulder, CO: Lynne Rienner, 1993.

Jamal, Shawqī 'Atā'Allāh al-. *Siyasat Misr fi al-bahr al-achmar fi al-nisf al-thani min al-qarn al-tsi' 'ashar* [The Egyptian Policy in the Red Sea in the Second Part of the Nineteenth Century]. Cairo: Wizarat al-Takafa, al-Maktaba al-'Arabia, 1974.

———. *Al-Wathā'iq al-ta'rikhiyya li-siyāsat Misr fī al-bahr al-achmar, 1863–1879* [Historical Documents of the Egyptian Policy in the Red Sea, 1863–1879]. Cairo: Matba'at lajnat al-bayan al-'arabi, 1959.

Jansen, Marius B. "The Meiji Restoration." In *The Cambridge History of Japan*. Vol. 5, *The Nineteenth Century*, edited by Marius B. Jansen, 308–66. New York: Cambridge Univ. Press, 1989.

Jesman, Czeslaw. "Egyptian Invasion of Ethiopia." *African Affairs: Journal of the Royal African Society* 58, no. 230 (Jan. 1959): 75–82.

Koehn, Peter, and Sidney R. Waldron. *Afoca: A Link between Community and Administration in Harar, Ethiopia*. Syracuse, NY: Maxwell School of Citizenship and Public Affairs, Syracuse Univ., 1978.

Labrousse, Henri. "Rivalité entre L'Égypte et L'Éthiopie dans la Mer Rouge à la fin du XIXe siècle." In *Proceedings of the Seventh International Conference of Ethiopian Studies*. Addis Ababa: Institute of Ethiopian Studies; Uppsala: Scandinavian Institute of African Studies, 1984.

Landes, David S. *Bankers and Pashas: International Finance and Economic Imperialism in Egypt*. Cambridge, MA: Harvard Univ. Press, 1958.

Lane, Paul, and Douglas Johnson. "The Archaeology and History of Slavery in South Sudan in the Nineteenth Century." In Peacock, *Frontiers of the Ottoman World*, 509–53.

Legesse, Asmarom. *Gada: Three Approaches to the Study of an African Society*. New York: Free Press, 1973.

Lenci, Marco. "Antonelli, Pietro." In Uhlig, *Encyclopaedia Aethiopica*, 1:283.

———. "Cecchi, Antonio." In Uhlig, *Encyclopaedia Aethiopica*, 1:704.

"Lettre de Lucereau au Président de la Société de Géographie Commerciale de Paris, Harar, le 12 août 1880(?)." *Bulletin de la Société de Géographie Commerciale de Paris* 3 (Paris: Oct. 1880–Oct. 1881): 47.

Lewis, Herbert S., and Dirk Bustorf. "Mooti." In Uhlig, *Encyclopaedia Aethiopica*, 3:1015–16.

Lewis, Ioan M. *A Modern History of Somalia: Nation and State in the Horn of Africa*. London: Longmans, 1988.

———, ed. *Nationalism and Self-Determination in the Horn of Africa*. London: Ithaca Press, 1983.

———. *A Pastoral Democracy*. London: Oxford Univ. Press, 1982.

Linsly, James Frank. *The Unknown Horn of Africa: An exploration from Berbera to the Leopard River*. London: George Philip, 1888.

Longrigg, Stephan A. *A Short History of Eritrea*. New York: Oxford Univ. Press, 1945; repr., Westport, CT: Greenwood Press, 1974.

Makdisi, Ussama. "Ottoman Orientalism." *American Historical Review* 107, no. 3 (Jun. 2002): 768–98.

Mallinson, Michael, Laurence Smith, Colin Bren, Wes Forsythe, and Jack Phillips. "Ottoman Suakin 1541–1865: Lost and Found." In Peacock, *Frontiers of the Ottoman World*, 469–92.

Marlow, John. *Cromer in Egypt*. New York: Praeger, 1971.

Marston, Thomas E. *Britain's Imperial Role in the Red Sea Area 1800–1878*. Hamden: Shoe String Press, 1961.

Martin, Percy F. *The Sudan in Evolution: A Study of the Economic, Financial and Administrative Conditions of the Anglo-Egyptian Sudan*. London: Constable and Company Ltd., 1921.

Maryam, Jara Haile. "An Approach to the Conservation of the Historical Town of Harar." In *Proceedings of the First National Conference of Ethiopian Studies, Addis Ababa, April 11–12 1990*, edited by Richard Pankhurst, Ahmed Zekaria, and Teddese Beyene, 403–7. Addis Ababa: Institute of Ethiopian Studies, Addis Ababa University.

———. "Historic Town of Harar: An Approach to Its Conservation." Master's thesis, Institute of Advanced Architectural Studies, University of New York, 1989.

Melbaa, Gada. *Oromia: A Brief Introduction*. Finfine, Oromia: Gada Melbaa, 1980.

Mengste-ab, Adhana. "The Occupation of Keren by the Egyptians, 4 July 1872–10 April 1885." In *Proceedings of the First International Conference of Ethiopian Studies*, edited by Richard Pankhurst, 367–81. Addis Ababa: Institute of Ethiopian Studies, Addis Ababa Univ., 1990.

Minawi, Mustafa. *The Ottoman Scramble for Africa: Empire and Diplomacy in the Sahara and the Hijaz*. Stanford, CA: Stanford Univ. Press, 2016.

Miran, Jonathan. "Bardey, Xavier Alfred." In Uhlig, *Encyclopaedia Aethiopica*, 1:476.

———. "Mohammed Mokhtar, officier égyptien et explorateur." In *Les orientalistes sont des aventuriers: guirlande offerte à Joseph Tubiana par ses élèves et ses amis*, edited by Alain Rouaud, 130–35. Paris: Sépia, 1999.

———. "Muḥammad Muḫtār." In Uhlig, *Encyclopaedia Aethiopica*, 3:1054.

———. "Muḥammad Nādī." In Uhlig, *Encyclopaedia Aethiopica*, 3:1054–55.

———. "Muḥammad Ra'ūf." In Uhlig, *Encyclopaedia Aethiopica*, 3:1056–57.

———. *L'Occupation Egyptienne de Harar (1875–1885)*, Mémoire de Diplôme de Recherche et d'Etudes Appliquées Est-Africaines et Malagaches. Paris: Institut National des Langues et Civilisations Orientales, 1993.

———. *Red Sea Citizens: Cosmopolitan Society and Cultural Change in Massawa*. Bloomington: Indiana Univ. Press, 2009.

Miran, Jonathan, and Emeri van Donzel. "Nā'ib." In Uhlig, *Encyclopaedia Aethiopica*, 3:1116–18.

Mitchell, Timothy. *Colonizing Egypt*. Cambridge: Cambridge Univ. Press, 1988.

———. "Orientalism and the Exhibitionary Order." In *Colonialism and Culture*, edited by Nicholas B. Dirks, 309–14. Ann Arbor: Univ. of Michigan Press, 1992.

Moktar, Mohammed. "Notes sur le Pays de Harrar." *Bulletin de la Société Khédiviale de Géographie* 1, no. 4 (1876): 351–97.

Moore-Harell, Alice. *Gordon and the Sudan: Prologue to the Mahdiyya 1877–1880*. London: Frank Cass, 2001.

Morin, Didier. "'Afar." In Uhlig, *Encyclopaedia Aethiopica*, 1:115–16.

———. "Dankáli." In Uhlig, *Encyclopaedia Aethiopica*, 2:89–90.

———. "Gadabuursi." In Uhlig, *Encyclopaedia Aethiopica*, 2:639–41.

———. "'Issa." In Uhlig, *Encyclopaedia Aethiopica*, 3:218–19.

Müller, C. Detlef G., and Wolbert G. C. Smidt. "Munzinger, Werner." In Uhlig, *Encyclopaedia Aethiopica*, 3:1070–73.

Muth, Franz-Christoph. "Aḥmad b. Ibrāhīm al-Ġāzī." In Uhlig, *Encyclopaedia Aethiopica*, 1:155–58.

———. "Nūr b. Muǧāhid." In Uhlig, *Encyclopaedia Aethiopica*, 3:1209–10.

Myntti, Cyntia. *Paris along the Nile: Architecture in Cairo from the Belle Epoque*. Cairo: American Univ. in Cairo Press, 1999.

Nicolas, Andrea. "Bokkuu." In Uhlig, *Encyclopaedia Aethiopica*, 1:602.

Ofcansky, Thomas P. "Dir ethnography." In Uhlig, *Encyclopaedia Aethiopica*, 2:166–67.

———. "Gundät." In Uhlig, *Encyclopaedia Aethiopica*, 2:921–22.

Osterhammel, Jürgen. *Colonialism: A Theoretical Review*. Princeton, NJ: Markus Wiener Publishers, 1997.

Pankhurst, E. Sylvia. "Harar under Egyptian Rule." In "Special Issue on Harar," edited by Sylvia E. Pankhurst, *Ethiopia Observer* 2, no. 2 (1958): 56–59.

Pankhurst, Richard. "Č̣əqa Šum." In Uhlig, *Encyclopaedia Aethiopica*, 1:707–8.

———. "Harar in the Old Days." In "Special Issue on Harar," edited by Sylvia E. Pankhurst, *Ethiopia Observer* 2, no. 2 (1958): 47–56.

———. "Harris, William Cornwallis." In Uhlig, *Encyclopaedia Aethiopica*, 2:1036–37.

———. *History of Ethiopian Towns*. Vol. 2, *From the Mid-Nineteenth Century to 1935* (178–273). Wiesbaden: F. Steiner Verlag, 1985.

———. *Travelers in Ethiopia*. London: Oxford Univ. Press, 1965.

Paulitschke, Philipp. *Ethnographie Nordost-Afrikas: Die Materielle Kultur der Danakil, Galla und Somal*. Berlin: Dietrich Reimer, 1893.

———. *Harar: Forschungsreise nach den Somal und Gallaländern Ostafrikas*. Leipzig: F. A. Brockhaus, 1888.

———. "Le Harar sous l'administration égyptienne (1875–1885)." *Bulletin de la Société Khédiviale de Géographie du Caire* 10, no. 2 (Mar. 1887): 575–91.

Peacock, A. C. S., ed. *The Frontiers of the Ottoman World*. Oxford: Oxford Univ. Press, 2009.

Perret, M. "Voyage sans Retour: Henri Lucereau en Ethiopie, 1879–1880." In "*L'Africa ai tempi di Daniele Camboni*," Atti del Congresso Internazionale di Studi Africani, Roma, 19–21 Nov. 1981, 194–201. Rome: Istituto italo-africano, 1981.

Peterson, Andrew. "The Ottoman Conquest of Arabia and the Syrian Hajj Route." In Peacock, *Frontiers of the Ottoman World*, 81–94.

Porter, Denis. "Orientalism and Its Problems." In *Colonial Discourse and Post-Colonial Theory*, edited by P. Williams and L. Chrisman, 150–61. New York: Columbia Univ. Press, 1994.

Ramadan, Muhammad. *Wad'a al-Sudan fi nitaq al-'alaqat bin Misr wa al-du'al al-Ottmaniya hata 1863* [The Position of Sudan in the Relations between Egypt and the Ottoman Provinces until 1863]. Cairo, 1955.

Revault, Philippe, and Serge Santelli, eds. *Harar: A Muslim City of Ethiopia*. Paris: Maisonneuve and Larose, 2004.

Rimbaud, Arthur. *Oeuvres Complètes*, edited by André Guyaux. Paris: Gallimard, 2009.

Robecchi-Bricchetti, Luigi. *Nell'Harar*. Milan: Galli, 1896.

Rubenson, Sven, ed. *Acta Ethiopica*. Vol. 3, *Internal Rivalries and Foreign Threats 1869–1879*. Addis Ababa: Addis Ababa Univ. Press, 2000.

———. "The Adwa Peace Treaty of 1884." In *Proceedings of the Third International Conference of Ethiopian Studies*, 1:225–36. Addis Ababa: Institute of Ethiopian Studies, Haile Selassie I Univ., 1969.

———. *The Survival of Ethiopian Independence*. London: Heinemann Educational Books, 1976.

Sabry, Muhammad. *L'Empire égyptien sous Ismail et l'ingérence anglo-française (1863–1879)*. Paris: Paul Geuthner, 1933.

———. *L'Empire égyptien sous Mohamed Ali et la Question d'Orient (1811–1849).* Paris: Lib. Orient. Paul Geuthner, 1930.

———. *Al-Imbarraturiya al-Sudaniya fi al-Qarn al-Tasi''Ashar* [Imperial Sudan in the Nineteenth Century]. Cairo, 1948.

———. *Le Soudan égyptien: 1821–1898.* Cairo: Imprimerie Nationale, 1947.

Sacconi, Pietro. "Il Governo Egiziano e le tribu Galla e Somali." *L'Esploratore* 7 (Milan, 14 Feb. 1883), 169–73.

Said, Edward W. *Culture and Imperialism.* London: Vintage, 1993.

———. *Orientalism.* London: Vintage, 1978.

Salvadore, Matteo. "Porro expedition." In Uhlig, *Encyclopaedia Aethiopica,* 4:178–79.

Samatar, Said S. "Ogaden." In Uhlig, *Encyclopaedia Aethiopica,* 4:8–9.

Sammarco, A. *Précis de L'Histoire D'Egypte,* 4 vols. Cairo: Imprimé par l'Imprimerie de l'Institut français d'archéologie orientale du Caire, 1933.

Sayyid Marsot, Afaf Lutfi al-. *Egypt in the Reign of Muhammad Ali.* New York: Cambridge Univ. Press, 1988.

Scarin, Emilio. *Hararino: Ricerche e Studi Geografici.* Florence: G. C. Sansoni, 1942.

Sharkey, Heather. *Living with Colonialism: Nationalism and Culture in the Anglo-Egyptian Sudan.* Berkeley: Univ. of California Press, 2003.

Shibayka, Makki. *Al-Sudan fi Qarn 1819–1919* [Sudan in 1819–1919]. Beirut: Dar al-Jil, 1991.

———. *Ta'rikh Shu'ub wadi al-nil* [The Nile Valley Peoples' History]. Beirut, 1965.

Shukry, Muhammad Fuad. *Al-Hukm al-Misri fi al-Sudan, 1820–1885* [The Egyptian Regime in Sudan, 1820–1885]. Cairo: dar al-fikr al-'arabi, 1947.

———. *The Khedive Ismail and Slavery in the Sudan: A History of the Sudan from the Egyptian Conquest of 1820 to the Outbreak of the Mahdiist Rebellion of 1881.* Cairo: Renaissance d'Egypte, 1938.

Shuqayr, Na'um. *Ta'rikh al-Sudan* [The History of Sudan]. Beirut: dar al-thaqafa, 1981.

Smidt, Wolbert. "Cartography from the 18th Century Onward." In Uhlig, *Encyclopaedia Aethiopica,* 1:688–90.

———. "Hamasen." In Uhlig, *Encyclopaedia Aethiopica,* 2:987–90.

———. "Təgray." In Uhlig, *Encyclopaedia Aethiopica,* 4:888–95.

Smidt, Wolbert, and Denis Nosnitsin. "Gura'." In Uhlig, *Encyclopaedia Aethiopica,* 2:922–24.

Spivak, Gayatry Chakravorty. "Subaltern Studies: Deconstructing Historiography." Chap. 12 in *In Other Worlds: Essays in Cultural Politics*, 197–221. New York: Routledge, 1988.

Stanton, E. A., ed. "Secret Letters from Khedive Ismail in Connection with an Occupation of the East African Coast." *Journal of the Royal African Society* 34 (1935), 269–82.

Starkie, Enid. *Arthur Rimbaud*. London: Faber and Faber, 1961.

Stitz, Volker. "Arabic Town Records and the Economic and Population History of Harar during the 19th Century." Paper presented to a conference of the History Society of Ethiopia, Addis Ababa, Jun. 1975.

Tafla, Bairu. "Yohannəs IV." In Uhlig, *Encyclopaedia Aethiopica*, 5:73–80.

Talhami, Ghada H. "Massawa under Khedive Ismaíl 1865–1879." In *Proceedings of the Fifth International Conference of Ethiopian Studies*, 13–16 Apr. 1978, edited by Robert Hess, 481–93. Chicago: Office of Publications Services, Univ. of Illinois in Chicago Circle, 1979.

———. *Suakin and Massawa under Egyptian Rule, 1865–1885*. Washington, DC: Univ. Press of America, 1979.

Tarsitani, Simone. "Ḏikr in Harär: Zikri." In Uhlig, *Encyclopaedia Aethiopica*, 2:158–59.

Tedeschi, Salvatore. "L'emirato di Harar secondo un documento inedito." *IV Congresso Internazionale di Studi Etiopici*. Rome: Accademia Nazionale dei Lincei, 1974.

Tesfai, Ebreab. "The Causes and Effects of the Dogali Encounter." In *The Centenary of Dogali: Proceedings of the International Symposium, Addis Ababa-Asmara, January 24–25, 1987*, edited by Taddesse Beyne, Taddesse Tamrat, and Richard Pankhurst, 91–102. Addis Ababa: Institute of Ethiopian Studies, Addis Ababa Univ., 1988.

Toledano, Ehud R. *The Ottoman Slave Trade and Its Suppression 1840–1890*. New Jersey: Princeton Univ. Press, 1982.

———. *State and Society in Mid-Nineteenth Century Egypt*. New York: Cambridge Univ. Press, 1990.

Trimingham, J. Spencer. *Islam in Ethiopia*. London: Frank Cass, 1952.

———. *Islam in Ethiopia*, 2nd ed. London: Frank Cass, 1965.

Troutt Powell, Eve M. *A Different Shade of Colonialism: Egypt, Great Britain and the Mastery of the Sudan*. Berkeley: Univ. of California Press, 2003.

Tubiana, J. "Le Patron de Rimbaud." Preface to *Barr Adjam—Souvenirs d'Afrique Orientale 1880–1887*, by Alfred Bardey, vi–ix. Paris: ed. du SNRS, 1981.

Uhlig, Siegbert, ed. *Encyclopaedia Aethiopica*, 5 vols. Wiesbaden: Harrassowitz Verlag, 2003–14.

Vatikiotis, Panayiotis J. *History of Modern Egypt*, 2nd ed. London: Johns Hopkins Univ. Press, 1980.

Vérain, Jérôme, ed. *Arthur Rimbaud—Lettres du Harar*. Paris: Mille et Une Nuits, 2001.

Wagner, Ewald. "Abādir 'Umar ar-Riḍā." In Uhlig, *Encyclopaedia Aethiopica*, 1:4–5.

———. "'Alī b. Dā'ūd Dynasty." In Uhlig, *Encyclopaedia Aethiopica*, 1:199–200.

———. "Ǧildessa." In Uhlig, *Encyclopaedia Aethiopica*, 2:797–98.

———. "Harär City Structure and Buildings." In Uhlig, *Encyclopaedia Aethiopica*, 2:1013–15.

———. "Harär History till 1875." In Uhlig, *Encyclopaedia Aethiopica*, 2:1015–19.

———. "Mugād." In Uhlig, *Encyclopaedia Aethiopica*, 3:1038.

———. "Muḥammad b. 'Alī b. 'Abdaššakūr." In Uhlig, *Encyclopaedia Aethiopica*, 3:1049–51.

———. "Three Arabic Documents on the History of Harar." *Journal of Ethiopian Studies* 12, no. 1 (1974): 213–24.

Waldron, Sidney R. *Ethnicity as Epiphenomenon: Foundation of Harar-Oromo Relations under the Empire*. New York: State Univ. of New York, Cortland, n.d.

———. "A Farewell to Bab Haji: City Symbolism and Harari Identity, 1887–1977." In *Working Pages on Society and History in Imperial Ethiopia: The Southern Periphery from the 1880s to 1974*, edited by Donald L. Donham and Wendy James, 47–270. Cambridge: African Studies Center, 1980.

———. "Harar: The Muslim City in Ethiopia." In *Proceedings of the Fifth International Conference of Ethiopian Studies, 13–16 April 1978*, edited by Robert L. Hess, 239–57. Chicago: Office of Publications Services, Univ. of Illinois in Chicago Circle, 1979.

———. "The Political Economy of Harari-Oromo Relationship, 1559–1874." *Northeast African Studies* 6, no. 1–2 (1984): 23–40.

———. "Social Organization and Social Control in the Walled City of Harar, Ethiopia." PhD diss., Columbia University, 1974.

———. "Within the Wall and Beyond: Harari Ethnic Identity and Its Future." Paper presented at the Harari Studies Conference, Addis Ababa University, Jun. 1975.

Waller, John H. *Gordon of Khartoum: The Saga of a Victorian Hero*. New York: Atheneum Books/Macmillan, 1988.

Warburg, Gabriel R. *Historical Discord in the Nile Valley.* London: Hurst; Evanston, IL: Northwestern Univ. Press, 1992.

———. *Islam, Sectarianism and Politics in Sudan since the Mahdiyya.* London: Hurst, 2003.

Weeks, Jeffrey. "Foucault for Historians." *History Workshop Journal* 14, no. 1 (Oct. 1982): 106–119.

Wehr, Hans. *A Dictionary of Modern Written Arabic.* Wiesbaden: Otto Harrassowitz, 1974.

Wolde-Mariam, Mesfin. *An Introductory Geography of Ethiopia.* Addis Ababa: Berhanena Selam H.S.I. Printing Press, 1972.

Wood, Denis. *The Power of Maps.* London: Guilford Press, 1992.

Wylde, Augustus B. *Modern Abyssinia.* London: Methuen, 1901.

Yahya, Jlal. *Misr al-ifriqiya wa al-itmaʿa al—istiʿmariya fi al-Qarn al-Tasi'ʿAshar* [African Egypt and the Colonial Aspirations in the Nineteenth Century]. Cairo, 1967.

Yapp, Malcolm E. *The Making of the Modern Near East.* London: Routledge, 1987.

Zekaria, Ahmed. "ʿAbdullāhi b. Muḥammad." In Uhlig, *Encyclopaedia Aethiopica,* 1:38–39.

———. "Harari Coins: A Preliminary Survey." *Journal of Ethiopian Studies* 24 (Nov. 1991): 23–45.

———. "Harar: The Land of Ziyara, Pilgrimage." *Institute of Ethiopian Studies: First Interdisciplinary Seminar of the Institute of Ethiopian Studies,* 6–7 Jun. 1998, 1–9. Ethiopia: Nazareth, 1998.

Zitelmann, Thomas. "Qottuu." In Uhlig, *Encyclopaedia Aethiopica,* 4:301–3.

Index

Italic page numbers denote illustrations and tables.

Avishai Ben-Dror is a research fellow at the Harry S. Truman Institute for the Advancement of Peace and the Hebrew University of Jerusalem, and is a member of the academic teaching faculty and lecturer at the Department of History, Philosophy and Judaic Studies, the Open University of Israel. In addition, he is an adjunct lecturer at Ben-Gurion University of the Negev.